Fifth Edition

CRIMINAL JUSTICE
in Canada

A Reader

Fifth Edition

CRIMINAL JUSTICE
in Canada

A Reader

Julian V. Roberts, Ph.D.
UNIVERSITY OF OXFORD

Michelle G. Grossman, M.A., M.S.W.
UNIVERSITY OF OXFORD

NELSON
EDUCATION

Criminal Justice in Canada: A Reader, Fifth Edition
by Julian V. Roberts and Michelle G. Grossman

Vice President, Editorial
Higher Education:
Anne Williams

Publisher:
Leanna MacLean

Marketing Manager:
Terry Fedorkiw

Senior Developmental Editor:
Liisa Kelly

Permissions Coordinator:
Rachel Eagen

Production Project Manager:
Hedy Sellers

Production Service:
Cenveo Publisher Services

Copy Editor:
Maria Jelinek

Proofreader:
Rajasekaran N

Design Director:
Ken Phipps

Managing Designer:
Franca Amore

Interior Design:
Peter Papayanakis

Cover Design:
Martyn Schmoll

Cover Image:
samxmeg/Getty Royalty Free

Compositor:
Cenveo Publisher Services

Library and Archives Canada
Cataloguing in Publication

Criminal justice in Canada : a
reader / [edited by] Julian
V. Roberts, Michelle G. Grossman.
— Fifth edition.

Includes bibliographical
references.
ISBN 978-0-17-655789-8 (pbk.)

1. Criminal justice, Administration
of—Canada. I. Grossman, Michelle
G., editor II. Roberts, Julian V.,
editor

HV9960.C2C75 2015
364.971   C2014-907755-6

ISBN-13: 978-0-17-655789-8
ISBN-10: 0-17-655789-x

The editors dedicate their work on this and all editions to the memory of Kathleen Ducker (1917–2005)

Contents

PART THREE   CURRENT ISSUES IN CRIMINAL JUSTICE   *127*

PREFACE

Julian V. Roberts, Ph.D., and Michelle G. Grossman, M.A., M.S.W.

Welcome to the fifth edition of *Criminal Justice in Canada*. A decade ago, teachers in the field of criminology and criminal justice who sought a text for their students had few Canadian works from which to choose. That has since changed: several excellent books are now available. Finding a collection of critical readings, however, remains a challenge. Although several readers exist, they deal with crime rather than criminal justice or specific topics, such as crime control policy. Instructors looking for a more general collection of primarily introductory readings are often forced to cobble together a collection of readings and package them through commercial or university print shops.

This work simplifies this task. The fifth edition is aimed at any course with a primary or secondary focus on the criminal justice system. We have designed this book to accompany standard criminal justice and criminology texts by providing a diversity of views: some articles take a critical approach to criminal justice; others report findings from a more "mainstream" perspective. Many readings have been commissioned especially for this new edition and most of the existing chapters have been revised and updated. The readings have been selected to achieve three goals: (1) to provide some essential information on the structure and function of criminal justice; (2) to hear from people who are working in or who have passed through the criminal justice process, because the voice of practical experience has greater value than mere theory; and (3) to draw upon empirical research that sheds light on the way that the justice system functions in Canada.

ACKNOWLEDGMENTS

First and foremost we thank the contributing authors whose work is represented here. We would also like to acknowledge the important contributions of all the individuals involved in the production of this volume at Nelson Education Ltd.

Julian V. Roberts and Michelle G. Grossman
At Oxford, July 1, 2014

A Note from the Publisher

Thank you for selecting *Criminal Justice in Canada*, eds. Julian V. Roberts and Michelle G. Grossman. The editors and publisher have devoted considerable time to the careful development of this book. We appreciate your recognition of this effort and accomplishment.

 ## ABOUT THE NELSON EDUCATION TEACHING ADVANTAGE (NETA)

The **Nelson Education Teaching Advantage (NETA)** program delivers research-based instructor resources that promote student engagement and higher-order thinking to enable the success of Canadian students and educators. Be sure to visit Nelson Education's **Inspired Instruction** website at **http://www.nelson.com/inspired/** to find out more about NETA. Don't miss the testimonials of instructors who have used NETA supplements and seen student engagement increase!

INSTRUCTOR RESOURCES

Downloadable Instructor Supplements

All NETA and other key instructor ancillaries are provided in the *Instructor's Resources at* http://www.nelson.com/criminaljusticereader5e, giving instructors the ultimate tools for customizing lectures and presentations. Instructor materials can also be accessed through http://www.nelson.com/login and http://login.cengage.com.

NETA Test Bank: This resource was written by Sheri Fabian and Aynsley Pescitelli of Simon Fraser University. It includes over 400 multiple-choice questions written according to NETA guidelines for effective construction and development of higher-order questions. The Test Bank was copy-edited by a NETA-trained editor.

Image Library: This resource consists of digital copies of figures and tables used in the book. Instructors may use these jpegs to customize their own presentations.

DayOne: Day One—Prof InClass is a PowerPoint presentation that instructors can customize to orient students to the class and their text at the beginning of the course.

ABOUT THE CONTRIBUTORS

EDITORS

Julian V. Roberts holds a Ph.D. from the University of Toronto and is currently a professor of criminology in the Faculty of Law at the University of Oxford. His recent books include *Popular Punishment* (Oxford: Oxford University Press, 2014); *The Role of Previous Convictions at Sentencing* (Oxford: Hart, 2010); *Principled Sentencing* (with von Hirsch and Ashworth; Oxford: Hart, 2009); *Punishing Persistent Offenders* (Oxford: Oxford University Press, 2008); *Understanding Public Attitudes to Criminal Justice* (with M. Hough; Maidenhead: Open University Press, 2005); and *The Virtual Prison: Community Custody and the Evolution of Imprisonment* (Cambridge: Cambridge University Press, 2004).

Michelle G. Grossman has graduate degrees in criminology and social work from the University of Toronto. She has held both clinical and research/policy positions with a particular focus on victims and child victims. As the manager of a clinical program at a nonprofit organization in Toronto, she worked with child victims of sexual assault and with adult male sex offenders. She has also worked in a policy/research capacity for the Government of Canada at the Department of Justice, Research and Statistics Division, where she was senior research officer for the Policy Centre for Victim Issues, and as a policy officer at the Department of Public Safety Canada (formerly the Solicitor General Canada). She is currently undertaking a D.Phil. in the Faculty of Law, University of Oxford.

CONTRIBUTING AUTHORS

Daniel Antonowicz received his Doctorate in Psychology from Carleton University and is an associate professor in the Department of Criminology at Wilfrid Laurier University (Brantford Campus), Canada. His research on effective offender rehabilitation appears as a chapter in *Cognitive Behavioral Interventions for At-Risk Youth* (2nd ed.). He has also co-edited a book entitled *Going Straight: Effective Delinquency Prevention and Offender Rehabilitation*.

Nicholas Bala has been a law professor at Queen's University in Kingston since 1980. His research and teaching focus on families and children involved in the justice system. Much of his work is interdisciplinary and collaborative, addressing young offenders, post-separation parenting and alienation, family violence and high-conflict separations, familial support obligations, and child witnesses.

Shereen H. Benzvy Miller, M.A., LL.B, is a human rights lawyer by training and inclination. She has taught courses in law, criminology, and sociology at Carleton University, the University of Pennsylvania, and York University. She is a trained mediator and has written on restorative justice and governance. Previously a criminologist and criminal defence lawyer, she worked on a multitude of law reform files, including development of the statement of purpose and principles of sentencing for inclusion in the *Criminal Code of Canada*, and with the Correctional Law Review, which drafted the *Corrections and Conditional Release Act*. While her focus has been on criminal justice and human rights, she views the essence of her work as contributing to the support of democratic processes and values that improve Canada for Canadians.

Stephen Bittle is an assistant professor in the Department of Criminology at the University of Ottawa. His recent publications include *Still Dying for a Living: Corporate Criminal Liability after the Westray Mine Disaster* (UBC Press, 2012); "Beyond Corporate Fundamentalism: A Marxian Class Analysis of Corporate Crime Law Reform" (*Critical Sociology*, 2013); and (with L. Snider) "Examining the Ruggie Report: Can Voluntary Guidelines Tame Global Capitalism?" (*Critical Criminology*, 2013). His current research funded by the Social Sciences and Humanities Research Council of Canada examines the growing international interest in corporate criminal liability.

Gillian Blackell is Senior Legal Counsel with the Family, Children, and Youth Section of the Department of Justice Canada. She has worked on legal policy issues related to violence against women and children for 10 years, has been involved in the development of legislative reforms, and has had the privilege of participating in negotiations at the United Nations.

Paul Burstein started his own practice in 1992 specializing in criminal and constitutional litigation. He has argued appeals before the Supreme Court of Canada, the Ontario Court of Appeal, and the Federal Court of Appeal. Paul has appeared before parliamentary committees dealing with various criminal legislative proposals and has been the director of Osgoode Hall Law School's Criminal Law Intensive Programme since 1999. He is also involved with the Trial Advocacy courses offered by the Law School to both students and practitioners and is an adjunct professor at Queen's Law School, teaching both trial and appellate advocacy.

Kathryn M. Campbell is an associate professor in the Department of Criminology at the University of Ottawa. Her major research and teaching interests cover the study of youth justice, Aboriginal justice issues, and mis-carriages of justice. In 2012, she cofounded Innocence Ottawa, a pro bono student-run innocence project seeking exoneration for Canadian prisoners who have been wrongly convicted. She has a forthcoming publication with University of Toronto Press entitled *Miscarriages of Justice in Canada: Causes, Responses, Remedies*.

Peter J. Carrington is a professor of sociology at the University of Waterloo and has been a member of the Sociology and Legal Studies Department at the University of Waterloo since 1984. He is interested in the interplay between criminal careers and criminal networks, and in social networks and the juve-nile and criminal justice systems. He is editor of *Canadian Journal of Criminology and Criminal Justice* and co-editor of *Sage Handbook of Social Network Analysis*.

Carla Cesaroni is an associate professor and assistant dean, graduate studies at the University of Ontario Institute of Technology. She received her Ph.D. from the Centre of Criminology, University of Toronto. For the past 16 years she has studied the experiences and adjustment of incarcerated adolescents. Her recent research is a comparative study of young adults (18- to 21-year-olds) in Scottish and Canadian prisons.

Judge David P. Cole was appointed to the Ontario Court of Justice in 1991. He currently presides at Metro West court in Toronto. From 1992 to 1996, he was seconded to the Commission on Systemic Racism in the Ontario Criminal Justice System. He teaches the law of sentencing and penal policy at the Faculty of Law and the Centre of Criminology, both at the University of Toronto. He is the coauthor of *Release from Imprisonment: The Law of Sentencing and Parole*, and the co-editor of *Making Sense of Sentencing*. He also is a member of the edi-torial board of the *Canadian Journal of Criminology and Criminal Justice*.

Myriam Denov holds the Canada Research Chair (Tier 1) in Youth, Gender, and Armed Conflict and is professor of social work at McGill University. Her current research is exploring the militarization and reintegration experiences of former child soldiers in Sierra Leone and Colombia, as well as war-affected youth living in Canada. She is the author of several books including *Child Soldiers: Sierra Leone's Revolutionary United Front* (Cambridge University Press) and *Children's Rights and International Development: Lessons and Challenges from the Field* (Palgrave Macmillan Press). She currently leads a multi-institutional and multidisciplinary research team on children and global adversity, and is a 2014 recipient of the Trudeau Fellowship.

Chris Giacomantonio is an analyst with RAND Europe, working primarily in the security and justice domain. He completed his doctoral work at the University of Oxford's Centre for Criminology, where he studied police coor-dination in British Columbia's Lower Mainland. He has also been involved in research on police effectiveness, neighbourhood and public order policing, and ethics in security settings.

Holly Johnson is an associate professor of criminology at the University of Ottawa. She was principal investigator on Statistics Canada's national surveys on crime victimization and violence against women and is the author of many publications in that field. She also provides advice to community-based researchers and governments internationally on the development and design of surveys to measure violence against women. She acts as adviser to the *International Violence Against Women Survey*, a multi-jurisdictional project coordinated through the UN. She received her Ph.D. from the University of Manchester.

Barry N. Leighton is a criminologist specializing in policing in Canada. He teaches or has taught at a number of universities, including Carleton University and the University of Ottawa.

Savvas Lithopoulos is a senior research advisor at the Department of Public Safety Canada. Among his primary areas of research are policing, Aboriginal justice, comparative international criminal justice, policing isolated Aboriginal communities, public perceptions of the criminal justice system, and the economics of policing.

James D. Livingston is a criminologist and assistant professor in the Department of Sociology and Criminology at Saint Mary's University, Halifax, Nova Scotia. He studies issues of social inclusion and social justice for people with mental illnesses, with a special focus on the criminal justice and legal systems.

Brian Manarin is an assistant Crown attorney prosecuting criminal matters in Windsor, Ontario, after many years of practice with the Ministry of the Attorney General in the Greater Toronto Area. He was called to the Ontario Bar in 1988, and his prosecutorial experience has run the gamut of matters criminal. An internationally published author, he has written numerous articles on various legal topics.

Marie Manikis is a professor in the Faculty of Law, McGill. She completed her doctorate at the University of Oxford and an LL.M. at Osgoode Hall Law School, where she taught a course on the *Charter of Rights and Freedoms*. Prior to this, she practised law in Montreal, completing her law degree at the University of Montreal while clerking for a Superior Court Justice.

Susan McDonald is principal researcher with the Research and Statistics Division of the Department of Justice Canada. She is a lawyer and has a doctorate in Adult Education. In her position with the Department of Justice she is responsible for all sociolegal policy research on victims of crime. She also works on issues such as public confidence in the justice system, access to justice, and gender and diversity.

Peter McKnight is an award-winning columnist and editorial writer with the *Vancouver Sun* and an adjunct professor in the School of Criminology at Simon Fraser University. He holds a B.A. in psychology, a law degree, an M.A. in journalism, and an M.A. in philosophy, all from the University of Western Ontario, and has held fellowships at the University of Cambridge and MIT. A member of the Ontario Bar and a former probation and parole officer, he writes and speaks on a wide variety of topics, including law and justice issues, science and medicine, and philosophy, religion, and ethics.

Karen Middlecoat graduated from University of Toronto with a B.A.H. with a double major in criminology and psychology and a minor in English. She started working in the Ministry of Correctional Services as a correctional officer, then spent a year at the Metropolitan Toronto Forensic Services (METFORS), working with psychiatric staff to conduct assessments on individuals to determine their fitness to stand trial. She became a probation and parole officer in 1985 and worked in the field until 1997, when she was asked to work at the Toronto courts as the administrative probation liaison.

Eugene Oscapella completed an undergraduate degree in economics at the University of Toronto (1974), obtained his law degree from the University of Ottawa (1977), and received his Masters of Laws from the London School of Economics and Political Science (1979). He was called to the Ontario Bar in 1980. From 1982 to 1985, he was Director of Legislation and Law Reform for the Canadian Bar Association. He is a founding member of the Canadian Foundation for Drug Policy, and was a former chair and member of the policy committee of the Canadian Criminal Justice Association. He lectures in criminology at the University of Ottawa.

Holly Pelvin is a Ph.D. candidate at the Centre for Criminology and Sociolegal Studies at the University of Toronto. Her dissertation work examines the experience of the remand custody through in-depth interviews with 120 male and female prisoners at four maximum-security facilities in Southern Ontario.

Judge Gilles Renaud has been a member of the Ontario Court of Justice since 1995. Previously he served as a prosecutor and defence counsel. He is a prolific author, having written eight books on evidence, advocacy, and sentencing, including two in French, and a collection of humorous short stories.

Rick Ruddell is a professor and Law Foundation of Saskatchewan Chair in Police Studies at the University of Regina. Prior to this appointment he served with the Correctional Service of Canada and held faculty positions in California and Kentucky. He has authored, coauthored or edited 9 books and 75 peer-reviewed articles, technical reports, and articles in professional journals.

Rick Sauve: After serving 17 years in prison he worked as a cabinetmaker, then for Toronto Boys' Home as a child and youth worker with inner-city youth. While incarcerated, he finished high school as well as degrees in psychology and criminology. He has been active in prisoners' rights and led the successful court challenge in the Supreme Court of Canada for prisoners' right to vote. He lives with his wife Michele in the countryside near Lindsay, Ontario.

Sheldon Schwartz received a B.A. from York University, majoring in economics. He worked in the field of public accounting and auditing for several years before entering the field of social work. After three years working for an agency providing supervision services under contract to the Correctional Service of Canada (CSC), he was hired by the Government of Canada for another department (Human Resources Development Canada, formerly Employment and Immigration). After six years in various HRDC roles, he transferred back to CSC in 1996, where he has been ever since. He received a Bachelor of Social Work degree from York University and a Masters in Social Work from the University of Toronto and is now a registered social worker. He is also trained as an expert witness, representing the federal correctional system in certain types of sentencing hearings.

Rashmee Singh is an assistant professor in the Department of Sociology and Legal Studies at the University of Waterloo in Canada. Her previous research examines the civil-society state relations that are fundamental to the governance of gender violence in Toronto, Ontario. Her current research project explores the governance of sex workers through specialized prostitution courts in the United States. She is also involved in a collaborative study examining the use of photographic evidence in prosecutions of domestic violence.

Simon N. Verdun-Jones is a professor of criminology at Simon Fraser University. His major interests are criminal law, mentally disordered offenders, plea bargaining, sentencing, victim participation in the criminal justice system, the International Criminal Court of Justice, and violence and aggression in mental health facilities. Among his recent books are *Introduction to Criminal and Civil Law* (2006); *Criminal Law in Canada: Cases, Questions, and the Code*, 6th ed. (2015); and *Canadian Criminal Cases: Selected Highlights*, 4th ed. (2015).

Michael Waby is an assistant Crown attorney working for the Ministry of the Attorney General in Ontario. He is currently also the vice-president of the Ontario Crown Attorneys' Association. He joined the Metropolitan Police in 1986 and worked in West London for the balance of his service. Upon qualifying as a barrister, he left the police service in 1996 and then worked as a criminal barrister in a set of chambers in Temple doing a mix of defence and prosecution work before moving to Canada in 2001. After a brief period working as a defence counsel in Toronto, he became a Crown attorney in 2003, prosecuting those charged with criminal conduct ranging from homicide to property offences.

Richard Weisman is associate professor in the Law and Society Program at York University in Toronto. He has recently published a book on the role of remorse in law, using cases and other data from Canada, the United States, and South Africa.

John A. Winterdyk Since graduating from Simon Fraser University in 1988, Professor John Winterdyk has taught in the Department of Justice Studies at Mount Royal University (MRU)–Calgary. In addition to his position at MRU, John holds adjunct positions at several other universities and he is the former director of the Centre of Criminology and Justice Research at MRU. John has published/researched extensively in the areas of youth justice, human trafficking, international criminal justice, and criminological theory.

Introductory Readings

PART ONE

CHAPTER 1

Criminal Justice in Canada: An Overview

This introductory chapter provides context for the rest of the volume. It begins by noting two alternative models of criminal justice and then reviews research on public opinion about criminal justice. Many Canadians believe they know how the criminal justice system works (and have strong opinions about how it *should* work); but as we shall see, there is often a considerable gap between the public's ideas about how the system works and how it actually works. One of the main purposes of any course or text in the field of criminology is to correct public misperceptions. A good place to start, therefore, is to document the extent of public knowledge of crime and justice.

Julian V. Roberts
University of Oxford

Criminal justice in Canada—as elsewhere—involves a complex system of checks and balances in which responsibility for a criminal case is divided among many different decision makers. To complicate matters further, these decision makers are guided by somewhat different mandates. Judges are guided by the *principle of proportionality* when imposing a sentence. This means they attempt to ensure that the severity of the sentence imposed reflects the seriousness of the crime committed (and the offender's level of culpability). Parole boards, on the other hand, have a different mandate. When deciding whether a prisoner should be allowed out of prison to spend the remainder of her sentence in the community under supervision, a parole board is concerned about whether that offender will benefit from release on parole and whether that person represents a risk to the community. The seriousness of the crime plays little role in the decision—unless it sheds light on the issues of rehabilitation or risk to the community. Thus the length of the sentence is determined largely by the seriousness of the crime, while the portion of the sentence served in prison is often determined by other criteria. This is just one example of the system's complexity.

The justice system is also complex because it must respond to a wide diversity of human behaviour. If crime comprised only a limited number of proscribed acts, the system could develop a far more focused (and predictable) response to it. But the variability in criminal conduct is immense, and the system needs to vary its responses to it accordingly. The criminal justice system must be able to respond to cases of premeditated murder, minor acts of vandalism committed by bored teenagers, and all forms of offending between these two extremes. In addition, even when they have been convicted of the same category of crime, no two offenders are ever alike. Two people convicted of burglary may have very different backgrounds, and one may be more blameworthy than the other. Consider a case of break and enter in which one offender is 35 years old and has four previous convictions for breaking into houses; whereas the other offender is 18 and has no previous convictions. Even if they have committed the crime together, their cases are very different, and it is surely appropriate that the justice system treat them differently.

MODELS OF CRIMINAL JUSTICE

Two competing perspectives underlie our criminal justice system. These perspectives give rise to alternative models of justice that are closely associated with the writings of Herbert Packer, who coined the terms *crime control* and *due process* (see Packer 1968). As the name implies, the crime control model stresses the importance of controlling crime and favours providing criminal justice professionals with considerable powers for responding to crime. Thus crime control advocates support giving police wide powers to search suspects, enter people's houses, and detain persons accused of a crime.

In contrast, the due process model limits the powers of the criminal justice system to prosecute accused persons. Due process advocates argue that if the state—which has unlimited resources to prosecute suspects—is not subject to some limits, society will become intolerable, as people will be subjected to constant surveillance and police interventions. For this reason, we create specific rights that must be respected by the police, and indeed by all agents of the criminal justice system.

How are these limits on the powers of the state established? One example is by requiring police to obtain permission from a court prior to placing a wiretap on a suspect's telephone line. Similarly, police officers cannot stop a person and search him without reasonable grounds for doing so. In these and many other ways the due process model prevents the state from having unlimited power over the lives of suspects and accused persons. The due process model is therefore more concerned with protecting the rights of the accused and following correct legal procedure. For almost every important issue in criminal justice, one can find crime control as well as due process approaches.

For example, when determining the limits on the powers of the police, crime control advocates argue that the police should have wide powers to gather evidence and to question and interrogate suspects and accused persons. Due process advocates, on the other hand, want such powers limited in order to ensure that individual rights are not compromised and that innocent people are not stopped and detained by the police. The conduct of criminal trials also provides many examples of the conflict between due process and crime control models of criminal justice. During a criminal trial, an accused person is not obliged to take the stand and testify in her own defence. The onus is on the state, through the prosecutor, to establish the guilt of the accused beyond a reasonable doubt, without any help from the testimony of the accused. The due process model defends this procedural rule by arguing that the accused should not have to cooperate with the state's case. In contrast, crime control proponents would argue that the accused *should* have to testify because this may be the only way to get to the truth.

A criminal justice system founded exclusively on due process or crime control principles would be problematic. Pursuing crime control to the exclusion of due process considerations would inevitably result in an increase in the number of persons wrongfully convicted, because due process procedural safeguards provide the innocent with a protection against a false accusation and subsequent prosecution. However, a system that stresses due process considerations to the extreme would result in a higher number of wrongful acquittals: guilty people would evade punishment because the police would be hampered in their search for incriminating evidence. For this reason, the Canadian justice system has elements of both perspectives. But even a balanced approach can result in miscarriages of justice. As we shall see later in this volume, wrongful convictions can—and do—occur, resulting in the imprisonment of innocent people, sometimes for many years.

The ultimate arbiter of conflicts between the two models of criminal justice is the Supreme Court of Canada, the decisions of which are binding upon Parliament and all courts in Canada. The Supreme Court often hears arguments regarding the constitutionality of specific pieces of criminal justice legislation and decides whether a particular law is consistent with the rights guaranteed by the *Canadian Charter of Rights and Freedoms*. A law that goes too far in the direction of controlling crime may violate one of the provisions of the *Charter*. (The impact of the *Charter* on the criminal justice system is discussed in the next chapter by Marie Manikis.)

PUBLIC OPINION AND CRIMINAL JUSTICE

The public in Canada (as elsewhere) tends to be quite critical of their criminal justice system. Many people view the system as overly lenient and biased more toward the interests of the accused or offender than toward those of the victim. This perception, however, is often false. The media, furthermore, increasingly report that Canadians have lost confidence in their criminal justice system. But is this true? What do the polls say about the issue? Two surveys, both conducted in 2002, asked Canadians to express their degree of satisfaction with or confidence in the justice system (see Roberts, Crutcher, and Verbrugge 2007). In one of these surveys, respondents rated the degree of confidence they had in "the justice system in Canada" using a 7-point scale, where 7 represented a great deal of confidence and 1 no confidence at all. Leaving aside the 22 percent in the midpoint category (4), 46 percent of the respondents expressed confidence in the system, while 32 percent expressed little or no confidence—a difference of 14 percent. On balance, this poll suggests that Canadians are more positive than negative about their justice system.

The other survey conducted that same year asked respondents to express their level of satisfaction with the system. The response options were "very satisfied," "satisfied," "dissatisfied," or "very dissatisfied." This range of options permits a comparison of the proportion of respondents with positive or negative views. Just over half (54 percent) were satisfied, and 41 percent were dissatisfied. Thus, the surveys suggest that more Canadians are positive than negative about the system.

How do confidence trends for criminal justice compare to those for other public institutions? Table 1.1 shows that compared to other public institutions, the justice system attracts lower confidence ratings. However, the proportion of respondents expressing a great deal or quite a lot of confidence in the justice system is not significantly lower than the proportion expressing similar levels of confidence in the education system. Moreover, confidence levels in criminal justice are significantly higher for the justice system than for Parliament.

We should also not lose sight of the fact that the healthcare and educational systems have mandates very different from that ascribed to the justice

TABLE 1.1 *Public Confidence in Selected Public Institutions, Canada, 2003*

	A great deal of confidence	Quite a lot of confidence	Not very much confidence	No confidence at all
Local business	19%	61%	11%	1%
Banks	19	49	21	6
Healthcare system	19	48	24	4
Educational system	17	48	21	3
Justice system	14	43	27	7
Corporations	8	38	33	10
Parliament	8	35	35	10
Welfare system	9	32	29	9

Source: Adapted from Roberts, J.V., Crutcher, N., and Verbrugge, P. 2006. "Public Attitudes to Sentencing in Canada: Some Recent Findings." Canadian Journal of Criminology and Criminal Justice.

system. The healthcare system exists for the benefit of the health consumer: the patient. Its activities are directed toward one goal: improving the well-being of the patient, without any competing interests. In contrast, the justice system has a more complex mandate to fulfill; it must respond to the interests of multiple parties. Offenders, victims, and the families of both groups have rights and needs that sometimes conflict. It is therefore unreasonable to expect confidence levels to be comparable for the justice and health systems. In addition, the healthcare and educational systems share a mandate to help members of the public. In contrast, the mission of the criminal justice system is not *primarily* to help victims, but rather to promote public safety and impose appropriate punishments. Judges must discharge multiple mandates, one of which is to ensure that defendants receive a fair trial. Similarly, prosecutors must act in the public interest, which may mean discontinuing a prosecution or not launching an appeal against acquittal or sentence. Predictably, nurses, educators, and military personnel receive higher ratings from the public than lawyers, judges, or members of the parole board (see Roberts 2007). The public may lose sight of the complexity of the justice system's mandate, which may explain why justice professionals receive somewhat lower ratings of public confidence.

CONFIDENCE IN BRANCHES OF CRIMINAL JUSTICE

The public may be more positive than negative about the justice system as a whole, but people respond very differently when asked to rate the performance of, or express confidence in, specific branches of the justice system. In general, the public has great confidence in the police yet less confidence in other criminal justice professionals. For example, a survey conducted in 2002 found that over two-thirds of respondents rated the police as doing an "excellent" or "good" job, whereas only half expressed the same level of support for judges (Roberts 2002).

Table 1.2 summarizes findings from this survey of public ratings of four criminal justice professions. As the table shows, people rate the police more positively than they rate other criminal justice professionals. Moreover, this finding is not restricted to Canada: similar trends emerge in all other countries in which such surveys have been conducted (see Roberts 2007).

TABLE 1.2 *Public Evaluations of Criminal Justice Professions in Canada*

	Excellent or good	Average	Poor or very poor
Police	67%	25%	7%
Defence Counsel	56%	36%	6%
Prosecutors	53%	40%	5%
Judges	50%	31%	17%

Source: Public Safety Canada. Public Confidence in Criminal Justice: A Review of Recent Trends 2004-05. Table 15. Found at: http://www.publicsafety.gc.ca/res/cor/rep/2004-05-pub-conf-eng.aspx. Reproduced with the permission of the Minister of Public Safety and Emergency Preparedness Canada, [2014].

Explaining Variations in Confidence Levels

Several explanations can account for this hierarchy of confidence. With respect to Packer's (1968) two models of criminal justice, the public is more sympathetic to crime control than to due process. Support for this proposition can be found in the results of a number of surveys. A British poll found that four out of five respondents agreed with changing the law to permit the state to retry individuals who have been found not guilty (*Observer* 2003). An American survey found that nearly half of those interviewed believed that the criminal justice system treats defendants better than victims (National Victim Center 1991). Although these issues have not been explored by pollsters in Canada, it is likely that many Canadians share these views.

The public is equally intolerant of obstacles to prosecuting (and convicting) defendants. The judicial system can make two kinds of "classification" errors: it can convict innocent people, and it can acquit guilty parties. The aphorism is well engrained in legal thinking that it is better to acquit ten guilty individuals than allow an innocent person to be convicted. In other words, one kind of error is considered much worse than the other. The desire to ensure that the innocent are acquitted explains the many criminal procedures designed to avoid such a judicial mistake. The public, however, appears to be less concerned about the occurrence of wrongful convictions. A British

Attitudes Survey asked people whether it was worse to convict an innocent person or to let a guilty person go free. Almost half (42 percent) of the sample believed that letting a guilty person go free was worse (Dowds 1995). This finding reflects the crime control orientation of the public. Although it was a British survey, research on related issues makes it clear that Canadians would respond in the same way. In short, most people favour a justice system that gives police and prosecutors significant powers rather than a system that follows procedural safeguards to ensure that due process is maintained.

Thus, the police are more closely allied in the public mind with a crime control mandate and for this reason receive higher ratings. While the police have to observe constitutionally based rules regarding the surveillance of suspects and the collection of evidence, police practices are ultimately regulated by the courts through constitutional challenges. The judiciary has a more complex mandate. Unlike their counterparts in the systems of justice found in Europe, judges in common law jurisdictions such as Canada must remain neutral while the parties to the proceedings conduct the case. In the popular mind, judges are probably associated far more closely with a due process model of justice—one that, as we have seen, attracts less support from members of the public.

In popular opinion, therefore, the mandate of the police is closer to the crime control model of justice. Judges, on the other hand, must strive to protect the rights of the accused during a trial, and prosecutors must consider the interests in justice, not simply pursue the conviction of the defendant. The public is seldom aware of the true nature of the prosecutorial role. Research has shown that many people see the prosecutor as the "victim's lawyer" (Roberts 2002), and they may be disappointed when Crown counsel takes a position at odds with the opinion of the crime victim. Members of the public are less familiar with and have less sympathy for these elements of justice; and this lack of familiarity may be reflected in their perceptions of the courts and prosecutors.

One final explanation for the higher public approval ratings of the police is more mundane than theoretical. From many perspectives, the police are the most visible of all criminal justice professionals: they wear uniforms, drive (usually) marked vehicles, and perform their duties in public, on the streets of the nation. The public nature of policing contrasts the work of other professionals, such as judges or lawyers, whose duties are discharged out of the public eye. A significant proportion of the population has contact with a police officer at some point; the MORI poll in the United Kingdom found that almost one-third of the respondents reported having some contact with the police in the previous year. Yet how many people have contact with a judge, a member of a parole board, or a probation officer? Higher levels of exposure to the police likely promote confidence in the policing branch of criminal justice. The movement towards community policing in recent years reflects this relationship between exposure and confidence. The premise underlying community policing is that increasing the visibility of the police in the community promotes public confidence.

PUNISHMENT AND PREVENTION

Although the news media focus on punishment as a goal of criminal justice, the system also attempts to prevent crime. The public are often described as wanting simply to punish offenders. However, polls reveal that there is widespread support for crime prevention. In fact, given a choice between punishment and prevention, Canadians have always supported prevention. A number of polls have asked respondents to choose between two responses to crime: punishment or prevention. In 2003, Canadians were asked to identify "the main goal of the criminal justice system"; their responses are summarized in Figure 1.1. As can be seen, there was more support for prevention than for punishment (41 percent compared to 23 percent). Moreover, as Table 1.3

FIGURE 1.1 *Public Perceptions of the Primary Goal of Criminal Justice in Canada*

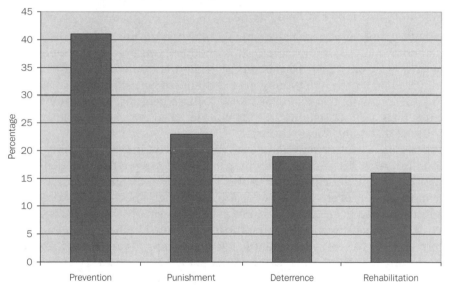

Source: Based on Ekos Research Associates. Canadian Attitudes Towards the Prevention of Crime, 2000.

TABLE 1.3 *Support for Different Approaches to Crime*

	(Percentage of Respondents Supporting Prevention vs. Enforcement)		
	1994	1997	1998
Crime prevention	73%	73%	57%
Law enforcement	22%	22%	37%

Source: Roberts, J.V. and Hastings, R. 2007. Public Opinion and Crime Prevention: A Review of International Findings. Institute for the Prevention of Crime. Vol. 1: Pg. 199.

reveals, Canadians have always expressed more support for prevention than for punishment. The most recent survey reported by Focus Canada found that almost two-thirds of the Canadian public believe that the emphasis should be on prevention (Focus Canada 2014). This is the highest level of public support for crime prevention in 20 years.

PUBLIC KNOWLEDGE OF CRIMINAL JUSTICE

This section summarizes findings from a review of public opinion polls in Canada about crime and criminal justice issues. I start by discussing one of the most important public misperceptions affecting attitudes toward the justice system. (For the sake of brevity, full bibliographic citations for some works have been omitted in this section of the chapter; they can be found in Roberts and Hough [2005]).

Public Perceptions of Crime Trends

Public opinion surveys in many nations show that the public generally thinks that crime rates are rising, regardless of whether crime is going up or down or remaining stable. Public perceptions of crime trends are unrelated to actual trends. Thus in the 1980s, most people were correct when they responded to polls by saying that crime rates were rising. Then, throughout the 1990s, crime rates declined significantly; yet polls revealed that most Canadians still believed that crime was on the rise.

A more recent survey—conducted in 2010—confirmed these perceptions of crime rates. The Angus Reid company asked a representative sample of Canadians whether crime rates in this country had increased, decreased, or remained stable over the past five years. Almost half the sample believed that crime rates had increased, when in fact they had declined (Angus Reid 2010). When Canadians were asked about the level of crime in their neighbourhood compared to five years ago, almost two-thirds of the sample expressed the view that the level of crime had remained stable (Brennan 2011). Official statistics reveal that crime rates had been stable or declining.

Police statistics and trends from victimization surveys tend not to reach the general public because downward or stable trends are not particularly newsworthy. The resulting misperception has important consequences for public attitudes toward the criminal justice system: if most people believe that crime rates are steadily increasing, then they may well also believe that the system has failed in its principal function—namely, to prevent crime. This misperception of crime trends, then, is probably responsible for much of the public criticism of the criminal justice system. Finally, most members of the public believe that a relatively large proportion of crime involves violence when in reality violent crime accounts for a relatively small percentage of crimes reported to the police. Most crime involves non-violent criminal conduct, but people tend to focus primarily on the most serious offences—namely, those involving violence.

Sentencing

Opinion polls often ask the public to rate the court system and, specifically, the severity of sentences imposed. The percentage of Canadians who feel that sentences are too lenient has been high for more than 20 years. In 1970, approximately two-thirds of Canadians endorsed the view that sentences were not harsh enough. In 1992, the proportion expressing this view was 85 percent. A more recent poll (conducted in 2005) found that 73 percent of Canadians felt that the justice system was "too soft" toward people convicted of crimes (Roberts, Crutcher, and Verbrugge 2007). However, this perception is often founded upon inaccurate knowledge of the actual severity of sentences imposed. People tend to underestimate the severity of sentencing practices. For example, approximately 90 percent of offenders convicted of robbery are sent to prison; yet fully three-quarters of respondents to a representative survey of the public estimated the incarceration rate for this crime to be under 60 percent (Canadian Sentencing Commission 1987). Similar results emerged for other offences. Thus, the perception of leniency in sentencing at the trial court level is based upon a misperception of the actual severity of sentences imposed.

Many people also mistakenly believe that increasing the severity of penalties will have an appreciable impact on crime rates. The reality is that such a small percentage of offenders are actually sentenced that the ability of the sentencing process to reduce crime is very restricted. This point has been made repeatedly in the sentencing literature. Ashworth (2010) notes that English courts deal with no more than about 3 percent of the offences actually committed. Statistics Canada reports similar trends in this country: a sentence is imposed in fewer than 5 percent of crimes committed because of case attrition in the criminal justice process. The term *case attrition* simply means that cases drop out of the criminal justice system. Only some crimes are reported to the police, and of these, only some are deemed by the police to be *founded*. Of the founded incidents, some do not result in the laying of a criminal charge. Of the charges actually brought to court, some are dropped or stayed, and the remainder do not all end in the conviction of an accused. If such a small percentage of crimes result in the imposition of a penalty, the nature of the sentence will have little impact on the overall volume of crime. Clearly, then, the sentencing system is limited in its ability to reduce the crime rate.

Use of Incarceration as a Sanction

Notwithstanding how difficult it is to compare international sentencing because of the differences between criminal justice systems (e.g., offence definitions and early release provisions), statistics show that incarceration rates in Canada are high relative to those in most other countries. Even with the incarceration rates declining in recent years, in 2005 the incarceration rate in Canada was still significantly higher than in many other Western nations (Public Safety and Emergency Preparedness Canada 2005). In 2013 the Correctional Investigator noted that the total offender population increased by 7 percent over the previous five years—at a time when crime rates were declining (Office of the Correctional Investigator 2013).

Commissions of inquiry as well as the federal government have long acknowledged that Canada relies too heavily on imprisonment as a sanction. Yet the public is often unaware of this reality. In 1999, a poll asked Canadians whether the incarceration rate in this country was higher, lower, or the same as in most other Western countries. Only 15 percent of respondents knew that the incarceration rate was higher here than elsewhere. Most respondents believed that the incarceration rate was lower in Canada (Roberts, Nuffield, and Hann 2000). Most people would be surprised to learn that over three-quarters of the prison admissions in 2010–11 were for non-violent crimes (Dauvergne 2012).

Corrections

There is a significant gap between public perception and the reality of prison life. Many Canadians feel that an inmate's life is an easy one and are not aware of the privations and difficulties suffered by incarcerated offenders. Most people are also unaware of the high rates of homicide, suicide, and assault in correctional institutions. One Gallup survey conducted in 1991 found that half the respondents felt that conditions in penal institutions were "too liberal," although fewer than 5 percent reported any first-hand experience in a correctional institution. In addition, many members of the public believe that if prison conditions were much harsher, prisoners would be less likely to reoffend. However, research has shown that making prisons more austere and taking away privileges may make prison life more unpleasant, but it does not result in lower reoffending rates. Simply put, making a prison a very inhospitable place to live will not mean that prisoners will be less likely to return to a life of crime. Preventing reoffending involves ensuring that ex-offenders get jobs and have a stake in the community.

Parole Grant Rates

The correctional issue that generates most public criticism concerns early release from prison. Most Canadians believe that too many inmates are released from prison too early. This view is based largely on misperceptions about the purpose of the parole system. In general, the public believes that most prisoners are granted release on parole and that parole is easy to obtain. One poll found that half the respondents overestimated the federal parole rate. In reality, less than half the applications for full parole release at the federal level are approved (Public Safety and Emergency Preparedness Canada 2005).

In addition, prisoners applying for parole must convince the Parole Board that they are not a risk to the community and that their progress toward rehabilitation would be assisted by release.

Success Rates of Parolees

The gap between public perception and reality is probably greater for parole and early release issues than for any other criminal justice topic. Intense media coverage of the small number of cases in which a parolee is charged with a serious offence likely contributes to widespread public concern about prisoners released on parole. High-profile incidents influence public knowledge about parole and subsequently affect public attitudes toward early release programs. Moreover, the public tends to believe that a significant percentage of these parolees commit further offences. In fact, the failure rate of offenders on parole tends to be quite low. Public misperceptions regarding parole recidivism may also fuel public opposition toward the early release of inmates serving terms of imprisonment for violent crimes.

Costs of Incarceration versus Supervision in the Community

A Gallup survey found that fewer than 20 percent of respondents were able to accurately estimate the cost of keeping an offender in prison. Few Canadians realize that it costs $357 a day to house an offender in a penitentiary (Dauvergne 2012). Most people believe it costs a lot less than this amount. At the same time, just as people underestimate the cost of incarceration, they also overestimate the cost of supervising an offender in the community. On average, it costs approximately $25,000 per year to supervise an offender in the community—one-fifth the cost of imprisonment. If the public knew how much money the system could save by punishing offenders in the community rather than in prison, they would probably be more supportive of community-based sentences and parole.

SUMMARY

Most people have a great deal of interest in criminal justice stories. However, this does not mean that they are necessarily well informed about the system. While expecting the public to have accurate views of all aspects of crime and justice would be naive, and while there are areas in which public awareness has increased in recent years, there remain important issues for which further public education is imperative. Crime provokes a great deal of public concern and debate over the nature of appropriate crime control policies. However, when evaluating public support for these policies, criminologists should bear in mind what people actually know about crime and criminal justice. Only when the public has a realistic understanding of crime and justice can an informed debate over crime control policies take place.

PLAN OF THE FIFTH EDITION

This fifth edition of *Criminal Justice in Canada: A Reader* contains a diverse collection of contemporary readings in criminal justice. **Part One** contains chapters dealing with general issues associated with criminal justice, while **Part Two** consists of contributions from participants in the criminal justice system. Criminal justice professionals draw upon their own experiences to comment on the system. Textbooks in criminal justice and even the most carefully conducted research cannot replace the experience of those actually participating in the criminal process. (This is why I always encourage students to observe the practice of the system directly whenever possible by going on "ride alongs" with the police or by sitting in court as an observer.) This section of the reader was conceived with this purpose in mind: to provide a view of the justice system drawn directly from the participants themselves.

The remaining chapters in **Part Three** address some of the most important criminal justice issues being discussed in Canada today. The contributors explore a wide range of topics, including the successes and failures of the criminal justice system. Many problems confront criminal justice in Canada, including the persistently high rate of incarceration of Aboriginal Canadians, to name but one problem that has yet to be adequately addressed. In 2012, Statistics Canada reported that adults sentenced to custody were disproportionately Aboriginal: the Aboriginal custody rate was eight times higher than the percentage of Aboriginal peoples in the general population (Dauvergne 2012). It is important not to lose sight of the failings of the system, and for this reason one of the issues explored is the problem of wrongful convictions. All justice systems make mistakes and no error is more serious than convicting a person who is innocent. Regrettably, a number of individuals have been convicted of a crime they did not commit, and this is discussed from the perspective of research and also the individual who is victimized in this way.

Further Readings

Goff, C. 2014. *Criminal Justice in Canada*. 6th ed. Toronto: Nelson Education Ltd.

Griffiths, C. 2014. *Canadian Criminal Justice: A Primer*. 5th ed. Toronto: Nelson Education Ltd.

Roberts, J.V., and M. Hough. 2005. *Understanding Public Attitudes to Criminal Justice*. Maidenhead: Open University Press.

References

Angus Reid. 2010. *Americans, Britons, and Canadians Take a Harsh Stance on Crime*. Toronto: Angus Reid.

Ashworth, A. 2010. *Sentencing and Criminal Justice*. 5th ed. Cambridge: Cambridge University Press.

Brennan, S. 2011. *Canadians' Perceptions of Personal Safety and Crime, 2009*. Ottawa: Statistics Canada.

Canadian Sentencing Commission. 1987. *Sentencing Reform: A Canadian Approach*. Ottawa: Supply and Services Canada.

Dauvergne, M. 2012. Adult Correctional Statistics in Canada, 2010–2011. *Juristat*. Cat. no. 85-002-x. Ottawa: Statistics Canada.

Dowds, L. 1995. *The Long-Eyed View of Law and Order: A Decade of British Social Attitudes Survey Results*. London: Home Office.

Focus Canada. 2014. *Highlights on Crime and Justice*. www.environics.ca/environics-in-the-news?news_id=115.

National Victim Center. 1991. *Citizens' Attitudes About Victims' Rights and Violence*. New York: National Victim Center.

Observer, The. "Crime Uncovered." April 27, 2003.

Office of the Correctional Investigator. *Annual Report, 2012–2013*. Ottawa: Office of the Correctional Investigator.

Packer, H. 1968. *The Limits of the Criminal Sanction*. Stanford: Stanford University Press.

Public Safety and Emergency Preparedness Canada. 2005. *Corrections and Conditional Release Statistical Overview*. Ottawa: Public Safety Canada.

Roberts, J.V. 2002. *Public Evaluations of Criminal Justice Professionals in Canada*. Ottawa: Department of Justice Canada.

Roberts, J.V. 2007. "Public Confidence in Criminal Justice in Canada: A Comparative and Contextual Analysis." *Canadian Journal of Criminology and Criminal Justice* 49: 153–85.

Roberts, J.V., N. Crutcher, and P. Verbrugge. 2007. "Public Attitudes to Sentencing in Canada: Some Recent Findings." *Canadian Journal of Criminology and Criminal Justice* 49: 75–107.

Roberts, J.V., and R. Hastings. 2007. "Public Opinion and Crime Prevention: A Review of International Findings." *Revue de l'Institut pour la Prevention de la Criminalite* 1: 193–218.

Roberts, J.V., and M. Hough. 2005. *Understanding Public Attitudes to Criminal Justice*. Maidenhead: Open University Press.

Roberts, J.V., J. Nuffield, and R. Hann. 2000. "Parole and the Public: Attitudinal and Behavioural Responses." *Empirical and Applied Criminal Justice Research* 1: 1–29.

CHAPTER 2

Criminal Justice and the *Canadian Charter of Rights and Freedoms*

Who ultimately determines the way the justice system functions? To a large degree it is Parliament, which is composed of the elected representatives of the people. In Canada, the federal Parliament creates and amends criminal laws, while the provinces and territories administer the criminal justice system. But that does not mean that Parliament can legislate any kind of law it likes, or that the provincial and territorial governments can run the system as they like. Courts have the authority to review legislation as well as the actions of criminal justice professionals to ensure these are consistent with Canada's supreme law—the *Canadian Charter of Rights and Freedoms* (hereafter "the *Charter*"). This chapter reviews the role the *Charter* has played in shaping the criminal justice system in Canada. It discusses how the daily decisions of criminal justice practitioners such as police officers and prosecutors have been influenced by this fundamental law, which protects our rights.

Marie Manikis
McGill University

The courts ensure that all criminal justice laws and practices are consistent with the *Charter*. If the judiciary finds that a particular law violates an individual's rights, it may strike the law down; Parliament should then comply with the ruling and make sure the law is consistent with the *Charter*. For example, the Supreme Court of Canada decided to strike down the entire *Criminal Code* section that criminalized abortion, since it violated women's *Charter* right to security (see *R. v. Morgentaler* 1988). Ever since this ruling, Parliament has avoided enacting any criminal laws on abortion in order to respect the *Charter*. More recently, the Supreme Court of Canada also decided to strike down all provisions in the Criminal Code that criminalized activities that relate to prostitution since they breached the *Charter* (see *Canada [Attorney General] v. Bedford* 2013). The *Charter*'s impact on the criminal justice system has been and continues to be strong. For this reason, anyone interested in the Canadian criminal justice system—all readers of this book—need to know about the role of the *Charter*.

The enactment of the *Charter* substantially changed the Canadian criminal justice system: Canada has developed into a state with an entrenched Bill of Rights similar to the American individual rights–based model. This model depends on a system of checks and balances in which the judicial branch has the power to verify that laws and state conduct are in accordance with the rights contained in the *Charter*. This important step toward a due process model of rights has provided individuals with an instrument for addressing the power imbalances and abuses that exist between them and the state—including prosecutors and the police.

This chapter reviews the *Charter*'s impact on the criminal justice system. It then considers the objectives of certain rights and their impact on participants in the criminal justice system. Finally, it explores some of the *Charter*'s limits as well as the challenges this instrument may still need to address.

THE *CHARTER*'S IMPACT ON THE POLICE

The Right to Privacy: Modifying Police Conduct during Search and Seizure

The *Charter* has constitutionalized the right to security against unreasonable search and seizure. In so doing it has established privacy as one of the most important values in our society. According to the decision in *Hunter v. Southam Inc.* (1984), privacy rights require, in most cases, that police officers obtain a warrant before searching a house, car, or any other location where a person has a reasonable expectation of privacy. More recently, the Supreme Court of Canada has devised a specific framework that recognizes stronger privacy protections for personal computers and similar devices (*R. v. Vue* 2013).

In other words, the police cannot just walk into someone's house whenever they want and search for incriminating evidence. A search of a home performed without a warrant is presumed to be abusive in the sense of violating the residents' rights. To address such cases, the Supreme Court (in *R. v. Collins* 1987) created an elaborate framework that requires the state to prove that the search was not abusive and was based on reasonable grounds. The police must have reasonable grounds to believe that the person is carrying an illegal object or substance on her person or inside her belongings.

Prior to the *Charter*, search powers existed but were not scrutinized, and this often led to abuses of power. Police and prosecutors sometimes obtained evidence in breach of individual rights, often without a warrant or reasonable grounds. Such evidence was then admissible in criminal court proceedings. For example, police officers were able to enter homes at any time and search people on the premises for illegal drugs. Or if they suspected that public washrooms were being used for "indecent" acts, they were permitted to hide behind air ducts and covertly observe individuals in stalls.

A notable example of a search that violated an individual's rights took place in 1974 in a Fort Erie tavern. During a "raid," the police physically searched almost all of the 115 individuals present and subjected 35 women to strip and body cavity searches. This search resulted in the discovery of six ounces of marijuana, most of it found on the tavern's floor instead of on these individuals. The Supreme Court considered this police raid to be legal. Police abuses would remain mostly out of sight until the *Charter* was enacted.

The *Charter* provides individuals with privacy protections in cases of abusive police conduct. Individuals now possess rights that are enforceable through the courts, which have the power to provide suitable remedies. Clearly, the *Charter* has increased citizens' sense of privacy as well as their security from unwarranted state interference. It has also enabled the courts to scrutinize police behaviour and contributed to the discovery of abusive situations, thereby bringing these practices out of the shadows.

Despite the *Charter*'s important contribution to privacy rights, concerns remain regarding searches and seizures, particularly for certain groups. Systemic racism is a reality that the criminal justice system faces—one that has affected the exercise of all police powers, including the search power (Rosenberg 2009). Although the *Charter* is in place to ensure that minorities and youths are treated fairly by the state, evidence in the lower courts suggests that police still abuse privacy rights (Stuart 2008). In addition, constitutional guarantees against unlawful searches seem to be less effective in contexts involving the poor and the homeless. For example, it is harder to ensure an individual's privacy rights when she lives in public housing, or if she is homeless and living on the street. This remains an important challenge for future *Charter* developments to address.

The Right to Counsel: Modifying Police Conduct during Detention, Arrest, and Interrogations

The right to consult a lawyer upon arrest is one of the most frequent subjects of *Charter* appeals. Section 10(b) of the *Charter* states that "[e]veryone has the right on arrest or detention ... to retain and instruct counsel without delay and to be informed of that right." The Supreme Court has interpreted this simple sentence quite broadly and requires police to provide suspects with (a) detailed, practical information about their rights (and how they can exercise them effectively) and (b) a reasonable opportunity to talk to a lawyer by providing them with the necessary means to contact one should they express a desire to do so (Penney 2004). To ensure that these requirements of fundamental justice are met, legal aid authorities have organized facilities that provide immediate and free advice for suspects who have been detained or arrested.

The right to counsel renders the complex criminal justice system more accessible to individuals. It recognizes the importance of legal counsel as a means to achieve more just results. The purpose of this right is to give criminal suspects a fair opportunity to exercise their right to silence and to refrain from self-incrimination. Hence, a person will be told that she does not have to collaborate with the prosecuting authorities. This places great importance on defence lawyers, who advise individuals on their right to silence. Furthermore, the police must refrain from searching for evidence when a person detained or arrested asserts the right to counsel, until she is given a reasonable opportunity to contact a lawyer (see *R. v. Bartle* 1994).

Despite the importance of the right to counsel, its impact is limited. First, the police's duty to inform the individual of his right to counsel is triggered solely at the outset of an investigative detention, immediately after the individual is detained or arrested (see *R. v. Grant* 2009; *R. v. Suberu* 2009). After that, most individuals must rely on their own resources, unless they qualify for legal aid, which is rare. Also, individuals who invoke their right to counsel must only be given a "reasonable opportunity" to do so. There is no requirement that they actually talk to a lawyer (Penney 2008). And once this opportunity has been taken, police are permitted to question the detainee, even if that person protests that he does not want to participate in the interview (see *R. v. Hebert* 1990). In addition, police are permitted to encourage individuals to disregard their lawyer's advice, as long as they do not unduly persist or impugn the integrity of counsel.

Commentators have expressed concerns about the police's commitment to providing the right to counsel in the context of routine, everyday police–citizen encounters (Rosenberg 2009). In some poorer neighbourhoods, visible minorities are routinely stopped on the streets for questioning. On those occasions they must rely solely on their wits and resources, without counsel. Administering the criminal justice system in such a manner can lead to problems, since the enforcement of justice in those circumstances relies heavily on the stopped person's ignorance of his rights and on his inequality of opportunity to assert those rights (Rosenberg 2009). Access to justice thus remains an important societal challenge in a society in which racial profiling in the streets persists (see Rudin 2008; Tanovich 2008).

To summarize, the *Charter* has had a profound impact on police practices. The police are required to respect people's privacy rights during searches and to inform arrested or detained individuals of their right to consult a lawyer. This development deters abusive police practices; it also reduces the power imbalance between the suspect and the state by providing individuals with more information about their rights. This information empowers individuals, who enjoy greater protection from self-incrimination and from the possibility of being wrongfully convicted. Yet despite these developments, there is much room for improvement. Access to justice should be unaffected by class or social status.

THE *CHARTER*'S IMPACT ON PROSECUTORIAL CONDUCT: THE DISCLOSURE OF EVIDENCE

One of the most important contributions that the *Charter* has made to the criminal justice system involves changes to prosecutorial "disclosure" practices. At present, in order to prepare his defence, the defendant has a right to full disclosure of all the evidence against him. This means that the prosecutor (the Crown) must provide the accused with all relevant information gathered during the investigation, whether or not the prosecutor intends to introduce it as evidence, and whether or not it suggests guilt or innocence (see *R. v. Stinchcombe* 1991). This requirement enables the defendant to prepare a proper defence and reduces the risk of wrongful convictions. Indeed, inadequate disclosure has been identified as one of the leading causes of wrongful convictions (see, for example, the Nova Scotia, Royal Commission on the Donald Marshall Jr. Prosecution). This obligation on the prosecution to disclose the case has revolutionized the process by modifying the pre-*Charter* paradigm, which held that the results of investigations in the Crown's possession belonged to the Crown to secure a conviction. The results of investigations are now considered public property that must be provided to the accused in order to achieve greater justice.

Prior to the *Charter*, disclosure issues were decided by Crown counsel (prosecutors) and thus were almost entirely discretionary. Curiously, civil cases in Canada were subject to a much more generous regime of disclosure, even if the interests at stake were far less crucial to the individual than the liberty interests at stake in criminal cases. The criminal regime presumed that the accused would use this disclosure to fabricate evidence that would facilitate perjury. In rare cases, limited disclosure was provided, but the quality of disclosure varied from one jurisdiction to the next and from one prosecutor to the next. No remedy was provided in cases of insufficient disclosure, except for disciplinary proceedings, which were rare.

This state of affairs contributed to wrongful convictions (discussed in later chapters of this book) and deprived some accused individuals of the means to demonstrate their innocence (Rosenberg 2009). For example, Donald Marshall Jr. was wrongfully convicted of murder and sentenced to life in prison. The Marshall Inquiry in 1989 revealed that the prosecutor's failure to provide full disclosure contributed to his wrongful conviction (see Nova Scotia, Royal Commission on the Donald Marshall Jr. Prosecution). Other inquiries relating to wrongful convictions reached similar conclusions (see Ontario, Commission on Proceedings Involving Guy Paul Morin; Manitoba, Commission of Inquiry into Certain Aspects of the Trial and Conviction of James Driskell). The *Charter* has certainly helped reduce the risk of wrongful conviction.

THE *CHARTER*'S IMPACT ON VICTIMS AND WITNESSES

The *Charter* has had an impact on participants other than the accused and criminal justice officials (Barrett 2008). Judges have recognized that vulnerable victims and witnesses (such as children, people with developmental disabilities, and people who have been sexually assaulted) can benefit from certain constitutional protections.

It can be very difficult—sometimes traumatic—for children and sexual assault victims to testify in criminal trials. For this reason the Supreme Court has recognized the importance of several measures in the *Criminal Code* (R.S.C. 1985, c. C-46) to facilitate victim participation in the process (see *R. v. Legoviannis* 1993). For children, Section 486.2 allows certain victims to testify outside the courtroom or behind a screen to avoid being seen by the accused, which was held to respect the *Charter* (see *R. v. J.Z.S.* 2008, 2009). The court has stated that since child witnesses have rights and require protection from emotional harm during criminal proceedings, protective measures like these should be employed (see Bala 2008).

In addition, cross-examination practices by the defence counsel regarding sexual assault victims have changed. Judges have recognized that victims have security, privacy, and equality rights; as a consequence, the content of cross-examinations has been restricted. For example, in sexual assault trials, evidence and cross-examination questions based on stereotypes, such as the victim's/witness's prior sexual history and sexual reputation, are now prohibited. Furthermore, to encourage victim testimony and to avoid discriminatory conclusions based on stereotypes, the court has recognized that victims of sexual assault have privacy rights regarding their medical and therapeutic records. Thus the accused generally does not have access to these records for his defence (*R. v. Mills* 1999).

To summarize, victims qualified as "vulnerable," such as people who were sexually assaulted, have benefited from their rights in court. Conversely, rights for victims who are not considered vulnerable are exceptional and more limited. Victims' rights were never explicitly entrenched in the *Charter,* and the courts remain a less than welcoming place for them. Judicial reform and education could greatly enhance participation and access to justice for these individuals.

THE *CHARTER*'S IMPACT ON JUDGES

Charter Remedies and the Exclusion of Evidence

Arguably, one of the most important elements the *Charter* has brought to criminal law is the possibility of obtaining remedies in cases of rights violations. Judges are the protectors of rights and have the ability to devise the remedies they see fit as a response to violations. In effect, under Section 24(1) of the *Charter*, judges have been given wide and unfettered discretion to provide any remedy that they consider "appropriate and just in the circumstances."

These remedies include stays of proceedings (permanently terminating proceedings) against the accused—the equivalent of an acquittal. This remedy is only awarded when other remedies cannot adequately redress a certain breach. For instance, it has been awarded in cases where a defendant's *Charter* right to be tried within a reasonable time was breached (see *R v. Askov* 1990) and more recently in a case of egregious breach of a defendant's *Charter* rights, where a prison guard grievously assaulted a defendant who was chained, shackled, handcuffed, and defenceless (*R. v. Bellusci* 2012). Further, under Section 24(1) courts can also order government officials and institutions to pay damages to people whose rights have been violated. For instance, a damage award of $5,000 was given to an individual following an unconstitutional strip search that was made by the police (see *Vancouver v. Ward* 2010). Moreover, most courts have also accepted that sentence reductions can also be ordered under Section 24(1) when rights are breached. Prior to the *Charter*, the way evidence was obtained was not important; even in cases of abuse, remedies were not available, except for disciplinary sanctions, which were virtually never imposed.

The power to exclude unconstitutionally obtained evidence (also known as the exclusionary rule) pursuant to Section 24(2) of the *Charter* has been one of the most powerful and drastic *Charter* remedies in the context of criminal trials, since the exclusion of evidence often results in the defendant's acquittal. That section's main objectives include the preservation of the justice system's integrity and the protection from wrongful convictions.

Initially, this remedy was used more often, notably in cases of right-to-counsel breaches, abusive searches and seizures by police, illegal detentions, and abusive interrogations that led to confessions. In certain cases, the exclusionary rule was quasi-automatic. Many academics and civil rights activists welcomed this groundbreaking remedy, contending that it was a defining feature of any legal system committed to the protection of individual due process rights in criminal law (see Packer 1964; Stribopoulos 2008). In the past few years, however, the public has expressed dissatisfaction with these numerous exclusions—at least when they have resulted in acquittals. Public opposition has been particularly vocal in cases where serious crimes remained unpunished.

Public discontent may have in part contributed to the Supreme Court's decision in *R. v. Grant* (2009), in which judges decided to exclude unconstitutionally obtained evidence less frequently. In most cases, where state officials have not intentionally breached the defendant's rights and the evidence obtained is reliable, the evidence will not be excluded. Since that decision, the judiciary has been confronted with the difficult task of finding the right balance between the discovery of truth related to a crime in criminal proceedings and the exclusion of evidence obtained in breach of the accused's fundamental *Charter* rights. The complexity often arises when evidence that renders the accused factually guilty of a serious crime has been obtained in violation of the accused's rights. It has been argued that evidence is more easily excluded when the accused has committed a minor offence without causing injury than when the accused was in possession of a dangerous weapon such as a gun (Rosenberg 2009). For example, if the police stop an individual without a motive and discover a hidden gun, the evidence (the gun) has been obtained unconstitutionally; yet its discovery suggests that the individual is guilty of a serious crime: the possession of a gun. In such cases, to facilitate convictions, judges may be tempted to allow the evidence despite the way in which it was obtained. Many *Charter* scholars have warned against this practice, since rights violations should be taken seriously and denounced whether the individual is factually guilty or not (see Quigley 2008).

The *Charter*'s Impact on Sentencing

Finally, it is interesting to note that the *Charter*'s impact has only recently been felt in the area of sentencing. Several constitutional provisions can be invoked: Section 9, which guarantees protection from arbitrary detention and imprisonment; Section 12, which guarantees protection from cruel and unusual punishment and treatment; and Section 15, which guarantees the right to equality. The *Charter*'s protections against unreasonable punishment (Section 9) have rarely been applied, but, in more recent years, protection from cruel and unusual punishment (Section 12), as well as equality protections for Aboriginal offenders (Section 15) were successfully invoked in appellate court cases that challenged the constitutionality of mandatory minimum sentences (see, for example, *R. v. Nur* 2013; *R. v. Smickle* 2013; *R. v. Lloyd* 2014; *R. v. Anderson* 2013). Since 1982, Parliament has legislated mandatory sentences of imprisonment for a number of crimes, and in 2008 new mandatory minimum sentences were introduced for firearm crimes and impaired driving offences.

A considerable body of literature has demonstrated over the years that most minimum sentences of imprisonment are unfair and ineffective, as well as unduly harsh in certain cases (see, for example, Roberts 2001; Roach 2001). Further, it has been argued that mandatory minimum sentences would disproportionately affect the incarceration of Aboriginal offenders, which would be contrary to the right to equality protected under Section 15 of the *Charter* (Chartrand 2001). Despite this, the Supreme Court has traditionally not interfered with Parliament's plans and has refrained from considering them to be contrary to the *Charter*. The debate at the Supreme Court level will take place soon, as the court will be deciding whether a specific mandatory minimum provision breaches Aboriginal offenders' rights to equality under Section 15 of the *Charter* (see *R. v. Anderson* 2014). Hence, it will be interesting to see whether the *Charter* will continue to have an impact of these types of sentences.

In the context of youth justice and sentencing, the *Charter* has also had an impact. The Supreme Court of Canada recently constitutionalized the principle of "diminished moral blameworthiness" for young offenders (see Bala 2009; *R. v. D.B.* 2009). Since youth have limited capacities (relative to adults), they are considered less blameworthy than adults guilty of similar crimes. Young offenders should not therefore be sentenced like adults. For these reasons, the Supreme Court found that elements of the *Youth Criminal Justice Act* (*YCJA*) would breach the *Charter*. Indeed the YCJA, as passed by Parliament in 2002, included a presumption that youth 14 or older found guilty of certain serious violent offences would receive an adult sentence. Based on the principle of diminished moral blameworthiness protected by the *Charter*, this presumption of adult sentencing for youth in cases of serious offences was considered contrary to the young offender's *Charter* rights. Moreover, youths also benefit from special measures to prevent their identity from being publicly exposed even in the most serious crimes.

PRACTICAL MEASURES TO FACILITATE THE IMPLEMENTATION OF *CHARTER* RIGHTS

The *Charter*'s contribution to the advancement of individual rights constitutes a significant development in criminal justice. However, the *Charter* is not perfect and cannot solve all the problems identified in this chapter. Legal education and governmental services are important elements that need to be developed concurrently with *Charter* rights to address these systemic concerns and to ensure the *Charter*'s effective implementation.

First, despite the *Charter*'s enactment, police still engage in racial profiling of visible minorities. It has been argued that the criminal justice system has failed to address these issues in the courts or to adopt appropriate critical race standards in judicial reasoning (Tanovich 2008). Also, youth and visible minorities are subjected to proactive tactics by police that often result in *Charter* breaches. Education and police training can be good starting points to achieve the effective implementation of equality rights free from discrimination based on gender, race, age, or income. Moreover, legal education is an important measure that can contribute to meaningful legal reform. For example, it can promote recognition that marginal groups—notably, victims of crime—also deserve *Charter* protections.

CONCLUSION

It is safe to say that the *Charter* has had a profound impact on virtually every stage of the criminal justice system. Key developments since the *Charter*'s enactment include changes in police and prosecution practices regarding individual rights. Police forces currently have constitutional duties to respect an accused's right to privacy and to inform that person of the right to counsel during detention and arrest. Prosecutors also have the important obligation of disclosing to the accused *all* elements of the investigation. The *Charter*'s impact on victims, young offenders, and vulnerable witnesses, as well as the important remedial powers vested in courts to address *Charter* breaches, have made an important contribution to the recognition and protection of fundamental individual rights. But despite these important positive changes, systemic concerns remain. Access to justice and *Charter* litigation is harder for certain marginal groups, which are subjected to racism, discrimination, and inequalities; consequently, there is room for further *Charter* developments to address these issues. Unless *Charter* rights and developments are accompanied by education, and by governmental resources and services, systemic problems will remain and the implementation of *Charter* rights will be illusory for certain individuals.

Further Readings

Roach, K., and R. Sharpe. 2005. *The Charter of Rights and Freedoms*. 3rd ed. Toronto: Irwin Law.

Stribopoulos, J. 2006. "Has Everything Been Decided? Certainty, the Charter, and Criminal Justice." 34 *Supreme Court Law Review* (2d) 34: 381–408.

Stuart, D. 2005. *Charter Justice in Canadian Criminal Law*. 4th ed. Toronto: Carswell.

References

Bala, N. 2008. "Youth as Victims and Offenders in the Criminal Justice System: A *Charter* Analysis—Recognizing Vulnerability." *Supreme Court Law Review* 40: 595–625.

——. 2009. "*R. v. D.B.*: The Constitutionalization of Adolescence." *Supreme Court Law Review* 47: 211–34.

Barrett, J. 2008. "Expanding Victims' Rights in the *Charter* Era and Beyond." In J. Cameron and J. Stribopoulos, eds., *The Charter and Criminal Justice: Twenty-Five Years Later*. Markham: LexisNexis.

Chartrand, L.N. 2001. "Aboriginal Peoples and Mandatory Sentencing." *Osgoode Hall Law Journal* 39: 449–67.

Packer, H. 1964. "Two Models of the Criminal Process." *University of Pennsylvania Law Review* 113: 1–68.

Penney, S. 2004. "What's Wrong with Self-Incrimination? The Wayward Path of Self-Incrimination Law in the Post-Charter Era—Part II: Self-Incrimination in Police Investigations." *Criminal Law Quarterly* 48: 280–336.

——. 2008. "Triggering the Right to Counsel: 'Detention' and Section 10 of the *Charter*." In J. Cameron and J. Stribopoulos, eds., *The Charter and Criminal Justice: Twenty-Five Years Later*. Markham: LexisNexis.

Quigley, T. 2008. "The Impact of the *Charter* on the Law of Search and Seizure." In J. Cameron and J. Stribopoulos, eds., *The Charter and Criminal Justice: Twenty-Five Years Later*. Markham: LexisNexis.

Roach, K. 2001. "Searching for Smith: The Constitutionality of Mandatory Sentences." *Osgoode Hall Law Journal* 39: 367–412.

Roberts, J.V. 2001. "Mandatory Minimum Sentences: Exploring the Consequences for the Sentencing Process." *Osgoode Hall Law Journal* 39: 305–28.

Rosenberg, M. 2009. "Twenty-Five Years Later: The Impact of the *Canadian Charter of Rights and Freedoms* on the Criminal Law." *Supreme Court Law Review* (2d), 45.

Rudin, J. 2008. "Aboriginal Over-Representation and *R. v. Gladue*: Where We Were, Where We Are, and Where We Might Be Going." In J. Cameron and J. Stribopoulos, eds., *The Charter and Criminal Justice: Twenty-Five Years Later*. Markham: LexisNexis.

Stribopoulos, J. 2008. "Has the *Charter* Been for Crime Control? Reflecting on 25 Years of Constitutional Criminal Procedure in Canada." In M. Beare, ed., *Honouring Social Justice: Honouring Dianne Martin*. Toronto: University of Toronto Press.

Stuart, D. 2008. "*Charter* Standards for Investigative Powers: Have the Courts Got the Balance Right?" *Supreme Court Law Review* 40: 1–53.

Tanovich, D. 2008. "The Charter of Whiteness: Twenty-Five Years of Maintaining Racial Injustice in the Canadian Criminal Justice System." *Supreme Court Law Review* (2d), 40: 655–86.

Cases Cited

Canada (Attorney General) v. Bedford, 2013 SCC 72.

Hunter v. Southam Inc., [1984] 2 S.C.R. 14.

R. v. Anderson, 2013 NLCA 2; 2014 SCC No. 35246.

R. v. Askov, [1990] 2 S.C.R. 1199.

R. v. Bartle, [1994] 3 S.C.R. 173.

R. v. Bellusci, [2012] 2 S.C.R. 509.

R. v. Collins, [1987] 1 S.C.R 265.

R. v. D.B., [2008] 2 S.C.R. 3.

R. v. Grant, [2009] 2 S.C.R. 353.

R. v. Hebert, [1990] S.C.J. No. 64.

R. v. J.Z.S., 2008 BCCA 401; 2010 SCC 1.

R. v. Levogiannis, [1993] 4 S.C.R. 475.

R. v. Loyd, 2014 BCPC 0008.

R. v. Mills, [1999] 3 S.C.R. 668.

R. v. Morgentaler, [1988] 1 S.C.R. 30.

R. v. Nur, 2013 ONCA 677.

R. v. Smickle, 2013 ONCA 678.

R. v. Stinchcombe, [1991] 3 S.C.R. 325.

R. v. Suberu, [2009] 2 S.C.R. 460.

R. v. Vue, 2013 SCC 60.

Vancouver v. Ward, [2010] 2 S.C.R. 28.

Reports

Nova Scotia, Royal Commission on the Donald Marshall Jr. Prosecution, *Commissioners' Report, Findings and Recommendations 1989*, vols. 1–7 (Halifax: 1989) (Chair: Justice T. Alexander Hickman).

Ontario, *Commission on Proceedings Involving Guy Paul Morin, Report* (Toronto: Queen's Printer for Ontario, 1998) (Commissioner: Hon. Fred Kaufman).

Manitoba, *Report of the Commission of Inquiry into Certain Aspects of the Trial and Conviction of James Driskell* (Winnipeg: 2007) (Commissioner: Hon. Patrick J. LeSage, Q.C.).

CHAPTER 3

The Funhouse Mirror: Media Representations of Crime and Justice

Chapter 1 of this volume noted the existence of many public misperceptions about crime and criminal justice. These misperceptions exist in all Western nations. The public tends to perceive crime rates as constantly rising and to believe that the justice system is far more lenient than is in fact the case. The same public also has a very distorted view of important criminal justice trends such as imprisonment and parole rates. Where do these misperceptions come from? This chapter discusses the source of many public misperceptions about crime and justice: the news media. Peter McKnight, a highly experienced journalist as well as a lawyer by training, discusses how the media represent crime and the justice system's response to crime.

Peter McKnight
Vancouver Sun

Crime is epidemic and growing across the country. The overwhelming majority of crimes involve violence, and the most common form of violent crime is also the most serious: murder. Murderers, who are intelligent, otherwise upstanding members of the middle class, plan their crimes meticulously. Victims, who never know their killers, are typically young, affluent, Caucasian women. The murderers are usually caught, but justice is rarely achieved as offenders are either acquitted on a technicality or handed a slap on the wrist by lenient judges. And so the crime epidemic continues to grow and grow.

This scenario sounds like it was lifted from a dystopian science fiction novel. Yet to regular consumers of the newspapers or television or radio news the scenario will be instantly familiar: it is the world the news media have built. Even a brief review of the news media reveals that crime—and especially violent crime—is rampant and that we are all at great risk of becoming the next victims in an unstoppable crime wave. The picture is not entirely false. Rather, it is simply not the whole truth: violent crimes do occur, but not that often, especially relative to non-violent property crimes. Some murders are carefully planned by high-status offenders, but most are the result of spontaneous acts committed by people under the influence of drugs, alcohol, or intense rage. White, affluent women are sometimes victims of murder, but most victims come from other demographic and socio-economic groups. And while some people charged with murder are acquitted in court, most are convicted. Finally, all defendants convicted of murder in Canada receive a life sentence, and prisoners serving a life sentence for murder typically spend more time in prison than people convicted of murder in other Western nations.

The picture of crime painted by the media is therefore a distorted one. Or, to use the metaphor most commonly applied to the media—they simply hold a mirror up to the world and reflect what is there—we must conclude that it is a *funhouse mirror*, one that accentuates certain aspects of the world, and of crime, at the expense of others. This distorted picture of crime takes on added importance in light of the exposure that crime receives in the media. In a study of American broadcast news, for example, Dorfman and Schiraldi (2001) found that throughout the 1990s, the national networks ABC, CBS, and NBC all devoted more time to crime than to any other type of story. Similar results were found for local U.S. television stations, with as much as 30 percent of news time devoted just to violent crime.

A series of studies (Ericson et al. 1987, 1989, 1991) of major news outlets in Toronto found even more striking results, with upwards of half of all stories dedicated to deviance. It should be noted, however, that in focusing on deviance, Ericson and his colleagues considered not merely stories involving crime, but also those covering departures from "organisational procedures and violations of common sense knowledge." We must be careful, then, not to infer too much about crime coverage in the media from Ericson and colleagues' studies (Reiner 2007). But the studies do show that deviance is "the defining characteristic of what journalists regard as newsworthy." And this leads us into a contemplation of what journalists consider newsworthy, of how the media paint a distorted picture of crime through their selection of certain stories from the vast array that present themselves to journalists each day.

ELEMENTS OF NEWSWORTHINESS

Since Chibnall's classic *Law-and-Order News* (1977), many scholars have sought to identify the factors that lead the media to consider a story newsworthy. Chibnall identified five factors: novelty, immediacy, personalization, dramatization, and titillation. Since then, others have suggested at least a dozen more (Jewkes 2004). Let's consider some of the most often cited elements of newsworthiness.

Characteristics of the Offence

As noted above, deviance is itself newsworthy, but most forms of deviance or crime will not make it onto the evening news or the pages of a daily newspaper. To be worthy of coverage, a crime must meet a certain threshold of significance, and violent crimes are the most likely to meet that threshold. Marsh reviewed research on crime news in the United States and other countries between the 1960s and 1980s (Marsh 1991; Reiner 2007). All studies revealed that the media overemphasized violent offences and underemphasized property crimes. In the United States there were four times as many stories about violent crimes as property crimes, even though according to official statistics there were nine times as many property offences.

Violent crimes are, therefore, more likely to make it into the news; but not all violent crimes are equal. Murder, the most serious and one of the rarest of violent crimes, is most likely to attract coverage; one study revealed that murder accounted for between one-quarter and one-third of crime stories on American television news (Dorfman and Schiraldi 2001). Offences of a sexual nature also receive a disproportionate amount of press attention. In one month in Britain in 1981, crimes involving sex and violence accounted for nearly half of newspaper coverage, despite comprising little more than 2 percent of reported incidents (Ditton and Duffy 1983; Jewkes 2010).

Unlike Britain and the United States, media coverage of violent crime in Canada has not been the subject of exhaustive study. But crime reporting in Canada does appear similar, as murder stories are commonly seen on the front pages of newspapers and on evening newscasts, despite making up less than 1 percent of violent crime (Statistics Canada 2009b). Similarly, violent crime is more frequently covered than property crime, even though five times as many property crimes are reported to police, and even this likely underestimates the problem, since many property crimes go unreported.

Finally, given their novelty, "new" crimes—behaviours that have only recently been conceptualized as crimes—also tend to preoccupy the press. The 1960s, 1970s, and 1980s witnessed increased reporting of what were then new crimes, including drug offences, child sexual offences, and domestic violence. Today, crimes such as road rage, carjacking, and "grow rips"—breaking into a building in which marijuana is being grown—fill the pages of newspapers and the schedules of evening news broadcasts.

Characteristics of the Offender

Although official crime statistics suggest that the majority of offenders are young, low-income males, many studies have revealed that news reports overemphasize crimes committed by older, well-to-do men (Roshier 1973; Graber 1980). This suggests that sex is perhaps the only characteristic of offenders that the media reflect accurately. However, given the relative novelty of female offenders, crimes committed by women tend to receive a disproportionate amount of attention, particularly if the female offender is young and her crime involves violence. For example, in 1997, 14-year-old British Columbia resident Reena Virk was swarmed and killed by eight teenagers, all but one of whom were girls. Two of Virk's assailants were subsequently convicted of murder. The case received unprecedented press coverage from coast to coast, in large part because most of the assailants were girls. A national discussion on violence among teenage girls ensued, with sociologists suggesting that the event had prompted a "moral panic" over adolescent female violence (Barron and Lacombe 2005). The age of the offenders in the Virk case contributed to the media feeding frenzy, as the media typically overemphasize crimes involving child and youth offenders. Most infamously, news outlets around the world presented lengthy in-depth coverage of the James Bulger case, in which a two-year-old boy in England was abducted and murdered by two ten-year-old boys (Muncie 1999). Aside from age and sex, the offender's social status also plays a significant role. Almost any crime committed by a celebrity is deemed newsworthy, given that the public is already familiar with the offender (Greer 2003), and in the United States entire television shows are dedicated to the crimes of celebrities. The televised murder trial of O.J. Simpson was followed by huge numbers of viewers, and the announcement of the verdict in that case attracted millions of people to the screen.

While this trend toward celebrity crime is less common in Canada (given the limited number of bona fide celebrities), the news media do emphasize crimes committed by people who enjoy high social status, particularly politicians. In 2010, for example, Rahim Jaffer, a former Member of Parliament and husband of a sitting cabinet minister, was charged with possession of cocaine and driving with a blood alcohol level over the legal limit. Jaffer pleaded guilty to a lesser offence, which is not unusual; but, given his position, the plea bargain received extensive press coverage. A year earlier, news media across the nation devoted great attention to the criminal charges laid against Michael Bryant, Ontario's former Attorney General. He had been charged with criminal negligence causing death and dangerous operation of a motor vehicle causing death (CBC News 2009).

Characteristics of the Victim

Although many violent crimes, in particular homicides, involve offenders and victims who know each other, the media are much more likely to report stranger-on-stranger crimes (Reiner 2007). This serves to cast offenders as "predatory outsiders" rather than family members or friends (Beckett and Sasson 2000).

Consider the case of Wendy Ladner-Beaudry. In 2009, Ladner-Beaudry, the sister of a former Vancouver mayoral candidate, was found dead after jogging through a public park. Although her killer has not been apprehended, it has been assumed that she was killed by a stranger. Largely for that reason, the Vancouver media—and to a lesser extent, the national media—covered Ladner-Baudry's death extensively, with the case becoming the lead story on many nightly newscasts. The statistics reveal just how rare cases like Ladner-Beaudry's are. According to the latest Statistics Canada data, fewer than 10 percent of female homicide victims were killed by a stranger (Statistics Canada 2009a). In contrast, 92 percent of female homicide victims knew their killer, and in upwards of 60 percent of these cases the killer was a current spouse or ex-spouse or a boyfriend of the victim. Yet homicides resulting from domestic violence receive scant attention in the press compared to those committed by an assailant unknown to the victim. Similarly, the media pay less attention to cases involving "innocent" victims. Gang violence in Toronto, Montreal, and Vancouver has received significant press coverage in recent years; yet it is not often noted that the majority of homicides in those cities have been committed by and against gang members. The media have therefore paid little attention to individual victims' stories, beyond noting their gang affiliations.

When an innocent bystander—particularly a child—gets caught in the crossfire, however, the case frequently becomes a *cause célèbre* (Jenkins 1992). For example, a 1990s turf war between two Montreal motorcycle gangs caused the deaths of scores of people; but media coverage intensified considerably when 11-year-old Daniel Desrochers was killed by shrapnel from a car bomb in 1995. Similarly, after 15-year-old Jane Creba was killed by a stray bullet on Toronto's Yonge Street on Boxing Day 2005, unprecedented media coverage of the event led to intense discussions about gun crime, which likely had a significant effect on the 2006 federal election.

Even when victims are not affiliated with gangs, they may not be seen as innocent, and their deaths may therefore slip under the media radar. Between the early 1980s and 2002 more than 60 women went missing from Vancouver's impoverished Downtown Eastside, but those disappearances received relatively little attention at first, possibly because many of the women were Aboriginal sex workers battling mental health and substance abuse problems. To the media's credit, though, a series of articles in the *Vancouver Sun* did call attention to the disappearances. Robert Pickton was eventually convicted of six murders and stands charged with twenty more. The case led to widespread discussion about how the characteristics of the victims affected the amount of attention their disappearance attracted from the press, the police, and the public.

Characteristics of the Sentence

There has been extensive research on media coverage of crime, offenders, and victims; in contrast, relatively little research has been conducted on media reporting of sentencing decisions. But there is some evidence that just as the media tend to overemphasize rare and unusual crimes, they similarly selectively report rare and unusual sentences—that is, sentences that appear to be unusually lenient. In response to public concerns that sentencing in British Columbia is less severe than other provinces, Doob and Webster (2008) compared sentencing patterns across Canada. While finding little reason to believe that B.C.'s sentencing practices are lenient compared to those of other provinces, they noted that popular belief "in sentence leniency is supported, if not strengthened" by the media.

Several studies conducted in the 1980s bear this out (Doob and Roberts 1983; Roberts and Doob 1990). These studies revealed that people who read judges' reasons for sentences are much more likely to consider sentences appropriate than those who read newspaper reports about sentences. For example, in one study, half the participants read the court documents from a sentencing decision, while the other half read the newspaper story describing the sentencing hearing and the sentence. Afterwards both groups were asked what they thought about the sentence, the offender, and the judge. People who had read the newspaper account were significantly more likely to see the sentence as too lenient and to criticize the judge for not considering all the appropriate factors. This study suggests that just as the media selectively attend to certain sentences, they also tend to over- or underemphasize certain facts about the law, the offence, and the offender. These facts are generally ones that lead people to believe that the sentence imposed was too lenient.

FACTORS AFFECTING DETERMINATIONS OF NEWSWORTHINESS

We have thus far considered various elements that the media believe make a crime story newsworthy. But we have yet to consider *why* the media value these elements. Many factors have been suggested to explain media determinations of newsworthiness. We will concentrate on two: news values, and the organizational structure of news organizations and news making (Reiner 2007).

News Values

Perhaps the single most important news value—and hence the most important factor in deciding on newsworthiness—relates to a common definition of news: news is that which is new, rare, and unusual (Hall 1979). By this defini-tion, events that occur all day, every day, simply do not count as news. This is the case with property crime, except perhaps in small towns, where property crime may be rare enough to warrant press coverage. But in large cities and at the national level, commonplace events like property crimes are unlikely to receive coverage unless there is something unusual about them. For example, the theft of art from a museum might garner media attention, given its nov-elty. The theft of a number of famous paintings from a Paris art gallery in 2010 attracted widespread media coverage.

This emphasis on novelty also explains why the press focuses most intensely on the rarest of violent crimes. Similarly, female violent offenders are sufficiently rare to warrant inclusion, as are stranger-on-stranger crimes and ostensibly lenient sentences. Much of what the media consider newsworthy, therefore, arises directly out of the popular definition of news. This definition itself arises out of presumptions about what news consumers want to read and see. Few people are interested in hearing about things that happen all the time; consequently, news outlets strive to give them something different. And with profit margins dwindling, news organizations are ever mindful of the wishes of their readers and viewers. Every major news outlet conducts regular reader and viewer surveys, and these surveys typically reveal signifi-cant interest in crime, but also a great desire for personalization: readers and viewers want to know how the news, whether it concerns crime, health, or finance, affects them personally.

The overemphasis on violence is a form of personalization, since the average news consumer is much more concerned about becoming the victim of a violent crime than of having his wallet stolen. The media's emphasis on offenders who are reasonably well-to-do also stems from an attempt at per-sonalization, since stories involving relatively high-status offenders are likely to resonate with many readers and viewers, given their similarities to such offenders. Similarly, the media's tendency to overemphasize crimes involving reasonably affluent, innocent victims also likely resonates with the audi-ence members, most of whom are—or like to believe they are—affluent and innocent.

Organizational Structure

According to what is sometimes referred to as the "dominant ideology model," the media reinforce existing power structures; thus the emphasis on deviance is an inevitable consequence of the media's desire to maintain law and order (Hall 1979). While there is some truth to this model, much of the media's apparent law-and-order stance stems not from ideological commitments but rather from the organizational structure of news organizations and the pres-sures of news reporting.

The newsroom is governed by headlines and deadlines and is an intensely high-pressure environment. Reporters work under severe time constraints and typically have only a few hours to file their stories. On an average day, a reporter is assigned a story in the morning and must then familiarize herself with the issue, speak to the people involved, and by early afternoon produce a story that is accurate, fair to those involved, and accessible to the audience. The difficulty of this undertaking is compounded by the fact that many justice reporters have limited experience and knowledge of the justice system.

Consequently, reporters rely heavily on government officials and the police to provide them with information about crime. Besides the fact that such sources are often seen as trustworthy and authoritative, justice system officials hold scheduled press conferences, which allow journalists to schedule their day and which ensure that they have an opportunity to speak to interested parties. Also, courthouses function according to schedule and provide many interesting stories. Stationing reporters at courthouses therefore helps reporters manage their time, since they need not dig for stories or search for people to interview (Jewkes 2010).

These practices do, however, mean that reporters will receive the official version of events—typically from politicians and government officials, or from the police. And since these people are interested in defending their measures and actions, there is always the danger that they will shape their stories for the media in ways that reflect positively upon them (Schlesinger and Tumber 1992). Good reporters know to look skeptically upon the pronouncements of officials, but the serious time constraints under which they work sometimes result in a privileging of the officials' versions of events. Officials can therefore play a significant role in determining what the media cover and the way they cover it. This is not necessarily the result of media and justice officials sharing an ideology; rather, it is the result of officials' awareness of the nature of journalism, and their willingness to work within that to get their word out.

Impact of the Media

The media's preoccupation with violent crime has led to concerns that media coverage can cause crime to rise. This long-standing debate is receiving renewed attention owing to concerns about the impact of violent video games on children and teenagers. Thus far the research on the "criminogenic" impact of crime news has been inconclusive (Livingstone 1996), in large part due to the difficulty of establishing real-world causal connections between news consumption and crime (Reiner 2007).

Given these difficulties, we might instead consider a more recently expressed fear: that media coverage of crime leads the public to support a more punitive approach to criminal justice (e.g., Roberts et al. 2003). Surveys suggest that people who consume a lot of news tend to think that crime is much more prevalent than it is; that crime rates are rising even during periods when they are falling; and that "innocent" people—people not involved in criminal activity—are much more likely to be victims of crime that official statistics would suggest. Furthermore, there is some evidence that frequent consumption of television news is associated with higher degrees of fear (Chiricos, Eschholz, and Gertz 1997). It is not entirely clear, though, whether consuming television news causes fear or whether fearful people are more likely to watch the evening newscast.

In light of the media's emphasis on stranger-on-stranger crime and on offences that involve victims who share many characteristics with news consumers, it would not be surprising to find a causal connection between frequent consumption of news and fear. And when the media simultaneously highlight ostensibly lenient sentences, the public might easily conclude that there is a causal connection between high crime rates and lenient sentences. In this way the courts are portrayed as being responsible for stopping crime and then condemned for failing to do so. Needless to say, this can result in decreased public respect for the courts—and, by extension, decreased respect for the Constitution, the rule of law, and the administration of justice. And it can lead to increased public support for more punitive measures, particularly those that limit judicial discretion in sentencing, such as mandatory minimum sentences, which serve to increase prison populations but which have not been shown to reduce crime rates.

CONCLUSION

We have seen that the media paint a distorted picture of crime thanks to their overemphasis on serious, violent crime, and that this can lead to increased and irrational fear as well as to support for counterproductive punitive measures. But seeing is the easy part; the difficult question is how to respond to this systematic distortion of reality. Changing news values won't be easy. It's unlikely that the media will cease publicizing novel events instead of common ones: serious, violent crimes will always receive more attention than trivial property crimes. But it is important that journalists understand the ways in which their business distorts reality, and to write and speak about it, or at least provide context for the stories they cover. The media will also always try to give the public what it wants, and this is where people can have a real and sustained impact on media coverage of crime. Journalism is not a monologue; it is a dialogue in which the press and the public speak to each other. For example, if the public object, loudly and vociferously, to sensational coverage of violent crime, the media will respond by at the very least toning things down. Similarly, if the public demands a broader range of stories, with a more penetrating analysis of crime, the media will comply. There is little that influences the media more than the desires of its consumers.

More than anyone else, courts and judges bear the brunt of the media's distorted picture of crime. This is not surprising, given that, in contrast to other justice system officials, judges typically avoid talking to the media and the public—as the saying goes, they "speak through their judgments." But if judges were more available to the media they could help shape the media's representations of their decisions. In short, we all have the ability to influence the media, to decide what is newsworthy, and to shape the stories the media tell. In this sense, we are all responsible for the distorted picture of crime we see, and we are all responsible for changing the picture. The media might always reflect reality like a funhouse mirror, but anyone can reshape its contours.

Further Readings

Mason, P. 2003. *Criminal Visions: Media Representations of Crime and Justice.* Cullompton: Willan.

Reiner, R. 2007. "Media-Made Criminality: The Representation of Crime in the Mass Media." In M. Maguire, R. Morgan, and R. Reiner, eds., *The Oxford Handbook of Criminology.* New York: Oxford University Press.

References

Barron, C., and D. Lacombe. 2005. "Moral Panic and the Nasty Girl." *Canadian Review of Sociology and Anthropology* 42, no. 1.

Beckett, K., and T. Sasson. 2000. *The Politics of Injustice.* Thousand Oaks: Pine Forge.

CBC News. 2009. "Former Ontario AG Bryant Charged in Cyclist's Death." http://www.cbc.ca/canada/toronto/story/2009/09/01/toronto-cyclist-collision-death481.html#ixzz0nLeqlafr

Chibnall, S. 1977. *Law-and-Order News.* London: Tavistock.

Chiricos, T., S. Eschholz, and M. Gertz. 1997. "Crime, News, and Fear of Crime." *Social Problems* 44, no. 3: 342–57.

Ditton, J., and J. Duffy. 1983. "Bias in the Newspaper Reporting of Crime News." *British Journal of Criminology* 23, no. 2: 159–65.

Doob, A.N., and J.V. Roberts. 1983. *An Analysis of the Public's View of Sentencing.* Ottawa: Department of Justice.

Doob, A.N., and C.M. Webster. 2008. *Concern with Leniency: An Examination of Sentencing Patterns in British Columbia.* A Report to the Province of British Columbia. Vancouver: Attorney General's Office.

Dorfman, L., and V. Schiraldi. 2001. *Off Balance: Youth, Race, and Crime in the News.* Washington: Building Blocks for Youth.

Ericson, R., P. Baranek, and J. Chan. 1987. *Visualizing Deviance.* Milton Keynes: Open University Press.

——. 1989. *Negotiating Control.* Milton Keynes: Open University Press.

——. 1991. *Representing Order.* Milton Keynes: Open University Press.

Graber, D. 1980. *Crime News and the Public*. New York: Praeger.

Greer, C. 2003. *Sex, Crime, and the Media*. Cullompton: Willan.

Hall, S. 1979. *Drifting into a Law and Order Society*. London: Cobden Trust.

Jenkins, P. 1992. *Intimate Enemies: Moral Panics in Contemporary Great Britain*. Hawthorne: Aldine de Gruyter.

Jewkes, Y. 2004. *Media and Crime*. London: Sage.

——. 2010. *Media and Crime*. 2nd ed. London: Sage.

Livingstone, S. 1996. "On the Continuing Problem of Media Effects." In J. Curran and M. Gurevitch, eds., *Mass Media and Society*. London: Arnold.

Marsh, H.L. 1991. "A Comparative Analysis of Crime Coverage in Newspapers in the United States and Other Countries from 1960–1989: A Review of the Literature." *Journal of Criminal Justice* 19, no. 1: 67–80.

Muncie, J. 1999. *Youth and Crime*. London: Sage.

Reiner, R. 2007. "Media-Made Criminality: The Representation of Crime in the Mass Media." In M. Maguire, R. Morgan, and R. Reiner, eds., *The Oxford Handbook of Criminology*. New York: Oxford University Press.

Roberts, J.V., and A.N. Doob. 1990. "Media Influences on Public Views of Sentencing." *Law and Human Behaviour* 14, no. 5: 451–68.

Roberts, J.V., L.J. Stalans, D. Indermaur, and M. Hough. 2003. *Penal Populism and Public Opinion: Lessons from Five Countries*. New York: Oxford University Press.

Roshier, B. 1973. "The Selection of Crime News by the Press." In S. Cohen and J. Young, eds., *The Manufacture of News*. London: Constable.

Schlesinger, P., and H. Tumber. 1992. "Crime and Criminal Justice in Media." In D. Downes, ed., *Unravelling Criminal Justice*. London: Macmillan.

Statistics Canada. 2009a. *Family Violence in Canada: A Statistical Profile*. Cat. no. 85-224-X. Ottawa.

——. 2009b. "Police-Reported Crime Statistics in Canada, 2008." *Juristat* 29, no. 3.

Voices of Actors in the Criminal Justice System

PART
TWO

CHAPTER 4

Scenes from the Life of a Police Officer

As members of the public we often see police officers going about their business—in cruisers or on the beat, as it were. But these fleeting glimpses of the police tell us little about what it is like to be a police officer. The profession is a very demanding one that requires officers to act quickly in response to a wide variety of calls for service. In this chapter, Michael Waby, who served as a police officer in Canada and the United Kingdom, describes some of the challenges facing people in this job.

Michael Waby
Ministry of the Attorney General of Ontario

Police officers are perhaps the most readily identifiable professionals in the criminal justice system, and for this reason alone they can attract strong views from the public. While many people may have little, if any, contact with judges or lawyers throughout the course of their life, most people will have some personal contact with a police officer, whether it be as a motorist, a lost tourist, the victim of a crime, or a suspect or accused in a criminal case. The circumstances of this encounter, as well as the conduct of the individual officer, will determine the impression that a person takes away from the encounter and the impressions that they make both of the individual officer and of the police service as a whole.

Impressions of the police may be held with a genuine sense of conviction but they may not be entirely accurate or fair. Conversely, they may be entirely justified. Familiarity with something often tends to make us think we know more about it than we actually do. The aim of this chapter is to provide a window onto some of the realities of life as a police officer. While the range of duties and posts to which officers may be assigned are hugely varied and specialism plays an ever increasing part, this chapter concentrates on aspects of the routine working life of a uniformed police officer—the kind of police officer most people are likely to encounter on the street.

Not only is the uniformed constable the face of the police service with which most members of the public are most familiar, but before going on to wear a detective's badge, ride a police horse, or be promoted, all officers are required to begin their careers in this manner. The concept of beginning on the street, as it were, is at the heart of policing. It is the common starting point for all police officers. Some officers happily spend their entire service as a uniformed officer patrolling the streets; others work as hard as they can to escape from this particular role.

The uniformed patrol officer is typically the first to attend at the scene of an incident, the first to see the blood, hear the screams, offer comfort and help to victims, or start trying to pick up the pieces. It is this man or woman who will be racing to the scene of a "disturbance"—not always knowing where it lies on the continuum between a noisy but happy drunk making his way home or a violent street fight or shooting.

Unfortunately for the officer, it is surprising how often and how rapidly the feuding parties are prepared to set aside their respective differences in order to jointly turn on the person sent to help them. Aggrieved spouses will quickly leap to the defence of their partners at the point that they see them being handcuffed—despite the fact that, battered and bruised, they called for help in the first place! Similarly, an angry crowd may quickly become hostile towards the uniformed authority figure who turns up to try to restore peace and order to their part of the community. Police recruitment materials frequently emphasize the variety that police work can provide in the course of a working day. Since the role of uniformed police officers is largely reactive (as opposed to proactive), up to a point this is often true. Part of the enjoyment of the work lies in not knowing with any certainty what the next radio call will bring with it when you arrive on the scene. One winter's night I encountered a man who had apparently tried to kill himself by jumping off a six-storey building. As I launched into administering my finest police first aid skills, a neighbour approached us and calmly told me that the man who had just thrown my "attempted suicide" off the sixth-floor balcony lived with the victim in apartment 608. As an ambulance crew arrived, I ran up six flights of stairs to encounter a man wearing only a large pair of underpants, carrying an even larger kitchen knife. He did nothing to set me at my ease when he informed me that his name was "Peter, Peter the Apostle." Thankfully, no one else exited the building via the balcony and "Peter" found secure accommodation for some time thereafter. Needless to say, I had not anticipated this particular scenario when I first arrived at the scene.

Although an ever-increasing amount of time is spent by officers on questionable paperwork and red tape, much of their work still involves dealing with the people in the communities they serve. It is this element that provides the real variable in the nature of police work. Five different people may react in five entirely differently ways to a similar set of circumstances, and it is part of a police officer's role to respond appropriately to each, often with very little time to process what is happening. Not every victim of crime is hysterical or cooperative, and some people respond quite irrationally to police interventions.

It is inevitable that mistakes will be made, especially by those new to this often daunting role of police officer. Sometimes such mistakes are understandable while on other occasions they are unforgiveable. Officers frequently discover that lessons are learned the hard way, often under harsh public scrutiny. Woe betide the officer who, to the great amusement of an assembled crowd, reverses his car into a stone pillar, or forgets that when directing traffic you don't suddenly stop the Mini directly in front of the large truck (the resulting collision acts as a firm reminder to the officer that the braking distances of these two vehicles are markedly different). These mistakes tend to be made only once.

Much of the role is about at least presenting a credible show of confidence to those with whom you are dealing. New officers, often younger in age, will have impressed upon them by their more experienced colleagues the fact that it doesn't matter how awful or chaotic the scene of an incident is—the one thing that has to remain constant in the eyes of the public is the apparently calm and authoritative figure of the attending police officer. Simply put, if you are busy vomiting or swooning at a gory or unpleasant sight, you are not doing your job.

Inevitably it is only with time and experience that officers are able to develop the necessary confidence and resistance to tackle some of the more unpleasant aspects of their work. If they are doing their job properly, no one should suspect that they may later be losing sleep over the unpleasant incident which they have just dealt with. Projecting this image of a calm individual in control is a skill that, like so many others in life, takes time to acquire. Indeed, while to some officers it appears to come effortlessly, others never manage to acquire it.

Having joined the Metropolitan Police force in London, England, at the tender age of 19, I can still vividly recall admiring myself in my new uniform in the reflection of a series of shop windows on my first few days out on foot patrol by myself. My belief in the invincible, professional image that I was sure I outwardly presented lasted until the first member of the public walked up to me to ask me for directions, at which point a sense of panic gripped me and the limits of my knowledge seemed overwhelming. I have subsequently been informed by officers in both England and Canada that this pattern of dread alternating with bursts of self-confidence is common to most new officers. Thankfully most live through it.

The learning curve of most officers is usually fairly steep. Especially in metropolitan areas, in a fairly short space of time, a great deal of knowledge and hands-on experience is gained. They will also be able to rely on the accumulated wisdom and experience of their longer-serving colleagues. Advice is seldom far away if you have the sense to ask for it and may often be there when you least want it. Of course, part of the learning curve is to know who to listen to and, frankly, who to ignore. As societal attitudes have evolved, some officers have coped better with these changes than others. While the "common sense" advice of one long-serving officer may well sometimes be a quick route to discipline or disaster, most experienced officers are invaluable in terms of providing supervision, support, and essential advice to their younger colleagues. Their accumulated wisdom frequently disproves the maxim that you can only learn through your own mistakes, and it is often only more experienced colleagues to whom one can turn after a particularly bad day. Many young officers have been saved from themselves by their colleagues.

For the majority of officers, the most enjoyable aspect of their work encompasses actually dealing with the wide variety of people and situations that they encounter. Whether it is helping the vulnerable, bringing order from chaos, or arresting an apparently guilty party, it is this "hands-on" activity that drew most to the job in the first place. Very few officers relish the ever-increasing burden of paperwork that now accompanies their role. It is the perennial complaint of officers that their time is increasingly occupied by filling in forms, many of which appear to duplicate their predecessor, rather than being out on the streets. It is also a concern increasingly and legitimately shared by many members of the public.

It is something of a paradox that the multifarious initiatives by various police services designed to address this concern seem not to have had the desired effect. Whether it is under the supposed rubric of the *Charter of Rights* or a product of a corporate police interpretation of our increasingly bureaucratic societies, the amount of paperwork that accompanies the most routine tasks that police officers now have to complete is quite remarkable. Notwithstanding the computer age that we now occupy, the time it takes to process a simple arrest today as opposed to 20 years ago is vastly longer.

As a case in point, in the early years of my police service, it was a matter of personal pride among officers that a simple arrest for an offence of theft or mischief, for example, would be properly processed from start to finish within an hour. The prisoner would be booked in, the officer would write his statement or notes surrounding the event and subsequent arrest, and then the officer would return to patrolling. A comparable event nowadays can easily see the officer completing paperwork for four or five hours.

Unfortunately it does not take much for an officer to make an arrest at the start of the shift and not make it back out for the remainder of that day's shift. Some would contend that this increase in paperwork is necessary to better safeguard the rights of the accused and to provide valuable and useful statistics. These arguments frequently seem to overlook not only the sheer duplication of effort that is created, with its attendant implications for police and civilian resources, but also the fact that if an officer is inclined to be creative in his note writing or evidence of an arrest, then this theme will inevitably continue throughout all of the paperwork he completes. It is really only when and if his evidence is forensically examined in court that meaningful scrutiny may occur. A dishonest or sloppy officer will neither be discovered nor reformed under reams of red tape and mandatory box ticking.

THE NEED FOR HUMOUR

As the job can often be emotionally demanding, police officers frequently take refuge in the notoriously macabre sense of humour that many of them share, or quickly develop. Whether this is through habit or necessity, the ability of police officers to laugh at things that would make many people cry is an enduring aspect of police life. Police slang can also lend to otherwise serious or sad situations what can appear to outsiders as a flippant air. This coping mechanism can certainly be a double-edged sword. Between colleagues it can provide an essential release of tension and enable you to perform the delightful task of collecting body parts at the scene of an accident or dealing with a failed suicide attempt. Unfortunately, to the uninitiated it can often appear cold and cruel.

I know of one former colleague who, to lighten the mood for a young officer dealing with his first dead body, placed his police hat on the head of the elderly gentleman who had quietly passed away in his pyjamas. This act certainly achieved its desired effect, until the deceased's son walked unannounced into the room and witnessed the spectacle. Similarly, attaching to photographs a faux judge's scorecard that marked the perceived merits of the swallow dive of the poor unfortunate who leaped to his death from the end of a crane is an act that is legitimately open to mixed reviews.

DEALING WITH VICTIMS

Notwithstanding this tendency towards gallows humour, most police officers, most of the time, have a sense of propriety. This is particularly required when dealing with the victims of crime in all its many forms. At the more routine end of the scale is the patience that needs to be shown to those who have been the victim of a theft or a loss of some personal property. It is a depressing reality that many such offences are never likely to be solved, and thus the reporting exercise is one principally conducted to facilitate an insurance claim. However, it is never very politic to be as blunt as this to the person who has just had a wallet or purse stolen. The fact that it is the fourth such report that the officer has completed in as many hours is quite rightly of little consequence to the latest victim that the officer encounters.

Unsurprisingly, more tact and diplomacy is required when dealing with the victims, or relatives of victims, of violent criminal offences. There will often be a need to explain in detail what action the police are taking and why, or conversely what action they are *not* taking and why. Officers will encounter victims who are angry, afraid, or numb. Frequently the victims of crime, or witnesses to it, may not initially wish to provide a statement to police in respect of what has happened. This may be through fear or indifference but it remains part of a police officer's job to work with the victim as early as possible in order to obtain as much useful information as they can. The interests of the victim and the police will usually, but not always, coincide, but police officers should always remember that the impression that a victim of crime takes away with them can have a significant impact upon whether they choose to voluntarily get involved with the police in the future. No matter how frustrated or busy the officer may be, leaving a victim of crime angry, upset, or confused is always counterproductive.

Sometimes there is no magic to the interaction between police officers and victims. It is simply a product of common humanity. Officers may simply do nothing more than hold a person while she cries. My father, who was a police officer some 50 years ago, was the first on the scene of a woman pedestrian who had been fatally struck by a car as she crossed the road. Knowing that she was dying my father cradled her. She asked him to say a prayer for her. Not a particularly religious man, the only prayer that my father knew was the Lord's Prayer. He recited this over the woman as she died in his arms.

SHIFT WORK

Shift work is a necessary and well-established aspect of police work and can frequently set the rhythm of what officers may expect to encounter. Morning and afternoon shifts will invariably bring with them different types of calls. This may be reflected in responding to numerous calls to banks and other business premises as staff arrive for work and inadvertently trigger alarms or a wide range of property-related crimes from shoplifting to street robberies. Many of these calls enable police officers to engage in an aspect of the job that always seems to retain its appeal, and that is the opportunity to race to the scene of a call in their police car with sirens blaring and lights flashing. Even the most jaded of officers seldom seem to tire of this act. The downside of course is the capacity to cause injury or damage on the way to deal with the original incident. Regrettably this does happen from time to time, and sometimes enthusiasm can outstrip an officer's driving ability. It is the perpetual nightmare of officers responding to an emergency call. Navigating a busy city's pedestrian-filled streets in the middle of the afternoon on the way to deal with a bank robbery can be a fraught experience. Driving to respond to an urgent call—often in heavy traffic and sometimes in appalling weather— requires considerable skill and judgment. So too does the vehicular pursuit of people who have a very great incentive to flee and often have no regard for those around them.

Typically, many more people are abroad during the working day than at night. This inevitably increases the number and variety of calls that officers on a day duty may receive. A direct consequence of this is the element of havoc than can be created when large numbers of people are present. Unfortunately few people and even fewer crowds are as patient as police officers would like them to be. In most instances people's curiosity with what is going on soon gives way to impatience about getting on with their own business. Any police officer who has had to seal off a street or a building can attest to this impatience on the part of the public. It is sometimes quite remarkable how people will react to even the most serious of situations. I have witnessed and even participated in arguments with people who have *insisted* that they are the exception to the rule and should be allowed to walk through a police cordon, or enter a particular building even when it is known that to do so would mean walking past the bomb disposal team working to diffuse an explosive device.

People's tendency to believe that they are the exception to the rule is one of a number of truths that officers discover at an early stage of their career. It goes along with other so-called golden rules such as "the rudeness of the driver is directly proportionate to the value of their car"—the more expensive it is, the ruder the driver will inevitably become. Similarly, it is a universal truth that if the location of a call is situated on the upper floors of a building, the elevator will invariably be out of service.

COURT WORK

Another regular aspect of police work during the daytime is that of attending court. Officers often have to appear as witnesses, and sometimes as victims themselves. I know officers who would far sooner deal with an armed suspect than attend at court to give evidence as it can be one of the more nerve-wracking aspects of an officer's job. Detached and insulated from the heat of the moment, judges and lawyers have the luxury of analyzing in detail and at leisure the actions of officers involved in dynamic incidents that may have lasted only a few seconds. The theatre of the courtroom and the sometimes intense, yet entirely proper, spotlight that it shines on the police can be a terrifying or frustrating experience for some officers. I have witnessed police officers so unnerved by the prospect or experience of testifying in court that they have variously walked into the dock instead of the witness box, fainted while giving evidence, and in one memorable incident a young officer even forgot his own name.

Before I began to practise as a barrister and became rather more sanguine about appearing in court, as a young officer I once repeatedly forgot to inform the court of the fact that I had found a suicide note next to a body I had discovered. Slightly overawed by the occasion of giving evidence, I provided all the other information I could but neglected to mention this fairly useful detail. I was immune to the increasingly desperate attempts by counsel to elicit this from me, and it took an intercession by the coroner who had previously read my statement to confirm that we were probably not dealing with a homicide.

It is just as important for police officers not to seem too confident when giving their evidence. This seldom goes down well, although few go as far as one seasoned officer I encountered some years ago who, when asked which oath he wished to take prior to giving his evidence, produced, with a suitably theatrical flourish, his own copy of the bible from his breast pocket, which, he informed an amused if disbelieving judge, he carried with him at all times. However traumatic the experience may be, most officers quickly learn the necessity to provide their evidence in a professional manner. As with all witnesses, and police officers are no different, a nervous disposition while testifying does not necessarily mean that they are being untruthful, and nor is confidence always consistent with accuracy. It is unfortunate—given its obvious importance—that in the modern era less time seems to be spent educating officers in how to properly and effectively present their evidence in court.

Of course the travails of giving evidence in court are only compounded when an officer does so following a 10- or 12-hour night shift and turns up at court bleary-eyed after, at best, a couple of hours sleep. While potentially quite lucrative in terms of overtime payments for the officer, attending court "off-nights" is an exhausting experience undertaken after what can often prove to be an extremely busy tour of duty and with the prospect of yet another night shift ahead.

POLICING AT NIGHT

There is something very particular to policing by night and perhaps unremarkably it is the most unique of the shifts. If there is truth in the old adage that "bad weather is the best policeman," then it is also the case that the darkness can often be the best friend of those intent on breaking the law. Most cities and towns appear to assume a completely different identity by night, and you could often be forgiven for thinking that they are occupied by an entirely different population. For many officers there is a tension between the excitement that can accompany policing by night and the adverse effects on their body clock. As a general rule, younger officers tend to be far more enthusiastic about night duty work than their older colleagues, but many officers of any length of service recognize that it gradually becomes harder and harder to make the transition from days to nights and then back to days again.

By night, partygoers fill the bars and streets and inevitably problems occur where people celebrate well but not wisely. Without doubt a significant percentage of police work at night is linked to alcohol and/or drug use and abuse. Indeed, if alcohol was removed from the equation there would be a lot less work for all of the participants in the criminal justice system. Tempers, bravado, and fights all flare up more suddenly and, even if unintended, the associated consequences can be substantially worse.

Officers quickly learn to distinguish the happy, if annoying, drunk, from the dangerous one. Breaking up incidents in pubs and bars can carry great risks for the police. The amount of glass that is readily available to hand in a bar will typically make most officers nervous as they wade in to a crowded space with a tense or hostile atmosphere. Fortunately Canada generally lacks the apparent Anglo-Saxon compulsion prevalent in some to become as drunk as possible within the shortest possible time and then go on to wreak as much havoc as they can. Pub fights are a depressingly familiar aspect of policing in much of England, as are the marauding groups who frequently terrorize many town centres late on a Friday or Saturday night. A great many of the injuries sustained by officers are as a result of them dealing with drunken, aggressive young males.

The different perspective that night work can bring can certainly be useful as it enables officers to appreciate and discover aspects of the communities that they police that they would never otherwise come across. However, one of the greatest downsides of night work can arise when the bars have closed and the city finally begins to fall asleep. The absence of any apparent activity—or of any calls with which to deal—does nothing to help keep you awake, and at four o'clock in the morning it can be very difficult to stay motivated, let alone on your feet. The irony is that, half asleep, an officer can suddenly be expected to respond to a serious incident, sometimes involving life or death decisions. Racing to the scene of a call in your police car in this semi-comatose state can be demanding enough. More especially, not many of us would wish to be placed in the situation of having to decide whether or not to shoot someone, but unfortunately this is not an infrequent occurrence for police officers. Trying to decide in a tense and fast-moving situation whether to pull the trigger is an incredibly difficult decision at the best of times. It is certainly not made any easier if the incident happens at night, with little or no warning and after exhaustion has begun to set in.

Along with many of our institutions, police services (they used to be called forces) increasingly find that, especially at night, they are less able to rely on traditional respect or deference for the work they do. There is no doubt that there are a number of complex explanations for this, some eminently justifiable, but the reality is that whatever combination of reasons that exist for this change, policing is not becoming either a safer occupation or an easier one to perform than it once was.

POLICE AND FIREARMS

In Canada our police officers are all armed. The United Kingdom remains perhaps the last major police service in the world to not routinely arm its officers. In 1986 when I joined the Metropolitan Police, if an armed incident arose one of two things occurred. Those nearest the scene typically chased after the armed individual or ran into the bank that was apparently being held up, armed only with their wooden truncheon and a childlike faith in the fact that they probably wouldn't be shot. If this sounds particularly remarkable, it is not meant to be. It was simply the typical response of most officers at that time. The alternative was, and I kid you not, to drive or run back to your police station and sign out one of the handful of aging revolvers that were kept under lock and key by the duty inspector. Having done this you then ran or drove back to the scene of the incident and hoped it wasn't already over.

Thankfully things have improved somewhat since then, although most police officers in the United Kingdom are not trained in the use of firearms and do not carry them. This prevents many officers there from encountering some of the terrifying dilemmas experienced by their Canadian colleagues. Conversely though, the two most pointless words to shout in the English language are "Stop, police" if you have neither a gun nor a police dog to hand.

That being said, police officers across the country experience situations on a daily basis that can be frankly terrifying. Moreover, they are not expected to turn tail and flee but to engage and deal with it. In the same way that we expect our firefighters to routinely run into blazing buildings, we legitimately expect our police officers to tackle dangerous situations and armed criminals. Coming out on top can be exhilarating but as we all know this is unfortunately not always the case. Often, pure blind luck may be the factor between triumph and disaster.

However, a very common theme that has developed for all police officers is the ever-increasing amount of equipment that they are now routinely expected to carry. Preparing to begin a shift takes longer than ever before as an officer has to ensure that he or she is properly, if exhaustingly, equipped for the tour of duty ahead. Whether armed or not, most officers now sport body armour (welcome, but often heavy, hot, and uncomfortable) and a utility belt that would be the envy of your average superhero and comprises pepper spray, handcuffs, surgical gloves, and a panoply of other items. The net result of this accumulation of kit is that police officers are certainly better equipped than ever before, even if they are 30 pounds heavier and far less likely to catch a motivated suspect in a foot-chase.

Thus encumbered, officers then leave their respective stations or divisions for the day or night ahead. Unless assigned to the often mind-numbing tedium of a fixed post duty, typically most uniformed police officers will have little idea of what a "routine" shift will hold in store for them. Within a few minutes of starting work they may be engaged in the completion of routine but necessary paperwork in respect to a recent break-in or attempting to comfort a stranger to whom they have just delivered the devastating news that their child has been killed. They may find themselves running along dark alleys or rooftops while chasing a suspect who, generally, has a great reluctance to be caught or providing first aid to someone knocked down by a streetcar. Their reality on any given day may prove to be exhilarating or mundane in the extreme or any combination of the two.

Their role is that of a veritable jack-of-all-trades. Police officers have to be prepared to be mediators, counsellors, peacekeepers, and enforcers. They are expected to perform any of their required roles at a moment's notice and will frequently be pilloried by at least one if not all of the parties involved. They will become depressingly familiar with people routinely lying to them, even when it makes no sense to do so, and will see some of the very best and worst aspects of human nature. Yet we will still expect them to retain their humanity, good manners, and, ideally, a sense of humour.

The "job" is a job unlike any other and yet it is mostly the same the world over.

The Role of the Prosecutor

Most people are familiar with the role and function of a defence lawyer: to argue the accused's side against the case of the state. This means rebutting evidence against the accused wherever possible and advancing the interests of the accused right through to the sentencing hearing (in the event of a conviction). At the sentencing hearing, the defence proposes a sentence that would be in the best interests of the accused, and his representation of the accused may not stop here if an appeal of the conviction or sentence is launched. The role of the Crown is less well known. In this chapter, Brian Manarin, a senior assistant Crown attorney in the Province of Ontario, illustrates the role of the Crown or prosecutor. He discusses the various decisions that confront a Crown counsel, such as which charge should be laid (including whether it is in the public interest to proceed with a prosecution at all), whether the accused should be granted release on bail, and what evidence to submit on sentencing.

Brian Manarin
Crown Counsel[1]

The vast majority of criminal cases in Canada are prosecuted in the lower-level provincial division courts. If one pictures an inverted funnel, with the provincial courts representing the wide opening at the bottom and the Supreme Court of Canada representing the narrow spout at the top, one can better appreciate just how busy the provincial courts really are.

Crown attorneys (and any assistant Crown attorneys in their charge) are lawyers responsible for preparing and prosecuting cases for alleged criminal and quasi-criminal offences occurring within the province in which they are employed. Although countless statutes govern allegations of criminal conduct, the pre-eminent legislation that governs the prosecution of criminal offences in Canada is known simply as the *Criminal Code*.[2] Within this lengthy federal statute is a detailed sketch of what Parliament considers to be acceptable and unacceptable conduct in civilized Canadian society. Canada's *Criminal Code* can be considered the catalyst behind all criminal prosecutions that take place in the country.

The majority of prosecutors earn their living in the courtroom. Their role focuses on searching for the truth during the trial process. However, many issues that are integral to the administration of justice are dealt with far from the courtroom. Other prosecutorial responsibilities include drafting court documents and providing professional advice to the police, related agencies, and the general public on criminal matters. In addition, prosecutors must possess a thorough knowledge of criminal law and procedure and the rules of evidence, as well as a strong comprehension of the workings of the *Canadian Charter of Rights and Freedoms*,[3] which is the supreme law of Canada (see Chapter 2 of this volume). Finally, prosecutors must bring sound judgment and a healthy degree of common sense to their workaday duties.

What distinguishes prosecutors from any other type of lawyer is their role in the trial process. The parties to any criminal prosecution are Her Majesty the Queen on the one side and those accused of committing the offences on the other (Wijesinha and Young 1978). The prosecution must ensure that the accused receives a fair trial. The end goal is not to achieve a conviction but, rather, to come to a just result born out of the evidence presented at trial. Without a doubt, the best definition of the role of the Crown can be found in the often-quoted words of Mr. Justice Rand of the Supreme Court of Canada in the case of *R. v. Boucher*:[4]

> It cannot be over-emphasized that the purpose of a criminal prosecution is not to obtain a conviction, it is to lay before a jury what the Crown considers to be credible evidence relevant to what is alleged to be a crime. Counsel have a duty to see that all available legal proof of the facts is presented: it should be done firmly and pressed to its legitimate strength, but it must also be done fairly. The role of the prosecutor excludes any notion of winning or losing; his function is a matter of public duty: in civil life there can be none charged with greater personal responsibility. It is to be efficiently performed with

an ingrained sense of the dignity, the seriousness, and the justness of judicial proceedings.

The goal of every prosecutor is to meet the high standards that Justice Rand emphasized in his classic statement on the subject. However, prosecutors are human and are thus subject to the same foibles and fallibility as any other person in any other walk of life. Putting aside one's passions to make way for moderation and impartiality requires constant effort.[5] Maintaining neutrality does not, however, translate into a lacklustre effort. To the contrary, the Crown counsel, like any other advocate, is entitled to advance her position forcefully and effectively.[6]

In contrast, the role of the defence counsel is to be openly partisan toward his client. The defence has a duty to protect the client from being found guilty of a criminal offence and, to that end, the defence may use all the available evidence and defences as long as they are not false or fraudulent. Therefore, the defence is not obligated to assist the prosecution at trial. In fact, the defence is entitled to assume an entirely adversarial role toward the prosecution.[7] Whereas the prosecution must, with very few exceptions, disclose the case in its entirety to the other side, the defence does not need to state in advance what specific defence will be made against the accusation, who the witnesses are, or what they will say on the witness stand. Distilled to its most fundamental, a person accused of committing a crime is presumed to be innocent until the prosecution proves her guilt beyond a reasonable doubt. As a result, an accused person has a right to remain silent to avoid the potential for self-incrimination. The burden of proving guilt always rests with the prosecution.

Thus, the prosecution and the defence each have different roles and responsibilities in the trial process. In order to illustrate the typical duties and obligations of a prosecutor practising in the provincial courts, the remainder of this chapter will describe three sets of tasks that a Crown attorney deals with during a normal week: (1) charge screening and disclosure, (2) bail hearings, and (3) sentencing. The trial process itself will not be dealt with in any direct way.

CHARGE SCREENING AND DISCLOSURE

Although there is always a need for policing in Canadian society, it is neither necessary nor desirable to prosecute all alleged offenders. The decision to continue or terminate a prosecution is among the most difficult Crown counsel must make (*Crown Practice Memorandum* [2002] No. 5, Charge Screening, October 1: 1). At this early stage of the proceedings, prosecutors need to remember the true function of their job:

> A Crown attorney must be ever alert to prevent abuses of the criminal process. He [or she] must stand independent between the accused and overzealous police. He [or she] must recognize and prevent

vexatious or multifarious charges being laid or prosecuted. He [or she] must recognize unworthy or vindictive complainants and not become wittingly or unwittingly an instrument of persecution. He [or she] must remain objective, exercising his [or her] own discretion and judgment, especially in cases that have caused public outrage or incensed his [or her] community. Cases that have political overtones, cases that have attained a great deal of publicity, or cases that appeal to prejudices, such as race or religion, must be dealt with in the same fashion (Bynoe 1968, 102).*

Screening occurs when the prosecution receives a brief of the allegations from the agency responsible for laying the charge or charges—usually the police or an individual. Screening is an ongoing process and must be completed before a date can be set for a preliminary inquiry or trial. The Crown attorney screens each charge to decide (among other things) the following:

(1) whether there is a reasonable prospect of conviction;
(2) whether it is in the public interest to discontinue a prosecution even if there is a reasonable prospect of conviction;
(3) whether the proper charge has been laid;
(4) whether the investigation is complete; and
(5) whether an offer of diversion should be made to the accused** (*Crown Practice Memorandum* [2002] No. 5, Charge Screening, October 1: 2–3).[8]

If there is no reasonable prospect of conviction, then the Crown attorney must terminate the prosecution. The test objectively considers the availability and admissibility of evidence, the credibility of witnesses, and the viability of any apparent defences. After considering the issue of reasonable prospect of conviction, the prosecutor must then contemplate the public interest. Although deciding what is in the public interest can be a daunting task even for a seasoned prosecutor, the following questions guide the screening process:

• Is the incident in question grave or trivial?
• What are the victim's views?
• What is the age and health, both physical and mental, of an accused or witness?
• Would public confidence in the administration of justice be maintained by the screening decision?
• Are issues of national security or international relations involved?
• What is the degree of culpability for the accused in the grand scheme of the particular offence being alleged?
• Is the offence widespread in the community?

---

* © Queen's Printer for Ontario, Crown Policy Manual - Charge Screening, March 21, 2005. Province of Ontario, Ministry of Attorney General. Reproduced with permission.
** Bynoe, B. 1968. "The Role and Function of Crown Counsel." 3 C.R.N.S. 90. Crown Policy Manual. 1994. Policy # C.S.-1, Charge Screening, January 15. Province of Ontario, Ministry of Attorney General. Reproduced with permission.

- Would a conviction be unduly harsh or oppressive in relation to this particular accused person?
- Has the accused cooperated in the police investigation, or is the accused willing to do so now?
- How strong is the Crown's case?
- How old are the allegations?
- How long and costly will the prosecution be compared with the likely sentence for the crime?
- Are alternatives to prosecution available?
  (*Crown Practice Memorandum* [2002] No. 5, Charge Screening, October 1: 5–6).*

An example at this point will help illustrate when a prosecution would not be in the public interest, despite the Crown having a strong case. Assume a scenario where an octogenarian widower, presently in poor health but without a criminal record, is found to have continued to receive and cash his deceased wife's Canada Pension Plan (CPP) cheques for 17 months after her demise. He was depressed during this time and stopped his fraudulent conduct after receiving grief counselling. Indeed, the allegations are from six years in the past. The defendant used his wife's CPP funds to pay for the daily placing of a bouquet of flowers on her grave. When confronted with the allegations by the investigating detective, the defendant immediately confessed. However, the detective is now retired and has moved from Canada to Italy. Given the age, health, and circumstances of the defendant, it would not be in the public interest to fly the police officer back to Canada from Europe to testify at a trial. The fact that the offence was six years old before it was detected must also be taken into consideration when assessing the recollections of witnesses and the availability of other evidence.

The public would understand the reasoning of the Crown in the above-described case, but often there is no bright line to guide the prosecutor in making these difficult and, ultimately, discretionary decisions. However, as long as sound judgment is underpinned by objective fairness, critics of the screening process will be scarce.

Although police officers are required to have a sufficient working knowledge of criminal law to allow them to make arrests and lay charges, Crown counsel must ultimately decide at the screening stage whether the proper charge has in fact been laid or whether another charge should be substituted. Often a changing of charge can result in reducing duplicate charges, since one single action can result in the commission of many criminal offences. In other circumstances, substituting one charge for another can save valuable resources by keeping a case within the jurisdiction of a provincially appointed judge. Additionally, when prosecutors notice more subtle legal nuances, they can recommend that the police lay a more (or less) serious charge than they originally contemplated.

---

* © Queen's Printer for Ontario, Crown Practice Memorandum [2002] No. 5 – Charge Screening – October 1, 2002, 5–6. Province of Ontario, Ministry of Attorney General. Reproduced with permission.

In addition, neither an accused person nor a prosecutor can truly assess the strengths or weaknesses of a particular case until the police investigation is complete. For this reason, the prosecutor must be satisfied that all avenues of a police investigation have been exhausted before completing the screening process. If not, then Crown counsel must direct the police to complete the areas of the investigation that are incomplete. At this point, the prosecution should invite the defence counsel to point out any other oversights by the police.

Finally, Crown counsel has the opportunity to divert a criminal charge away from the criminal justice system. This means that no prosecution will proceed and the person accused of the offence will not acquire a criminal record. Historically, a prosecutor has always had the discretion to withdraw a charge or charges against an accused, as described in the *Criminal Code*. Today's prosecutors have the option to use diversion programs devised by the Attorneys General, Lieutenant Governors in Council, or their respective designates in each province, collectively recognized as "alternative measures" by the *Criminal Code*.[9] Generally speaking, if an accused person admits to his involvement in the commission of an offence and does not wish a trial, the prosecutor may recommend alternative measures—as long as they are not inconsistent with the protection of society. The interests of society and those of the victim are weighed against each other. Similarly, the prosecutor makes efforts to protect the interests of the accused in this process by (1) ensuring that he fully and freely consents to the alternative measures, and (2) ensuring that a trial is actually held if that is what the accused desires.

Alternative measures programs may involve the diversion of charges for mentally disordered accused, prostitutes and their patrons, Aboriginal Canadians, young offenders,[10] and minor (and generally first-time) offenders. Each diversion requires the accused to complete a program or act of contrition that satisfies the prosecution's terms and conditions. By offering alternatives, the prosecutor discourages the offender from offending again and prevents the creation of a criminal record. Also, the state is spared the necessity of a costly trial.

BAIL HEARINGS

Bail, or "judicial interim release" as it is referred to in the *Criminal Code,* means the release from custody of accused persons so that they can maintain their liberty while awaiting trial. In certain circumstances, a police officer or a justice of the peace can arrange a person's release (Trotter 1998). However, this chapter will concentrate on bail hearings conducted in court where a prosecutor is called upon to make a decision whether an accused person should be detained in custody until trial.

The decision for or against bail is often difficult. Picture, if you will, bail court on a Monday morning where, in addition to the normal volume of weekend arrests, there have been raids on illegal establishments and final "take-downs" of various special police crime prevention projects, resulting in further large-scale arrests. The courtroom is full. As can be imagined, to make intelligent, fair, and informed decisions about the release or detention of each detainee can be an overwhelming task. Digesting the allegations pertinent to each accused person, considering the positions of the police, defence, and complainants, and considering strategy for the bail hearings in such circumstances requires a cool head and great confidence.

The outcome of a bail hearing is often pivotal to the outcome of the case itself. Statistics show that over 80 percent of all charges dealt with in the lower-level provincial courts result in guilty pleas (Martin 1993, 15). Moreover, experience has shown that persons detained without bail are much more likely to plead guilty so that they may start serving their sentence immediately. Justice through trial seems much less appealing when a person is waiting for her "day in court" without a release on bail. As such, it is perhaps at the bail hearing that the prosecutor is under the most intense pressure to be firm but fair.

What are the fundamental concerns at a bail hearing? The court will grant an accused person a form of bail unless the prosecution can show why the detention of the accused person is justified. In fact, the law requires that the least onerous form of release be granted to an accused person unless the prosecution can show why a more stringent form of release should be imposed.[11] However, no less than 11 scenarios can shift the onus onto the accused to show why his detention is *not* justified. The scenarios that are relevant to a provincial-level bail hearing, generally described, include:

1. Has the accused person allegedly committed another indictable offence while on release?
2. Has the accused person allegedly committed an offence involving organized crime?
3. Has the accused person allegedly committed an offence that involved the financing of terrorism?
4. Has the accused person allegedly committed an offence that involved communicating governmental information to a foreign entity or terrorist group contrary to the *Security of Information Act*?
5. Has the accused person allegedly committed an offence that involved harbouring or concealing persons, committing preparatory acts, or attempting or conspiring to commit acts that contravene the communication of governmental information sections of the *Security of Information Act* as they relate to a foreign entity or terrorist group?
6. Has the accused person allegedly committed an offence that involved the importing, exporting, or trafficking of weapons?
7. Has the accused person allegedly committed certain serious bodily harm, bodily endangerment, or domination offences with the aid of a firearm?
8. Has the accused person allegedly committed an offence that involved the use of a firearm, ammunition, or another serious form of weaponry while under an order prohibiting the possession of such an item/s?

9. Has the accused person allegedly committed an indictable offence and is not ordinarily resident in Canada?

10. Has the accused person allegedly failed to attend court as required on a previous outstanding release or failed to otherwise live up to the terms of the previous release?

11. Has the accused person allegedly committed or conspired to commit an offence that involved the production, trafficking, or importation of certain controlled drugs?[12]

Whether the burden is on the accused or the prosecution, bail hearings consistently address three different areas of concern: (1) Is the accused person's detention necessary to ensure her attendance in court in order to be dealt with according to law? (2) Is the accused person's detention necessary for the protection or safety of the public? (3) Is the detention necessary to maintain confidence in the administration of justice, having regard to all the circumstances, including the apparent strength of the prosecution's case; the gravity of the offence; the circumstances surrounding its commission, including whether a firearm was used; and the potential for a lengthy term of imprisonment, including a mandatory minimum punishment of imprisonment where a firearm was used?[13]

Although the *Criminal Code* clearly defines when a prosecutor may seek to detain a person in custody until trial, a prosecutor should not apply these criteria automatically. By rigidly following the rules, a Crown counsel can fall short of the standards of fairness that are expected from his office. The following three examples illustrate the point.

Example 1

A refugee claimant has come to Canada to escape a repressive regime where he had been a vocal opponent of the government. He has left family and friends behind. Six months into his stay in Canada, he is charged with a street robbery that occurred in an area of Toronto plagued by this type of offence. The identity of the perpetrator of this crime is clearly an issue at trial. No significant injuries were suffered by the victim. No weapon was used during the offence. Although the accused person has no real roots in the community, he has no criminal record and has two sureties who will guarantee his release on bail and who will, in addition, offer a cash deposit.

Although protection of the public is important, and it is recognized that this type of offence generally commands a term of imprisonment upon conviction, the foremost concern in this situation tends to be whether the accused will flee if granted bail. Since this accused has no ties to the community, it would appear that flight from prosecution should be a concern. Should Crown counsel simply point out that because the accused is not normally resident in Canada, he should be detained, and that it is up to the accused to demonstrate why he should be released? Or do the facts require more detailed consideration?

Although the accused has not yet established himself in Toronto, the prosecution is clearly aware that he has come to Canada to escape his homeland. Why would a person flee back to a country where he knows he faces likely persecution? Moreover, there are weaknesses in the Crown's case, because the accused has not been clearly identified as the culprit. The fact that the accused has no criminal record bodes well for his release. For these reasons, in this case the Crown could suggest a form of release without abdicating its duties as a minister of justice.

Example 2

The police are called to a residential dwelling, the scene of an earlier domestic assault by a husband on his wife. The accused had been drinking heavily at the time of the incident but is now sober and remorseful. The accused has no criminal record, and the police discover from family sources that his behaviour was an aberration likely stemming from the loss of his job. Although there are no apparent injuries, the victim is concerned that her husband broke a sacred trust between them, and she fears that he may repeat this conduct if he is granted bail. The victim is financially dependent on her spouse and has two small children to care for. The accused has a surety who will allow him to live at his home, far away from the family abode, while awaiting trial. He will also get the accused some treatment for what appears to be an alcohol problem.

Society's general abhorrence for spousal assault cannot be overstated. What was once considered a problem to be worked out within the family is now understood to be a serious criminal offence that brings with it significant criminal sanctions. Both police and prosecutors realize that an inordinate number of homicides result from domestic violence. However, the truly objective prosecutor must not be influenced by her disgust for certain alleged conduct. Although it is understandable that the spouse may fear a repetition of the abuse, all indications reveal that this assault was an isolated incident.

The fact that a strong surety has come forward who can put some physical distance between the abuser and the victim should also alleviate certain concerns. Despite the seriousness of this kind of violence, the Crown counsel really has no choice but to immediately concede that this accused person is a candidate for bail. Although complete protection of the victim can only be achieved in certain situations by denying the abuser any form of release, in this case, a carefully crafted bail order would meet the ends of justice.

Example 3

The accused person is on a police release for taking a motor vehicle without the owner's consent. One of the terms of his release is that he abide by a curfew that requires him to be in his place of residence between 11:00 p.m. and 6:00 a.m. every day. He is seen by the police staggering down the road at 3:00 a.m. on the morning in question and, upon investigation, it is discovered that he is in violation of his curfew. The accused is clearly guilty of failing to comply with a fundamental condition of his release. Although this is a reverse-onus situation, the accused seeks another bail and can produce a substantial surety to the court. At the time, the accused has no criminal record.

Prosecutors can fall into the habit of rationalizing that since an accused will likely be found guilty at trial, the notion of release pending that foregone conclusion is inappropriate. Certainly, the strength of the prosecution's case is an important consideration when deciding whether bail is a viable option, but in a situation like this one, other factors must be considered. Except for his curfew violation, this accused would be a candidate for the alternative measures program for his property-related offence. As for the curfew violation itself, despite the fact that violating a release condition is a serious offence, it is highly unlikely that the accused would be sentenced to a period of custody. As such, a detention order at the accused's bail hearing would be overly harsh given what he could expect as a just punishment for either or both offences. Sound judgment dictates a further release for this accused person, but with more restrictive conditions.

SENTENCING

Arguably nothing is more challenging for a prosecutor than making submissions on sentence. By definition, the accused now stands convicted as a result of a guilty plea or after being found guilty at trial. In either situation, the accused is at his most vulnerable, and so is the Crown counsel. The former is vulnerable because the passing of sentence can result in the loss of liberty as well as the stigmatization of the offender for several years. The latter is vulnerable since the quality of justice is often measured by the submissions of the prosecution on sentence. A lack of impartiality at this most emotional stage of the proceedings can tarnish the entire office of the Crown attorney, not just the reputation of the individual prosecutor. For this reason alone, the role of Crown counsel has been measured on the strength of the following statement: "With the result, as with the verdict at the trial, he is enormously unconcerned" (Humphreys 1955, 748). In other words, prosecutors must remain unemotional in their role, without any appearance of desiring a particular outcome.

The purpose and principles of sentencing are now largely incorporated into Canada's *Criminal Code*.[14] Entire texts have been written on the subject of sentencing, which makes the topic too complex to discuss in a single chapter (see Manson 2001; Roberts and Cole 1999). However, hearings are governed almost entirely by the facts presented, rather than by laws or theories. Therefore, no two proceedings are ever exactly the same, despite efforts to treat similar offenders in a comparable fashion.

One area of sentencing worthy of special comment pertains to the *conditional sentence*.[15] Amendments to the *Criminal Code* in 1996 created a new type of sentence in Canada. When a person is convicted of an offence that does not have a minimum term of imprisonment spelled out in the *Criminal Code*, the court may order that the offender serve the sentence in the community. The sentence contemplated by the court must be less than two years of imprisonment and must not be for an offence that, if prosecuted by way of indictment, could potentially yield a maximum term of imprisonment of 14 years or life. Indeed, certain named offences, due to their seriousness, automatically preclude the imposition of a conditional sentence. In addition, the court must be satisfied that the offender will not be a danger to the community. As well, the court must be satisfied that serving the sentence in the community would be consistent with the fundamental purpose and principles of sentencing as set out in the *Criminal Code*. It is clearly a complex area of the law.

The advent of the conditional sentence means that some offenders who traditionally went to jail are now able to serve their sentences in the community subject to conditions. Yet even today, many prosecutors and members of the general public still have difficulty accepting the conditional sentence as a reasonable alternative to traditional incarceration, perhaps for these two reasons: (1) It is hard to appreciate how the value systems in Canadian society have shifted so dramatically in recent times that Parliament has allowed offenders, who would have been jailed before, to serve their sentences in the same community whose trust they violated; and (2) Due to scarce resources, the administration of criminal justice is ill equipped to monitor or prosecute those offenders who do not live up to the conditions of their sentences in the community. A shortcoming of the conditional sentence is that many judges, defence counsel, and prosecutors view it as a second-class form of punishment. It is bandied about more as a tool for plea-bargaining purposes than as a legitimate form of sentence. Anecdotal evidence suggests that conditional sentences are more often imposed for a guilty plea than they are for a guilty verdict.

How should Crown counsel remedy the misuse of the conditional sentence? The answer is obvious. The prosecution has a positive duty to apply the law as expressed by Parliament and to actively urge conditional sentences upon the court whenever the circumstances dictate. This would be in keeping with the highest traditions of the Crown and entirely consistent with the expected objectivity that goes with the office. To lead by example is to conscientiously discharge the duties of the prosecution.

CONCLUSION

The prosecution plays an essential role in making the busiest of all Canadian courts a functional role model for the administration of justice. By maintaining an objective frame of mind, Crown counsel ensures that the adversarial process works. It is not always an easy task.

Further Readings

Brockman, J., and G. Rose. 1996. *An Introduction to Canadian Criminal Procedure and Evidence*. Toronto: Nelson Canada.

Manarin, B. 2009. "Bedeviled by Delay: Straight Talk about Memory Loss, Procedural Delay and the Myth of Swift Justice." *Windsor Review of Legal and Social Issues* 27: 117.

Stenning, P.C. 1994. "Current Issues concerning the Court Process." In C.T. Griffiths and S.N. Verdun-Jones, eds., *Canadian Criminal Justice*, 2nd ed. Toronto: Harcourt Brace Canada.

References

Bynoe, B. 1968. "The Role and Function of Crown Counsel." 3 C.R.N.S. 90. *Crown Policy Manual*. 1994. Policy # C.S.-1, Charge Screening, January 15.

Crown Practice Memorandum, Charge Screening [2002] No. 5, October 1.

Humphreys, C. 1955. "The Duties and Responsibilities of Prosecuting Counsel." *Criminal Law Review* 739: 748.

Manson, A. 2001 *Sentencing*. Toronto: Irwin Law.

Martin, G. 1993. *Report of the Attorney General's Advisory Committee on Charge Screening, Disclosure, and Resolution Discussions*. Toronto: Queen's Printer.

Roberts, J.V., and D. Cole. 1999. *Making Sense of Sentencing*. Toronto: University of Toronto Press.

Trotter, G. 1998. *The Law of Bail in Canada*. 2nd ed. Toronto: Carswell.

Wijesinha K., and B.J. Young. 1978. *Aids to Criminal Investigation*. Scarborough: Panju Canada.

Endnotes

1. The comments found herein are solely those of the author, made in his personal capacity.
2. R.S.C. 1985, c. C-46, as amended.
3. S. 33, Part I of the *Constitution Act*, 1982, being Schedule B to the *Canada Act* 1982 (U.K.), 1982, c. 11.
4. *R. v. Boucher* (1955), 110 C.C.C. 263 at 270 (S.C.C.).
5. *R. v. Bain* (1992), 10 C.R. (4th) 257 at 264 (S.C.C.), wherein Mr. Justice Cory recognizes that passions are not easily stilled, even when considering counsel for the Crown: "[T]hey, like all of us, are subject to human frailties and occasional lapses … I do not make these observations in order to be critical of Crown Attorneys. Rather they are made to emphasize the very human frailties that are common to all, no matter what the office held."
6. *R. v. Daly* (1992), 57 O.A.C. 70 at 76, para. 32 (C.A.).
7. *R. v. Stinchcombe* (1991), 68 C.C.C. (3d) 1 at 7 (S.C.C.).

8. Contained therein is a more exhaustive list of considerations that must be addressed by the Crown attorney's office. Note that the *Practice Memorandum* in question was incorporated into the new *Crown Policy Manual* as of March 31, 2006.

9. *Supra* note 2, ss. 716, 717. Note that the present incarnation of the diversion program in Ontario is called the "Direct Accountability Program," which was implemented as part of the provincial government's 2008 "Justice on Target" initiative.

10. See the *Youth Criminal Justice Act,* S.C. 2002, c. 1, as amended.

11. *Supra* note 2, s. 515(1).

12. Ibid., s. 515(6).

13. Ibid., s. 515(10).

14. Ibid., ss. 718–718.2.

15. Ibid., ss. 742–742.7.

CHAPTER 6

The Role of a Defence Counsel

Of all criminal justice professions, the one most people are familiar with is the defence counsel. Although people know what defence lawyers are, they don't necessarily have a good understanding of their role in the criminal justice system. Moreover, when asked to rate the performance of different criminal justice professionals, Canadians assign relatively poor ratings to members of the defence bar. People appear to overlook the vital role that defence lawyers play in the adversarial system of justice. In this chapter, Paul Burstein, an experienced criminal defence lawyer practising in Toronto, discusses the professional life of a defence counsel.

Paul Burstein
Queen's University and Osgoode Hall Law School

As a criminal defence lawyer, I have often been asked by friends and family whether it bothers me to work so hard in the defence of someone whom I know is guilty. For reasons that I hope to make clear a little further on, I have never found this to be a very difficult question to answer. However, many years ago, my then seven-year-old daughter asked me a slightly different question, one that I found myself struggling to answer.[1] She asked me how I could defend bad people. My daughter's question led me to rethink the soundness of the explanations that I had long offered to critics of criminal defence lawyers. Fortunately, after some long periods of thought, I have managed to once again come to terms with this skepticism with respect to the importance of criminal defence work for our society.

In order to emphasize the importance of what criminal defence lawyers do, I think it is necessary to first explain what it is that we do. Simply put, criminal defence lawyers represent people who find themselves accused of crimes. As a result of the proliferation of television legal dramas, most people mistakenly perceive a defence lawyer's job as beginning and ending with their work at a trial. In fact, most of a criminal defence lawyer's time is spent helping clients long before their cases actually get to trial. Indeed, the vast majority of criminal cases never go to trial. Although the numbers have varied over the past couple of decades, no more than 5 to 10 percent of criminal charges are resolved through trials. If so few criminal cases result in trials, what are all those criminal defence lawyers doing hanging around the courthouses? It may sound trite, but they are trying to help their clients stay out, or get out, of jail.

THE CLIENT AT THE POLICE STATION

Typically, a criminal defence lawyer's "job" begins long before the client's case even gets to trial. In fact, a criminal defence lawyer often becomes involved in a case even before the client goes to court. In Canada, s. 10(b) of the *Canadian Charter of Rights and Freedoms* provides that:

10. Everyone has the right on arrest or detention ...
    (b)   to retain and instruct counsel without delay and to be informed of that right....

Canadian courts have interpreted this constitutional right to mean that the police must tell someone who has been arrested that he or she can immediately contact a lawyer for free legal advice.[2] Where a "detainee" (i.e., a person who has been detained) requests to speak to a lawyer, our courts have also held that the police are obliged to help that detainee get in touch with a lawyer right away, such as by providing her with a phone and a phone book.[3] For those detainees who call a lawyer from the police station (not all of them do), the defence lawyer will almost always urge the detainee to assert her right to remain silent.

Contrary to a popular misconception, even detainees who are not guilty can end up "confessing" to the police while being held in detention. In effect, these innocent[4] people provide the police with a false confession. In addition, detainees who are not guilty of the charge sometimes end up providing the police with an account of the events that is confused or mistaken. After all, these people are being held in custody and are being interrogated by very skilled and experienced questioners. More often than not, those police interrogators confront the detainee with overblown claims of a case against the person in the hope of stimulating some sort of incriminating statement. These overblown accusations can frighten an accused into agreeing to a lesser accusation, even if it is untrue. Thus, to prevent the creation of unreliable "confessions," the law guarantees a detainee the right to remain silent upon arrest. The defence lawyer must not only remind the detainee of this right during that first phone call but also help the detainee build the courage to maintain that silence in the face of any subtle or confrontational police questioning. In my experience, the vast majority of police officers, when told by the criminal defence lawyer of the detainee's desire to remain silent, will do the honourable thing and refrain from questioning that detainee any further. To the chagrin of many defence lawyers, certain clients, no matter how many times they come in contact with the criminal justice system, never seem to be able to learn what it means to "shut up"![5]

RELEASE OF THE CLIENT ON BAIL

The other task of a criminal defence lawyer during that first phone call from the police station is to attempt to persuade the police to allow the client–detainee to be released on bail. While the police usually have already made a decision about bail, a defence lawyer's input can help satisfy the arresting officer that it is appropriate to release the detainee directly from the police station. If not, then the defence lawyer will ask where and when the client–detainee will be brought to court for a hearing before a justice of the peace to determine whether or not the client should be released on bail. The *Criminal Code* requires that a person who has been arrested and who has not been released at the scene or at the police station be brought before a justice of the peace within a day or two of the arrest for a bail hearing. Many lawyers believe that the bail issue is the most important one in the criminal process. Given the long delays that occur between the time of the arrest and the time of trial, some people will have a strong incentive to plead guilty to their charge(s), even when they are not in fact guilty, simply to avoid a lengthy wait in a pre-trial remand facility for their trial date.

In preparation for a bail hearing, a defence lawyer will need to help his client find a *surety*—someone who is willing to pledge a sum of money as a guarantee of that person's ability to supervise the detainee if released. In many cases, defence lawyers also must function as social workers or counsellors and help arrange for their clients to obtain treatment, secure employment, or re-enroll in school, since the justice of the peace will want to know that the client isn't sitting at home watching television until the trial date arrives. I cannot tell you how many times I have been in bail court and have heard the expression "the devil finds work for idle hands."

DEFENCES

Win or lose, the bail hearing does not end the case for a person who has been charged with a criminal offence. The next stage in the process involves trying to determine whether the client has a defence to the charge(s) she faces. At the risk of grossly oversimplifying what I do, criminal defences can generally be divided into two categories: *factual defences* and *legal defences*. The factual type of defence involves a challenge to the evidence that the police have gathered in the course of the investigation that resulted in the charge(s) against the client. Perhaps the witness is lying. Maybe he implicated the accused in order to benefit himself, such as through a lesser sentence for his own charges or for a monetary reward. Maybe the eyewitness is mistaken. As noted elsewhere in this book (see Chapter 18 by Campbell and Denov), eyewitness identification is notoriously unreliable.

The other type of defence, the legal kind, focuses on whether or not what the person is accused of doing should be considered "criminal." For example, there may be no dispute that my client shot her husband, but it may have been in self-defence and, thus, is legally justified. In trying to determine what (if any) defence a client has to a criminal charge, the defence lawyer needs to gather information relevant to the case. That information comes from the police reports and witness statements, which the prosecutor is legally obliged to disclose to the defence in advance of the trial,[6] as well as any information the client and other potential witnesses provide. (This practice is known as the Crown providing "disclosure" to the defence.) In addition, the defence lawyer may have to do some research into the law that governs the features of the client's case—for example, whether the police have engaged in an illegal search, whether self-defence includes the defence of one's property, or whether two lovers in a parked car are in a "public place." Once the defence lawyer has determined the nature and extent of the available defences, the lawyer is ready to advise the client how next to proceed.

At this juncture, the defence lawyer presents the client with two options: plead guilty in the hope of obtaining a more lenient sentence from the court as a reward for sparing everyone the time and expense of a trial, or schedule a date for a trial, at which time the client can plead not guilty and contest the prosecutor's case. As noted above, in the vast majority of cases, persons charged with criminal offences opt to have their lawyer try to negotiate a plea bargain with the prosecutor.

The term *plea bargain* connotes exactly what it means: in exchange for giving up the right to a full trial, the accused receives the prosecutor's recommendation for a more lenient sentence than would normally be sought in a trial sentencing. This bargaining is often done at the prosecutor's office and is sometimes mediated by a judge. Upon learning the bottom-line offer of the prosecutor, a defence lawyer must always seek the input of the client before accepting or rejecting it. When asked by clients whether I would take the plea bargain if I were in their shoes, I am always left to explain that my risk–benefit analysis of trial versus guilty plea will, by definition, be different from theirs. As I tell them, given the nature of my work, I am quite used to spending my days in jail and am quite comfortable hanging around with criminals. If, on the other hand, the client is one of the minority who decide to reject the plea bargain in favour of a trial, the court will schedule a trial for some time down the road.[7]

PREPARING FOR TRIAL

Preparing a case for trial is very much like producing a film or a play. First, you have to develop the story on which the play will be based. By this, I certainly do not mean that lawyers help clients fabricate stories in order to avoid conviction. I am simply referring to the development of the narrative that takes into account the evidence that the defence lawyer believes will be accepted by the jury (or judge) at the end of the case *and* that is consistent with innocence. That is what a criminal defence lawyer does in representing a client at a trial: develop an "innocence" narrative to compete with the "guilty" narrative constructed by the police. For instance, the police may not have interviewed all of the potential witnesses, some of whom may not only cast doubt on the claim by others that a client is the guilty party but also shed light on the true identity of the perpetrator.

However, to develop a competing narrative is no easy task. By the time a defence lawyer becomes involved in a case, the prosecution narrative has already been constructed. The raw material (i.e., the evidence) is rarely still sitting at the scene waiting to be collected and examined. Nevertheless, a defence lawyer must visit the scene of the crime to discover the competing innocence narrative. Perhaps the one feature of criminal defence work that is fairly reflected on television is the sleuthing that criminal defence lawyers do in the preparation of their clients' cases.

I recall once going to a seedy hotel in downtown Toronto in preparation for a murder case where my client, a young female prostitute, had been charged with stabbing her customer to death. The case was about whether she had acted in self-defence. Thus, her opportunities to escape would play a critically important role in the jury's decision. After waiting for the elevator for 10 minutes down the hall from the room where the stabbing had occurred, I decided to take the stairs back down to the lobby. It was only then, when I saw that the staircase had been locked (apparently to prevent prostitutes from servicing clients in the stairwell and thereby avoiding the $50 room charge) that I better understood why my client would have felt that there was no means of escaping her attacker. This visit provided me with evidence to present at trial.

The next element of the trial drama is the cast of characters, and some are indeed characters. Who are the people who will tell the story to the jury? What are their backgrounds? Are they neutral and impartial, or are they motivated by revenge against the client? Do these people have a criminal record or a history of substance abuse? Usually, as part of the disclosure, the defence lawyer receives this sort of information about the proposed witnesses. However, in some cases, a defence lawyer must hire a private investigator to gather information about the witnesses. Unfortunately, even with the assistance of a private investigator, a criminal defence lawyer will never have the investigative resources that were (and are) available to the police and prosecutor. This is one of the principal justifications for insisting that the prosecutor bear the burden of proving guilt beyond a reasonable doubt, rather than asking the accused to prove that she is innocent.

With the storyline developed and the cast of characters defined, the defence lawyer must then turn to "directing" the play. In stark contrast to television legal dramas, most criminal defence lawyers do not simply stand up after the prosecutor finishes questioning a witness and begin cross-examination of that witness. Cross-examination must be carefully thought out and planned so that it does not do more harm than good. Moreover, a criminal defence lawyer must also maintain the jury's interest in the case: important points that arise in the middle of a long and meandering cross-examination of a witness will be lost if the jury are daydreaming. In an effort to maintain the jury's interest, lawyers also use visual aids to illustrate the testimony of the witnesses, such as by diagrams, photographs, or computer simulations. The ultimate efficacy of the "production" in the courtroom depends on the time invested in its planning.

CONSTITUTIONAL ISSUES

While the outcome of the majority of trials depends on the narrative created by the witnesses and the evidence, some trials are not about who did what, where, why, and to whom. Occasionally, a trial focuses instead on the law itself.

One of the most famous Canadian examples is the trial of Dr. Henry Morgentaler. Most Canadians recall that in 1988, the Supreme Court of Canada declared that anti-abortion laws violated Section 7 of the *Canadian Charter of Rights and Freedoms*. What most laypeople do not appreciate, however, is that this ruling was made in the context of Dr. Morgentaler's trial on criminal charges for performing abortions. Dr. Morgentaler never denied that he had performed the abortions on the women in contravention of Section 251 of the *Criminal Code*. Instead, his defence focused on the constitutional validity of the law itself. In other words, Dr. Morgentaler's lawyer argued that it did not matter whether or not his client had done what the prosecutor was alleging because even if he had done those things, the *Charter* prohibited the Government of Canada from making it a crime to do those things.

Section 52 of the *Constitution Act, 1982,* known by lawyers as the "supremacy clause," states:

> 52(1) The Constitution of Canada is the supreme law of Canada, and any law that is inconsistent with the provisions of the Constitution is, to the extent of the inconsistency, of no force or effect.

In plain English, this means that the Canadian government is not entitled to make laws that violate the rights that are set out in the *Canadian Charter of Rights and Freedoms*. Accordingly, a trial judge has the power to strike down a provision of the *Criminal Code* that is inconsistent with the *Charter*, just as the Supreme Court of Canada did when it struck down Section 251 of the *Code* in Dr. Morgentaler's case. This means that a lone criminal defence lawyer, armed with nothing more than a solid legal argument, can make (or rather, unmake) law, a feat not possible even for the prime minister.

It was not long into my career as a criminal defence lawyer before I started to raise "Section 52 challenges" to criminal laws that I (and my clients) felt were oppressive and unfair. In 1993, about a year and a half after being called to the bar, I launched a challenge to Canada's criminal prohibition on marijuana on behalf of a client who was charged with growing some plants in his house for his own personal use. As a result of a very good plea bargain that quickly followed that challenge, the court was never given the opportunity to decide the issue. However, less than two years later, along with my friend and mentor Professor Alan Young, I became involved in another challenge to Canada's criminal prohibition on marijuana that had wound its way up to the Supreme Court of Canada, before finally being dismissed (by six of the nine justices; see *R. v. Clay*, [2003] S.C.J. No. 80). If the Supreme Court of Canada had agreed with our reasoning that the law violates the rights enshrined in Section 7 of the *Charter*, it would have declared the law to be "of no force or effect" pursuant to the supremacy clause in Section 52 of the Constitution. This would have meant that the marijuana offences with which our client had been charged back in 1995 would have been dismissed. More important, though, it would have meant that no other Canadian could henceforth have been convicted of breaking that law because the law itself would have been effectively erased from the books.

In some instances, criminal defence lawyers instead challenge only the *scope* of a particular criminal law, as opposed to the law itself. For example, in the marijuana case, one alternative argument was that the criminal prohibition on cannabis, as it is referred to in the legislation, should be limited to the type of cannabis that people can use to get high. While it may sound silly to think that people could be convicted of possessing hemp, the non-intoxicating form of cannabis, the law is unfortunately not so clear. Indeed, the drug analyst who testified at the trial admitted that based on the testing protocol, he would willingly certify a piece of hemp clothing as cannabis, since the clothing would contain all of the elements that the law required for something to be certified as cannabis. Rather than compelling the court to strike down the entire law, this argument would simply have required the court to redefine the law in a way that would have produced a more appropriate (and narrowed) definition of the "crime."

In a similar vein, I was also involved with Alan Young in a challenge to the breadth of the criminal law that prohibited the "Thornhill Dominatrix" from offering her clients sadomasochistic services for hire. She had been charged with operating a common bawdyhouse on the basis that the sadomasochistic services were the equivalent of criminally proscribed sex-for-hire. On the strength of expert evidence concerning its sociological, psychological, and cultural dimensions, we argued that the nature and purpose of S&M activities is not sexual but rather psychological stimulation—namely, the thrill associated with the anticipation and experience of pain (and/or humiliation).[8] Therefore, we argued, the criminal prohibition should not apply as it was properly limited to activities that were specifically aimed at providing sexual stimulation in exchange for money. But despite the inferential support to the argument provided by prior case decisions, the courts reaffirmed their monopoly on being paid to administer punishment and rejected these arguments.

In December of 2013, on behalf of that same "Thornhill Dominatrix" (a.k.a. Terri-Jean Bedford), Professor Young successfully persuaded the Supreme Court of Canada that the criminal prohibition on various prostitution-related offences violated the *Charter* as they unnecessarily endangered the safety of women who chose to engage in acts of prostitution (a legal activity). The Supreme Court nullified those laws, but gave the Canadian Government 12 months in which to try and draft new criminal laws governing prostitution-related activities that would be compliant with the *Charter.*

My involvement in these constitutional challenges highlights another important feature of being a criminal defence lawyer: the need (or opportunity) to study new disciplines beyond the confines of law. For the constitutional challenge concerning marijuana, I had to educate myself on the psychopharmacological, sociological, criminological, botanical, and historical perspectives on the criminal prohibition of marijuana. For the Dominatrix case, I had to become versed in the culture of S&M in order to be able to explain it to the court and, more important, to be able to demonstrate why the stereotypical perception of this practice is misguided.

For other cases, I have had to learn about psychiatry, literature, chemistry, toxicology, biology, and even entomology (i.e., the study of bugs). This pursuit of knowledge can be a burden of the criminal defence lawyer's job. Indeed, I recall having to spend all of my Friday evenings, for weeks on end, sitting on a stool in the cramped office of our engineering expert in the Toronto "Just Desserts" murder case to learn all about digital image processing in preparation for the trial. Then again, this is probably one of the great benefits of being a criminal defence lawyer: the opportunity to learn about things in the world to which I might never otherwise have been exposed.

DEFENDING PEOPLE WHO MAY BE GUILTY

Despite the very long hours, the limited financial rewards, and the general lack of respect from the public, most of the time I love my job. I meet interesting people, learn fascinating new things, and visit places I would otherwise likely never have gone. In many ways, the job of a criminal defence lawyer is exotic and exciting.

Having explained why someone might want to be a criminal defence lawyer and what it is that criminal defence lawyers do, I am left to answer the question as to how I could defend someone whom I "know" is guilty. To begin with, it is important to remember that the Canadian criminal justice system, while good, is far from perfect. One need only pay heed to the increasing number of wrongful convictions that are emerging in Canada (and in the United States as well). Indeed, look back to the media coverage of the arrest of Guy Paul Morin, a man now proved innocent of the murder with which he was charged. But back in 1985, the public "knew" he was guilty. It was not until almost a decade later that the public realized its mistake. Perception is not reality.

The only way to reduce the number of wrongful convictions is to ensure that the system never cuts corners, no matter how heinous the crime. If someone truly is guilty, the system should be able to arrive at that determination in a fair and just manner—that is, by following the usual rules. Everyone must be subject to the same set of rules, no matter who she is or what she has been accused of doing. Unfortunately, there are many countries where that is not the case. In those places, the rules depend upon who you are or the people you know. The ruling elites in those places exist, in part, because there are no defence lawyers to challenge the arbitrary detention and imprisonment of people who are unfairly labelled as "criminals." While Canada is a long way off from that paradigm, Canadians must never take for granted their rights and freedoms nor those whose job it is to defend those rights and freedoms. Defending the "guilty" is a necessary part of ensuring that *all* Canadians continue to enjoy their rights and freedoms.[9] In short, defence lawyers keep the criminal justice system honest and true.

That still leaves me with my daughter's question of how I can defend "bad" people, as opposed to people who have been accused of doing a bad thing. Why is it that "bad" people should benefit from all of my hard work as a criminal defence lawyer? Why should someone who has a long history of violating other people's rights be entitled to the same rights and freedoms as everyone else? The answer is that for better or for worse, the Canadian criminal justice system is one that seeks only to punish people for what they have done, not for who they are. It has to be that way.

Consider what it would mean to base punishment decisions on whether a person was "good" or "bad." Even in that sort of system, it would be unfair to punish those who were bad through no fault of their own—for example, those who suffered from fetal alcohol syndrome or those who had grown up being physically abused in group homes after being abandoned by their families. Instead, we would have to punish bad people only after having a trial to determine if they were bad by choice or by circumstances. If we did not care to make that distinction, we would have to be prepared to charge all those who may have contributed to the person's crime of being bad, such as parents, schools, peers, and government. Of course, when I explained all of this to my daughter, she was quick to agree and reminded me that by that logic, I should therefore be the one serving her detention at school, because it is my fault, not hers, that she was bad. Spoken like the daughter of a criminal defence lawyer.

Further Reading

Greenspan, E. 1980. "The Role of the Defence Counsel in Sentencing." In B. Grosman, ed., *New Directions in Sentencing*. Toronto: Butterworths.

Endnotes

1. Being the father of Courtney, now age 18; Nikki, age 15; Jaxson, age 7; Jazmyn, age 6; and Elle and Emme, ages 3, has taught me more about how to ask and how to answer more "tough" questions than my many other experiences in the criminal law sphere.
2. *R. v. Bartle* (1994), 92 C.C.C. (3d) 289 (S.C.C.).
3. You would be amazed at how many first-time detainees go about choosing the defence lawyer who will represent them by simply going to the section in the Yellow Pages that lists "criminal lawyers" and starting at the As. You would, no doubt, be equally amazed at how many criminal defence lawyers were named "ΛΛΛΛΛΛΛΛΛΛSmith" at birth!
4. Whether they are "factually" innocent (i.e., did not do what the police have alleged) or "legally" innocent (i.e., have not done something that actually amounts to a crime).
5. For example, in *R. v. Manninen* (1987), 34 C.C.C. (3d) 385 (S.C.C.), one of the seminal cases on the "right to counsel" in Canada, the accused, a "rounder," is savvy enough to assert his right to speak to a lawyer when arrested on a robbery charge. However, he then proceeds to engage in the following dialogue with the arresting officer:

   Q. Where is the knife that you had along with this [showing the accused the CO2 gun found in the car] when you ripped off the Mac's Milk on Wilson Avenue?

   A. He's lying. When I was in the store I only had the gun. The knife was in the tool box in the car.

   Q. What are these for?

   A. What the fuck do you think they are for? Are you fucking stupid?

Q. You tell me what they are for, and is this yours? [showing the grey sweatshirt]

A. Of course it's mine. You fuckers are really stupid. Don't bother me anymore. I'm not saying anything until I see my lawyer. Just fuck off. You fuckers have to prove it.

6. See *R. v. Stinchcombe* (1991), 68 C.C.C. (3d) 1 (S.C.C.).

7. The lag between the "set date" and the trial can range up to a few years. The length of the delay is dependent upon the jurisdiction and upon the nature of the case; more complicated cases require more court time and, thus, are harder to slot into already very busy schedules.

8. Apparently, much like bungee jumping, skydiving, or white-water rafting.

9. Throughout history, criminal defence lawyers have been accused of being unpatriotic. In one of the most eloquent descriptions of the importance of defence lawyers, Henry Brougham, defending Queen Caroline on charges of adultery before the English House of Lords many centuries ago, said: "An advocate, in the discharge of his duty, knows but one person in all the world, and that person is his client. To save that client by all means and expedients, and at all hazards and costs to other persons, and, among them, to himself, is his first and only duty; and in performing this duty he must not regard the alarm, the torments, the destruction which he may bring upon others. Separating the duty of a patriot from that of an advocate, he must go on reckless of consequences, though it should be his unhappy fate to involve his country in confusion" (*Trial of Queen Caroline*, by J. Nightingale, vol. II, The Defence, Part I (1821), at p. 8).

A Day in the Life of a Judge

Many people think that judges simply supervise trials and sentence convicted offenders; but judges have a great deal more to do than that. Judges are required to perform many judicial functions over the course of a typical day. In addition to their in-court activities, they also supervise pretrial conferences, meet with lawyers, see police officers about search and other kinds of warrants, write judgments (quite lengthy at times), and stay current with a large number of areas of the law. The professional life of a judge is not helped by the backlog of cases. In this reading, a very experienced provincial court judge in one of Ontario's busiest courts describes a typical day in his professional life.

Judge David P. Cole
Ontario Court of Justice, Toronto

I became a lawyer in 1975, practising exclusively as criminal defence counsel until my appointment as a judge of the Ontario Court of Justice (Provincial Division)[1] in 1991. What follows is a narrative of a typical day in one court at the Metro East (Scarborough) Court facility in Toronto, including its major phases, players, and communications with one another and before the bench. In order to better present what happens in a judge's life, the following explains—from one judge's perspective—daily life in court as court personnel and I go about our duties in dealing with the accused.

When I arrive at the court building each morning, I find on my desk in my office the list of the cases scheduled to be heard that day (the "docket"). On the day that I shall describe (September 1, 1998), I had to deal with the following charges: failing to appear (Mr. Ashbury); impaired driving (Ms. Andrus); breach of probation (Mr. Burns); assault (Mr. Fisher); mischief to private property/prowl by night (Mr. Goode); and two young offenders (K.B. and R.S.[2]). On this particular day, Ms. Crisante[3] was the Crown assigned responsibility for prosecuting all the new cases on the trial list. Normally—though, regrettably, by no means always—the trial Crown is given the Crown files ("briefs") for preparation the afternoon before the court hearing.

The paperwork for even the simplest cases is often voluminous. For example, the charge of failing to appear against Mr. Ashbury was legally quite simple: could the Crown establish to my satisfaction that Mr. Ashbury had an obligation to appear in court and that he had failed to do so? Once the Crown could prove these things, the *Criminal Code* directed that Mr. Ashbury would be found guilty of this offence unless he could establish that he had a lawful excuse for not appearing. However, there is considerable paperwork necessary to prove such a charge; at a minimum, the Crown would need certified copies of the form of the accused's release on bail, a certified copy of the charge that he failed to appear, and a certificate of the court clerk indicating that he had not appeared on the scheduled date. The trial Crown would then have the responsibility for checking to see that the investigating police officer (or, in this case, the accused's probation officer) had included all the necessary documents in the brief. Failure to do so would likely result in an aborted prosecution.

The Crown brief for the impaired driving charges against Ms. Andrus might be several centimetres thick, depending on the facts and issues raised. It would usually contain the statements of police officers and civilian witnesses, a computer printout of the accused's breath readings, reports from a toxicologist explaining the significance of those readings, and a videotape of some of the time she was in the police station. Also likely to be included would be photocopies of precedents from other cases that Crown counsel thinks the defendant might submit in arguing her case.

Unlike some European systems in which the presiding judge is deeply involved in investigating every detail of cases from their outset, the Canadian justice system is designed in such a way that the judge is supposed to know as little as possible about the cases he is assigned. Thus, I would not usually see much, if any, of this paperwork prior to the trial. Similarly, fairly elaborate steps are taken to ensure that I would not be assigned to try cases of which I have any previous knowledge.

Before going into court, I normally do not look at the docket of the new cases I am about to try. On this day, the only cases with which I was familiar ahead of time were those concerning the two young offenders, K.B. and R.S. I had already started these cases on prior occasions, and these were the only cases to which Mr. Kerr, the other Crown listed on the court docket, had been assigned. As the day developed, he dealt with some of Ms. Crisante's cases in order to maximize efficient use of court time. She prepared herself to respond to last-minute arguments that defence counsel in Ms. Andrus's impaired driving case (driving with over .80 milligrams of alcohol per millilitre of blood) had announced he was going to raise.

As the first item of business, the Crown usually calls up the cases that defence counsel or the investigating police officer has not spoken to her about in order to determine the status of the cases. When Mr. Burns's case was called, he told me that he had not been able to arrange for a lawyer to represent him on the charge of breaching a probation order because he could not afford the $25 fee to process his application for legal aid. He asked to have his case adjourned. I examined the paperwork, which disclosed that Mr. Burns was charged with not paying the restitution that was part of a previous probation order. It also revealed that he had agreed several months earlier that he would proceed to trial on September 1 regardless whether he had counsel. If I were to find Mr. Burns guilty, he faced the possibility of going to jail (depending on the circumstances of the breach and his previous record). Nevertheless, given his previous indication that he was prepared to proceed to trial without counsel, I ruled that unless there was some extraordinary reason for him to have another chance to get a lawyer, I would not grant a further adjournment.

Mr. Burns then told me that since the charge had been laid, he had paid off the outstanding order for restitution. At this point, Crown counsel intervened, saying that her brief indicated that while partial restitution had been made, a balance of $200 remained outstanding at the time the brief had been prepared, and that unless she received further information, she was not prepared to withdraw the charge. Mr. Burns said, "My old lady took a hundred dollar money order down to my PO [probation officer] last week."

I told the accused that while, in his mind, it might be true that he had "fixed it ... with his PO," could he please explain how he could have done this while $100 apparently remained outstanding? In response, Mr. Burns simply stared at the floor. The Crown explained to the accused that the probation officer had caused the accused to be charged because, in the probation officer's opinion, Mr. Burns had willfully declined to complete paying restitution when he was in a position to do so. I told Mr. Burns that it was up to the Crown, not his probation officer, to decide whether the charge would proceed, but that we should wait for the probation officer to arrive at court (due to pressure of work, they are almost always late) to further update the Crown.

Mr. Burns then told me that he could not wait because he had to go to work and asked what he "would get ... if I cop [plead guilty] to the charge." Such an inquiry by an accused is quite common and raises several difficult issues for the court system. First, while I told Mr. Burns that I would not and could not tell him in advance what I might do if he were to plead guilty, strictly speaking, this was not true. There are many cases in which I am consulted in advance if a plea bargain is contemplated. I did not feel comfortable doing so in this case because Mr. Burns had neither his own counsel nor duty counsel to advise him. For this reason, I sent him off to the duty counsel office in the hope that the standby duty counsel might be able to advise him. Unfortunately, he returned to court a few minutes later, saying that he had been told that the standby duty counsel was busy and would not be available for some time, if at all.

Surprising as it may sound, many accused enter pleas of guilty despite the fact that they may have legal or factual defences to the charge. They decide for their own reasons, which often seem very sensible to them, that they are not interested in presenting a defence. As a judge, I cannot accept a plea unless the accused makes an informed waiver of his rights and is prepared to admit to all the elements necessary to support the Crown's case. In this case, had Mr. Burns insisted on pleading guilty, because he was not represented by counsel, I would have conducted what is termed a *plea comprehension inquiry*, reviewing with him his understanding of his right to contest the allegations and his willingness to admit to each element of the Crown's case. If he had balked at any stage, I would likely have struck the plea and remanded the case to another trial date. The practical difficulty that arises is that on the next date, the accused may go through the same process, this time pretending that he is making an informed waiver and conceding the elements of the case just so he can get it over with.

Luckily, by this time, Mr. Burns's probation officer arrived. Crown counsel suggested that the case be "held down" to allow the parties the opportunity for some brief discussion. Although I was not privy to discussions among the accused, the probation officer, and Crown counsel, they eventually presented me with a compromise. Mr. Burns's case would be adjourned for 30 days. If he voluntarily performed 25 hours of community service prior to the return date by way of extra punishment for not having done what he was supposed to do, the parties agreed that the criminal charge would be withdrawn on the next appearance.

This case neatly illustrates several of the time allocation dilemmas regularly faced by the criminal justice system (and the extent to which the professionals are driven by the need to use court time as efficiently as possible). Given the relative unimportance of this case compared with the others on the list, the Crown likely had very little interest in prosecuting Mr. Burns that day, particularly since, being unrepresented, his case would probably take about 90 minutes to try. According to the Ministry of the Attorney General's current guidelines, a court day is supposed to consist of eight hours of trial time.[4]

After extensive discussion in our court's delay reduction committee, our trial coordinator has been instructed to "load" 14 hours of trial time per day into a court such as this one. This is based on assumptions—well understood by court professionals though not by some accused and the general public—that a substantial number of cases will not proceed to trial despite having been scheduled as if they would be. As will be learned from what follows, Mr. Burns's case was the first of several that day to be diverted away from a trial.

Moreover, by the time the trial date comes up, Mr. Burns's probation term will have expired, thus making the agreement negotiated on the court date virtually unenforceable. If Mr. Burns does not perform the agreed-upon community service, all that can be done when his case next came before the court (on September 30) would be to process the original charge of breaching his probation by failing to make restitution. Once again, Crown counsel assigned to this court on that date, facing another list containing at least 14 hours of cases, would not likely have much interest in prosecuting the charge.

Did Mr. Burns know or guess some or all of this? Did he put off the day of reckoning by luck or by design? I do not know for sure. Ironically, in our adversarial system, the judge in the courtroom is usually the person who least knows the accused. Apart from the brief series of questions I asked in response to his request for an adjournment, I am not supposed to engage in much dialogue with an accused. (And if Mr. Burns had had counsel there to represent him, he would likely have stood mute, leaving it up to his lawyer to speak on his behalf.) Because of this, over the years, I have learned to try as hard as I can to resist the human temptation to speculate and judge without sufficient evidence.

Although this example illustrates an acceptable way of proceeding, problems can and do occur when cases are not completed the same day that they start. This is particularly the case when the evidentiary portion of a trial has to be remanded to another day, as in the case of Ms. Andrus. The accused's lawyer brought a pretrial motion to dismiss the charges on the basis that she had not been given her constitutionally guaranteed right to counsel.[5] Because of the time needed to deal with the cases ahead of hers, her case could not be started until the afternoon (this is quite typical). The defence counsel's evidence on the motion to stop the proceedings (on the basis that her *Charter* rights had been violated) was already completed. In reply, the police testifying had given most of their evidence. Unfortunately, because of insufficient time, I had to defer the remainder of their testimony (including cross-examination by the defence) to March 4, 1999. After taking ten minutes of court time to deal with the trial coordinator's concerns and those of the lawyers, I determined that this was the earliest date that the time required could be matched with the schedules of the witnesses, the lawyers, and me.[6]

In such cases, in addition to taking what I hope are accurate notes of what is said by witnesses as they give their evidence, as soon as I leave court at the end of the day, I try to make notes immediately of how I am responding to the evidence as it is unfolding (recognizing, of course, that my preliminary impressions may change during the case). This includes such things as whether

I think there is an adequate connection between Fact A and Fact B, why certain questions have not been asked (or properly answered), and, most importantly, what I think of the witnesses' credibility. While I try not to make up my mind until I have heard all the evidence and the lawyers' submissions, the reality of the situation is that given these lengthy delays and the danger of wrongly convicting an innocent person, most judges in this position would be more likely to acquit when the case is resumed six months later. This kind of ongoing resource problem is something that all court professionals are well aware of, and that is likely why the Crown seemed resigned or disappointed while the defence seemed quietly elated when the conclusion of the case is put off like this.

Why were more consecutive days not scheduled to avoid such unreasonable delays? This is a constant systemic problem that can be solved if more resources are available. As a result of aggressively pre-trying cases, Scarborough's courts have made significant efforts toward reducing the backlog of case.[7] However, despite repeated requests, no more resources are likely to be made available in the near future. As a result, cases such as this one tend to "slip through" the system.

What happened in Ms. Andrus's case was this: as soon as defence counsel decided that he wished to launch a "right to counsel" constitutional challenge, the court rules required him to serve a formal "Notice of a Constitutional Question" on the Crown and with the court. This notice must be filed at least 15 days prior to the trial date in order to give Crown counsel an opportunity to prepare to respond to the motion. He did not do so, asking that I permit him to proceed with his motion despite his failure to file it on time (which I have the power to do). He claimed that the reason he did not do so was simple inadvertence on his part. Crown counsel responded by saying that this was "too bad. The rules are there for a purpose. I am sick and tired of defence counsel going about their business as if the rules don't exist."

While I appreciated the defence counsel's apparent candour, how did this help me in deciding whether to allow him to argue the motion? Although I have not seen him for many years, the defence counsel was known to me as someone whose word could be accepted. Was he subtly reminding me, as an ex-defence counsel, that I, too, might have made such a slip and that I should not show him up in front of his client? Was he signalling me that he wasn't really serious about the motion and was just going through the motions of presenting a defence? (After all, "right to counsel" issues are probably the most frequently argued motions under the *Charter*. A counsel as experienced as he surely would have noticed the issue earlier. From what I know of the case to date, that should have been easy.) Or was he signalling perhaps that his client was not paying him as quickly as he would have liked and that he was "playing hardball" with her, refusing to file the motion until she had completed paying his retainer?

And how should I have responded to the Crown's position? Should she, as soon as she realized that the defence had filed a motion, have filed a written application to dismiss it as being beyond the time frame allotted by the rules of procedure? That is doubtful unless this was an extremely serious case; and apart from the clerk in the office making sure that the motion was put in the Crown brief, no one in the Crown's office would have looked at the motion until late on August 31. What if the motion ultimately turned out to be valid, and the charges were dismissed for a breach of the accused's constitutional rights? Should I have refused to hear it simply because it was not filed on time?

What have I learned about this for the future? Should I be more careful with this particular lawyer if I see him in the future? Should I modify my practice in such cases to penalize counsel for sloppy conduct by saying that I will hear only out-of-time motions if they agree to pay for a complete transcript if the case has to be remanded to another date? Or might that only penalize the poor? Should I have ordered a transcript so that I am not forced to rely on my substantive notes of the evidence when the case is resumed?

The court clerk occupies a very important position. In addition to ensuring that all the various court documents are located and brought to court each day by the scheduled start time, she ensures that each time I make an order, it is accurately reflected in the court records. This may be as simple as ordering that a case be remanded to another date, or it may be very complicated, such as ensuring that varying terms of imprisonment or probation are properly apportioned to each charge. As I write this, the newspapers have reported an apparently appalling case in which an accused wrongly spent a week in jail. This took place despite several supposedly fail-safe procedures designed to protect against this very kind of miscarriage of justice. Apparently, someone had ticked off the wrong box on a court form designed to record judicial orders. Instead of recording that the accused had been given a year to pay his fine of $1,000, it was recorded that the accused had been sentenced to jail for a year. No one, including the justice of the peace who made the order, noticed the mistake.

In order to protect against this very type of error, many of the orders that I make—particularly penalties of various forms—are presented to me at least twice for signature: once when the court clerk writes up what I have said, and again when the formal order has been typed. On a very busy day, I might be asked to sign upward of 50 orders. Although I suppose I could refuse to sign them until I have an opportunity to check them against my notes, the reality is that if I do that, everything will be delayed. If I delay signing remand papers for incarcerated accused, the jail will refuse to accept them, which means that the backlog of incoming prisoners to the jail at the end of the day will be extensive. If I decline to sign probation orders immediately, those placed on probation may tire of waiting and leave the court, not knowing when and where they are supposed to report next. Because I have realized that it causes all kinds of problems if I stop to read each paper in detail, like many other judges, I have tacitly condoned the practice of agreeing to sign them as they are prepared. The result is that I am constantly having such papers thrust at me throughout the day, even when I am on the bench trying to concentrate on the proceedings. In practice, this means that the judge relies heavily on the court clerk and the support staff who type the orders to ensure their accuracy.

The problem does not end there. Despite the best efforts of the court personnel, errors occur because the staff are simply not trained to pick up some types of errors. This week, our court probation officer saw me about a case from some months ago. She pointed out that I had clearly made an error by imposing a period of probation in circumstances in which I had no power to do so. I did not spot the error at any stage (the day had been a particularly busy one), nor did the lawyers (who had urged this disposition on me). What is even sadder is that the accused, a man of limited intelligence, was clearly in no position to realize that he had been improperly dealt with.

According to ministry statistics, in 1997, I dealt (however briefly) with some 2,400 cases. Like other judges, I often worry about cases in which I may have made mechanical errors (such as errors writing the warrant), which may have resulted in an improper process being applied (or not applied[8]) against an accused. As I have previously mentioned, the trial coordinator has been instructed to put more cases onto a trial list than can actually be dealt with. What happened with the rest of the cases is a good illustration of how this kind of daily gamble works.[9]

While Ms. Crisante was outside the courtroom "brokering" Mr. Burns's case, as usually occurs, she was also able to plea-bargain or divert all but Ms. Andrus's case. Some of the cases were relatively simple for her to deal with. In Mr. Fisher's case, the alleged assault victim (complainant) did not turn up at court, which happens in about 40 percent of cases. There may be many reasons for this: the complainant may have moved since the charge was laid on December 30, 1997, and may not have received the mailed subpoena; or the complainant may simply have decided that, having called in the police to intervene, he is not interested in proceeding with the charge.[10]

Even when complainants do come to court, as occurred in Mr. Goode's case, they may tell the Crown that they would be satisfied with a reduced charge. In that case, Mr. Goode, the accused, while drunk[11] and despondent about breaking up with his girlfriend, had hung around her townhouse one night intending to persuade her to resume their relationship. When she spurned his advances, he smashed the windshield of what he assumed was her new lover's car. In fact, the vehicle belonged to, as I was told, "her religious advisor."[12] What the ex-girlfriend wanted was an order for the accused to stay away from her. What the male complainant wanted was the cost of repairing his car. After verifying that the accused had lived up to the term of his bail order that required him not to communicate with his ex-girlfriend, Crown and defence counsel jointly proposed that I order the accused to post a "peace bond." In exchange for having the charge withdrawn, the accused would promise to keep the peace and be on good behaviour for one year. If he did not live up to the conditions of the order (staying away from the two complainants and making restitution for the windshield), he would stand to lose $500 (the amount of the peace bond) and would be liable to be prosecuted for being in breach of the bond. All parties left the courtroom content.

Mr. Ashbury's case raised different issues. Given the carnage on our roads, police forces tend to be very intolerant of suspected drunk drivers. Even where there are few signs of impairment and the accused's breath reading is just over the limit (as happened here), police are under instructions to lay charges rather than sending the accused home in a cab. Because of aggressive lobbying by groups such as MADD (Mothers Against Drunk Driving), for many years, Crown counsel have been under a directive to prosecute vigorously all drinking and driving charges. In part because of their lobbying, the severity of the mandatory minimum penalties has been increased considerably.

Unlike most other criminal charges, large numbers of middle-class people are charged with drinking and driving offences. As they wish neither the inconvenience of being without a licence (up to a year for a first offender) nor the stigma of a criminal record, they are often prepared to invest considerable resources in defending themselves against these charges. Thus, in most cities, there are specialist defence counsel who devote much of their practices to defending impaired drivers.[13] They frequently employ expert toxicologists whose role is to uncover technical flaws in the Crown's case.

Once again, Crown counsel was faced with a dilemma that day. As only one other court had offered help (by now it was about noon), she could not send out Mr. Ashbury's case (or that of Ms. Andrus) to another court. Thus, she was virtually forced to enter into a plea bargain with Mr. Ashbury's very skilled defence counsel. Although I was not present during the plea bargaining (which all happened in Crown counsel's office), having done it myself for some 16 years, I can imagine that the conversation went something like this (salty language deleted):

Crown: If I agree to drop the charge of failing to appear, will your client plead to the over .80?

Defence: Forget it, I've got my tox [expert toxicologist] on standby, and he'll be able to provide "evidence to the contrary."

Crown: Well, in that case, I'll proceed on both, one at a time. Even if I lose one, if we don't finish today, you'll just have to come back. I've got to get something out of this.

Defence: You might lose both. You know these charges have been going since '92, and they might get thrown out for undue delay.

Crown: Yeah, but that's only because your client disappeared and wasn't rearrested until '97. Besides, you haven't filed a motion under the new rules, so you can't argue it anyway.

Defence: Judge Cole will let me abridge the time. You know these ex-defence counsel....

Investigating Officer: Look, I've got better things to do than watch you two try to out-macho one another. I've been talking to the accused outside. He isn't a bad guy. He's got no other driving record that I know of and the [breath] readings were pretty low. I'm not interested in blood. I'll be content as long as he gets a big fine.

Crown: All right, with this reading, the new directive allows me to let him plead to careless driving under the provincial *Highway Traffic Act*. But he'll have to plead to the fail to appear.

Defence: Sounds good to me. At least, this way, he'll keep his licence. Give me ten minutes to talk to him.[14]

The bargain ultimately proposed was as follows: The Crown would allow the accused to plead guilty to the lesser charge of careless driving. Both parties would agree that the accused should be fined $1,000. The accused would plead guilty to failing to appear; in exchange, Crown counsel would agree not to ask for jail but would join in asking for a fine of $300. The accused would be given six months to pay.

According to the rules that are expected to guide me, I may depart from plea bargains if I find them offensive; but in order for all parties to know what to expect, I normally go along with them. I was entirely content to do so in this case. On the basis of what I was told (unlike some other cases, the first I heard of the contents of the plea bargain was in open court), the proposed disposition seemed entirely sensible, having been made by experienced counsel well aware of the strengths and weaknesses of their case.

During the time that Ms. Crisante had been negotiating outside court, Crown counsel Mr. Kerr was speaking to the continuing cases of the two young offenders (R.S. and K.B.) assigned to me. I describe these two cases in some detail not because young offenders are generally more violent (that is a myth unfortunately perpetuated by those who seek to make political hay through scaremongering), but because they illustrate the range of cases with which I deal on a daily basis.

In February 1997, I found R.S. guilty of armed robbery and aggravated assault. The accused had begun to demonstrate a variety of disturbed behaviours from about age ten. He was hospitalized from time to time, complaining that he had visual hallucinations and that demons were controlling him. He identified his parents as persecutors and from time to time had little to do with them, withdrawing to his room for days on end. One night in June 1996, just after his 14th birthday, he told his father he was going to the neighbourhood convenience store. He concealed a knife in his jacket, which he brandished at the proprietor. The accused fled the store, having taken 50 cents that happened to be sitting on the countertop. He was pursued by a friend of the proprietor. As they reached the other side of the road, R.S. was tackled to the ground. He stabbed his pursuer several times, necessitating some 40 stitches. Some of the victim's scarring was permanent.

The accused was arrested a few minutes later. When he was taken to the police station, he gave some coherent responses to questions asked by the officers. Sometimes, however, he spontaneously broke into monologues, claiming, "Kurt Cobain told me that the guy in the store was the Devil, and that I had to kill him or I would go to hell forever."

At first, there were questions about whether the accused was fit to stand trial. After some period of assessment in a psychiatric facility, during which he was diagnosed as suffering from a severe form of schizophrenic disorder, he was stabilized on medication so that he was deemed fit to stand trial. As the doctors who assessed him considered that he had been insane at the time he committed the offences, he raised the defence of insanity at his trial. I rejected that defence[15] and sentenced him to two and a half years.

The *Young Offenders Act*[16] provides that an accused in these circumstances has the right to have his status reviewed every six months. R.S. has insisted on availing himself of that right (I suspect because it gives him a day out of the facility he is being held in) despite the fact that, for many months, he refused to take the medication that he so obviously needed. In his untreated state, he was prone to assaulting other prisoners and staff, which of course meant that he could not put together any release plan that had any hope of success. According to a report that was forwarded to me as part of his review, progress seemed to have been made. He was now taking a medication that agreed with him (many schizophrenia medications have unpleasant side effects), and the social workers reported that he had become much easier to manage. Through his counsel, he agreed that his case should be remanded for another six months. I assumed that if his counsel felt that R.S.'s progress was sufficient, he would request a substantial hearing, at which time I could be asked to release him on probation.

The second young offender I dealt with that day was K.B. She was born in another country, and her father died in an accident when she was a few months old. Because her mother objected to that society's deeply rooted custom that women should not remarry, she elected to come to Canada, leaving the six-month-old K.B. in her grandparents' care. Although K.B. saw her mother every year for a few weeks, she did not live with her until she was six years old. Both agreed that, as unfortunately happens so frequently in these situations, mother and daughter did not bond well. This was compounded by the fact that soon after they began to live together, the mother became involved with a man she ultimately married.

Sometime after K.B. started high school, she began to go through teenage rebellion, albeit in a very moderate form. Her parents objected to the fact that she began to go out with J.C., a boy from a different culture. They told her that she could not continue the relationship. There were fights, often of a physical nature, between mother, stepfather, and daughter.

In April 1998, the parents told K.B. that she would be grounded until she stopped seeing J.C. The young couple met secretly and persuaded one another that the only way out was for them to murder her parents and get their money so that they could flee to the United States, where they "could live happily ever after."[17] After discussing this for a few days, K.B. let J.C. into her house in the middle of the night. By pre-arrangement, he had a mask and was armed with a large knife that he had taken from home. He crept into the parents' bedroom and started to slash at them while they were sleeping. He nearly severed the mother's thumb and stabbed both parents numerous times, fortunately not fatally. All the while, K.B. remained outside the room, listening to what was going on. After J.C. escaped, the police were called.

Since the parents were initially unclear as to whom their assailant was, K.B. was asked by the police to provide a description of the intruder. She told them that it was a "black youth with a Jamaican accent."[18] On the basis of her description, the police conducted an investigation. As the case had attracted some public attention, they issued a public warning containing this description and handed out fliers to neighbours warning them to be vigilant. Two days later, K.B. was questioned again, and this time she admitted that she had lied. J.C. was arrested and charged with attempted murder. (Ironically, he had confessed to his parents, who had assisted him in disposing of the knife and mask. They, too, were arrested and charged with obstructing justice.)

As this was an important case, one Crown counsel was immediately assigned to all three cases. The Crown applied to have J.C. transferred to be tried as an adult (he was fifteen); that hearing would take place before another judge at Scarborough court.[19]

Crown counsel Mr. Kerr realized from the outset that he had considerable legal hurdles in the prosecution of K.B. The only evidence against her on potential charges related to the attempted murder of her parents was her own confession to the police. Because the officers dealing with the case had not been fully trained in taking statements from young offenders, they had taken the incriminating statement from her as though she had been an adult. Unbeknown to these officers, the Supreme Court of Canada had recently insisted on very high standards of informed waiver before a statement taken from a young person could be admitted into evidence. It did not take long for Mr. Kerr to realize that he could not use K.B.'s statement to convict her.

The only other way the Crown could hope to convict K.B. would be to call J.C. as a witness against her. This could be very risky for the Crown. If J.C. was called without the Crown's knowing what he might say on the stand (he would likely refuse to cooperate with the Crown unless he got some benefit from it), he could say anything, some of which might hurt the Crown's case against K.B. If he was to be a cooperative witness, the Crown would likely secure his cooperation only by agreeing to some reduced charge against him, which it was not prepared to do given the circumstances and the severity of the injuries caused. For these reasons, Crown counsel proposed (and defence counsel was only too happy to accept) to proceed only on a charge of public mischief (lying to the police) against K.B.

Although I was not the scheduled pretrial judge on the day the parties came to their proposed plea bargain, they asked to see me in chambers. This happens regularly at the Scarborough court. The lawyers "judge shop" as part of their plea bargain, seeking to find a judge who will agree in advance to commit to a range of sentence.[20] They told me that the Crown would ask for a sentence of 12 to 18 months, but that I should make some allowance for the amount of pretrial custody that the accused would have served by the time I ultimately sentenced her. The defence would ask for probation, arguing that the amount of pretrial custody was equivalent to some ten months,[21] and that was sufficient given her age and Parliament's view of the seriousness of the offence, as expressed by the maximum possible penalty of two years. I agreed that counsel's suggestions were in the range, and that so long as mental health assessments (which I would order as soon as she pleaded guilty) were not devastating, I would not exceed the sentence sought by the Crown.

The accused entered her plea of guilty that same day, and the case was remanded so that mental health assessments and a predisposition report (a social history of the accused prepared by a youth probation officer) could be obtained. On September 1, the parties made their formal submissions based on the facts and what was disclosed in the various reports. Having heard what they said, I told the lawyers that I needed time to think about what they had said and put the case over until after my next chambers day on September 4.[22]

During the sentencing hearing, a joint victim impact statement was filed on behalf of both parents. I accepted it because both parties agreed that it should be filed. As I thought more about the case, I wondered if I should have done so. The report documented the devastating impact their daughter's behaviour has had on the parents' lives. They are both physically and mentally unable to work; it appears that because they cannot pay their mortgage, they will lose their home, their only form of substantial saving. However, because of the accused's guilty plea, I was not, strictly speaking, sentencing her for her part in causing harm to her parents. I concluded that what happened on that awful night only provided the backdrop for the lies that she told the police. As a result, I decided that I should factor in the victim impact statements only to the extent that they would give me some sort of clue to the accused's likelihood of reoffending (the psychiatric report concluded that it was low) and only because they told me that her parents were not prepared to offer her any support at this time.

On September 10, I gave oral reasons, sentencing the accused to 10 months of open custody, followed by 12 months' probation. The lengths of the various terms were tailored around the accused's schooling (school is a real strength for her). Like R.S., she could come back to ask me to review her status after six months of open custody.

This, then, is part of a day in the life of a busy court. It is usually intense, sometimes tragic, always human, and endlessly fascinating. It may even be socially useful.

Endnotes

1. At the time of writing, the Provincial Division of the Ontario Court of Justice comprises about 260 judges, about 180 of whom preside over 95 percent of the criminal cases in the province.

2. Initials are used because the *Young Offenders Act* provides that no young offender's name may be published.

3. As of the date of writing, this particular Crown's office employs almost 50 percent women, up from about 30 percent when I started as a judge in Scarborough in 1991. This reflects the general trend in the Ontario bar, where now over 50 percent of recent graduates are women. Currently in Ontario, the percentage of Provincial Division women judges is still less than one-third, and even fewer in the Superior Court.

4. I have no idea where the bureaucrats come up with this notional figure. To allow for the movement of prisoners from remand centres to the court (some may be transported as much as 40 kilometres through rush-hour traffic), experience demonstrates that it is almost impossible to start a trial court before 10:00 a.m. Because it is very difficult for court reporters to be able to concentrate for longer than about 90 minutes at a time, on the best of days, morning court goes from 10:00 a.m. to 1:00 p.m. with a 15- to 20-minute break. Court normally resumes at 2:00 p.m., again with an afternoon break. Court usually recesses at 4:30 p.m. to allow court staff to finish their paperwork and prisoners to be returned to their remand centres.

5. Section 10(b) of the *Canadian Charter of Rights and Freedoms* provides, "Everyone has the right on arrest or detention to retain and instruct counsel without delay and to be informed of that right." The Supreme Court of Canada has generally interpreted this to mean that an accused should have the right to telephone a lawyer as soon as practicable following arrest or detention. Police forces have responded to this by providing private access to duty counsel or a private lawyer by telephone from the police station.

6. The reason that this cumbersome process took place on the record in open court was that, in fact, there were some earlier dates available. Knowing that the case was already on the verge of being dismissed for taking too long to come to trial, everyone (including myself in an oblique way) felt the need to protect his position by saying that, while he could be available, it was the other party's "fault" that they could not take advantage of those dates. Some of the final compromises were interesting. The police officer had to telephone his staff sergeant to get approval to come to court on a date he was scheduled to be away, thereby being eligible to "pick up a court card," entitling him to be paid at double the normal shift rate. He was obviously delighted. Defence counsel and the accused were also content because they could defer the potential day of reckoning by another six months (if convicted, Ms. Andrus stood, at the very least, to lose her licence for a year). Crown counsel, who is currently working part-time, seemed mostly concerned to adjourn this to a date when her child-care needs could be accommodated (so that another Crown attorney would not be forced to take over the case). For myself, March 4 was a scheduled "chambers day," a regularly scheduled time during which I am supposed

to read the approximately 500 pages of case law, legislative updates, and other items of interest that cross my desk each week, or to write judgments or articles (such as this one). One of my concerns was whether the trial coordinator could find me another chambers day.

7. Since January 1996, as a result of the police, the Crowns, the Legal Aid Plan, and the judges finding new resources or diverting existing staff, we have cut our backlog by 32.5 percent. However, because we have done so well, the bureaucrats have deemed that we are no longer on the chronic list of courts experiencing extreme delays, and it has been difficult for us to argue that our Crown and judicial complement should be maintained. As a result, both complements have been somewhat cut back, and we are beginning to slip again, as this delay signifies.

8. An example of this arose here. As I was typing this article, I realized that in the case of Mr. Ashbury's charge of failing to appear, I should have at least considered whether to impose a 15 percent victim surcharge to his $300 fine under the Criminal Code. These surcharges are to be applied to raise money for various forms of victim support services. Neither the Crown nor the clerk drew this to my attention, and I simply neglected to raise the issue.

9. I leave it to the reader to consider whether this fits the definition of a "working" criminal justice system. Some observers have questioned whether it is "a system" at all.

10. This seems particularly to be the case in charges of wife assault. Consistent with data from other jurisdictions, recent Toronto figures suggest that about 40 percent of complainants do not appear for trial. (Anecdotal evidence from Crowns who prosecute such cases puts the figure even higher.) This is the case despite police and prosecutorial directives mandating "no-tolerance" responses to such incidents.

11. There is some consensus among criminal justice professionals that alcohol or drugs figure in about 75 percent of criminal offences.

12. What he was doing there at 11:00 p.m. on a Saturday night was not made clear to me. Sometimes criminal court offers wonderful opportunities for creating fantastic fiction à la Marquez or for reciting Shakespearian verse à la Rumpole!

13. The going rate in Toronto for some of the top counsel at the time of writing is about $5,000 per case, not including the costs of various experts. It may even be higher in areas of the country where there is no public transit. Accused people willingly pay this fee because of the economic and social costs of doing without a licence.

14. Variants of this type of conversation occur every day. Depending on the exhaustion level of the lawyers, more bargaining (some would call it haggling) can take place over the amount of the proposed fine. Interestingly, the lawyers would be unlikely to bargain about the length of time the accused should have to pay the fine. For his part, the accused might be less concerned about the amount of the fine; he would likely be more

concerned about how long he would have to pay it. This illustrates one of the fundamental differences between lawyers and accused. The former tend to be more concerned about form, while the latter tend to be more concerned with substance.

15. Insanity pleas are quite rare. This is the only one I have had since my appointment. On the other hand, dispositions of "not criminally responsible" (another type of mental impairment defence) are relatively frequent. I probably hear one (usually on consent of both parties) about once every two months.

16. On April 1, 2003, the *Young Offenders Act* was replaced by the *Youth Criminal Justice Act*. The processes here remain the same under the new law.

17. K.B. later told the police that one of her other motivations for the offence was that her stepfather had sexually assaulted her on several occasions. She refused to provide the police with any further information and indicated that she did not wish to have her stepfather charged.

18. The racial stereotyping is particularly troubling.

19. Obviously, that judge and I refrain from talking with one another about our respective cases. Given the seriousness of the matters, each of us might have to solicit the advice of our colleagues who, as always, are generous with their advice. We have agreed to handle this by leaving the lunchroom whenever the other wishes to discuss the case with another colleague.

20. Appellate courts across the country have been very clear that, because plea bargains so obviously give the impression that what happens in open court merely rubber stamps what has been worked out in advance (the very term *plea bargain* is frowned on by the appellate courts, and judges usually prefer to use such neutral phrases as *pretrial discussions*), the judge should decline to agree to any particular sentence and agree only, if at all, to a particular range or type of sentence. Frankly, this is observed daily in the breach in busy provincial courts. Many of us consider that if we do not agree to precise plea bargains, our lists will likely be even more backlogged. Luckily, in this case, the parties came to me with a range of sentence rather than a precise sentence proposal.

21. Although, as a matter of law, I do not have to make any allowance for pretrial custody in the sentence ultimately imposed, the Supreme Court of Canada has ruled that an allowance should normally be made, usually on a "two-for-one basis." In other words, for each day spent in pretrial custody, two days should be taken off the normally appropriate sentence.

22. In fact, in addition to my chambers day, I spent a lot of time reading and thinking about this case throughout the Labour Day weekend. The judicial life may seem "cushy" to outsiders (our salaries are good, our pensions are excellent, we get 8 weeks of holidays and up to 36 chamber days per year, and we cannot be fired except in the most extreme circumstances). However, most judges I know spend much of their weekends and some of their holidays preparing for upcoming cases.

The Probation Officer's Report

When most members of the public think about the criminal justice professionals who run the justice system, lawyers, judges, and police officers come most readily to mind. Probation officers have a lower public profile than these other professions; yet in many respects, their role in the criminal justice system is critical because most offenders are sentenced to community-based sanctions. As Karen Middlecoat, an experienced probation officer in Ontario, describes in this chapter, members of the probation service supervise offenders on probation, offenders serving conditional sentences of imprisonment in the community, and provincial parolees.

Karen Middlecoat
Probation Officers' Association of Ontario

Several years ago, a distinguished justice at the Superior Court of Ontario was invited to be a guest speaker at a professional development day for probation and parole officers. He praised us for helping troubled individuals in times of dwindling social resources and expressed almost bewildered admiration for us. In fact, he confessed, "To be honest with you, when judges don't know what to do with someone, we put them on probation." The feelings of relief and validation in the room were practically palpable: finally, a judge was acknowledging what we had known all our professional lives.

CASELOAD OF A PROBATION OFFICER

In Ontario, approximately 1,000 probation officers supervise approximately 60,000 individuals, the vast majority of whom are adults. Young persons (aged 12 to 17) are actively supervised as extra-judicial sanctions, probation cases, and open custody residents. Adults (aged 18 and older) are probationers, conditional sentence cases, and provincial parolees. Probation officer caseloads vary significantly from small towns to major cities, and the duties of probation officers vary widely across the province. In parts of northern Ontario, probation officers have smaller caseloads but are required to fly into remote areas to see clients. In Toronto, probation officers have adult caseloads that average approximately 63 clients. Young person probation officers may have fewer clients, but their responsibilities are more extensive, because they must maintain ongoing contact with parents, schools, and counselling agencies.

Generally, most probation officers supervise adult offenders—defined as persons 18 years of age or over on the date of their offence. Adults report to probation officers for several reasons, but most are supervised on a *probation order*. A probation order is a legal document requiring the offender to comply with certain probation conditions for a specific period of time. An adult probation order cannot exceed three years, although some offenders can be on probation continuously for several years, if judges continue to place them on probation each time they are sentenced. Probation orders have three standard conditions:

1. The offender shall keep the peace and be of good behaviour;
2. The offender shall appear before the court when required to do so by the court;
3. The offender shall notify the court or the probation officer in advance of any change of name or address and promptly notify the court or the probation officer of any change of employment or occupation.

In addition, judges can impose other conditions designed to respond to the specific needs of the particular offender. For example, a court can order an offender to reimburse the victim or perform unpaid work for the community. Probationers may also be ordered not to go to certain locations. An example of this type of condition would be one prohibiting the offender from entering certain premises where the offence occurred. Someone found guilty of shoplifting could be forbidden from entering the store where the offence was committed, or a man convicted of assaulting his wife could be prohibited from returning to the marital home.

ENSURING THAT THE CONDITIONS OF PROBATION ARE OBSERVED

Despite the intent of the probation conditions to assist offenders while deterring them from committing further offences, these same conditions are fraught with enforcement difficulties. The enforcement of probation conditions is an important part of a probation officer's job. According to the *Criminal Code*, an adult has breached probation when he has failed or refused to comply with a probation condition "without reasonable excuse." Therefore, not every violation of probation results in the offender's return to court, and probation officers must make the final decision whether or not to charge an individual with breaching a probation order.

Discretion is often exercised regarding the reporting condition (the obligation to report to a probation officer) of a probation order, as it is the most common optional condition and therefore the most often violated. Probation officers will rarely charge a client who has missed one or two appointments, even if the reason is one of simple forgetfulness. However, if the offender establishes a pattern of missing scheduled appointments after having repeatedly been cautioned, a probation officer will pursue a charge, since this is clearly unreasonable. In the case of high-risk offenders, the probation officer would not wait for a pattern to be established because the safety of a victim or the general public would be of paramount concern. Conversely, in extenuating circumstances, a probation officer may choose not to charge an individual even if the reporting condition has been violated.

Difficulties can arise in some circumstances when the offender has mental health problems and doesn't understand the importance of keeping appointments. In these cases, a "reasonable excuse" is somewhat evident, but the probation officer will not take the risk of leaving such an individual in the community without some sort of ongoing supervision. Instead, the probation officer will override the reasonable excuse rule, err on the side of caution, and lay a breach of probation charge in order to protect the individual and the community, especially if medication or the lack thereof was of particular concern.

The case of Benjamin illustrates this issue. Benjamin was a 30-year-old who suffered from a bipolar affective disorder and refused to take medication. He was also in a wheelchair due to the amputation of both his legs following a suicide attempt at a subway station. He was on a two-year probation order for fraud accommodation and assault, resulting from a hotel stay for which he refused to pay and where he spat on one of the employees. Benjamin was ordered to report to a probation officer as often as directed, but he had no fixed address and could not be contacted. The probation officer made contact with Benjamin's parents and left messages for Benjamin, as he would phone his parents occasionally to ask for money. Benjamin called his probation officer twice and flatly stated that he had no intention of reporting. The probation officer decided to charge him for not reporting and issued a warrant for his arrest.

Approximately three months after the warrant was issued, Benjamin was arrested again in a hotel room for damaging furniture and smashing mirrors. He was sentenced in court several months later and received more probation with a condition to attend for psychiatric counselling. Unfortunately, he never reported and within two months had committed suicide. In this case, the probation officer had realized that Benjamin, given his medical condition, would probably never report or attend psychiatric counselling, regardless of how many probation orders he was given or how many times he was charged with breaching probation. Yet the probation officer still charged him in an attempt to protect Benjamin from himself and to fulfill probation services' responsibility to the community and to the justice system. Unfortunately, doing all the right things ultimately did not help Benjamin.

Community service work, which requires offenders to perform volunteer work, can cause problems for offenders who have full-time employment as well as other responsibilities that limit their ability to complete the hours ordered. Occasionally, community service work has been ordered on offenders who are long-distance truck drivers, construction workers who work 12-hour shifts, single mothers with full-time jobs, and young offenders in school with homework and part-time jobs. Individuals in these categories have difficulty performing the work ordered by the court.

Even more problematic is community service work that is imposed on individuals such as sex offenders and persons with disabilities who are difficult to place in a community service work agency. Community service is also imposed on individuals who are capable of performing the hours but who choose not to perform the prescribed hours. When community service becomes problematic, the probation officer must consider all the facts and decide whether or not to charge the offender, keeping in mind that the *Criminal Code* states that a breach of probation has been committed when the offender has failed or refused to comply with probation "without reasonable excuse."

The different situations of Charlene and David illustrate the discretion that a probation officer must exercise regarding community service work enforcement. Charlene was a 36-year-old single mother of a 6-year-old girl. She had been convicted of shoplifting and ordered to perform 100 hours of community service work at a rate of 10 hours per month during a one-year probation order. However, because she had a full-time job, Charlene had only limited time on weekends to perform community service at the food bank to which she had been assigned. She managed to perform community service every month but never completed the prescribed monthly rate of 10 hours. At the expiration of her probation, Charlene had completed only 68 of the

100 hours ordered but her probation officer decided to exercise her discretion not to return her to court. Given Charlene's circumstances, she had made a reasonable effort toward completing her community service work.

In contrast, David was a 20-year-old convicted of possession of stolen property. He lived with his parents who were aware of his offence and his probation term with its requirement to perform 100 hours of community service work at a rate of 10 hours per month during a one-year probation order. For the community service, he was placed at a church that provided hot meals and beds to homeless people. David was not in school and worked sporadically for a friend's roofing business when work was available. David failed to perform any hours for the first three months, citing forgetfulness, work opportunities, and vague references to insufficient time. He was cautioned that if he failed to begin his hours he would be returned to court and charged with failing to perform community service work at the monthly rate.

During the third quarter of probation, David performed a total of 22 hours and in the final three months, he completed another 15 hours, for a total of 37 hours. He was returned to court, found guilty of not completing community service work, and given another year's probation with a condition to perform an additional 100 hours of community work. One may assume that the judge's intention was to let David know that he could not avoid the imposition of community service work; certainly, David knew now that he had a second conviction on his criminal record. During his second probation order, David performed 53 hours, but his employment situation had not changed and his reasons for failing to complete the work remained vague and unsubstantiated. He was again returned to court and fined $400 with no more probation or community service work.

RESTITUTION

The court's intention when imposing a restitution condition is more straightforward, yet the "reasonable excuse" clause raises much more complex issues. When the amount of money is relatively small and the offender's ability to make restitution is established, then restitution is usually paid and no enforcement is necessary. However, if the amount is considerable and the offender is unable to pay the entire amount, then he is practically set up for failure and subsequent enforcement for breach.

Although the probation officer could exercise discretion and not breach the individual if the "reasonable excuse" clause is applicable, all restitution cases have victims, unlike community service work, and the recipients are often persons who have no recourse to reclaim their money except via the courts. In these cases, probation officers are very reluctant to deny the victims their entitlement to see the offender held accountable for nonpayment. For this reason the offender will be brought back to court and a judge will decide what the appropriate response to nonpayment should be.

The case of Edward is a good example of the way in which a court's best intentions can miscarry, creating a dilemma for the probation officer. Edward was a 46-year-old man convicted of defrauding his landlord of approximately $30,000. He was sentenced to the maximum of three years' probation to allow him as much time as possible to repay the victim. However, the court's restitution condition read as follows:

> ... to pay restitution at a monthly rate until the restitution is paid in full. A monthly amount will not be specified but a payment must be made each and every month until probation expires.

Unfortunately, the order did not stipulate that the full amount of restitution was to be paid by the end of the probation period, and as no monthly rate was given, the offender made a monthly payment, by money order, of one cent. In an attached letter that accompanied his first payment, the offender made it clear that he was not breaching the restitution condition in any way and even acknowledged that, although he had to pay five dollars every month to purchase a money order, he would still pay only one cent monthly to the victim.

Although the probation officer had the option to return the case to the original judge and request a variation in the payment schedule, the effort may not have gained the desired result and the offender, or his attorney, could express an objection to a more onerous payment system. Nevertheless, the probation officer was able to advise the victim that financial recovery was available to him through a civil court action. The victim agreed to pursue this remedy but expressed great frustration at the expense of time and money required to regain his own money.

Another example of an unsuccessful restitution case is that of Frank, a 33-year-old convicted of mischief to private property. Following an argument in a bar, Frank left the establishment and vandalized his opponent's truck. He was convicted and ordered to pay $1,800 restitution over a two-year probation period. Frank lived in the basement apartment of his parents' home but had very little interaction with them because his parents were aware that Frank sold drugs while receiving disability income. However, they felt somewhat protective of Frank as he had developed some brain damage from years of drug use and could not maintain regular employment. Over the two years of probation, Frank reported regularly but insisted that the victim would just keep the $1,800, as his insurance company would cover the cost of the repairs. Frank was advised repeatedly that he had still been held responsible by the court for damages and had a legal requirement to compensate the victim.

While on probation for mischief, Frank was arrested and convicted of cocaine possession and sentenced to two weeks' imprisonment and one year's probation. Upon expiration of his first probation order, Frank had paid only $350 of the total restitution and was returned to court for breaching probation. At the time of his trial Frank stated that he could not afford to pay the stipulated amount due to his limited income on disability, but had done the best he could. He was acquitted of the charge of breach of probation.

Cases such as Edward's and Frank's reinforce probation services' ongoing desire not to be utilized as collection agencies by the courts; however, when restitution is successful, it communicates a worthwhile lesson for the offender and provides the victim with a sense of closure rarely experienced by other victims in the justice system.

ENFORCING CONDITIONS THAT RESTRICT AN OFFENDER'S LIFESTYLE

Ironically, the easiest violations of probation to prove are also the most difficult on which to obtain convictions; these are the "lifestyle" conditions. Such conditions include requiring the offender to abstain from alcohol or drugs, or to see a mental health professional on a regular basis. Violations of these abstinence or treatment-related conditions are often discovered by the police, who apprehend the individual in an intoxicated state, or by the probation officer, who can determine a client's compliance with psychiatric treatment via a phone call to the relevant mental health professional.

Although the offender's non-compliance can be clearly established, determining that the offender breached the condition "without reasonable excuse" is very difficult, as some judges may consider substance abuse and mental illness medical conditions over which an individual has little control. As a result, a court that imposes a probation condition prohibiting the offender from consuming alcohol or nonprescription drugs can unintentionally bring the offender back into the system. Furthermore, requiring the offender to seek treatment for substance abuse, psychological difficulties, or even spousal abuse does not guarantee that the offender will comply with the condition, and a return to court for a breach of the treatment condition may hold the offender accountable without addressing the underlying problem that gave rise to the offending.

The most common cases are those involving substance abuse. George was a 48-year-old convicted of assault. After consuming alcohol, he slapped and pushed his wife, who called police. He was found guilty and placed on probation for 18 months with a condition to attend counselling for partner assault. However, the court acknowledged that alcohol was a factor in the assault and added a condition on the probation order that instructed the offender "to consume alcohol moderately." Unfortunately, no one advised the court that George was in fact an alcoholic, and that by his standards, moderation in alcohol consumption was not in all likelihood the standard that the court intended. The probation officer could not send George to alcohol counselling as only partner abuse counselling had been ordered, and George expressed no interest in going voluntarily. Therefore, although the probation officer arranged partner abuse counselling and cautioned George that failure to complete the program would result in a breach, his problem of alcohol abuse remained untreated.

Probation orders that require the offender to "abstain absolutely from the purchase, possession, or consumption of alcohol" also cause enforcement difficulties for probation officers. Monitoring these conditions is simply not possible, and violations are rarely discovered unless the offender is in public and arrested by police. Interesting exceptions, however, are cases like Harry, an admitted alcoholic, who was found guilty of impaired driving. He was fined $1,200, placed on probation for one year, required to attend a program, and prohibited from drinking for one year. Harry was self-employed in his own well-established renovations company and stated that he could not attend any residential program but agreed to attend weekly AA meetings held at the probation office.

Within a few months, Harry's wife notified the probation officer that Harry had been violating his abstinence condition. As she was the only person who could testify that Harry had been drinking, she was advised that she would be required to attend court as the sole witness. Immediately she stated that she would not go to court to testify against her husband. When the probation officer indicated that the incidents would be discussed with Harry at his next appointment, she begged the officer not to say anything to Harry as he would know she had informed the probation officer of his violations. In such cases, probation officers are placed in a difficult position: between confronting the offender on the one hand and violating the wife's request for secrecy on the other. Here, if the probation officer returned Harry to court to hold him accountable for violating his abstinence condition, the case risked a withdrawal if Harry's wife, who was the sole witness, failed to testify. Furthermore, once Harry's probation order expired, he would be able to resume drinking and cease attending AA meetings, and one could only hope that the program would have had a sufficiently positive effect on him to encourage him to seek out meetings in the community voluntarily.

Treatment and counselling conditions raise similar concerns, and no offence is a better example than domestic assault. Ian was a 32-year-old convicted of assaulting his wife. He was prohibited from returning home until he had completed a program for partner assault and had obtained written permission from his wife allowing him to return home. Ian attended two sessions of the 16-week program and then stopped, stating that he had no time to go. He was charged by the probation officer, returned to court, found guilty, and ordered to attend the program again. Again he failed to complete the sessions; he also began harassing his wife with phone calls and unscheduled visits. She called the police and again Ian was returned to court. He was sentenced to 30 days in jail and probation for one year, with a condition, for the third time, to attend counselling. He failed to attend the program and within weeks had seriously assaulted his wife, breaking her arm and nose. He was incarcerated for eight months but despite three probation orders, counselling conditions, and custodial sentences, Ian believed that his right to see his wife superseded any legal authority that stipulated otherwise. Cases like Ian's are common in the justice system, and despite the thorough work of police, probation officers, and the courts, Ian's wife and women like her continue to live in fear.

Indeed, all cases that involve high-risk offenders, high-need offenders, or persons with serious charges require more intensive supervision from the probation officer. Within the past five years, procedures regarding the supervision of sex offenders and domestic assault offenders, and mental health and substance abuse cases have become more complex and stringent, stressing ongoing contact with the offenders, victims, and treatment agencies. Although probation officers recognize the necessity of these standards, the resulting escalation in workload has detracted from their time spent with lower-risk clients, some of whom form a bond with their probation officers and grow to rely on them for support and guidance. Many probation officers choose their profession because they enjoy human interaction and genuinely want to "help people." Ironically, the ones they may be able to help the most are the ones with whom they can't spend enough time, due to ever-increasing workloads and the court's reliance on community supervision as the most frequently used sentencing option.

CONDITIONAL SENTENCE OFFENDERS

Probation officers also supervise offenders serving conditional sentences of imprisonment. Conditional sentences were introduced in 1996 as an additional sentencing option to fill the void between probation and incarceration. Conditional sentence offenders have committed crimes that warrant imprisonment, but because the court does not consider them a threat to the community, they are allowed to serve the sentence at home. Some examples are offenders who have committed serious frauds or violent offences but who may have full-time jobs and families to support.

The conditions of probation orders are also standard on conditional sentences, but the reporting condition that is optional on a probation order becomes a mandatory condition for a conditional sentence. Notably, the only additional mandatory condition on conditional sentences prohibits the offender from leaving the province without written permission from the probation officer. One important difference between probation orders and conditional sentence orders is that the latter will often include a condition of house arrest that confines the offender to his or her home, except for court-authorized exceptions. Unfortunately, when judges list exceptions beyond work, religious services, and medical emergencies, house arrest loses much of its perceived effectiveness. The recent case of John illustrates this problem.

John was given a one-year conditional sentence for aggravated assault and assault causing bodily harm against an ex-girlfriend and her new boyfriend. He was placed under house arrest, but among the exceptions to confinement was permission to maintain employment. Unfortunately, John was a taxi driver and the exception for the purpose of employment gave John free rein to be in the community, since he would have a ready explanation to be in the community for extended periods of time. Conditions with exceptions of this kind create problems for the probation officer and do not achieve the intended restrictions.

Theoretically, the enforcement of conditional sentences is intended to be a much swifter process than probation enforcement but in practice this is generally not the case. Unlike an alleged breach of probation, which is an entirely new criminal charge, an alleged breach of a conditional sentence simply results in a court hearing, during which the onus is upon the offender to prove that she did not violate the conditional sentence. If a breach is deemed to have occurred, the judge has four options:

1. Take no action;
2. Change the optional conditions;
3. Suspend the conditional sentence and direct that the offender serve a portion of the unexpired sentence in custody with the balance to resume upon release; *or*
4. Terminate the conditional sentence and direct that the offender serve the full balance of the conditional sentence in custody.

Unfortunately, the conditional sentencing process may be considered by some to be in its legal adolescence, and the implications of conditional sentence conditions are yet to be fully understood. An example is the case of Lloyd, who received a one-year conditional sentence for assaulting his wife for the second time in three years. Lloyd was ordered to attend partner abuse counselling and to complete it by the end of his conditional sentence. Due to an extensive waiting list and some delays on Lloyd's part, he began the program nine months after the conditional sentence started. Lloyd attended every session until his conditional sentence expired, at which point four sessions remained outstanding. Lloyd refused to complete the program but could not be breached by the probation officer because no balance remained on the order that could be converted to custody.

YOUNG PERSONS

Probation for young persons offers many of the options available to adults; however, the maximum period for young person probation is two years, rather than the three years for adults. The same issues exist for monitoring and enforcing young person orders; however, a notable distinction relates to the influence of peer groups—an effect seen regularly among young persons whose offences involve co-accused who occasionally are fellow gang members.

Mark was a 17-year-old found guilty of theft over $5,000 and possession over $5,000. He had stolen his parents' car and when police found him in a parking lot with two friends hours after the car had been reported stolen, all three were charged, although Mark's two co-accused eventually had their charges dropped. One of Mark's conditions prohibited him from having any contact with his two friends. However, information from the police indicated that Mark had stolen the car as part of his initiation into a gang and had met his friends to show successful completion of his task. Mark denied any connection to a gang during interviews with his probation officer, and his sense of loyalty to his group overrode any court-imposed non-association condition or any threat of enforcement that his probation officer could make.

Generally, the courts impose as few conditions as possible on young persons, favouring the restorative and rehabilitative aspects of probation as they relate to the offence. However, some conditions become onerous and present the probation officer with clear challenges.

Nagenthan was a 17-year-old found guilty of theft under $5,000 after he shoplifted a portable CD player from an electronics store. He was placed on probation for one year and prohibited from entering the electronics store. Nagenthan was also ordered to take classes, as recommended by the probation officer, in English as a Second Language. Although he was 17 at the time of the offence, he had turned 18 by the time of sentencing and had already graduated from grade 12, with plans to attend college the coming September. Because the ESL condition had no relevance to his offence and conflicted with his college schedule and part-time job at a local restaurant, the probation officer exercised his discretion and advised Nagenthan that the ESL condition would be set aside providing that the youth continue his education and employment.

Another notable difference between adult and young person supervision is the involvement of parents. The probation officer must establish contact with the parents or guardians to ensure that information is being exchanged regularly. However, some parents have the misplaced belief that once their child has been through the justice system and now has a probation officer to whom he must report and legal requirements with which to comply, discipline issues and behavioural problems at home will be corrected. Sadly, this is not the case. Probation officers explain to parents that, as agents of the court, they can only enforce the conditions of probation and offer the youth some guidance, not guarantee improvements in the youth's behaviour. Probation officers often receive calls from parents complaining that their child is out late, not doing house chores, or not telling them where he is going or with whom he is socializing. Indeed, a parent once called her son's probation officer and complained that he was still leaving dirty dishes in the kitchen sink and not cleaning his room, despite being on probation!

Obviously, the probation officer has no authority over the young person in these circumstances, although some parents believe that probation officers could fix problems in one year that had developed over the previous sixteen. Conversely, some probation orders will require the youth to "be amenable to the routine and discipline of the family home," and in many cases this stipulation will bring some sort of clear expectations into the household, especially if the probation officer meets with the youth and his parents and writes a contract that all parties sign.

Regrettably, this well-intentioned condition may not achieve its desired results, as in the case of Paula, a 16-year-old found guilty of assaulting her mother for refusing to give her money. Paula was placed on probation for 18 months and required to report to a probation officer, write a letter of apology to her mother, reside at home, and be amenable to the routine and discipline of the home. The probation officer met with Paula and her mother and wrote out a contract with four rules regarding curfew, chores, phone privileges, and respectful behaviour.

Approximately five months later, Paula's mother advised the probation officer that the home situation was deteriorating and that rules were not being followed. At the next probation appointment, Paula admitted that she was breaking rules but that her mother was becoming too unreasonable. The probation officer suggested family counselling but Paula refused. The probation officer then arranged for Paula and her mother to attend the next appointment together; however, Paula's mother called the officer within a few weeks and advised that money and jewelry were missing and that Paula's whereabouts were unknown.

Clearly, the probation officer had a difficult decision to make: either wait and hope that Paula would resurface, thus avoiding a return to the court system with more criminal charges; *or,* issue a warrant for her arrest and have the police actively look for her thus forestalling any harm she might encounter on the city streets. By the next week, Paula's mother called the probation officer. She'd heard from friends of her daughter that Paula was staying with various acquaintances and had no intention of returning home. Paula's mother was becoming extremely anxious about her daughter's safety and questionable companions, and the officer decided to issue the warrant. Paula's mother was advised and encouraged to tell Paula's friends of the warrant in the hope that Paula would contact the probation officer. Soon enough, Paula called her officer to question the existence of the warrant, but she refused to go to the local police station to address the outstanding charge and stated unequivocally that she had no intention of returning home.

Months later, Paula was arrested for shoplifting and the outstanding warrant came to light. Paula was found guilty of both offences and despite her mother's statement that she would accept Paula back home, Paula told the court she did not plan to return home. She was given another year's probation, and was instructed to report as required and to live at a residence approved by her probation officer. Since Paula had had no approved residence since her mother's, any friend's house or city shelter became an approved residence because the alternative was the street. Paula continued to report satisfactorily and was advised that the probation officer would be calling the residences she provided to confirm her housing. However, by the expiration of probation, Paula was 18 with no fixed address, no employment, and no family support, despite the best intentions and efforts of probation services.

SUCCESSES

Fortunately, not all cases end as bleakly as Paula's, and when an individual does appear to have benefited from probation supervision, the officer feels a rare sense of success, as in the case of Rick. Rick was a 25-year-old factory worker convicted of assault, arising from a fight outside a bar. He was placed on probation for one year, with conditions to report as directed, to maintain employment, and not to be on the premises where the offence had been committed. Rick reported regularly and complied with conditions, but the probation officer suspected that Rick had an alcohol problem, among other issues. However, she could not engage him in meaningful conversation. At the third appointment, the probation officer asked Rick about his activities and interests, and he expressed surprise that the probation officer would care about subjects that did not relate to probation supervision. She responded that he seemed somewhat troubled and unhappy and that she was willing to listen if he felt like talking. He again expressed surprise but offered little response. However, over the next few appointments, he spoke about his estrangement from his family, with the exception of his only sister, who lived in British Columbia; he even spoke fondly about his cat, Sully. He mentioned AA meetings that he'd attended in the past but had not found helpful and that he wasn't interested in resuming them.

The probation officer's next contact with Rick was a phone call. He was in a phone booth and admitted he'd been drinking. He planned to withdraw all his money from his bank account, buy alcohol, rent a motel room, and commit suicide. The probation officer asked what had happened, but Rick simply stated that he was fed up with life. As the probation officer continued to talk to him, she waved down a colleague passing in the hallway and wrote a note explaining the ongoing emergency. Rick's probation officer managed to learn that Rick was in a phone booth near his bank, as well as the bank's location and even what he was wearing. At one point, Rick stated, "I know what you're trying to do, but it won't work." The probation officer reminded him that his life mattered, to his family, his sister, and even his cat, which would be abandoned and neglected without him.

In the meantime, the probation officer's colleague had relayed Rick's description and whereabouts to police, and eventually, officers located Rick in the phone booth and transported him to hospital. Rick remained there for a few days and, upon his release, reported to his probation officer. He could not verbalize any event that had led to his suicidal thoughts—only that he had felt a general depression that became exacerbated by his alcohol consumption. Nevertheless, he thanked his probation officer for helping him that day and revealed that, after returning home from hospital he had phoned his sister in British Columbia and resumed contact. As Rick's probation came to an end, he decided that he was going to use his savings to move to B.C. to be near his sister, who was happily expecting him. A few months after Rick's probation terminated, his probation officer received a postcard. Rick was living with his sister temporarily and working at a landscaping company, and he had attended two AA meetings. He ended the note by thanking the probation officer again for caring. She heard from him only one more time: he sent her a Christmas card that year, enclosing a photograph of him and Sully.

Although cases like Rick's are somewhat outnumbered by less successful ones, these are the cases that make the probation profession worthwhile, and the opportunities to make a difference, and the challenges therein, never cease. Many cases are never resolved the way the courts intend and probation officers wish, but the desire to help individuals who've made mistakes to move beyond them and get their lives back in order remains. Like the judge at the professional development day, probation officers may not always initially know what to do with their offenders either, considering the challenges of each case and the complexities of the probation officer's role. We are responsible for ensuring that the offenders comply with their conditions, for returning them to court when those conditions are violated, for providing support, counselling, and direction to assist in rehabilitation, thereby reducing recidivism, and for keeping the victims and general public protected at all times to the best of our abilities. As long as probation officers continue to accomplish these goals, they continue to derive satisfaction from knowing they are doing the right thing.

Further Readings

Abadinsky, H. 1997. *Probation and Parole: Theory and Practice*. Upper Saddle River, NJ: Prentice Hall.

Bottomley, K. 1990. "Parole in Transition: A Comparative Study of Origins, Developments, and Prospects for the 1990s." In M. Tonry and N. Morris, eds., *Crime and Justice: A Review of Research*, 12. Chicago, IL: University of Chicago Press.

Petersilia, J. 1998. "Probation and Parole." In M. Tonry, ed., *Oxford Handbook on Crime and Punishment*. Oxford: Oxford University Press.

The Professional Life of a Federal Parole Officer

CHAPTER 9

Most prisoners leave prison before their sentence has expired to spend the rest of the sentence in the community under supervision. The most well-known form of "early release" is *parole*. Most inmates can apply for release on full parole after having served one-third of their sentence in prison. Once in the community, these individuals are supervised by parole officers. The professional activities of a parole officer are probably less well-known to the general public than are those of other professionals involved in the criminal justice system, such as defence lawyers. In this chapter, a federal parole officer with 18 years of professional experience describes his role in the criminal justice system.

Sheldon Schwartz
Correctional Service of Canada

Few Canadians understand the roles and duties of a parole officer (PO). The average person knows that a PO deals with offenders and monitors their behaviour. This represents a good start; however, it is also very general. I have been a federal parole officer with the Correctional Service of Canada (CSC) for 18 years. The federal correctional system deals mainly with individuals who are serving sentences of two years or more. Offenders serving sentences of less than two years fall under the jurisdiction of the provinces. There is one exception: in parts of Canada where there is no provincial correctional system in place, all offenders sentenced to a term of incarceration end up in the federal system. Additionally, offenders, when serving a Long Term Supervision Order (LTSO)—even if the custodial sentence is for less than two years—fall under the jurisdiction of the Parole Board of Canada (PBC) and the CSC during the LTSO portion of their sentence.

In dealing with offenders serving two years or more, federal POs work with every type of offender up to and including those serving sentences of life imprisonment. I should also mention that I am a community-based PO. Whereas some parole officers are assigned to prisons, I supervise only prisoners who have been released to the community. For example, a significant number of offenders who are serving life sentences have now been paroled. Assuming that they remain in the community (they may be returned to prison for a violation of their release conditions), POs will supervise them until their death.

Parole officer is a universal term in Western societies. In Canada, however, it may be somewhat misleading. The Canadian correctional system has both *day parole* and *full parole* releases of federal offenders. An individual released on day parole is required to reside in a community residential centre or a community correctional centre (better known as a *halfway house*). A full parole release is a conditional release to the community, with the offender residing in a location he has chosen and that the PBC has approved.

In Canada, there is also a form of release referred to as *statutory release* (SR). Offenders who have not applied for or been denied release on day parole or full parole will usually be released on SR at the two-thirds mark of their sentence. The release is also a conditional release to the community. It is a legislative right of offenders and only rarely is it denied. If a prisoner is believed to represent a certain type of risk to the community, she may be detained[1] in prison until the end of the sentence. My experience has been that few people know about SR and assume that any prisoner serving a portion of her custodial sentence in the community must have earned release on parole. However, for several reasons,[2] many offenders do not even apply for parole. Instead, they wait for their SR date. Generally speaking, offenders released on SR pose more of a risk than the average offender released on parole because the higher-risk inmates are either denied parole or don't bother applying for parole.

I am currently assigned to the Toronto East Parole Office. For 12 years, I worked with the Team Supervision Unit (TSU) in Toronto. This unit was dedicated to dealing only with the highest-risk offenders. Almost all the individuals we supervised left prison on SR. As a result of the recommendations of a number of inquests in the early 1990s, the TSU was developed to focus on the higher-risk offenders and to provide more intensive supervision of these individuals. While stable federal offenders who are supervised by a regular parole unit may be required to meet with their PO only once a month (or even once every three months in some cases), offenders in the TSU program were seen by their POs at least twice a week. In addition, the POs conducted unannounced curfew checks at night, showing up at individuals' residences to verify that they are in fact at home as required by the conditions of the release. This concept and model of intensive supervision has now been carried over to individual parole offices in the Toronto area. I continue to specialize in high-risk offenders, using the same intensive supervision strategy. I am part-nered with another parole officer and we continue to perform unannounced evening curfew compliance checks.

Another public misconception is that the CSC and the PBC are the same organization. In fact, these agencies are separate. The PBC is composed of appointed members who decide which inmates are to be granted release on parole and who determine the conditions of parole and statutory release. In contrast, the CSC provides an assessment report about each prisoner applying for parole. Such reports usually contain recommendations regarding whether or not the prisoner should be granted parole. However, the PBC is not bound by CSC recommendations. While usually agreeing with those recommenda-tions, the PBC may vote against a CSC-recommended course of action. The CSC also has the power to temporarily re-incarcerate a released offender (i.e., suspend a release). However, the PBC has the final say on the suspension.

The CSC is the agency responsible for managing and enforcing an offender's sentence of imprisonment. In the community, the PO enforces the conditions of release and the offender's adherence to a correctional plan. The development of the offender's correctional plan commences soon after the offender has been sentenced. By the time the offender is released, the plan represents a finely tuned blueprint of what is required for an offender's risk to be considered manageable in the community and what he needs to do to reintegrate successfully both during the sentence and in the long term. The principal duties of a PO include monitoring an offender's behaviour, performing ongoing risk assessments, and taking timely and effective action when necessary.

The CSC in the Toronto community is multidimensional. Front-line POs managing and working with released offenders also work with a Programs Department, a Psychology Department, a contracted psychiatrist, a mental health component, Aboriginal liaisons, and a Chaplaincy Section. Additionally, the CSC works closely with mental health and addictions abuse agencies, an employment service, and various other social service agencies in Toronto. It also works in partnership with local, provincial, and federal police services and other law enforcement agencies such as the immigration service. In particular, there is an ongoing dialogue (including meetings and training) between POs and specialized police units, such as the Robbery Squad, the Sex Crimes Unit, the Gangs and Guns Unit, and the Outlaw Biker Unit. There are also police officers (referred to as CCLOs—Community Corrections Liaison Officers) assigned to various parole offices.

The cases of offenders on PO caseloads (all of whom are serving sentences of two years or more or are under Long Term Supervision Orders) are multifaceted. While we do categorize offenders (sex offenders, organized criminals, street gang members, property offenders, and so forth), within each category no two cases are alike. I have supervised every type of offender, from one who had consumed a human body part, to those who had sexually abused their own children, to property offenders who could not walk a city block without being tempted to steal something. Many offenders fall into more than one category.

POs must get to know the individuals they supervise by being aware of all significant areas of an offender's life. People may wonder what a property offender's relationship with his girlfriend has to do with his risk of reoffending. However, there is considerable evidence that this risk is affected by interpersonal relationships. Individuals in stable relationships are less likely to relapse into the kinds of habits that give rise to offending. In addition, offenders who are in meaningful relationships have more to lose if their parole status is cancelled and they are recalled to prison. I have rarely had a problem overcoming the objections of an offender about needing to know about significant areas of her life, once I explain the reason.

What does a PO do? To supervise a caseload effectively, a PO must consider many issues—for example, medications and their effects, medical diagnoses, physical and mental diseases and disorders, legal requirements and legislation (corporate, offender, family, etc.), law enforcement, psychology, and financial accounting. Legally, POs are peace officers who enforce the conditions of an offender's release. To a large degree, the PO is also a broker who refers the offender to relevant resources in the community and who engages other professionals to assist with case management. Whether these other professionals realize it or not, they become extensions of the case management team. For instance, if an offender is on a program of methadone (a legal medication that helps an offender overcome heroin addiction), the relevant methadone doctor is an essential resource not only for the offender but also as a consultant for the PO. In many instances, that doctor will learn before the PO does that an offender has breached his drug abstinence condition.

Parole officers meet with offenders both at and away from the office. While it is easiest to meet with offenders in the office, it is also important to observe offenders in other environments, particularly at home and at their place of employment. It is also useful to communicate with *collateral contacts* in the community in order to get other perspectives on an offender's performance. Examples of these collateral contacts include police officers, employers, family members, friends and acquaintances, program delivery officers, psychologists, and landlords. Collateral contacts have varying degrees of reliability when it comes to providing accurate information on the offender and his other activities; that said, the greater the range of collateral contacts, the more accurate the overall picture will be. Of course, contradictory information will lead the PO to further investigate the matter.

The main objective of a parole officer is to protect the community. Ideally, this is achieved through the successful reintegration of offenders back into the community. In such cases, everyone is a winner, and this is the best long-term investment for society. However, sometimes protecting the community is achieved by taking measures of varying degrees of severity, up to and including removal of an offender from the community. Partnerships with other law enforcement agencies, such as the police and immigration authorities, are ever evolving and being improved. All of these professionals ultimately have the same objective; thus timely sharing of information, improved communication mechanisms, and awareness of all our roles in the justice system help make everyone's work more successful.

To meet the objective of protecting the community and to perform his or her duties, a PO must meet minimum standards as described in the Commissioner's Directives. These standards that prescribe operating practices have been developed over the years and are continually being refined and amended, based on experiences with cases and "best practices" models.

Most POs would agree that one of the main challenges of the job is to balance time management with meeting professional standards. If a PO ever says, "I'm all caught up," there is a problem. I can honestly say that I have never been "all caught up." While a PO may have reached certain standards for that week and may have met relevant deadlines, I can guarantee that there are more file reviews, collateral contacts, and case conferences that need to be done. So time management is a key skill, as is prioritization of job-related duties; both of these come with experience on the job. The Government of Canada has screened applicants for time-management skills using the "in-basket" simulation test. This test gives applicants a list of outstanding matters that need to be resolved. Applicants must prioritize these matters and indicate the actions they would take as well as how much time they would spend on each. Such screening helps ensure that new POs have good time-management skills.

As with any other job, a PO has a daily/weekly/monthly agenda. However, each day can be full of surprises—in this environment, not generally positive ones. Learning that the offender has failed a drug test, receiving a phone call from a spouse claiming she has been assaulted by an offender, being contacted by the police who are investigating an offender for new charges, and not being able to locate an offender are just some examples of typical surprises. Depending on the type of new information, an entire day or more may end up being dedicated to one situation, and the original agenda goes out the window.

A PAROLE OFFICER'S CASELOAD

In a regular supervision unit, a PO supervises caseloads averaging 20 to 25 cases. These offenders are required to report to their PO anywhere from once every three months to eight times per month. This frequency of contact is determined in a structured manner and depends on the rating of a case, the level of risk, and the needs of the offender. However, in supervising only high-risk cases, the caseload tends to reach a maximum of 10 cases. Each PO has two or three face-to-face interviews per week with each offender. Additionally, the POs must make numerous collateral contacts in order to gain accurate perspective and observation on the offender's community functioning.

Safety and Security Concerns

I am regularly asked about the dangers of the job and whether I carry a gun. (I do not.) It would be naive to not recognize that the job of a PO involves potential danger and risk. The safety and security of POs is always under discussion and examination. Within a prison, security systems and safety processes have greater structure and foundation; in the community, such systems are still evolving. For example, in supervising high-risk cases, curfew checks are performed by POs in partnered pairs. Indeed, where there is concern about risk, community-based contacts with an offender are usually conducted by POs in pairs (referred to formally as *tandem supervision*), and in some cases, this pairing is mandatory. At the office, POs must follow safety policies and know how to use emergency equipment such as personal alarms. There are also strict *call-in protocols* established for when POs are in the community performing their duties, in order to monitor their safety.

On October 6, 2004, PO Louise Pargeter became the first federal parole officer to be murdered in the community by an offender under supervision. The offender had previously been convicted of manslaughter. Since Pargeter's murder, safety and security systems and policies have been further amended and refined. This process continues to evolve. A PO should be extremely prudent, not only while on duty but when off duty as well. POs deal with individuals whose behaviour cannot always be predicted. For example, I go out of my way to protect my personal information. As well, even when walking through a mall on my own time, I try to be aware of what's going on around me at all times.

Dangerous situations sometimes stem from the most unlikely sources. For example, one evening during June 2004, my partner and I had just completed a curfew check on an offender in a high-rise apartment building. We left the apartment unit, and while we were waiting for the elevator, doors at both ends of the hallway simultaneously burst open and two police officers from each end ran toward us with guns drawn, screaming "Get down, face down!" I thought this was some kind of joke, but it didn't take long to realize that the officers were deadly serious. We hit the floor. They seemed somewhat nervous themselves. Within seconds, my partner and I had four semi-automatics pointed at our heads at close range. On the way down to the floor, my partner was able to get out the words: "We're parole officers."

Once we were lying flat, one officer asked for ID. I said that I had this in my pocket. He told me to get it. As I placed my hand in my pocket, I was praying that the officers on the other side of the hallway had heard their colleague tell me to reach into my pocket. I took out my badge and slid it to the officer as instructed. They immediately apologized, there was some chuckling by all, and the officers were quickly on their way. My partner and I then had to descend 18 stories on foot, since the elevators had been shut down. We later learned that there had been a report of an individual pointing a gun at others in the building.

Professional Instincts

Instincts play a large role in supervising offenders. Parole supervision is a "people" business; thus, individuals who are interested in working as a PO are "people persons" and have good instincts. Good instincts help a PO anticipate an offender's behaviour. Effective supervision often involves staying one step ahead of the offender. This trait can help a PO gather, process, and assess information and can possibly help predict what is about to happen, thereby preventing further crime. It is one thing to take action after a crime has occurred or when an event is known to have happened; it is better to prevent such an event. A PO's action (such as re-incarcerating the offender) is often taken based upon an assessment of the offender's deteriorating behaviour before an actual negative event has occurred. In such cases, the PO may never know what actions he or she prevented. The probability, though, is that it was something undesirable.

However, instincts cannot be defined easily and certainly cannot form the basis of an action taken or a recommendation on a case. A PO's actions and recommendations must be based on facts and credible information. In some cases, the action or recommendation is glaringly obvious; in other less obvious circumstances the PO must make a case to support an opinion. The case management team forms opinions and recommendations that represent several perspectives. Where there is dissenting opinion, the PO and his supervisor have the final recommendation, since the supervisors are accountable for the enforcement of the release conditions and for the management of risk. When the PO and parole supervisor (PS) disagree, the PS has the final say.

Supervising offenders also involves controlling some basic instincts. A PO may want to believe what an offender is saying; however, experience dictates that much of what offenders say must be verified. Years ago, I worked in public auditing. There was an audit principle employed that was referred to as *reasonable skepticism*—that is, you should always exercise a reasonable degree of skepticism in the workplace. I still apply this principle in my work as a PO. Most offenders sit in front of me, especially at the commencement of their release, and tell me about all the plans they have for life after release from prison. When high-risk offenders present these plans many of them fail to materialize. I often tell the offender: "Every offender sitting across from my desk tells me the same thing. Why should I believe you?" This will also set the ground for an offender understanding why a PO has to keep on verifying information the offender is providing. Eventually, an offender's word becomes credible after a pattern of honesty and openness has been established. However, this level of trust takes time.

The Balancing Act

Parole officers have numerous roles to perform, although some are more significant than others. The role a PO plays in supervising and managing a case is to a large degree determined by the offender. Part of my initial interview with a newly released offender is to convey this message to him. I tell the offender that my role and style of interaction depend on her performance and response to supervision. I explain that her case presents positive signals or negative ones. An experienced PO learns to balance the good with the bad and knows what role to play and when. Supervising a case without the right balance can upset the case and raise the risk to the community. Thus, the PO must learn about the offender and become aware of her reactions to certain structures, interventions, and communication styles. In the end, the offender is responsible for her own behaviour. However, case management can help create a positive outcome when the PO's style and interventions complement an offender's positive behaviours and when that PO is able to monitor and take timely action in response to an offender's negative behaviours.

In addition, decision making in a case can be quite complex. The complexity of decision making explains why there is a case management team. Here is an example of a very common situation that can create a difficult decision-making process:

A parole officer is supervising an offender, 25 years of age, who is serving time for multiple robberies. The offender has no drug addiction history, and the robberies were committed strictly for financial gain. Correctional planning has identified that the offender's attitude is a matter of considerable concern because he tends to make impulsive and antisocial decisions when he is under financial pressure. Another area of considerable concern is employment. The offender has never held a job for any significant period and has very few marketable skills. During his community release, he has secured employment as a landscaper. An employer has taken him under his wing and is teaching the offender landscaping skills and the skills of operating a small business. The landscaping job requires workers to work long hours in the spring, summer, and fall. The workday often extends well into the evenings. The employer has made it clear that he requires the offender for all of these hours, as his right-hand man.

The strategy for returning this offender to the community includes placing him on a waiting list for a CSC program that teaches offenders about changing their values to more pro-social ones by thinking about and avoiding situations that can lead to undesirable consequences. Several weeks into the offender's employment (which has been going very well), the PO receives a call from CSC programming saying that the program the offender is waitlisted for is about to commence. The program will run three evenings per week for 12 weeks beginning at 6:00 p.m. The offender will have to leave work by 4:00 p.m. on these days in order to get to the program on time. However, the employer cannot accept this schedule; thus, the offender would have to quit his job to participate in this program. What should the PO do?

Should the PO have the offender quit his job for the sake of the program, or should the PO endorse the employment—contrary to a component of the offender's correctional plan? Obviously, there is a choice to be made, since the offender cannot do both. Which plan stands to benefit society more in the long run? Quitting work to attend the program will likely cause a great deal of frustration for the offender. However, a decision by the PO to maintain the employment and not force the offender to participate in the program may become be a source of disagreement among the PO, the programs department, and management. What should the PO do? If it were me, I would stress that the development of work ethic, marketable skills, and business acumen would form a more solid foundation and a better long-term investment than a program would. However, this assessment is subjective.

Another complex task for a PO arises when disclosure about the nature of an offender's offences needs to be made in order to protect the community. The criterion used here is *foreseeability of risk*. When a team assesses an offender and determines that his release meets this criterion, disclosure regarding the nature of the relevant offences needs to be made. Disclosure may need to be made to a potential girlfriend, an employer, a relative, or a landlord. When it has been determined that disclosure needs to be made in order for risk to be managed, I usually allow offenders a short period of time to make the disclosure themselves. However, I tell them that I will be confirming what they told the relevant party and that I will fill in any gaps if I need to, in order to ensure that the individual has an adequate level of awareness to make an informed decision. Here is a practical example of such a situation.

An offender with an extensive history of property theft lands a job with a computer business that carries an extensive inventory of computer products. This situation presents a foreseeable risk, and the employer will have to be informed accordingly. However, there is also a significant chance that the employer will not want to hire the offender after being notified of his situation. There is the duty to notify the employer, but is there a way to do so that would be less likely to jeopardize the offender's employment? In this scenario, the PO may offer to meet the employer together with the offender so that, in addition to notifying the employer about the offender's history, the employer can be reassured that the offender is under supervision. Plenty of employers are willing to give a known offender a chance—as long as he or she is reassured that community supervision is in place.

In some such situations, the employer may decide to terminate the offender's employment. Obviously, this can have a very negative effect on the offender's confidence and attitude. However, the bottom line is that the community must be protected. There are many other situations where difficult decisions have to be made. Allowing an offender to leave his jurisdiction for a family event, waiving a curfew for employment purposes, and allowing an offender with a history of domestic violence to date a woman (a degree of disclosure would have to be made to the woman) all represent situations where there may be a perceived conflict between flexibility in allowing an offender the opportunity to reintegrate successfully into the community on the one hand, and potential risk to the community on the other.

DOCUMENTATION AND REPORT WRITING

In addition to travelling, meeting with offenders and collateral contacts, attending staff and professional meetings, investigating incidents, and receiving training, a significant amount of time must be spent on documentation and report writing. All relevant contacts (including telephone contacts) and meaningful discussions about a case must be recorded. Additionally, at regular intervals POs have to complete reports and applications for the PBC regarding the offender's progress or regarding other significant developments. There are time frames and deadlines for all of these reports, everyday case notes included. The PO's job and the correctional environment in general are very documentation oriented. The premise is that any event could become relevant in a future court case or other legal proceeding. Thus, documentation must be accurate and precise and include all dates and times.

Consider the following scenario. A PO has a scheduled appointment for an offender to report to him at the PO's office. The offender phones him in advance of the appointment time and complains that the transit system is currently slow and that he may be a few minutes late. In the background, the PO can hear the sound of subway trains. However, the PO doesn't write down the phone call and therefore doesn't record its time. The offender shows up at the PO's office on time. The PO records the details regarding the meeting. The next day, the Hold-Up Squad contacts the PO and reports that the offender is a suspect in a bank robbery that occurred the previous day during a period just prior to the offender's meeting with the PO. The PO has the precise time of his meeting with the offender. He also recalls the phone call *before* the meeting, but he does not have the precise time of the call. Obviously, this time could be critical information to the police investigation. Could the robbery have occurred between the offender's phone call to the PO and the meeting? Maybe the phone call was planned this way to provide an alibi for the offender. How should the PO respond to questioning by the police regarding the time of the phone call?

In my opinion, the worst thing the PO could do in this scenario is guess about the time of the phone call and offer it as fact. This could actually provide an alibi for the offender based on the PO's estimate. In responding to the police investigation, any estimate of time should be qualified as such. It is better to say, "I don't know for sure—I inadvertently forgot to record it," than to state something as factual when it is not.

POs render opinions and are sometimes called upon to predict future behaviour. That said, if an element of current and past dynamics has not been verified as factual, it cannot be recorded as a fact. Words such as "apparently" and "seemingly" are very important to use when conveying unverified opinion. An offender's self-disclosure is not always taken at face value, for obvious reasons. It is a good idea to complete documentation with the attitude that it could make its way to court. While this may seem overly cautious on the surface, it is prudent conduct for a PO. There is a healthy concept that I refer to as "reasonable paranoia": a PO ought to function, not with undue fear, but prudently enough to cover her backside when documenting.

WORKING WITH VICTIMS OF CRIME

In recent years the CSC and the PBC have placed greater emphasis on communicating with victims, providing relevant information about offenders, and listening to victims' concerns. Victims may formally register as victims so that they can receive information about offenders and their locations and supervision and ensure their own safety and peace of mind. Victims or potential victims who are not formally registered can contact the CSC to express concerns and ask questions. While respecting the privacy rights of the offender, the CSC can discuss what he is allowed to discuss and can take effective and timely action when necessary. The main objective is to protect the community. Parole officers are trained to be mindful of victims, both past and future.

CONCLUSION

The job of a federal parole officer is challenging, stressful, and at times thankless. However, it is also rewarding and fulfilling. Most POs would say that there are no two days alike in this job. My colleagues would also tell you that they are clock watchers; but unlike the clock watchers who want time to go more quickly, the POs I know want it to slow down. When they see it is 2:00 p.m., they wish it was still noon. It sounds strange, but I believe it speaks to the challenge of time management, always being busy, and finding the job challenging and interesting.

Further Reading

The Correctional Service of Canada website at http://www.csc-scc.gc.ca is comprehensive and includes relevant legislation, policies, standards, and a list of publications.

Endnotes

1. In order to detain offenders to the end of their sentence, correctional authorities must have reasonable grounds to believe that offenders are likely to commit one of the following crimes before the expiration of their sentence: a sexual offence involving a child, an offence causing death or serious harm to another person, or a serious drug offence.

2. Some prisoners may not wish to go through the steps to apply for parole or may believe their chances of getting released on parole are slim. Instead, they will just wait until the two-thirds mark, and then leave prison on statutory release, as they are entitled to by law (unless correctional authorities deem and can establish that the prisoner meets the criteria for detention as described above).

A Life Prisoner's Perspective

In this chapter a life prisoner describes his experience in prison and his subsequent release on parole as a result of the "Faint Hope clause," a provision of the *Criminal Code of Canada* that permitted some life sentence prisoners to apply for a jury review of their parole eligibility dates. If the jury found merit in an application, it had the power to allow the prisoner to apply to the Parole Board earlier than would otherwise have been the case. This release mechanism has now been abolished, except for prisoners sentenced before the reform was introduced who are still eligible. Rick Sauve talks about his educational achievements while in prison and his life after release from prison. His story illustrates the importance of rehabilitation, and the transformation that people can make in their lives, given the chance to do so. The chapter also illustrates the important contributions that prisoners have made to the correctional system in this country.

Rick Sauve
Prisoners' Rights Activist

My name is Rick Sauve, and I am currently serving a life sentence while living in the community. In this chapter I am going to do two things. First, I am going to tell you about my life in prison—how I spent my 17 years inside. Second, I am going to describe my life after release, and offer some reflections on the role of education and the need to reform Canada's prison system.

LIFE IN PRISON

When I was sentenced to prison with a life sentence with no parole eligibility for 25 years I decided early on that the only way I could survive the prison experience—both physically and psychologically—was to take control of my environment in a productive way. I was fortunate as I had good family support to supply me with hope and encouragement while serving my sentence. I realized early in my sentence that in order to earn parole I would have to try and remain positive and actively work toward that goal. One of the hurdles I knew I would face was that I refused to accept my conviction and was determined to fight it. I maintained my innocence and as a result my case management team constantly told me that the only way I would ever get out of prison was to admit guilt. But how could I admit guilt to an offence I never committed? In the end, all of this actually strengthened my determination to succeed, and to avoid becoming immersed and lost in the prison subculture.

Going to School in Prison

One of the first things I did when I got to Millhaven, a maximum-security prison, was enrol in school. Prior to prison I had not completed my Grade 10, so I took the opportunity to complete my education. In open society, students of all kinds attend university and community colleges. They probably take their education for granted since they have easy access to instructors, libraries and computers, and other resources. Prisons are different. It's not easy getting an education inside prison.

Besides gaining an education there were other benefits to enrolling in school. First, the school setting itself offered a sanctuary that took me out of the prison environment. At school I was able to see myself as a student rather than just as a prisoner. It also provided me with the opportunity to interact with teachers rather than uniformed institutional staff. Furthermore, it provided me with some sense of control, in the sense that I was able to deviate from the regimentation of daily prison life. I was able to select the courses I wanted to take. Finally, school allowed me to share these experiences with my family—in particular my daughter. This allowed me to share a normal kind of routine that wasn't necessarily prison-related.

After completing my high school requirements, I was accepted into a degree program offered by Queen's University. I completed two courses in psychology from Queen's while serving time at Millhaven. When I applied for a transfer to a medium-security prison, the transfer board had some concerns because I wouldn't admit guilt; nor would I discuss my conviction, because I was still fighting my case. However, because of my good behaviour in prison, my positive attitude, and my educational achievements, I was eventually granted a transfer to Collins Bay, a medium-security prison.

Once at Collins Bay I was determined to finish my degree. I also became involved in other activities that took me out of the routine prison environment. One of these was the Exceptional People's Olympiad, which was sponsored by prisoners inside the prison on an annual basis. I became part of the executive. This allowed me to be productive and also gave me a sense of giving back and being a part of the outside community. Another important step I took was to co-found the "Lifers' Group" at the institution. We were an active group of like-minded prisoners serving life sentences who wanted to create a more positive environment inside the prison. We became affiliated with faculty members and students from the Criminology Department at the University of Ottawa. Together we shared a desire to make prisons more productive and more positive, and to help prisoners take the necessary steps to achieve rehabilitation and a successful return to open society.

I continued my studies and graduated from Queen's University in 1987 with a B.A. in psychology—the first prisoner from Collins Bay to do so. As a result I was granted permission, with the Solicitor General intervening on my behalf, to attend my graduation ceremonies on an Escorted Temporary Absence (ETA). This happened after the Solicitor General was contacted by Mick Lowe, a journalist who had written a book chronicling my case and conviction. Initially the institution had refused to let me attend my own graduation but after the intervention by the Solicitor General my application to attend was granted by the National Parole Board.

The next stage in my education came when, with the support of Dr. Robert Gaucher, I was accepted into the graduate studies program in criminology at the University of Ottawa. Thus I became a graduate student—not a bad achievement for someone who had entered prison without Grade 10! I had met Robert in my capacity as chairperson of the Lifers' Group. This affiliation with the University of Ottawa became important not only to me but also to the students, faculty, and guests. A symbiotic relationship developed: the students and guests learned first-hand from our prison experiences, while prisoners gained links to the community. Together we wrote papers and articles about a variety of criminal justice issues, including sentencing. We regularly invited outside guests—ranging from politicians and activists to senior corrections officials. I developed many lasting friendships from this experience.

Voting Rights for Prisoners

It was also at Collins Bay that I launched the legal challenge for the prisoners' right-to-vote case under the *Charter of Rights and Freedoms*. At the time, prisoners in Canada did not have the right to vote in federal elections. The fact that you are serving time should not mean you lose this basic democratic right—as has been recognized by the European Court of Human Rights. If society wants prisoners to rehabilitate themselves, it should encourage prisoners to take part in the electoral process—not exclude them. The case eventually made its way to the Supreme Court of Canada, where the court ruled that prisoners have the right to vote.

After several years at Collins Bay, I was approached by the warden who told me that the Commissioner of Corrections wanted to start a pilot program to send lifers serving a minimum of 25 years to a minimum-security camp, and that I had been selected as one of the first candidates to go. I was then transferred to Frontenac, a minimum-security institution, where I continued with my graduate studies, completing my honours year and all the requirements for a Masters degree in Criminology.

I also became much more involved in community projects. I organized and chaired the Conwalk, a fundraiser for muscular dystrophy during which one group of prisoners went into communities to collect money for the Muscular Dystrophy Association and a second group walked a marathon back to the institution, beginning at Parliament Hill in Ottawa. In four years we raised almost $130,000 for this worthy cause. I also became involved in the Ontario Special Olympics. I organized a group of inmates and staff to build bleachers for the event and to provide volunteers to assist.

I also created the Straight Talk program, designed for young offenders and youth at risk. This followed a two-pronged approach. The first part involved going to schools, group homes, and other community organizations to talk about the experience of imprisonment. At two of these events I paired up with the community's police chief to make presentations to students. The other part of the Straight Talk program was more structured—an eight-week program for young offenders that my wife and I developed. We would have the youth come into the prison and, with other lifers we had trained, we would work on a variety of problem areas affecting their lives. We ran this program for about four years while I was at Frontenac, and continued some elements of it after I was released on parole.

My Application for Release

After serving 15 years inside, I became eligible for a Faint Hope hearing, which, as noted at the beginning of the chapter, has now been abolished. This process involved applying to a court for a jury to hear about my life in prison, with a view to determining whether I could apply to the National Parole Board before having spent 25 years in prison. At my hearing, the activities I had been involved in were described for the jury who then determined whether I should be eligible to have my parole date changed—from 25 years down to something sooner. I was able to call witnesses to testify about these activities, including family members, friends, community associates from my volunteer work, one of my professors, and the warden from Frontenac. They all gave evidence under oath before the jury. They were able to paint a picture of who I really was for the jury to consider. I attest here that throughout my sentence I never involved myself in any activities to gain favour for my review or for my eventual parole. I involved myself because I believed I could make a positive contribution to my community both inside prison and beyond its walls. After hearing all the evidence, the jury—composed of members of the public—recommended that I be considered for parole immediately. This did not mean that I could leave prison—a jury does not have that power. What it meant was that I could then apply to the Parole Board, which would conduct its own review of my case. As you can see, it is not easy to get released from prison.

Applying for Parole

I still had to appear before the National Parole Board to present my case and to prove to the board members that I would not pose a risk if I was released into the community. The board decided to initially grant me four unescorted temporary absences over a six-month period. These all went well. I then applied for and was granted day parole to a halfway house. After six months I again appeared before the board, which this time granted me release on full parole.

LIFE AFTER RELEASE FROM PRISON

After leaving prison I worked for a year as a cabinetmaker. I then secured employment as a child and youth worker for the Toronto Boys' Home for three years. There I worked with open detention and open custody youth, many of whom were involved in street gangs. I shared with them my background and experiences, hoping they might gain some insights from what I had been through. While I was employed there I received two promotions and developed a good rapport with both the youth and other staff. I continued speaking at schools and to groups across the province.

For 14 years I worked for the LifeLine program, going back inside various prisons as an Inreach worker. LifeLine is a uniquely Canadian concept that was developed at St. Leonard's as a result of a tripartite agreement between St. Leonard's, the Correctional Service of Canada (CSC), and the National Parole Board. There were initially 26 Inreach workers across the country. We provide institutional services in prisons at all security levels. Our focus is on providing hope to men and women who are serving life sentences.

All Inreach workers are paroled lifers or long-term prisoners. With periods of incarceration getting longer, it is difficult for many lifers to maintain hope and to develop realistic plans to some day return to the community. We help them in this regard, as we ourselves had to make that transition. To make the adjustment back into the community after 10 to 25 years (often longer) can be overwhelming. We also assist them with their parole hearings. We bring a unique perspective for the Parole Board to consider, as we have worked with our clients for many years in prisons of various security levels. We also assist them with their reintegration plans—for example, by helping them select halfway houses that fit their needs. We know first-hand how difficult that can be, as we ourselves have experienced it.

To give people a better understanding of what prison is like, we also speak at schools, as well as to community groups and the media. We see ourselves as a valuable resource to promote understanding about the system and to break down the myths and misconceptions that surround it. It is not easy for Inreach workers to go back into the prisons that they worked so hard to get out of and stay out of. For many of us it is a vocation, not simply a job.

The LifeLine program, despite being an award-winning and internationally recognized corrections program, was cancelled as part of government cutbacks. In the words of MP Vic Toews, who became justice minister in the Harper Conservative government, "We are not going to have convicted murderers helping other murderers get out of prison." The program has now changed into a similar program that is funded by St. Leonard's Society on a much-reduced scale. Although LifeLine was cancelled, St. Leonard's of Windsor, Peterborough, Hamilton, and Ottawa have provided funding to keep myself and one other worker to continue with this work. As one of the board of directors said, "We have a moral commitment to our community to know who is coming here, and you guys are one of the best resources for us to know who that is and who are in the best position to succeed."

To this day I continue to speak to youth at risk; I also make presentations to schools at all levels, victims' groups, other community groups and agencies, and correctional conferences, and I conduct many media interviews. I hope that by sharing my experiences I can help them make positive decisions in their lives. Sharing keeps me grounded and helps me make sense of my own life experiences. My career in this respect has not changed. I have never hidden the facts of my prison experiences or my journey through the justice system, including my experience with the Faint Hope clause. Not once has anyone among the thousands of people I have presented to over the years ever implied to me that I should not have been released on parole. To me that speaks volumes about the level of community acceptance. I believe that when people are properly informed and have a clear understanding of the issues, they are more accepting and understanding of them.

Reflection of The Past Twenty Years

It has been almost 20 years since I left prison via the Faint Hope clause. I have on many occasions taken time to reflect on what life on parole has been for me. I often have been asked how my life has evolved since being released from prison on parole. In reality, for me, at times it feels like I am still serving time, which in effect I am—a life sentence never ends. For the past 20 years I have worked or been involved with the criminal justice system. From the time I was released from prison until the present I have made numerous presentations; they have all involved reflecting on not only the prison environment but my "time," my life in prison, and serving my sentence in the community. I always feel that I am identified first and foremost as a lifer. For me it sometimes is difficult to have the sense that in these instances people don't see the distinction between my career and the ex-con.

In my career over the past 17 years I have testified in court, for youth sentencing hearings, and for Faint Hope applications by other prisoners still in the system. I have assisted at well over 300 parole hearings and continue to do so. Far too often in my dealings with parole officers (and in some cases with parole board members) it is noted that I know what is expected of a lifer on parole, and the consequences of not adhering to parole conditions. It is that constant reminder that I am a convicted person, that I was in prison for murder and that I am being held up to scrutiny.

Because my case is so widely known I am constantly asked about prison life. I often feel that I am part of the entertainment for the evening. I more often than not feel I can never get away from prison. It has become a double-edged sword: I know that I am doing well in my career but feel trapped because of my life sentence. My wife has pointed out to me that I have been consumed by prison life and that I have to escape, that I need to let go of prison and come home. She has pointed out that I need to achieve more balance in my life, that I need to distinguish my career from my life. It is difficult, however, to make that transition—particularly since my career has been so intrinsic to my identity.

Over the years while working with LifeLine and going back into prison I started having nightmares—I would often wake up in a sweat, wondering if I was in or out of prison. I started getting tremendous feelings of anxiety that I would be trapped there and never get out. It wasn't that I was afraid of prison; on the contrary I felt comfortable there in a strange way, I didn't feel different inside in the same way I far too often felt in the community. I would sometimes feel guilty when leaving the prison, I felt that there was always more that I could do, there was always one more prisoner that I could assist. I compare it to feeling like Frodo the Hobbit carrying the ring, it just kept getting heavier and heavier the more I carried it. On far too many occasions when I came home I would become depressed and sometimes break down in tears. I now have learned to search out sanctuaries, particularly my home in the country, with my cabinet shop where I can shut out the world and escape from prison.

I shared these experiences with a friend (Dr. Robert Gaucher) who pointed out that I was probably experiencing post-traumatic stress. His comment was like a light going on in my mind and allowed me understand what I was experiencing. I felt that I couldn't share this insight with my parole officer as I was concerned that it might be misconstrued and be seen as a risk factor. I don't see this as a risk for me; rather, I believe that I have learned to utilize it as a tool that I can use to better understand what other prisoners face upon returning to the community. I now share my insights with them to help them better understand what they will face, and for them to realize that this abnormal emotional roller coaster is actually normal and that they are not alone. I share with them effective coping strategies, and I believe that I also provide a safe environment, a sanctuary for them to discuss their experiences. Prison life is a traumatic experience, particularly for those that have served (or will serve) decades inside with the knowledge they may never get out. Not surprisingly, over the years I have had numerous clients share similar experiences with me and it is comforting to know they have that connection with others who share these experiences. I have raised the issue of post-traumatic stress disorder in my meetings with senior corrections staff from National Headquarters while working for LifeLine, and suggested that this could be an area where resources should be devoted to assist those returning to the community. Post-traumatic stress may well explain why some parolees breach special conditions such as abstinence from alcohol or drugs.

The Evolving Prison

Although prison life remains static, one day like the next, repeating itself for years on end, the correctional system has changed in Canada. The current government's "Get Tough on Crime" agenda has affected the prison community. The institutions have become much more secure and tend to shut out the outside community. Groups such as the Lifers' Groups that once flourished with many volunteers have greatly diminished or are no longer functioning.

A recent article in the *Toronto Sun* raised the issue of the cost of corrections. It noted that it costs on average approximately $120,000 per year to keep someone in prison in Canada. In the same article a government spokesperson said the government is reducing costs by closing down prisons. They did close Kingston Pen and Leclerc Prison, which they proudly announced would save 120 million dollars per year, and no new prisons have been built since 2006. The fact is, however, they have spent billions of dollars on construction of new units within existing prisons, adding 1,700 cells, including administration buildings, and other construction for maintenance support. This construction took place inside prison perimeters, which in effect added to construction costs. "Double bunking"—housing two prisoners in cells designed for single occupancy—is becoming more common. Longer prison sentences and more restrictive parole will lead to an increase in the prison population and significantly more issues to deal with in the future. The irony of all this of course is that the government is getting tough when crime statistics show that crime rates have been declining now for years. Why, you might ask, should Canadians spend more money housing prisoners for longer periods of time, when crime rates are falling?

Many of the initiatives and projects that prisoners had developed over the years to introduce some normalcy and humanity inside prison have been cancelled or curtailed. For example, consider the Exceptional People's Olympiad at Collins Bay Prison, which for over 25 years brought in hundreds of developmentally challenged individuals as well as community volunteers to be involved in games within the walls, with great success. It is no longer running. The LifeLine program, which was identified as a "Best Practice" in Corrections was cancelled almost two years ago. There has also been a downloading of costs onto prisoners who make minuscule pay, which has virtually remained the same since 1983. Prisoners' pay has been cut by 30 percent. After paying for medication and other healthcare needs, prisoners are left with little or no resources to pay for education programs or any kind of family support, or to have some money when they leave prison. How are these changes going to result in a safer society?

Many of the harsher sentencing laws affect the correctional environment. The abolition of the Faint Hope clause, the introduction of consecutive life sentences and life without parole will have a profound effect within the institutions. Changes in parole have also led to an increase in time served in prison. There has been an increased waiting time for those that have been denied parole before they can re-apply. Moreover, if parole is revoked (most often for a breach of conditions rather than for a fresh allegation of offending) it takes approximately two years before the next hearing is held.

There has been a significant degree of aging in the prison population. This will tax the resources within the prison environment and the community halfway houses and agencies that house prisoners upon return to the community. Halfway houses have had to accept more released prisoners on terms of a residency condition of release who would normally have been granted statutory release to the community. This has reduced bed space for prisoners who are being granted day parole, and has significantly increased waiting times for release to the community. Long-term prisoners—especially those serving life sentences—who have earned administrative unescorted temporary absences are being wait-listed for bed space, and this has also slowed down their reintegration.

I was recently asked by the Parole Board of Canada to provide my insight at a three-day seminar for their annual training on risk assessment. They are seeing more and more applicants at parole hearings that have spent 25, 30 years or longer in custody and want a better understanding of the issues and challenges that these prisoners face when reintegrating back into the community. I will be running three workshops over the three days for the board members from across the country. The Parole Board recognizes that with these ever-increasing sentences, an aging prison population, and the issues faced in reintegrating, assessing risk and release planning is a challenge for them. Neither the resources nor the programming available to address these needs currently exists within corrections, and it is stretching the community resources of both agencies and halfway houses. I am currently helping to prepare two men—both in their 80s and with obvious health issues—to develop a viable release plan.

In closing, it still feels like I am "doing time," and I still feel like a prisoner. Perhaps this feeling is a tool that I can utilize in my career to bring attention to these issues and to assist in developing effective responses. Still feeling like a prisoner has given me great insight into how these changes have affected the men and women within the prison walls, and the issues they will have to face when returning to the community. It has allowed me to work with correctional officials and community agencies to assist them in their work. It has also provided an opportunity for the audiences to whom I make presentations to better understand the world of corrections and the issues facing prisoners who will be returning to the community.

Current Issues in Criminal Justice

PART
THREE

CHAPTER 11

Community Policing in Canada: The Broad Blue Line

Community policing represents one of the most important developments in policing in Canada and elsewhere. The community policing approach re-emerged in the 1980s in response to a certain degree of disenchantment with traditional policing. At the heart of this movement is a desire to produce a closer connection between the police and the communities they serve. However, the so-called community policing revolution may have run its course, as there has been a return to more traditional policing following the 9/11 terrorism events and the growing attention paid to national security. In this article, policing expert Barry Leighton explores the nature and function of community policing.

Barry N. Leighton
Carleton University

The current and future challenge for public policing is whether to return to the proactive, "Blue" model of community policing, whether to continue reverting to the traditional, reactive, or "Brown" model, or whether to engage the full spectrum of policing styles in an integrated way.

The idea of community policing is almost 200 years old. Departing from the British military red uniform that symbolized the use of raw armed force, public police in the distinctive blue uniform was originally championed by Sir Robert Peel in 1829 when he established modern public policing in London, England. He argued that the "new police" merely formalized a local function that has its origins in common law. At the core of Peel's innovation lies the fundamental principle of the public police working in partnership with the community they serve to solve local crime and disorder problems.

The metaphor of a "broad blue line" against crime is an adaptation of the "thin red line" imagery used to describe the resilience of 19th-century outnumbered British forces withstanding attacks by Russian cavalry during the 1854 Crimean war. The troops were commanded to stand fast in ranks two-deep rather than in the customary four. This "thin red line" strategy succeeded and developed into a romantic picture of a beleaguered few, defying the odds and overcoming them. This "us against them" strategy using a small number of uniformed police spread thinly against a much larger number of criminals in defending the local community has become part of the rhetoric and imagery of traditional policing. However, community policing turns this on its head by placing the local police on the same side as society. Such an alliance between police and the empowered community they serve transforms the "thin blue line" of uniformed police into the coalition of a "broad blue line" of police and community.

To better explain the police–community alliance, this chapter discusses the following questions: How can we define *community policing*? What are its main strategies and tactics? What is the broader context of community policing? How does the Blue model of community policing contrast with the traditional or Brown model of policing? What theories help explain community policing? How is community policing practised in Canada? What is the empirical evidence showing that community policing works? Finally, what is the future of community policing?

DEFINITION AND CORE STRATEGIES

The term *community policing* has also been labelled *community-oriented policing*, *community-based policing*, *neighbourhood policing*, and *problem-oriented policing*, although there are only marginal, if any, differences between these terms. While the meaning of *community policing* may be in the eye of the beholder, it may be defined as "a philosophical, organizational, and operational approach to urban policing which emphasizes a police–community partnership to solve local crime and disorder problems" (Leighton 1991).

Problem solving means addressing identified local crime and disorder problems by finding patterns among similar incidents (Goldstein 1979). This may be seen as the "blue" part of the "broad blue line" to reduce crime at the local level. Rather than responding to each call from the public as a separate case, the police take appropriate crime reduction and prevention steps to proactively solve the common, underlying causes. For example, these actions may involve "target hardening" (e.g., installing better locks and lighting) and other prevention tactics prescribed by the *environmental design approach*, whose main strategy is to reduce opportunities for crime. Reducing crime opportunities may also include more intensive policing in crime locations at higher risk of crime. In these crime *hot spots*, or *hot places* at *hot times,* police routinely play the lead role in reducing opportunities for offending.

The second core strategy of community policing is a broad *community partnership* between the police and the community they serve. This may be seen as the "broad" part of the "broad blue line." Such a partnership usually takes the form of public engagement through participation and consultation. Partnership activities provide the focal point for identifying local crime and disorder problems, setting priorities for the problems, and developing solutions. Problems are viewed as shared problems with shared solutions which are provided by the police and other criminal justice agencies in partnership with social service agencies and other resources in the community. This partnership in identifying and ameliorating local crime and disorder problems make the police and the community "co-producers" of order and civility (Wilson and Kelling 1982) and "co-reproducers of order" (Ericson 1982).

These two strategies of problem solving and community partnerships also have a number of organizational prerequisites (Leighton 1991). In particular, decentralized police management and resource deployment empower police officers to work with their community to use whatever tactics are appropriate to the neighbourhood and its specific crime problems. Other innovations include a proactive approach to delivering services rather than knee-jerk responses to emergency calls or randomly cruising the streets in patrol cars in the hope of apprehending a crime in progress.

Within these two core strategies, community policing uses a variety of *tactics*. For a particular crime problem in a particular community, tactics may include a mix of one or more of the following: police mini-stations or storefronts; neighbourhood patrol by car, foot, or bicycle; dedicated beats or zones; "differential" or specialized response; interagency partnerships; and consultative committees. However, not all of them are appropriate for all communities; for example, foot patrol may not be very effective in low-density, spread-out suburbs. But because the objective of these tactics is to facilitate greater police–citizen contact, the right tactics must be chosen to reduce particular crime problems and they must be appropriate for the community's circumstances. Moreover, advances in social media technology may make some of these tactics almost obsolete, such as community storefront offices.

Consequently, community policing is "designer policing" because the specific tactics and police services delivered by the police are tailored to meet the needs of a particular neighbourhood, the local crime and disorder problem being addressed, and the solutions jointly developed by the police and the community. While there is no standard template or model, the appeal of community policing lies is its flexibility to deliver its two core strategies through a variety of tactics that differ from community to community and from problem to problem.

When talking about community policing, we should also clarify two key terms. Widespread confusion over the meaning of *community* can render the notion of *community policing* almost meaningless. This is because most traditional definitions of *community* focus on geographical space, such as neighbourhoods. But in a highly mobile society people are often more connected electronically than they are physically. Adopting a traditional definition transforms community policing into a romantic fiction of old-fashioned, self-policed communities with little crime. Modern definitions of *community* replace geography with local and non-local *social networks* that are increasingly national and global in scope. These new definitions allow community policing to embrace both local (neighborhood) and non-local (professional, business, and recreational) types of communities (Leighton 1988; Dupont 2004). We can then apply "community as network" to a whole range of alternative community types, including the electronic "global village" connected by social media tools such as the Internet, blogs, Facebook, YouTube, and Twitter. The notion of the networked community is also helpful in understanding how different types of non-local crime problems operate, such as transnational organized crime and terrorism.

In the same way that technological innovations have transformed the nature of community, they may also be seen in the history and development of public policing. The technologies of order maintenance have changed dramatically since the days when troops were called out to re-establish order in communities. For example, the Twenty-Sixth Cameronian Rifles quelled the Gavazzi Riots in Montreal during the summer of 1853 (Atherton 1914). Between community-based watch systems and troops with fixed bayonets, there were few options available to civil powers. But calling in the army was a very costly exercise, both in terms of expense and lives lost.

Peel solved the problem of finding alternatives to military force by offering two models of policing, both of which were readily adopted in Canada. The North West Mounted Police model for bringing order to Canada's sparsely populated West was borrowed from another of Peel's inventions, the Royal Irish Constabulary. However, it was his urban policing model that was adopted by Canada's municipalities.

Foot patrol of neighbourhoods quickly became the core urban policing strategy, eventually aided by the technological advance of police telephones on street corners so they could ask for help when needed. With the advent of police patrol cars, a rapid response to crimes in progress became the watchword for motorized patrol. The downside of this invention was that it distanced police from the communities they served. Two-way radios fostered more rapid responses, while on-board computers allowed police to check information on suspects. But it took the invention of smart phones and GPS to free police from the patrol car, allowing them to keep in touch electronically while patrolling neighborhoods on foot or bicycle.

On the other hand, these same technologies also served to enable supervisors at the police station to keep track of and control the otherwise independent police officers on patrol. The growing pressure to install video cameras on police vehicles to monitor police is partly a reaction to high-profile cases of serious misconduct associated with an inappropriate choice of tactic from the police *use of force continuum*, such as the 2013 shooting of a troubled youth in a Toronto streetcar. As well, bystanders with smart phones are recording police use of deadly force, such as when tasers were misused by police at Vancouver Airport in 2007 resulting in the death of a Polish-speaking immigrant. Communities observing the police while the police monitor the community is an outcome reflecting the double-edged sword of technology.

Meanwhile, other technologies may undermine the image of a friendly community police officer, particularly the bulky, bulletproof vest and other pieces of equipment previously used only by tactical or emergency response units. Moreover, in addition to firearms, police officers on foot now carry a variety of other weighty tools on their belts, all of which project quite a different image from what Sir Robert Peel originally envisioned: that of a member of the community wearing a simple dark blue uniform with a distinctive helmet. The combination of these two contrasting images—the community police officer and the tactical squad member in full battle dress—invites further exploration.

TWO MODELS OF POLICING

Community policing differs from other approaches to public policing, especially from the traditional (professional or bureaucratic) model of policing, which may represent idealized types in each end of a spectrum.

Under the *traditional policing* model, crime is the exclusive "property" of the police, who use a technology-driven, rapid-response strategy combined with random motorized patrol, all of which are designed to have a deterrent effect on potential criminal events (Kelling and Moore 1988). Usually associated with the crime control approach under which the police "own" crime problems and exercise a monopoly on the response to it (Christie 1977), the traditional police are seen as forming a "thin blue line" against crime. However, with crime as their exclusive professional domain, these police unfortunately may also end up forming a thin blue line against the community, especially when their tactics are questioned and community consent to be policed is withdrawn. In contrast, community policing forms a "broad blue line" or coalition against local crime and disorder problems, because the police–community partnership unleashes under-utilized community resources.

Many of the differences between the two models of policing are found in their tactics. Guth (1994) calls these two models the "Brown" to symbolize para-military policing and the "Blue" to denote community policing. The first reflects police organizations with "force" in their name whereas the second reflects those which changed their name to "police service." As well, the first model focuses on enforcing the law through "law enforcement officers" whereas the second favours "peace officers" (i.e., the legal status of police in Canada) who facilitate peace in the streets by using tactics—of which only one is enforcing the law. But some uncharitable critics have called these two models "real policing" and "social work."

The difference between the Blue or community policing model and the Brown or traditional model can be illustrated with a healthcare analogy. Traditional policing corresponds to a police force that works like a hospital operating exclusively as an emergency ward. Most of the time the staff would be patiently waiting for a 911 call for an ambulance to make a rapid response to a life-threatening incident, even though these incidents are relatively few in number compared with most hospital visits. Doctors would randomly cruise the streets in ambulances as a deterrent for accident-prone, high-risk people who are driving unsafely under the influence of alcohol or illegal drugs. On vary rare occasions, perhaps when cruising accident *hot spots*, they might come across an accident in progress and then be readily available for assistance. Consequently, most patients would arrive only by an emergency-response ambulance, regular wards would be used only for follow-up care, and the underlying causes of health problems would remain unaddressed.

In contrast, community policing is closer to preventive medicine, with an ambulance making an emergency response in only a small proportion of calls for health care. The focus of treatment and response is the individual, rather then the event or incident. This holistic approach to healthcare promotes and maintains good health through exercise and a balanced diet in much the same way that building a healthy community results in a safer community with a lower risk of crime and disorder problems. As a result, policing costs less, is more affordable, and is less of a burden on society in the long run. In short, community policing is *sustainable policing*.

But are these two, apparently conflicting, models incompatible for police on the beat? First, much of the glamour of policing, and what may attract many recruits, is "extreme policing," namely, para-military tactical units in combat gear responding to dramatic terrorist or hostage incidents or mass shootings. In contrast, much of routine policing is just boring, such as directing traffic, handing out parking tickets, checking false alarms, and driving around on patrol, all the while waiting for the "big call." So when police work involves being trained and ready to perform these two roles at the same time, there is a great deal of stress placed on the police.

THE POLICING SPECTRUM

Community policing can be also contrasted with other policing models, all of which fall within the broader concept of *social control*. During the last century, many sociologists theorized that, when the informal mechanisms of family, religion, school, and community failed to adequately socialize people with the appropriate norms and values of the dominant society to create internalized control, then "leakage" would occur and formal agents of societal control would take over. In one sense, citizens would move from being controlled by a "policeman in our heads" (i.e., internalized controls) to having a "policeman at our elbows" (i.e., in the streets). Because of the weakening of traditional societal institutions, the maintenance of order in society now relies more on formal social control mechanisms, including the police employing a full range of "active" (people-based) and "passive" (technology-based) surveillance tools.

At one end of this spectrum of social control agents, *private police* or *parapolice* serve the security needs of individuals and corporations, working as agents of property owners, largely for the protection of property such as mass private space (e.g., shopping malls). As well, high-risk politicians, business leaders, and celebrities also employ security guards for their physical safety. Next on the spectrum are the public police. In Canada, they are organized along jurisdictional grounds that reflect constitutional responsibilities at three levels of government: at the local level, public police serve a municipal function; regionally they may have a provincial function; and nationally, they serve a federal function where Canada's national police force, the RCMP, are joined by other federal agencies such as Canada Border Services Agency, to combat major crime. However, while these three levels have distinctive responsibilities, their operations are often closely linked, such as when the federal police combat organized crime where it has roots in local communities.

The national end of the policing spectrum, with a mandate to tackle terrorism, transnational organized crime, and other threats to national security, more clearly shows that the police act as agents of the state. This "higher" level of protecting Canada's national security has been called *high policing*, in contrast to *low policing* (Brodeur 1983). However, these terms are confusing, because those dedicated to community policing consider the pursuit of community safety to be the more noble or "higher" calling whereas agencies combating terrorism often get into serious skullduggery under the guise of national security.

COMMUNITY POLICING IN THEORY

While a comprehensive theory of community policing has yet to be developed, the *broken windows* argument advanced by Wilson and Kelling (1982) has academic credibility (Sparrow, Moore and Kennedy 1990; Kelling and Coles 1996) and widespread appeal. The broken windows argument mirrors the notion of the self-fulfilling prophecy, as developed in 1929 by sociologist W.I. Thomas: if people define a situation as real, then it will be real in its consequences.

The broken windows theory proposes that when potential offenders perceive neighbourhood decay and deterioration (such as broken windows, derelict cars, or graffiti), they conclude that the neighbourhood has few defences against crime and is "ripe for the picking." However, when the visible signs of crime and urban decay are removed, then the neighbourhood is more likely to be perceived as being low in crime because it is well defended, resulting in an actual reduction in crime. That is, when changes in perceptions and attitudes result in changes in reality, then crime is actually reduced, thereby making streets and homes safer.

But the idea that a neighbourhood in decay will inevitably lead to disorder and then to crime has been challenged (Greene and Mastrofski 1988). Critics argue that it "explains too much" and might better serve as simply an explanation for neighbourhood disorder and order maintenance, rather than overextending itself to cover crime as well. On the other hand, compelling research (Skogan and Hartnett 1997) demonstrates an empirical link between disorder and crime, thereby providing strong support for this theory.

COMMUNITY POLICING IN PRACTICE: DOES IT WORK?

An assessment of the state of community policing in Canada at the turn of this century suggests that it was fairly well accepted. First, it was officially endorsed by most police services. For example, it reflected the rhetoric and official positions of the majority of Canadian police chiefs and police boards; it was officially endorsed by Public Safety Canada (formerly Solicitor General Canada) as the preferred approach to modern urban policing (Normandeau and Leighton 1990); several provincial governments made it their official policy and the Ontario government formalized it in legislation (the *Ontario Police Services Act*); and, finally, Canada's national police service, the RCMP, formally adopted community policing.

Second, anecdotal evidence suggests that the core strategy of problem solving was working well in many cities and that the partnership strategy was evident through the widespread use of police–community consultative committees. Some police touted their own successes by publishing police- or government-sponsored reports, such as one about policing in Edmonton (Koller 1990) and in Montreal (Laudrum 1998). Community policing had gone beyond the stage of experimentation and program demonstration by becoming integrated into the daily operations of policing.

On the other hand, there were still some police services where (1) community policing remained marooned as an add-on program, a sideline on the organization chart; (2) the two core strategies of community policing were often disconnected; (3) the tailoring of a specific package of tactics to specific community needs was not widespread; (4) there was little support for community policing at the working level; (5) too few resources were invested in implementing and maintaining this model of policing; and (6) the integration of community policing into routine police operations is likely more rhetoric than reality.

But, regardless of how well it has been implemented, does community policing work? This question about its effectiveness in reducing and preventing crime is a key question (Rosenbaum 1994). Some critics claim there is very little proof that community policing works. But even if there is such proof, they say that instead of reducing or preventing actual crime, community policing just makes people "feel good" by simply changing their perceptions of crime and level of fear of being personally victimized.

Ideally, well-designed evaluations of the effectiveness of community policing programs would inform the "does it really work" question. While there are few robust evaluations of community policing effectiveness to answer this question (see Leighton 1994), studies of the Windsor Police Service found that community policing did have an impact on crime trends, despite little support by its member officers and mixed attitudes among management (Schneider et al. 2000). One study found that the first police mini-stations and storefront offices in Victoria, B.C., were not authorized to take calls for service from the public or do problem-solving projects (Walker and Walker 1989). Instead, they ended up being no more than stationary "grin and wave squads" or public relations outposts handing out crime prevention brochures, making school visits, or sending police out on patrol.

One of the most rigorous evaluations of a community policing program conducted anywhere is that of the Edmonton Police Service's Neighbourhood Foot Patrol Project, where 21 constables on foot were based in mini-stations strategically located in selected neighbourhoods (Hornick, et al. 1991). This evaluation concluded that the project (1) significantly reduced the number of repeat calls for service in the beat neighbourhoods with foot patrol; (2) improved user satisfaction with police services; (3) improved constables' job satisfaction; and (4) increased constables' knowledge of the neighbourhoods and their problems. This pilot project led to the department-wide implementation of community policing.

An experiment by the New York Police Department during the 1990s provides some insight into the "does it really work" question. Police Commissioner William Bratton claimed that reductions in crime were due to the effectiveness of community policing. He had just taken over the NYPD after significantly reducing crime on the New York subway by applying the broken windows strategy of cleaning up the signs of crime, especially graffiti. Beginning in 1983, the NYPD produced daily crime statistics for each precinct and then compared them in weekly meetings (called *compstats*, an abbreviation of "computer statistics") in order to provide feedback to precinct commanders on the relative success or failure of their problem solving and other community policing exercises. These statistics helped the commanders make decisions about reallocating resources to new crime hot spots at different times and places once previous ones were successfully handled (Silverman 1999).

Critics have suggested, however, that the NYPD emphasis on reducing crime statistics merely encouraged precinct commanders to lower, at almost any cost, the number of crime incidents reported to the police by the public.

Hence, the celebrated *compstat factor* may reflect the manipulation of crime and clearance rates as much as it does the success of problem-solving and related tactics. To further muddy the waters, official rates for serious and violent crime declined for five years in a row across the United States during this same period, not just in New York City. Consequently, it is difficult to untangle all the factors that contributed to a decline in crime. Some of the other factors include more affluent economic conditions, which reduce the motivations for engaging in criminality, as well as an aging society in which there are fewer young males at risk of offending. There were also tougher laws in the U.S., more aggressive law enforcement, more severe sentences, and extensive warehousing of offenders. So the jury is still out as to how much the decline in crime in New York City can be credited to community policing and how much can be attributed to right-wing criminal justice ideology and policies or to broader social trends. Nonetheless, the increasing use of crime analysis based on official crime and other statistics is a welcome trend that further extends the problem-solving strategy towards "evidence-based policing."

THE FUTURE OF COMMUNITY POLICING

In light of changes in public policing in Canada over the past few decades, it is reasonable to ask whether community policing has a future. Looking back, community policing was at its height in the 1980s after which many police forces integrated its two core strategies and multiple tactics into what came to be called *integrated policing*. This development made community policing far less visible as a way of operating and diluted it to a somewhat vague "operational philosophy."

During the 1990s, public policing increasingly focused on the more "serious" crimes, such as drugs and organized crime, which required prioritizing cases based on "criminal intelligence" from a variety of public and confidential sources, thereby earning the label of *intelligence-led policing* (see Deukmedjian and de Lint 2007). Then, in the wake of 9/11 terrorist incidents in 2001, governments panicked in the face of real and imagined national security threats and funded the retrenchment of public police into the traditional model's strategy of reactive policing. North America "circled the wagons" by hardening the borders to create a fortress in the hope of forestalling potential terrorists. As Murphy (2005) notes, Canadian police rapidly became "securitized." So there are signs that the Brown model of traditional policing once again has become the dominant model for policing in Canada.

Looking forward, several broad societal trends are now shaping the future of policing in Canada in even more complex ways than a simple public policy choice between the Blue and the Brown models of policing. Hybrid forms of policing appear to be emerging (Murphy 1998).

First, there is the continuing public expectation that the public police should respond to the needs of vulnerable sectors. In an aging society, isolated seniors turn to the police not only for criminal events but also in response to their fear of being victimized as well as for mundane non-crime matters, rather than to social service agencies and local community institutions. Adding to the core vulnerable populations of the elderly, women, and children as well as troubled youth in contact with the criminal justice system, the rapid increase in the population with mental disorders and challenges places an additional burden on police services. The hollowing out of the mental healthcare system has downloaded this vulnerable population onto police agencies and correctional services, which are generally not well prepared or trained for this challenge. When crisis situations arise, the police response is sometimes the "hammer" of a tactical emergency response unit rather than a more appropriate "social work" response. Indeed, as governments slash budgets of social service agencies that support crime victims, released offenders, etc., in an attempt to balance their overall budgets, there will be increasing pressures for the police to coordinate their efforts with the social support and volunteer sectors to help fill the gaps in demand.

The second broad societal trend raised here is the rapidly transforming, multicultural society in which Canadians of European origin become a minority while those with mother tongues other than the two official languages become a plurality. In an aging society, Canada will rely more on immigration than domestic population growth to sustain its economy and lifestyle. On humanitarian grounds, Canada will likely accept greater numbers of refugees in the face of overseas conflicts and environmental disasters. Consequently, there will be a continuing need for police agencies to better reflect the demographic characteristics of the communities they serve, not just through a gender balance but also through the ethnic and linguistic profile of those communities. Given that, on average, immigrants bring higher levels of education than Canadian-born workers, the needs of police agencies for a more diverse profile and capacity will likely be readily met. The changing multicultural face of communities will eventually be reflected in the changing multicultural face of community policing.

The third social trend addressed here is where the nature of crime and the *modus operandi* of sophisticated criminals is changing in response to the complexities of the information society, to rapidly evolving technologies, to a transnational social and business environment, and to rapidly changing social media. Private information and identity theft, new forms of fraudulent financial instruments, cyber attacks, and transnational organized crime are examples of emerging non-local challenges for public police agencies. To address these challenges, the police are increasingly faced with the need to reach beyond their jurisdictional boundaries to cooperate with other national and international agencies in a variety of ways. This not only involves establishing extra-jurisdictional law enforcement partnerships but also forming networks of national and international communities of practice, professional and business networks, and other extra-local, regional, and international organizations to meet the needs of extra-local, network-based communities. An interwoven "web of policing" (Brodeur 2010) is therefore a rational organizational response by police and security agencies to counteract the complex networks of criminals and criminal organizations and, indeed, to become more effectively organized than transnational organized crime.

Of the social trends selected for discussion here, the final one is the ongoing fiscal crisis of the state at all levels. As one of the big-ticket budget items of federal, provincial, and municipal governments, public policing competes for funding with the other demands, including the escalating demands for healthcare. For both the health and public safety sectors, composed of human services agencies, labour is the largest and fastest-growing cost. Moreover, the budgets of police agencies continue to rise while the need—but not necessarily the public demand—for these services continues to decline in terms of lower crime rates. Indeed, the public police may have priced themselves out of the market for delivering routine policing services to local communities. Sometimes this leads to reduced levels of service. For example, while "efficiently" allocating minimal patrol police numbers to shifts on quiet weekday nights with few emergency response demands, this low "tooth-to-tail" ratio of front-line police to management gives pause to those who prefer a more visible police presence and who raise questions about value for taxpayer dollars. With the growing price of public policing, the notion of affordable or financially "sustainable policing" forces the suppliers of police services and the users of these services to debate hard choices and alternative arrangements.

One option is to push for a division of labour between specialized emergency response agencies. For example, the apparent duplication of services in response to non-crime emergencies may be seen when fire-hall rescue vehicles attend residential crises along with ambulances and police cars. In the same way that mass private space is monitored by private police, the surveillance of mass public space may also be contracted out to private police using motorized patrol and passive technologies such as closed circuit cameras. Often called *tiered policing*, this integration of specialization of routine surveillance, emergency response, and other functions among a variety of public and private agencies would allow for differential pricing of these services and overall lower costs.

Internal tiered policing is also likely to evolve within public police agencies through differential pay scales for a range of police specializations and duties. This is similar to the hospital analogy discussed earlier where general practitioners, specialists, nurses, first responders, and para-professionals are differentially compensated and where there would be a much greater use of civilians for technical services. Under this scenario, newly qualified police officers would serve as "generalist constables" on traffic, routine patrol, and other core duties until their apprenticeship hones them for more demanding responsibilities. With further training and experience they may become "specialist constables" requiring more technical and sensitive skills, including more complex roles such as criminal investigation and major crimes (e.g., drug trafficking and people smuggling), if not community policing. Civilians would do much of the work not requiring peace officer status.

In light of these broad social trends and the developing police response to them, the question remains as to whether community policing or a similar form of public policing emerges to maintain and reproduce order across the varieties of local and non-communities that make up Canadian society. What will the future of policing in Canada look like: the Brown model of traditional policing, the Blue model of community policing, or a broad spectrum of colours reflecting the full variety of policing models?

Further Readings

Brogden, M., and P. Nijhar. 2005. *Community Policing: National and International Models and Approaches*. Portland, Oregon: Willan Publishing.

Murphy, C. 2005. "'Securitizing' Community Policing: Towards an Alternative Canadian Public Policing Model." *Canadian Review of Policing Research* 1.

References

Atherton, W. 1914. *Montreal, 1534–1914. Under British Rule, 1760–1914*, Vol. II. Montreal, QC: S.J. Clarke.

Brodeur, J-P. 1983. "High Policing and Low Policing: Remarks about the Policing of Political Activities." *Social Problems* 30: 507–20.

——— . 2010. *The Policing Web*. New York: Oxford University Press.

Christie, N. 1977. "Crime as Property." *British Journal of Criminology* 17: 1–15.

Deukmedjian, J.E., and W. de Lint. 2007. "Community into Intelligence: Resolving Information Uptake in the RCMP." *Policing and Society* 17, no. 3, 239–56.

Dupont, B. 2004. "Security in the Age of Networks." *Policing and Society* 14, no. 1, 76–91.

Ericson, R. 1982. *Reproducing Order*. Toronto: University of Toronto Press.

Goldstein, H. 1979. "Improving Policing: A Problem-Oriented Approach." *Crime and Delinquency* 25: 236–58.

Greene, J.R., and S. Mastrofski, eds. 1988. *Community Policing: Rhetoric or Reality*. New York: Praeger.

Guth, D.J. 1994. "The Traditional Common-Law Constable: From Bracton to the Fieldings to Canada." In R. Macleod and D. Scheiderman, eds., *Police Powers in Canada*. Toronto: University of Toronto Press.

Hornick, J., B. Burrows, D. Phillips, and B. Leighton. 1991. "An Impact-Evaluation of the Edmonton Neighbourhood Foot Patrol Program." *Canadian Journal of Program Evaluation* 6: 47–70.

Kelling, G., and C. Coles. 1996. *Fixing Broken Windows*. New York: Free Press.

Kelling, G., and M. Moore. 1988. "From Political to Reform to Community: The Evolving Strategy of Police." In J.R. Greene and S.D. Mastrofski, eds., *Community Policing: Rhetoric or Reality*. New York: Praeger.

Koller, K. 1990. *Working the Beat: The Edmonton Neighborhood Foot Patrol*. Edmonton: Edmonton Police Service.

Laudrum, K. 1998. "Measuring the Results of Community Policing." *Canadian Police Chief Magazine*, July, 10–20.

Leighton, B. 1988. "The Concept of Community in Criminology: Toward a Social Network Approach." *Journal of Research in Crime and Delinquency* 25: 351–74.

——. 1991. "Visions of Community Policing: Rhetoric and Reality in Canada." *Canadian Journal of Criminology* 33: 485–522.

——. 1994. "Community Policing in Canada: An Overview of Experience and Evaluations." In D. Rosenbaum, ed., *The Challenge of Community Policing*. Thousand Oaks, CA: Sage Publications.

Murphy, C. 1998. "Policing Postmodern Canada." *Canadian Journal of Law and Society* 13, no. 2.

——. 2005. "'Securitizing' Community Policing: Towards an Alternative Canadian Public Policing Model." *Canadian Review of Policing Research* 1.

Normandeau, A., and B. Leighton. 1990. *The Future of Policing in Canada*. Ottawa: Solicitor General Canada (now Public Safety Canada).

Rosenbaum, R. (Ed.). 1994. *The Challenge of Community Policing: Testing the Promises*. Thousand Oaks, CA: Sage Publications.

Schneider, F., P. Pilon, B. Horrobin, and M. Sideris. 2000. "Contributions of Evaluation Research to the Development of Community Policing in a Canadian City." *Canadian Journal of Program Evaluation* 15: 101–29.

Silverman, E. 1999. *NYPD Battles Crime*. Boston, MA: Northeastern University Press.

Skogan, W., and S. Hartnett. 1997. *Community Policing Chicago Style*. New York: Oxford University Press.

Sparrow, M., M. Moore, and D. Kennedy. 1990. *Beyond 911*. New York: Basic Books.

Walker, C., and G. Walker. 1989. *The Victoria Community Police Stations*. Ottawa: Canadian Police College.

Wilson, J., and G. Kelling. 1982. "Broken windows." *Atlantic Monthly*, March, 29–38.

CHAPTER
12

Who's Policing the Police? Police Governance and Oversight in Canada

Who's policing the police? The public police are supposed to operate under the rule of law. Yet to enforce laws and maintain order they are empowered to act in ways that would be otherwise illegal. Individual officers make choices between often very different courses of action, and are expected to use their own judgment to determine how to intervene, or not, in the lives of citizens. Their right to make these choices is a cornerstone of their ability to do their jobs in a complex and ever-changing environment. At the same time, when they make errors of judgment as individuals or as a group, a democratic society needs to find ways to hold them accountable; and when they abuse their power, there must be the potential for consequences. This chapter explores the paradoxical relationship between police discretion and the governance of police by citizens and governments in Canada, and reviews the available formal and informal mechanisms that keep police forces and officers accountable.

Chris Giacomantonio
RAND Corporation

INTRODUCTION: POLICE WORK AS LEGAL LAW BREAKING

The renowned Canadian criminologist Jean-Paul Brodeur (2010) argued that the public police are a unique organization in society insofar as they are licensed to break a great number of criminal and civil laws, and to use means otherwise prohibited to the public to promote a "defined order" in society. Under certain circumstances they may without fear of sanction drive at high speeds, breach individuals' privacy, engage in fraud and deceit, ingest illegal drugs, use physical force and firearms in public places, and potentially kill citizens in execution of their duties. Somewhat ironically, they do all of this to limit others' transgressions against law and order. Enforcement of the letter of the law is not always in line with maintaining order or indeed facilitating justice, and individual police officers are empowered to determine appropriate action with significant autonomy. The law as it exists provides a great deal of room for interpretation in all but the most straightforward of situations police may deal with. Bittner (1970) famously referred to the police as the people who deal with "something-that-ought-not-to-be-happening-and-about-which-someone-had-better-do-something-now!" There are obviously many situations that fit this description.

The choice to use one, or more, or none of the tactics available to police in a given situation cannot be explained entirely by the law about what the police *should* do. This is because such a body of law does not really exist. While Canadian law regarding police activity includes the federal *RCMP Act* alongside separate provincial police acts for each province; national, provincial, and local policy regulations and codes of conduct outlining rules for officers to follow; and decades of case law relating to police practice, there is no single coherent set of rules that police are required to observe. While both legislation and case law limit police activity in Canada, there remains a very wide and often unpredictable range of possible outcomes in any situation where police are called to act. The ability for police officers to make choices in these situations can be called constabulary independence or, more simply, discretion.

Discretion allows police to work between multiple "soft" and "hard" strategies ranging from community policing, partnerships with social services, and diversion and liaison programs with at-risk individuals, to "intelligence-led" targeted enforcement, zero-tolerance crackdowns, undercover work, deceit, wiretapping, and disruption and harassment of suspect individuals and groups. These are not, of course, mutually exclusive strategies, and represent some among many tools available to police. Discretion also means that police operate outside of the daily control of political actors, including legislators, ministers and deputy ministers, and political parties. As D'Ombrain (2008: 452) notes, the fact of police discretion and "investigative independence" mixed with the need for democratic control of police means that "there is no more complicated or difficult set of relationships in the entire machinery of government than those between governments and police."

Officers in Canada enforce laws under the command of their chief of police at the municipal level, or under the appropriate commissioner or designate at the regional, provincial, or federal level. Political control of police is normally held locally in Canada by police boards or similar bodies, with provincial oversight through the relevant ministry or, in the case of the RCMP, by a complex combination of the Treasury Board, Public Safety Canada, and the federal executive. Police boards and other oversight bodies are usually composed of elected politicians and appointed civilians. However, their authority normally extends only to hiring and firing chief officers and setting budgets and broad policy and priorities (Synyshyn 2008). Daily operations are meant to be at arms-length from the government to ensure, among other things, police officers' abilities to investigate members of political parties, high-ranking government officials, and friends of powerful people without fear of penalty.

Of course, this separation does not always work in practice. Sossin (2004), in a review paper for the Ipperwash Inquiry[1], noted problems of "multiple and overlapping forms of oversight" lacking "overarching vision and coherence" in the relationship between governments and police executives. There have also been many high-profile cases of government interference into police matters, as well as of political uses of police in service of a ruling party or parochial set of interests. This is typified by the activities of the RCMP in the 1970s, who at government behest engaged in a campaign of "provocation, disinformation and unauthorized surreptitious activities against separatist and left-wing groups in Quebec" (D'Ombrain 2008: 460).

While the deployment of police for overtly political ends has since been curtailed, some argue that "political" uses of the police may also include having police control political demonstrations and target individuals and groups engaged in civil disobedience. This still goes on today, as evidenced by the policing of the 2010 G20 Summit in Toronto. As Box 12.1 reveals, police in this case did more than try to keep the peace in a hostile environment; they contributed to disorder and adopted an attitude that equated protest to criminal activity.

However, there is much debate on this point, not least because police are also essential to facilitating protest and dissent in a democratic society, and regularly protect rights to free speech as well (Waddington 1994). Nonetheless, the separation of police from politics (or at least politicians) has been a central tenet in the design of policing within democracies, as it allows police officers to act with discretion—exercising their own judgment, within the broad boundaries of law—in highly complex and unpredictable social situations.

How you feel about discretionary police powers probably relates directly to your estimation of the state's intentions and capacity; if you think the police are the people and the people are the police, as Robert Peel did when he established the first modern Anglo-American police force in 1829 in London, then you probably trust the majority of police decisions in a democratic society. If you feel that the police are inescapably an instrument of a ruling class, you may wish these powers were severely limited (or you may wish they were turned primarily against the powerful, for example, against corporate

BOX 12.1   *Excerpt from* Policing the Right to Protest: G20 Systemic Review Report

Protesters were not the only ones who resorted to violence during the G20. Numerous police officers used excessive force when arresting individuals and seemed to send a message that violence would be met with violence. This reaction created a cycle of escalating responses from both sides.

Once the violence began on Saturday, June 26, police tactics changed. Crowds of protesters were surrounded and contained with no exit routes. The Incident Commander ordered the mass arrests of people at different "hot spots" throughout the city. On several occasions, people who lived in the area but were not part of the protest ended up being surrounded and contained.

Despite clear examples of non-protesters being rounded up, officers refused to let anyone leave, indicating that they were "following orders." The Office of the Independent Police Review Director knows of some occasions where officers on the ground personally removed non-protesters and peaceful protesters and allowed them to go home. Unfortunately, the vast majority of accounts are of officers blindly following orders—even those officers who questioned the orders that were given to them.

The Incident Commander at the MICC [Major Incident Command Centre] referred to crowds of protestors as "terrorists / protestors," leaving the impression that they were criminals. This attitude resulted in the decision to contain and arrest approximately 1,100 people during the summit, most of whom were peaceful protesters. (McNeilly 2012: x)

Source: McNeilly, Gerry. 2012. "Policing the right to protest: G20 Systemic Review Report." Ontario: Office of the Independent Police Review Director.

crime and political corruption). Whether or not you support all police powers as they currently stand in Canada, it is almost impossible to consider the job of policing existing in any form without also allowing operational discretion for those at the front lines of the job.

Mechanisms of Governance

The fact of discretion in police work does not grant police the right to do whatever they want, whenever they want. While police officers may be able to justify a broad swath of action or inaction in their decisions to intervene in the lives of citizens, they must nonetheless act within multiple limits. The current system is by no means perfect. Yet, within the system are various mechanisms that can keep police officers and organizations in line with acceptable police practice in a constitutional democracy. Beyond the limited powers of police boards and other political agencies discussed above, Canadian police may be held to account by disciplinary proceedings, the courts, complaints commissions and commissions of inquiry, informally by other members of their profession, and through emerging forms of accountability including direct community feedback, media scrutiny, and citizen surveillance. It remains an open question how well these measures work in holding police to high standards of practice, but at minimum they provide further checks against unfettered discretion and wanton abuse of power.

Internal Discipline

The first line of defense against police malpractice, abuse of power, or corruption at the more extreme end is normally internal discipline within police organizations. If police officers neglect their duties, act rashly or overzealously, or bring the policing profession into disrepute while on or off duty, their conduct will likely first be reviewed by their direct supervisor and, if it is serious enough, will warrant a disciplinary hearing. Discipline may be recommended by a supervisor or hearing panel, and usually requires the authorization of a chief of police or similarly senior officer. Officers can be disciplined through warnings or suspensions with or without pay, all of which create marks on employment records that can affect promotion and advancement. In more serious cases, organizations can demote officers for poor performance or misconduct, though the latter is far more likely to result in penalty than the former, as officers rarely lose rank for performance-related issues alone (Manning 2010). Finally, of course, police officers can be fired, though in Canada this only happens where officers commit a very serious, near-criminal or criminal breach of the law, and even where convicted of a minor offense an officer may retain his job.

An example of internal discipline can be found in the Box 12.2 excerpt from the Ontario Office of the Independent Police Review Director's Annual Report (OIPRD 2012), where an officer clearly tried to use his position to his advantage, threatened workers, and potentially put children at risk, all in violation of municipal policy. It is a matter of opinion whether 30 hours'—or around three days'—pay is an adequate penalty here, but one cannot imagine a punishment such as this one being a serious deterrent to minor abuses of authority.

Recent developments, such as the case of R. v. McNeil [2], may put pressure on police organizations to take internal discipline more seriously. In McNeil, a drug conviction was overturned on Charter grounds; the investigating officer had drug-related disciplinary marks on his record, which were considered relevant to his reliability as a witness. Consequently, any officers providing evidence now have to actively disclose any disciplinary proceedings against them (past, present, or forthcoming), and these can be used to question officers' credibility in court cases. Testimony of police officers who have been disciplined, however minor the penalties, may thus become impotent in court, and officers who are not reliable in court will not advance in their career. The consequences of McNeil are yet to be fully understood (see also Ives 2009).

BOX 12.2 *Abuse of Power? Ontario Provincial Police and Provincial Constable S.W.*

A complaint was filed in relation to Constable S.W.'s behaviour in an incident at his son's school. Constable S.W.'s wife was attending their son's school to pick him up between the hours of 2 p.m. and 4 p.m. During that time the pick-up and drop-off area at the school was a school bus–only zone and cars were not allowed. The school buses were parked in the bus zone blocking Constable S.W.'s wife's car. His wife spoke with one of the drivers and requested the bus be moved. The driver explained that it was a school bus–only zone and the drivers were not permitted to move the buses. Constable S.W.'s wife informed the bus driver she had called the police. Constable S.W. arrived shortly and asked the driver blocking his wife's car to move. The driver explained that it was against policy to move the buses while children were loading, and buses were not allowed to reverse in a loading zone. Constable S.W. moved his SUV to the centre of the road with lights flashing and ordered the driver to pull forward so his wife could leave. The bus driver did so and Constable S.W.'s wife left. Constable S.W. left the school but subsequently returned and had an argument with another bus driver indicating his displeasure that they would not help his wife. He threatened to write tickets for smoking on school property. Constable S.W. left but later saw one of the bus drivers on the road and pulled the bus over continuing to discuss the incident with his wife. Constable S.W. entered a guilty plea at the hearing and was found guilty of discreditable conduct. He was penalized 30 hours of pay by the hearing officer. (OPIRD 2012: 31–2)

Source: OIPRD. 2012. "Building a solid foundation: 2011–2012 Annual Report." Ontario: Office of the Independent Police Review Director. © Queen's Printer for Ontario, 2012. Reproduced with permission.

The Courts

Marie Manikis, in her contribution to this text, outlined the impact of the *Charter* on police practice. The *Charter* is enabled and enforced by Canada's courts; *Charter* principles are reflected in judges' willingness to include or exclude evidence, convict or acquit accused persons on the basis of police practice, and, in rarer cases, sanction police officers or organizations for their breach of *Charter* duties. The *Charter* is centrally important in public police work and in guiding the thinking of police officers, and has impacted heavily on officers' daily routines (Malm et al. 2005) as well as relationships between prosecution, courts, and the police. There are few more important developments in Canadian history regarding police accountability.

As well as curtailing or enabling police powers, courts can of course also punish individual officers who violate the law in the execution of their duties. However, most police work is never reviewed in court. Police recorded just over two million crimes in 2011 (Brennan 2012), which seems like a lot. But on a per-officer basis that amounts to only about 30 crimes investigated per year, given that we have almost 70,000 officers in Canada (Statistics Canada 2013).

Most of these crimes do not lead to arrest; only about 40 percent of known crimes are solved, and even less of these lead to charges or court cases for various reasons. When police are not arresting people (which is most of the time—generally a good sign in a democratic society), they may still be involved in helping to settle disputes, making decisions not to arrest, or disrupting the lives of suspects through interrogation, stop-and-search, or covert investigation and interdiction activities where no charge or arrest is intended.

Much of police work in any system involves "justice without trial," in Skolnick's (1994) famous phrase, which refers to the consequences of these discretionary decisions. Whose transgressions against law and order police choose to investigate, and whose they let slide on a daily basis, is perhaps the most fundamental choice in how certain people come into the justice system, others end up in diversionary programs, and still others are left without a mark on their record despite contravening the law. The courts may be able to limit or review police activities such as these, but they rarely intervene in police work where criminal charges have not been laid.

Civilian-ish Oversight: Complaints and Investigative Commissions

In most instances where a citizen feels they have been wronged by police conduct, they may have in the past complained directly to the police force in question in the hope that internal discipline processes would suffice. They may also have taken this route because no other meaningful venue for complaint existed. However, most provinces in Canada, as well as the RCMP, now have developed independent review boards, complaints commissions, or other similar mechanisms for reviewing complaints against police officers. Key agencies are listed in Table 12.1.

While the establishment of semi-independent review bodies represents an important step, these are not always effective. Complaints and investigative commissions are not always entirely citizen-led, and some of these agencies are primarily operated by or through police officers who undertake investigations into complaints. In the wake of a spate of police-involved deaths—the most prominent being the October 2007 taser-related death of Polish immigrant Robert Dziekanski at the Vancouver airport—a number of reports criticizing "police investigating police" were subsequently undertaken, including a review by the RCMP's then–Complaints Commissioner (Kennedy 2007). MacAlister (2010) has argued that review boards need to be (a) entirely civilian-led, including civilian investigators with no affiliation with the police; (b) universal in jurisdiction at the provincial level, including ability to investigate the RCMP and non-RCMP police within the same agency; and (c) given full powers of investigation. This is not currently the case.

Regarding (a), most investigation into alleged misconduct by police continues to be done by police. The logic is in many ways the same as within other professional bodies, such as lawyers and doctors, who investigate their own through peer review. In these cases, it is thought that knowledge of the

TABLE 12.1 *Canadian Police Oversight Agencies*

Alberta	Alberta Law Enforcement Review Board
	Alberta Serious Integrated Response Team (ASIRT)
	Calgary Police Commission Edmonton Police Commission
British Columbia	Office of the Police Complaint Commissioner
Manitoba	Manitoba Law Enforcement Review Agency (LERA)
	Manitoba Independent Investigation Unit
New Brunswick	New Brunswick Police Commission
Newfoundland and Labrador	Royal Newfoundland Constabulary Public Complaints Commission
Nova Scotia	Nova Scotia Office of the Police Complaints Commissioner
	Nova Scotia Serious Incident Response Team
Ontario	Special Investigations Unit
	Ontario Office of the Independent Police Review
	Ontario Civilian Commission on Police Services
Prince Edward Island	Office of the Police Commissioner
Quebec	Police Ethics Commissioner
Saskatchewan	Saskatchewan Public Complaints Commission
RCMP (Federal)	Commission for Public Complaints Against the RCMP (CPC)
	Canadian Military Police Complaints Commission (MPCC)

Source: Office of the Police Complaint Commissioner (British Columbia) website, at: https://www
.opcc.bc.ca/outreach/oversight_agencies.html

job can only really be held by people who have done the job. Another, possibly less defensible but pragmatic concern regards sensitive or confidential information; police investigations involve confidential information that is guarded by individual police officers and is essential to the craft of police work. To open up this information to external agencies is seen as an unjustifiable risk to police operations.

As for (b), only the federal Commission for Public Complaints Against the RCMP can investigate complaints against RCMP officers, even if those officers were working at a provincial or municipal level at the time. With respect to (c), even where investigations are done by civilian investigators, these investigators may lack full access to the facts of the case, as police forces often have a choice regarding their level of cooperation and information sharing with the review body. However, recent pressure has resulted in new review structures. Most importantly, it is now normally the case in Canada that instances of serious injury or death in police custody are at least investigated with the assistance of external police agencies, where before they may have been investigated by the force in which the injury or death occurred. As well, in British Columbia—which has the highest number of police-involved deaths in the country in recent years (MacAlister 2010)—the Independent Investigations Office was founded to investigate police-involved deaths or serious harm, with the proviso that its director could never have been a serving police officer. It is worth noting that most of its investigative staff consists of retired police officers, however.[3]

Virtually all complaints commissions and other similar bodies—the world over—have little or no power to order action by police forces. Rather, they bring facts to light, thus improving the transparency of the system, and also make recommendations on potential disciplinary actions or policy reforms. It is still up to the individual police forces to implement these recommendations, or not, which can create skepticism regarding the value of this system of oversight. Such skepticism may be justified in light of statistics from the commissions themselves. Most complaints received by complaints commissions are resolved without any action being taken against the officer or officers who are subject to the complaint. For example, of the 3,468 complaints against police received by OIPRD in 2011–12, 1,692 were "screened out,"[4] and of the remaining cases only 137 were referred to a disciplinary hearing (OIPRD 2012). In British Columbia in 2011, of 1,100 complaints received, only 87 were substantiated by the provincial complaints commission (Police Complaint Commissioner of B.C. 2011).

However, there are (at least) three possible explanations for the disparity between the numbers of complaints and those resulting in disciplinary action. The first, and most critical of the complaints system, is that police complaints commissions are more sympathetic to police than to complainants, and tend to support questionable practice because of an "insider" perspective on policing. The fact that investigators for these commissions are often current or former police officers themselves would lend credence to this point. The second explanation is that most complaints against police are probably better dealt with through other means, such as informal resolutions between the police and the complainant, which is less punitive for the officer and possibly more restorative overall. Indeed, in most provinces, many more complaints are resolved informally than through recommendations for discipline; and informal resolution requires consent of the complainant, suggesting satisfaction of complainants in at least some cases. A third explanation is that citizens who have been arrested feel wronged by the police (even if their arrest was justified), and use the complaints investigation as a way to punish the arresting officer and organization, as well as potentially add weight to claims they may make in court about wrongful treatment by the police. Each of these accounts probably has some merit, and there is no simplistic reading to be made of police complaints statistics.

COMMISSIONS OF INQUIRY

Large-scale or persistent failures of police operations or governance often lead to Commissions of Inquiry, which is something of a Canadian tradition regarding all sorts of government malfeasance. In some instances, these commissions result in significant organizational restructuring. For example, the curiously named *Royal Commission of Inquiry into Certain Activities of the RCMP*, colloquially known as the McDonald Commission (so named due to its Commissioner, Justice McDonald), found that the RCMP's then-existing Security Service was undertaking activities that were unacceptable for a domestic public police force, including domestic espionage and the use of *agents provocateurs* within political groups. In turn, the RCMP was stripped of a significant portion of its security intelligence capacity, and the Canadian Security Intelligence Service, a civilian agency with no enforcement capacity, was created.

Since the McDonald Commission, other commissions have been established with varying results. The Campbell Inquiry, which was held in the wake of Paul Bernardo and Karla Homolka's serial sexual assaults and murders in Ontario in the late 1980s and early 1990s, was concerned with inter-organizational breakdowns in communications between public police forces in Ontario. Due to an inability or unwillingness to cooperate between jurisdictions, Justice Campbell estimated that Bernardo and his accomplice were able to operate for more than two years past the time when Bernardo could have reasonably been identified as the prime suspect (Campbell 1996). A similar review has just taken place in British Columbia regarding B.C.'s Missing Women and the serial killer Robert "Willie" Pickton, where failures in police cooperation, coupled with institutional indifference regarding the largely poor, minority, and female victims in the case, again allowed the prime suspect to operate for years after he became known to police (Oppal 2012). These reports have led to both organizational restructuring and new information management systems in these provinces.

Other commissions have been less successful in promoting change in police practices and organization. For example, in 2007 a commission was created to investigate RCMP mismanagement of its pension and insurance programs. The subsequent Brown Commission report identified major areas of reform for the RCMP, including increasing independence from the federal government and other fundamental changes in RCMP governance. Commissioner Brown declared the management of the RCMP "horribly broken" and in need of major change no later than 2009 (Brown et al. 2007). Since the report, little has been done to implement these recommendations. There have also been a number of commissions of inquiry into wrongful convictions cases in Canada that are dealt with in relevant chapters elsewhere in this textbook, where police acted outside of the law to secure convictions in what is often referred to as "noble cause corruption" (see also Keenan and Brockman 2010).

SOFT POWER: INFORMAL GOVERNANCE MECHANISMS

Outside of formal mechanisms, such as disciplinary action and enforcement of rules to control police forces, there are a number of "soft" approaches that are increasingly important. These come from both inside and outside the occupation.

It has been argued by many who study the police that police officers are governed less by rules, laws, or fear of discipline, and more by internalized or cultural norms (Gordon, Kornberger, and Clegg 2009; Punch 2009). Despite some, and sometimes widespread, misconduct and corruption in police organizations, most police officers, at least in stable democracies, do not engage in excessive abuse of power or use their position for personal gain or graft. Police believe in the job they are doing, take their oath seriously, and keep one another in check to ensure legitimacy in the eyes of the community. The existence of a "blue wall of silence" regarding police misconduct may explain why so few complaints against police lead to serious discipline, but it also masks the fact that police who violate norms of good behaviour are often marginalized within their organizations to the detriment of their careers. This is by no means a perfect or particularly stable system of control, but this aspect of police culture—sometimes referred to as the *constabulary ethic*—is fundamental to understanding why police do not abuse their discretion more often. Such an ethic gives moral strength to the often vague legal structures that allow police to intervene in social situations; it is often the only real protection citizens have when directly confronted with police power.

Police also respond to community feedback received during the execution of their duties. Structured feedback mechanisms include community forums, neighbourhood offices, and police officers with community or school liaison responsibilities. These function to provide information regarding the acceptability of police practices within a community. These can in turn shape police cultural norms, especially to the degree that the police organization subscribes to a community policing ethos. Research also suggests that while police may not respond directly to community feedback in these forums, their attitudes about what constitutes a priority are shaped by community values and demands experienced in everyday interaction (Huey 2007), and that "communities get the policing they want" whether they recognize it or not. The continued importance of community feedback probably contributes to the generally high estimation of the public police in public opinion surveys (see Chapter 1), even within poor or minority neighbourhoods where police are in regular conflict with community members.

Other social factors bear on why police do, or do not, act in accordance with democratic principles such as due process, accountability, and transparency. It is no secret that police are a favourite subject in both news and entertainment media, with cop shows occupying an astonishing amount of daytime and primetime television, and police and crime-related stories often leading in both serious and tabloid newspapers and newscasts. The police are usually portrayed favourably, and police by and large retain control over their representation in mass media (Ericson 1989). However, mass media can also expose problematic police activity, and so this relationship is not only one-way (Mawby 2010).

Further, the advent of Web-based citizen journalism, ubiquitous cellphone cameras, and even the widespread presence of CCTV (closed-circuit television) cameras—often thought of as a policing tool, but equally useful in recording police action—has left cops relatively disempowered in hiding problematic activities when compared to the past. This was made obvious in the 1991 case of Rodney King, the motorist whose brutalization by the Los Angeles Police Department was caught on civilian camera, but the effect is more profound now due to the sheer volume of recording devices. The Dziekanski case in Canada gained international notoriety due in part to a video of the incident taken on the phone of civilian onlooker Paul Pritchard, who made the video available to the mass media. The video contradicted the official police story, and played a part in the resulting inquiry. Organizations such as CopWatch[5] who support videotaping of police encounters, and the use by some police forces of body-worn or vehicle-mounted cameras, increase the visibility of police in the discharge of their duties. This may improve police behaviour, at least in public or potentially public settings.

The fact of the digital record has forever changed the capacity of police as "primary definers" of their public image, although they have increasingly started to employ public relations officers to help them deal with this new form of transparency and regularly embrace websites, blogs, and even Twitter to develop their message on controversial events. Admittedly, citizens may misinterpret the content of videos of police using physical force against citizens, and taken out of context (as well as sometimes accurately in context) these kinds of videos can make police look thuggish or cruel. The violent aspects of the job are not particularly palatable at the best of times, and a video or picture of reasonable force may nonetheless evoke emotional responses. However, it also creates a form of accountability; for example, in a recent Vancouver case, a police officer was videotaped punching a handcuffed—and non-aggressive, if irreverent—man he had arrested for cycling through a red light. A passing driver stopped and recorded the incident on his phone, resulting in criminal assault charges against the officer involved (Canadian Press 2013). These recent developments in digital surveillance thus have the power to protect both law-abiding and law-breaking citizens from excessive force or other violations of their rights at the hands of police.

CONCLUSION

As legal lawbreakers—licensed to enforce the law through means prohibited to most other citizens—public police officers and organizations create a paradox for governance. Which laws they break, and how and why, are left to individual discretion in a system whose rules are unclear. Sometimes, police officers or their organizations will go too far in well-meaning execution of their duties, as in cases of noble cause corruption; or they may break the law in service of political interests, as in the RCMP's campaign against separatist groups in the 1970s. In other cases, they may not go far enough, as in the police failures to pursue Bernardo and Pickton. Finally, they may abuse their office for personal gain, treat citizens with disrespect or unnecessary violence, or believe they are above laws that are simply inconvenient. When this happens, a democratic society requires mechanisms to rein in police practice, create limits to discretion, and enforce consequences for police.

Police accountability processes in Canada differ between provinces, and they are not always effective. There is plenty of room for improvement in the formal system of internal discipline, courts, complaints, and review commissions, and a number of Canadian jurisdictions have implemented measures that increase civilian powers and decrease police insularity. In conjunction with these formal governance mechanisms, police practice is further constrained by officers' own occupational culture, as well as public opinion, community feedback, and citizen surveillance. While police in the public eye may not be breaking the law or overstepping acceptable boundaries of discretion, they may still do things that hurt their image and undermine public confidence. The need to maintain public consent, coupled with police officers' beliefs about their job and the need for good relations with citizens are thus powerful if informal ways of maintaining acceptable police practice.

References

Bittner, E. 1970. *The Functions of the Police in Modern Society*. Chevy Chase: National Institute of Mental Health.

Brennan, S. 2012. "Police-Reported Crime Statistics in Canada, 2011." *Juristat*. Ottawa: Statistics Canada.

Brodeur, J-P. 2010. *The Policing Web*. Oxford: Oxford University Press.

Brown, D.A., L. Black, N. Inkster, R. Drouin, and L. Murray. 2007. *Rebuilding the Trust: Report of the Task Force on Governance and Cultural Change in the RCMP*. Ottawa: Government of Canada.

Campbell, A. 1996. *Bernardo Investigation Review Summary*. Ottawa: Government of Canada.

Canadian Press. 2013. "Ismail Bhaba Charged: Vancouver Police Cyclist Punch Sparks Assault Case." Posted on HuffPost British Columbia, September 13, 2013, at http://www.huffingtonpost.ca/2013/09/13/ismail-bhabha-charged-vancouver-police-cyclist-punch_n_3922262.html, accessed March 8, 2014.

D'Ombrain, N. 2008. "The Federal Government and the RCMP." *Canadian Public Administration* 42, no. 4, 452–75.

Ericson, R.V. 1989. "Patrolling the Facts: Secrecy and Publicity in Police Work." *British Journal of Sociology* 40, no. 2, 205–26.

Gordon, R., M. Kornberger, and S.R. Clegg. 2009. "Power, Rationality and Legitimacy in Public Organizations." *Public Administration* 87, no. 1, 15–34.

Huey, L. 2007. *Negotiating Demands: The Politics of Skid Row Policing in Edinburgh, San Francisco and Vancouver*. Toronto: University of Toronto Press.

Ives, D.E. 2009. "Case Note: *R v. McNeil*—Narrowing the Gap between Disclosure and Production." *The International Journal of Evidence & Proof* 13: 225–31.

Keenan, K.T., and J. Brockman. 2010. *Mr. Big: Exposing Undercover Investigations in Canada*. Black Point, NS: Fernwood Publishing.

Kennedy, P. 2007. "Police Investigating Police—RCMP Investigations into Other RCMP Members in Cases Involving Serious Injury or Death." Ottawa: Commission for Public Complaints against the RCMP.

MacAlister, D. 2010. *Police-Involved Deaths: The Failure of Self-Investigation, Final Report*. Vancouver: British Columbia Civil Liberties Association.

Malm, A., N. Pollard, P.J. Brantingham, P. Tinsley, D. Plecas, P.L. Brantingham, I. Cohen, and B. Kinney. 2005. *A 30 Year Analysis of Police Service Delivery and Costing: "E" Division*. Abbotsford: Centre for Criminal Justice Research.

Manning, P.K. 2010. *Democratic Policing in a Changing World*. Boulder: Paradigm Publishers.

Mawby, R.C. 2010. "Police Corporate Communications, Crime Reporting and the Shaping of Policing News." *Policing and Society* 20, no 1, 124–39.

McNeilly, G. 2012. *Policing the Right to Protest: G20 Systemic Review Report*. Ontario: Office of the Independent Police Review Director.

OIPRD. 2012. *Building a Solid Foundation: 2011–2012 Annual Report*. Ontario: Office of the Independent Police Review Director.

Oppal, W. 2012. *Forsaken: The Report of the Missing Women Commission of Inquiry*. British Columbia: Missing Women Commission of Inquiry.

Police Complaint Commissioner of B.C. 2011. *2011 Year in Review* (Statistical Report). Victoria: Government of B.C.

Punch, M. 2009. *Police Corruption: Deviance, Accountability and Reform in Policing*. Collumpton: Wilan.

Skolnick, J.H. 1994. *Justice without Trial: Law enforcement in Democratic Society*. Oxford: Maxwell Macmillan International.

Sossin, L. 2004. *The Oversight of Executive Police Relations in Canada: The Constitution, the Courts, Administrative Processes and Democratic Governance: Discussion Paper*. Toronto: Government of Ontario.

Statistics Canada. 2013. *Police Officers, by Province and Territory* (CANSIM, Table 254-002). Ottawa: Statistics Canada.

Synyshyn, S. 2008. *Executive Summary: Civilian Oversight of Police in Canada: Governance, Accountability and Transparency.* Winnipeg: Manitoba Association of Rights and Liberties (MARL).

Waddington, P. 1994. *Liberty and Order: Public Order Policing in a Capital City.* London: UCL Press.

Endnotes

1. An inquiry into a controversial police operation; in this case, the Ontario Provincial Police mishandled a native land dispute, which resulted in the death of protester Dudley George by criminal negligence on the part of the police.
2. *R v. McNeil* 2009 SCC 3.
3. To their credit, this is a fact they make explicitly clear on their website (http://iiobc.ca/agency/).
4. "Screened out" means case management staff decided that a complaint was not suitable for investigation.
5. http://www.copwatch.org/

The Decision to Detain or Release: The Nuts and Bolts of Bail

When the state lays a criminal charge against an accused person, there may be reasons to detain that person in custody until the case comes to trial. For example, the individual may be considered a risk to the public, or there may be fears that the accused may not appear for trial. In these cases the accused will be held in custody. The decision to detain or release an individual pretrial is not taken lightly, however. After all, people are considered innocent until and unless the state proves the offence in court of law and beyond a reasonable doubt. In this chapter, Judge Renaud, a very experienced judge who has written a great deal on the criminal justice system in Canada, describes the law and procedures followed in the determination of whether to grant bail.

Judge Gilles Renaud
Ontario Court of Justice

Once they have been charged, most accused persons may safely be allowed to remain in the community until their first appearance in court to face the charge against them. These people are released on bail. For a small minority of people, however, the state may be justified in ordering their detention. The law of bail guides courts in determining whether an accused should be released on bail or detained.

To the public at large, the decision whether an accused who is presumed innocent should be jailed pending trial is made in a matter of seconds without input from the lawyers. At least this is how it appears in each episode of television shows such as *Law and Order*. In accordance with the nature of the criminal charge or the specific province involved, bail decisions are made by a justice of the peace, Provincial Court judge, or Superior Court judge. Some people believe that the court looks at the criminal charge, then the accused, and simply states "bail denied" or "bail granted: one million dollars," and with the bang of the gavel, the matter has ended. Nothing could be further from the reality of bail law in Canada.

In Canada, individual liberty is at the heart of a free and democratic society. Particularly in criminal law, the importance of this fundamental freedom is embodied in the presumption of innocence and more specifically in the notion of bail. Bail is a form of guarantee—usually an amount of money—undertaken by the accused or a surety to guarantee that the person in custody will appear for trial if released. Accordingly, bail must be set by the court at an amount within reach of the accused or the surety. A *surety* is a person who agrees to provide the guarantee for the accused and who is liable for the determined amount. If the accused fails to appear for trial, the money will be forfeit to the state. When a person is arrested for a criminal offence and taken into custody, the police must bring the person before court for a bail hearing, normally within 24 hours or as soon as possible thereafter. Since liberty plays a vital role in Canadian society, bail is usually a way to grant freedom to the accused, who, in exchange, agrees to respect certain conditions while awaiting trial. These conditions aim to ensure that the accused appears in court to face the charge.

To illustrate the importance that liberty plays in this context, Justice Iacobucci of the Supreme Court of Canada, in a famous and controversial case, stated:

> [47] At the heart of a free and democratic society is the liberty of its subjects. *Liberty lost is never regained and can never be fully compensated for*; [Emphasis added] therefore, where the potential exists for the loss of freedom for even a day, we, as a free and democratic society, must place the highest emphasis on ensuring that our system of justice minimizes the chances of an unwarranted denial of liberty.
>
> [48] *In the context of the criminal law, this fundamental freedom is embodied generally in the right to be presumed innocent until proven guilty, and further in the specific right to bail.* [Emphasis added] When bail is

denied to an individual who is merely accused of a criminal offence, the presumption of innocence is necessarily infringed. This is the context of this appeal, one in which the "golden thread" that runs through our system of criminal law is placed in jeopardy. And this is the context in which laws authorizing pre-trial detention must be scrutinized.

In light of Section 11(e) of the *Canadian Charter of Rights and Freedoms,* the court reminds us that judges, as guardians of liberty, must ensure "that pre-trial release remains the norm rather than the exception to the norm, and to restrict pre-trial detention to only those circumstances where the fundamental rights and freedoms of the accused must be overridden in order to preserve some demonstrably pressing societal interest" (*R. v. Hall*). In other words, courts must make every effort—consistent with a concern for public safety—to allow the accused to remain in the community until he is required to answer the charge.

Thus the accused should normally be granted bail, unless detention can be justified by one or more of the following three reasons found in the *Criminal Code*:

Three Grounds for Detention According to the Bail Reform Act

- To ensure that the accused attends court (detention is more likely to be ordered in cases where the accused has a history of failing to attend court or to respect other court orders);
- To protect the public (detention is more likely to be ordered if the accused has a criminal record for similar offences, a history of violence, or poses a risk to the community);
- To maintain confidence in the administration of justice (detention is more likely to be ordered in cases of serious offences, the potential of a lengthy jail term, or when it is justified by the circumstances surrounding the commission of the offence).

These legislative criteria must be taken in context and considered on a case-by-case basis when determining whether to grant or deny bail. Judges therefore have to be vigilant to ensure that a serious charge in and of itself, or a bad record of prior crimes, does not automatically lead to the detention of the accused before a trial is held. In this chapter these elements will be explored in greater detail.

The law of bail is of fundamental importance to all Canadians. My purpose in this chapter is twofold: to pull back the metaphorical veil that too often appears to shroud the pretrial proceedings devoted to the fundamental question of whether an accused person should be at liberty awaiting his criminal trial, and to explain in clear language what takes places in the thousands of bail courts operating each day across this country. Indeed, I aim to identify the "nuts and bolts" of the decision-making process at all levels, including the formal public hearing if one is held. As will be seen, the "law of bail" should be understood to be "the law of discretion" as to the conditions governing the behaviour of persons charged with a criminal act pending their trial.

DISCRETION: A LOOK BACK TO ASSIST IN UNDERSTANDING CONTEMPORARY EVENTS

Since the introduction of bail, legal discretion—instead of the strict words of the law—has been at the heart of much of the decision-making process in bail courts. In *Crankshaw's Magistrates' Manual being a Practical Guide to Police Magistrates and Justices of the Peace* (1921; 3rd ed.), by James Crankshaw, K.C., the author devotes most pages to the "discretion" that judges have regarding bail and states that magistrates—today's justices of the peace and judges—are asked to safeguard the public interest and the reputation of the administration of justice by locking up, until the day of their trial, individuals charged with crimes in situations where their release is thought to be contrary to the common good. Those who can be trusted should be released on conditions. This should be a well-grounded decision based largely on discretion. Despite the strict legislative criteria previously mentioned, judges today continue to rely on discretion when deciding whether to grant bail.

THE PIONEERING WORK OF PROFESSOR FRIEDLAND

Parliament brought numerous changes to the law of bail in 1972, chiefly as a result of the work of Professor Martin L. Friedland (1972), whose study, "Detention Before Trial," made it clear that detention prior to a quick guilty plea was the option chosen by many detainees in order to avoid prolonged pretrial detention. The legislation inspired by this study aimed to change certain practices by adopting measures that are still in place today. These measures relate to granting the police powers to avoid arrest or detention after initiating a legal accusation; the identification of clear legislative reasons establishing when detention is justified; and the onus that usually rests on the Crown to prove that bail should be denied.

1. The Primary Ground for Denying Bail: The Risk of Flight (s. 515(10)(a))

Having introduced the general lines for the exercise of discretion, it will be of assistance to draw direct attention to the legislative rules that are said to guide and control the exercise of that discretion. Parliament has directed that persons accused of crimes be detained pursuant to Section 515(10)(a) of the *Criminal Code* if they are not likely to be present at trial. In other words, the primary justification for refusing to grant bail rests on the common belief that judging from the person's record, past, contemporary actions, and possible lengthy jail period, the accused is at risk of fleeing the country or town.

Based on the severity of the offence and the limited spaces for detention, an accused with no prior record who faces a modest fine for a minor theft will not be detained no matter how likely it is that he will be convicted; on the other hand, a person accused of terrorism whose lifetime record displays an unrelenting crusade against state authorities, who has no ties to Canada, and who faces a lifetime jail sentence is unlikely to wish to attend a trial that will likely result in a finding of guilt. In fact, the courts will primarily examine elements such as the nature of the allegation; the record (if any), with particular attention to the accused's history of compliance with court orders; the strength of the accusation; the ties to the community; the likely sentence; and other factors, such as the possibility of living outside Canada. All these factors will be taken into account by the court when determining whether to detain or release the accused.

2. The Second Ground: The Risk of Further Crimes (s. 515(10)(b))

Parliament has ordered for reasons of public safety that all offenders ought to be granted bail, assuming they are not shown to be undue flight risks, unless "the detention is necessary for the protection or safety of the public, including any victim of or witness to the offence, having regard to all of the circumstances including any substantial likelihood that the accused will, if released from custody, commit a criminal offence or interfere with the administration of justice...."

In other words, courts are tasked with the unenviable duty of weighing the likelihood of further misconduct and assessing the risk that further crimes will be committed based on previous criminal charges or the accused's history. Once again, the risk analysis must take into account the legislative criteria but also the contextual background, including the limited number of "remand" places, the jail beds for those not yet convicted, and the constitutional limits briefly pointed out in the opening paragraphs and to be discussed below.

By contextual background I refer to the obvious fact that many offenders may breach their bail conditions because they are fighting addictions, mental illness, inadequate socialization in childhood, extreme poverty, racism, and a host of other "sad life" deficits. These problems make it harder for individuals to comply with bail conditions such as a curfew. Furthermore, many of the anticipated breaches may be of a minor nature—petty mischief, causing a disturbance, and so on.

Quite often, the fact of the matter is that an offender is granted two chances—two "strikes," if you will—prior to having the bail revoked, unless the matter is quite serious. In most of these instances, the prosecution bears the practical (if not the legal) onus of satisfying the justice of the peace or the judge that "old Charlie" or "poor Mary" should be "jugged" (i.e., detained in custody) until the trial, especially if the likely remand period will far exceed the anticipated sentence.

The best judicial example of the discretion conferred upon judicial officers tasked with deciding whether to grant bail under this provision is found in *R. v. Morales*, [1992] 3 S.C.R. 711. Former Chief Justice Lamer of the Supreme Court of Canada stated at page 737:

> … Bail is not denied for all individuals who pose a risk of committing an offence or interfering with the administration of justice while on bail. Bail is denied only for those who pose a "substantial likelihood" of committing an offence or interfering with the administration of justice, and only where this "substantial likelihood" endangers "the protection or safety of the public." Moreover, detention is justified only when it is "necessary" for public safety. It is not justified where detention would merely be convenient or advantageous. Such grounds are sufficiently narrow to fulfil the first requirement of just cause under s. 11(e).

However, despite this position, the legislation requires for certain more severe allegations—namely, violent offences involving firearms, murder, or drug trafficking—that the accused demonstrate that his freedom is justified pending trial. This is known as a "reverse onus." This means that although the onus is usually upon the state to justify the detention of the accused, for certain cases the obligation is upon the accused to justify his release on bail.

In discharging this legislative function, Parliament is merely seeking to protect the public by supporting the common belief that the more serious the accusation is, the greater are the chances of achieving public protection by detaining the accused. Stated otherwise, the lawmakers have chosen to place upon the accused, and not the state, the burden of demonstrating that detention is not required in the circumstances. This "reversal of onus" is in keeping with the traditional view that serious allegations of misconduct be treated with great concern for the public interest and also with the commonsense view that the accused is better placed to explain how her interim liberty is consonant with public safety. The reality is that most offenders are released pending trial, notwithstanding the serious allegations they face, as that is clearly Parliament's intention and consistent with the *Charter*, as will be discussed presently.

3. The Third Ground: Public Confidence in Justice (s. 515(10)(c))

As discussed at length in *Hall*, Parliament intended that a limited number of situations should result in the accused's detention even though the two first criteria that justify detention—namely, the risk of flight (515(10)(a)) and the risk of further crimes (515(10)(b))—have not been met. The remaining criteria that justify detention read as follows:

> (c) if the detention is necessary to maintain confidence in the administration of justice, having regard to all the circumstances, including (i) the apparent strength of the prosecution's case, (ii) the gravity of

the offence, (iii) the circumstances surrounding the commission of the offence, including whether a firearm was used, and (iv) the fact that the accused is liable, on conviction, for a potentially lengthy term of imprisonment or, in the case of an offence that involves, or whose subject-matter is, a firearm, a minimum punishment of imprisonment for a term of three years or more.

Similarly to reverse onus, this exceptional provision reverses the traditional exercise of discretion and appears to reflect the view that certain alleged offenders should be detained with a view to fostering public confidence in the administration of justice.

SECTION 518: EVIDENCE AT A HEARING INCLUDING HEARSAY

According to Section 518 of the *Criminal Code*, the justice who presides over the hearing may receive and base her decision on evidence considered credible or trustworthy. This allows the parties to introduce hearsay evidence. *Hearsay evidence* is defined as information that is not witnessed directly by the person testifying. For example, police officer A may testify that civilian B told her that her husband slashed her repeatedly in the torso area with a Rambo-style knife. The police officer did not actually see the assault—he is simply testifying about what the civilian told him regarding the knife attack.

Crown practices can vary considerably in each case and in practice must deal with the fact that most witnesses are not available to testify since hearings are often delayed or adjourned and at times are suspended after having started (see discussion in Weinper and Sandler 2003).

On the ground, technology is influencing the way information is received by courts. As a matter of practicality, many Crown and defence witnesses, particularly experts, testify using new forms of technology, thereby considerably reducing costs and delays. In addition, delays between the hearing of the original bail application and the appeal from the denial or refusal of bail are being reduced now that transcripts are being produced more quickly electronically. For example, a CD recording of earlier proceedings can be presented on the day the request is made (see *R. v. Pennell*).

SECTION 516: THE THREE-DAY RULE AND OTHER CAUSES OF DELAY

The long delay the accused often faces in custody before having a bail hearing is a problem the criminal justice system must address. Hamlet spoke of "the law's delays," and this aptly summarizes the plight of accused persons awaiting trial. Indeed, in more and more cases the accused is requesting that proceedings be ended (a judicial stay of proceedings) because of unreasonable delay before a bail hearing. In *R. v. Zarinchang,* a trial judge granted an order under the *Canadian Charter of Rights and Freedoms* staying the proceedings against Mr. Zarinchang on the ground that the judicial system had failed to provide him with a bail hearing for some 24 days from the time of his arrest. The trial judge further ordered the Crown to pay the court costs of the respondent. The Ontario Court of Appeal reviewed the decision and noted that stays may be granted in exceptional cases for such difficulties. The law is still evolving.

LEGAL MANOEUVRING AS A SUBSTITUTE FOR LEGAL COMPLIANCE WITH RULES

Another cause of delay relates to the tactics used by the two parties—the accused and the state. Each side seeks to gain a tactical advantage for the forthcoming trial as a result of, first, the emphasis placed on discretion in the legislation, and, second, the existence of the legal factor often referred to as "the strength of the Crown's case," by which the ultimate justice of pretrial detention is often justified. In most hearings that deal with serious accusations and grave circumstances, such as allegations of sexual violence, murder, or large-scale drug trafficking, lawyers wish to position themselves well to confront the other side's case and obtain the detention or release of the person in question. In most hearings, though, the result can be described as follows: the accused will be detained due to her record of previous breaches, *or* will be released based on the absence of a serious record or the presence of a sound plan of supervision reducing to an acceptable level the risk of further offending conduct.

A recent example of interest in the nuts-and-bolts element of tactical advantage in bail hearings can be found in *R. v. Badgerow*, in which the accused was charged with first-degree murder. One legal question that the court had to decide was whether the Crown attorney would be allowed to stop the investigating officer from being closely interrogated by counsel for the defence. As noted earlier, the *Criminal Code* allows the parties to lead hearsay testimony—that is to say, information that the witness did not perceive directly. The Crown often prefers to do so, for it is not realistic to have police officers or civilian witnesses appear in the bail court due to time constraints and scheduling concerns (a further topic of discussion). In *Badgerow*, the Crown did not wish the chief investigator to testify; but it was not because of these concerns, but rather to impede the defence counsel's ability to probe for weak points.

The judge referred to *R. v. John*, in which the defence argued that the Crown should be required to bring the officer in charge of the case to give evidence at the bail hearing. The Crown stated that a police officer without direct involvement in the investigation could present evidence at the bail hearing by reading aloud from the witness stand a statement or synopsis prepared by one or more of the officers directly involved in the investigation. In rejecting the Crown's position, Justice Casey Hill stated that according to paragraph 64:

> Where oral evidence is required, according to the submissions of certain Crown counsel in the history of this case, everything should be

done by the government to avoid calling a witness with any direct or personal knowledge of the investigation in order to prevent the defence from having the opportunity to cross-examine an individual who is likely to be a witness at trial. *While this "free crack at the witness" philosophy has meritorious attraction in the case of victims or complainants, beyond this it has little to recommend it.* [Emphasis added] Indeed, given the contribution of meaningful cross-examination to the truth-seeking process, the policy approach of conscripting an uninformed reader ("any" officer or a "court officer" or "court security officer") apart from serving convenience can, in certain circumstances, amount to a deliberate artifice designed to frustrate the court's pursuit of the truth. The Court has the authority to control questioning within relevant limits.

As a general rule, most practices during bail hearings serve tactical purposes instead of addressing whether the person accused should be detained or not. This development is a direct result of the highly discretionary nature of interpretations of the rules governing bail—notably, the importance given to the strength of the Crown's case, which is a highly illusory element. Parliament might be well served to consider removing this element from consideration in order to reduce the length of these hearings.

BAIL DECISIONS ON REVIEW: FURTHER EXERCISE OF DISCRETION

I turn now to the subject of appeals or reviews of bail decisions. Parliament has enacted an elaborate set of rules for reviewing the merits of earlier decisions, and it will suffice for present purposes to note that the reviewing court is granted a great deal of discretion. Guidelines on the review of bail orders are provided in *R. v. Moss* and suggest that a judge who reviews the bail decision must take a new look at the evidence submitted before the original judge and take into account any additional evidence offered by the parties. Once again, the judge may exercise discretion in deciding whether the accused has demonstrated that the previous decision should be overruled. The discretion, however, must be reasonable and fair to both parties.

BAIL DOES NOT AMOUNT TO FREEDOM: LIMITED LIBERTY IS THE NORM

Space constraints limit the discussion of this subject, but it must be understood that a decision to liberate an accused from custody pending trial (or appeal) does not result in the granting of freedom. On the contrary, most detainees who are released on bail are bound by stringent rules and often guarantee their pledge of good behaviour by means of monetary deposits and charges against real property. Unfortunately, most court dockets are replete with accusations of breaching these varied obligations. The public is regularly informed by the media about the electronic surveillance—including in-house cameras and electronic tagging—that many individuals under security certificates face. This practice may one day become the norm in bail decisions due to the lower costs entailed.

CONCLUSION

When a lawyer or a judge refers to "the law of bail," it sometimes puts a smile on justice officials' faces. Some are of the view that there is very little law involved around bail: at best, the legal requirements of the *Criminal Code* are viewed as providing the formal context to the proceedings, but local practices and experiences dominate the actual decision making. Indeed, most decisions affecting the potential release of a detained individual are made by police officers and not by lawyers or members of the judiciary. Also, when matters of release are debated, this tends to be on a case-by-case basis, leaving aside the legal jargon, to ensure that proceedings can be followed by lay witnesses, notably the families of the accused and victims.

Bail law should be a priority, given the fundamental issues of personal liberty and public safety. The law in this area should undergo an important reform, and the first element to be considered might well be the discretionary nature of decisions made whether to free (or not) a detained person accused of a crime.

Further Readings

Coughlan, S. 2009. *Criminal Procedure.* Toronto: Irwin Law.

Salhany, R. 2009. *Canadian Criminal Procedure.* 6th ed. Aurora: Canada Law Book.

Trotter, G. 1999. *The Law of Bail in Canada.* 2nd ed. Toronto: Carswell.

References

Crankshaw, J. 1921. *Crankshaw's Magistrates' Manual.* 3rd ed. Toronto: Canada Law Book.

Friedland, M. 1972. *Detention Before Trial.* Toronto: University of Toronto Press.

Trotter, G. 1999. *The Law of Bail in Canada.* 2nd ed. Toronto: Carswell.

Weinper, F., and M. Sandler. 2003. *Criminal Procedure Cases, Notes, and Materials.* 2nd ed. Toronto: Butterworths.

Cases

R. v. Badgerow, 2010 ONSC 932

R. v. Hall, [2002] 3 S.C.R. 309

R. v. John, [2001] O.J. No. 3396

R. v. Morales, [1992] 3 S.C.R. 711

R. v. Moss (2003), 229 Nfld. & P.E.I.R. 67

R. v. Pennell, [2006] N.J. No. 321, 2006 NLTD 185, 261 Nfld. & P.E.I.R. 339

R. v. Zarinchang, 2010 ONCA 286

CHAPTER 14

Plea Bargaining

Judges are often criticized for imposing lenient sentences, especially for crimes of violence (although the news media do not always give the full story). Another important source of public dissatisfaction concerns the practice known as *plea bargaining*. Many people were outraged when Karla Homolka was sentenced to only 12 years in prison for her role in the Bernardo murders. That sentence, which was universally denounced as too lenient, came about as a result of a plea bargain. As with sentencing, however, public perceptions of this phenomenon may well be at odds with reality. We should not let individual examples of plea bargaining that led to unpalatable consequences determine our reaction to all instances in which discussions take place between the Crown and the counsel for the accused. As this reading makes clear, plea bargaining involves more than a simple exchange in which the offender receives a lenient sentence for having agreed to plead guilty.

Simon N. Verdun-Jones
Simon Fraser University

Although the criminal trial is seen by many as occupying a pivotal position in the criminal justice system, the reality is that only a small minority of criminal cases in Canada proceed to a trial. Indeed, in 2008–9, 91 percent of all adult cases in Canadian criminal courts were settled without a trial (Thomas 2010). In about one-third of criminal cases, the charges are stayed (suspended for up to a year), withdrawn, dismissed, or discharged (primarily because there is insufficient evidence to proceed or because new evidence comes to light that suggests that the accused person will not be found guilty). However, the most common reason for a case not proceeding to a trial is the entry of a guilty plea. In 2008–9, 59 percent of accused persons who appeared in Canadian adult courts pleaded guilty (Thomas 2010). It is generally accepted that a significant percentage of these guilty pleas are the result of a so-called plea bargain between the prosecuting and defence lawyers, although the precise extent of the practice has not been documented by empirical research (Boyce 2013; Canadian Sentencing Commission 1987; Verdun-Jones and Tijerino 2005).

For many years, plea bargaining has been one of the most controversial—and, perhaps, least understood—practices in the Canadian criminal justice system (Griffiths and Verdun-Jones 1994, 317; Lippke 2011; Piccinato 2004). For criminal justice researchers, plea bargaining is a compendious term that describes a broad range of behaviours that may occur among actors in the criminal court system (Verdun-Jones and Hatch 1987, 1). The police, Crown counsel, and defence counsel may engage in conduct that ranges from simple *discussions* through to *negotiations* and on to concrete *agreements*, all of which are perceived to be binding on the parties. Of course, discussions and negotiations may not ultimately lead to any form of agreement between the parties; nevertheless, these activities have generally been considered by researchers to constitute components of the practice of plea bargaining (Griffiths and Verdun-Jones 1994, 318). In order to provide a clear focus for discussion, this chapter centres on the concept of a *plea agreement,* which constitutes the outcome of a successful process of negotiation between the Crown and the defence counsel.

One of the most useful definitions of *plea agreement* was furnished by the Law Reform Commission of Canada (1989, 3–4), which stated that a plea agreement is "an agreement by the accused to plead guilty in return for the prosecutor's agreeing to take or refrain from taking a particular course of action" (see also Cohen and Doob 1990, 85). The term *plea agreement* is more appropriate than *plea bargain* because, in Canada, there is no guarantee that any agreement will ultimately be carried into effect by the sentencing judge, who is not bound by any promises made by the Crown to the defence.[1]

Furthermore, some researchers have questioned whether the term *plea negotiations* is particularly appropriate, given the realities of the criminal justice process. For example, Ericson and Baranek (1982) asserted that the word *negotiate* is not meaningful in light of the stark imbalance of power between the police and the Crown on the one hand and the defendant on the other. These researchers argued that it is more realistic to view the accused's decisions within the criminal justice system as "coerced" or "manipulated" and that, therefore, the accused will scarcely perceive any accommodation with the Crown as constituting a genuine "bargain" (see also Brockman 2010; Caldwell 2011; McCoy 2005).

However, assuming that it is feasible for the Crown and the defence counsel to enter into a *plea agreement*, what may the Crown offer in order to persuade the defendant to plead guilty? Broadly speaking, the promises that may be made by Crown counsel fall into three overlapping categories: (1) promises relating to the nature of the charges to be laid (*charge bargaining*); (2) those relating to the ultimate sentence that may be meted out by the court (*sentence bargaining*); and (3) those relating to the facts that the Crown may bring to the attention of the trial judge (*fact bargaining*).

These three categories of plea bargaining encompass a considerable variety of promises that the Crown may offer the accused. For example, Verdun-Jones and Hatch (1985, 74–5) set out the following list of possible promises and agreements:

1. Charge bargaining
    (a) Reduction of the charge to a lesser included offence;
    (b) Withdrawal or stay of other charges, or the promise not to proceed with other charges;
    (c) Promise not to charge friends or family of the defendant; *or*
    (d) Promise to withdraw a charge in return for the defendant's undertaking to enter into a peace bond.[2]
2. Sentence bargaining
    (a) Promise to proceed summarily rather than by way of indictment;
    (b) Promise to make a specific sentence recommendation;
    (c) Promise not to oppose defence counsel's sentence recommendation;
    (d) Promise to submit a joint sentencing submission;
    (e) Promise not to appeal against sentence imposed at trial;
    (f) Promise not to apply for a more severe penalty (e.g., by not giving notice to seek a higher range of sentence based on the accused's previous conviction based on s. 727 of the *Criminal Code*);
    (g) Promise not to apply to the trial court for a finding that the accused is a dangerous offender (s. 753 of the *Criminal Code*) or a long-term offender (s. 753.1 of the *Criminal Code*);
    (h) Promise to make a representation as to the place of imprisonment, type of treatment, etc.; *or*
    (i) Promise to arrange the sentence hearing before a particular judge.

3. Fact bargaining
   (a) Promise not to "volunteer" information detrimental to the accused during the sentencing hearing;
   (b) Promise not to mention a circumstance of the offence that may be interpreted by the judge as an aggravating factor (see, e.g., the aggravating factors listed in s. 718.2(a) of the *Criminal Code*).*

THE RESPONSE OF CANADIAN JUDGES TO PLEA NEGOTIATIONS

Over the past 40 years, the extent to which the courts have been willing to accept plea negotiations as a legitimate component of the system of criminal justice in Canada has changed tremendously (Griffiths and Verdun-Jones 1994, 319–22; Verdun-Jones and Tijerino 2001, 2004, 2005). In 1995, the Supreme Court of Canada roundly endorsed the view that plea bargaining was indispensable to the functioning of the Canadian criminal justice system. Indeed, in *R. v. Burlingham* (1995, para. 23), Justice Iacobbucci stated:

> To the extent that the plea bargain is an integral element of the Canadian criminal process, the Crown and its officers engaged in the plea bargaining process must act honourably and forthrightly.

There is little doubt that the tolerant stance adopted by the Supreme Court of Canada toward the practice of plea negotiations was firmly embraced by the appellate and trial courts of the various Canadian provinces and territories. For example, in 2001, the B.C. Court of Appeal placed its seal of approval on plea negotiations and sent a clear signal to the trial courts that, since plea bargaining is vital to the efficient operations of criminal justice, trial courts should generally endorse the contents of plea agreements entered into by Crown and defence counsel. Indeed, in *R. v. Bezdan* (2001, para. 15), Madam Justice Prowse stated:

> It is apparent that the administration of criminal justice requires cooperation between counsel and that the court should not be too quick to look behind a plea bargain struck between competent counsel unless there is good reason to do so. In those instances in which the sentencing judge is not prepared to give effect to the proposal, I also agree that it would be appropriate for that judge to give his or her reasons for departing from the "bargain."

Why have the courts been willing in more recent years to accept the legitimacy of so-called plea bargaining in spite of its somewhat tarnished public image? The major reason seems to be pragmatic: namely, there is a perception among many judges and prosecutors that without a steady stream of guilty pleas, the criminal court system would collapse under the weight of a massive

---

* Library and Archives Canada/Plea Bargaining and Sentencing Guidelines/AMICUS 8304963/P. 74–75. © Government of Canada. Reproduced with the permission of Library and Archives Canada (2014).

backlog of delayed trials (Di Luca 2005; Lafontaine and Rondinelli 2005). In addition, the entry of a guilty plea "alleviates the workload of prosecutors, reduces the need for judicial resources and courtroom facilities and decreases all the other expenses necessitated by a trial" (Piccinato 2004). Judges may also support the practice of plea negotiations because a guilty plea will spare traumatized victims from the ordeal of testifying in a trial (Piccinato 2004).

The perception that plea negotiations are necessary was strongly rein-forced by the report of the Martin Task Force (Ontario Attorney General 1993), which was established to devise remedies for what was considered to be a serious crisis in the Ontario court system in the early 1990s. The Task Force recommended that, where appropriate, defendants should be routinely encouraged to plead guilty through the offer of sentence discounts (Roach 1999, 98–9). To this end, trial judges were exhorted to participate in pretrial conferences that would facilitate plea negotiations—primarily by giving an indication of the perceived appropriateness of any recommended sentence. Roach (1999, 99) concluded that the report of the Martin Task Force consti-tuted powerful evidence that "plea bargaining" in Ontario "was no longer a 'dirty secret' hidden in the corridors of the courtroom but was now openly facilitated in the judge's office."

It is significant that, in the same year as the release of the Martin Report, the Crown in Ontario negotiated a plea agreement that attracted a consider-able degree of public criticism (McGillivray 1998). In the notorious case of Karla Homolka (1993), the Crown accepted a plea from Homolka to a charge of manslaughter and advanced a joint sentencing submission to the effect that the accused should be sentenced to a term of imprisonment of 12 years. The Crown took the view that it was necessary to offer this plea bargain to Homolka, who was considered a willing accomplice to the killings of Kristen French and Leslie Mahaffy by her husband, Paul Bernardo. At the time the plea agreement was made, Crown counsel was apparently convinced that without Homolka's testimony against her husband, it would not be possible to convict Bernardo of the murders. In response to the public expressions of anger at the perceived lenience of Homolka's sentence, an independent inquiry was established to investigate the circumstances underlying the Homolka plea bar-gain. Ultimately, the inquiry found that, given its knowledge of the circum-stances at the time, the Crown had absolutely no choice but to enter into the plea agreement with Homolka's counsel if it wished to ensure the conviction of Paul Bernardo (Galligan 1996, 215–18; Piccinato 2004)[3]. There was wide-spread criticism of the sentence that was jointly recommended by the Crown and the defence; nevertheless, the *Homolka* case shows the extent to which plea negotiations had become accepted as a necessary—albeit somewhat unattractive—element in the administration of justice in Canada. Indeed, in *Boudreau v. Benaiah* (2000), the Ontario Court of Appeal upheld a trial court's ruling that an accused person was entitled to receive substantial damages from his counsel because the latter failed to properly communicate with him the contents of a proposed plea agreement with the Crown.

The extent to which Canadian courts have accepted the reality of plea negotiations is also demonstrated by their willingness to accept joint sentencing submissions advanced by both the Crown and the defence counsel (Manson 2001, 204–5). It is significant that joint sentencing submissions are generally predicated on the acceptance of a plea agreement by the accused. In *R. v. G.W.C.* (2000), the Alberta Court of Appeal forcefully articulated the view that trial courts should be reluctant to undermine plea negotiations by rejecting a joint sentencing submission that has been agreed upon by both Crown and defence counsel. However, it is important to recognize that Canadian courts have emphasized that sentencing judges do retain the discretion to reject a joint sentencing submission when it would not be in the interests of justice to do so.

SHOULD PROSECUTORS BE ABLE TO REPUDIATE A NEGOTIATED PLEA AGREEMENT?

It is clear that judges are not bound by any plea agreement reached between Crown and defence counsel. However, should the Crown be able to renege on an agreement reached with an accused person? If the Crown does repudiate a plea agreement, the accused person is placed in an extremely disadvantageous position because she has admitted factual guilt and her defence counsel will be severely constrained in mounting a viable defence, should the accused person wish to plead not guilty at trial. Indeed, as Linds (2012, 295) points out, "Crown withdrawal from a plea bargain is rare, but it can cause great prejudice to the accused and significantly undermine public confidence in the administration of justice."

In *R. v. Nixon* (2012), the Supreme Court of Canada ruled that, while it should be a rare occurrence, the Crown does indeed have the discretionary power to repudiate a plea bargain. In this case, the accused person had driven through an intersection, struck another vehicle, and killed a husband and wife, as well as injuring their young child. Crown counsel entered into a plea agreement in which the very serious *Criminal Code* charges of dangerous driving causing death/bodily harm and impaired driving would be dropped in exchange for the accused pleading guilty to the relatively minor provincial charge of careless driving under the Alberta *Traffic Safety Act*. There was also an agreement to make a joint sentencing submission for a fine of $1,800. Crown counsel made this agreement because he believed that there were serious flaws in the case against the accused person and that a conviction of the *Criminal Code* charges would be unlikely. However, Crown counsel's superior in the Office of the Attorney General disagreed with the assessment of the strength of the Crown's case and expressed the view that "a plea to careless driving in the circumstances was contrary to the interests of justice and would bring the administration of justice into disrepute" (para. 10). Crown counsel was ordered to withdraw the "resolution agreement" and proceed with the dangerous driving charges under the *Criminal Code*.

The Supreme Court of Canada affirmed (para. 63) the importance of plea agreements to the criminal justice system:

> As everyone agrees, it is of crucial importance to the proper and fair administration of criminal justice that plea agreements be honoured. The repudiation of a plea agreement is a rare and exceptional event.

The Supreme Court ruled that the repudiation of a plea agreement falls within the broad scope of the prosecutor's legitimate discretionary powers and, therefore, is not reviewable by the courts unless the prosecutor has behaved in a manner that abuses the process of the court:

> In the absence of any prosecutorial misconduct, improper motive or bad faith in the approach, circumstances, or ultimate decision to repudiate, the decision to proceed with the prosecution is the Crown's alone to make. (para. 68)

On the basis of the facts in the *Nixon* case, the Supreme Court ruled that the repudiation of the plea agreement by the Crown had not compromised the fairness of Nixon's trial and that there had not been any unfair or oppressive conduct by the Crown. Undoubtedly, the specific facts in the Nixon case were such that the public might well have lost confidence in the integrity of the judicial system if the plea agreement had been honoured by the Crown. The accused's conduct had caused the death of a mother and father and injured their child: a plea of guilty to a relatively minor provincial offence and a fine of $1,800 would undoubtedly have failed to recognize the catastrophic nature of the consequences of the accused's actions.

While the Crown may repudiate a plea agreement, it has been pointed out that it is very difficult for an accused person to do so by appealing a conviction that occurred as the result of a plea of guilty (Lippke 2013). This is problematic because one of the dangers associated with the practice of making plea agreements is that innocent accused persons may plead guilty in order to avoid the risk of a severe sentence if convicted at trial or because they may prefer to "get it over with" or to avoid a lengthy period of pretrial incarceration (Brockman 2010; Caldwell 2011; Jones 2011; Lippke 2012, 2013; Piccinato 2004; Sherrin 2012).

THE LACK OF A FORMAL PROCESS FOR REGULATING PLEA NEGOTIATIONS IN CANADA

The Canadian judiciary has accepted that plea negotiations play a significant role in the efficient administration of justice and has embraced sentencing policies that largely give effect to agreements negotiated by Crown and defence counsel. Yet despite the recommendations of the Canadian Sentencing Commission (1987) and the Law Reform Commission of Canada (1989), there is still no formal process that requires Canadian courts to scrutinize the contents of a plea bargain and to ensure that there is adequate protection for the rights and interests of all the affected parties—the Crown, the accused, the victim(s), and society in general (Verdun-Jones and Tijerino 2005).

In contrast, in the federal and state courts of the United States, trial judges are required to scrutinize plea agreements between the prosecuting and defence attorneys and have the power to accept or reject them (Bibas 2011; Levenson 2013; Pan and Kaiser 2001; Herman 2004). Judges are expected to examine the basic facts surrounding the charges laid against the accused and to consider the interests of all the affected parties, including society in general, the justice system, the accused, and the victim(s) of the offences (Verdun-Jones and Tijerino 2001, 2004). In many American jurisdictions, the victim of an offence is entitled to provide input to the court during a plea agreement hearing, although in no jurisdiction is the victim given a right of veto over a proposed agreement (U.S. Department of Justice 2002). Judges do not involve themselves in the negotiation process; their power is limited to accepting or rejecting the proposed plea agreement. The major advantage of this procedure is its transparency, since the existence of the plea agreement is openly acknowledged and is usually examined in open court. Furthermore, plea agreements are, by law, regulated by the judiciary.

Canada's *Criminal Code* (s. 625.1) does provide for formal pretrial hearings before a judge in order "to consider the matters that, to promote a fair and expeditious hearing, would be better decided before the start of the proceedings, and other similar matters, and to make arrangements for decisions on those matters" (Piccinato 2004). At these hearings, a judge may facilitate the making of a plea agreement by indicating the likely nature and extent of the sentence, should the accused person plead guilty. However, these pretrial hearings are not held for the specific purpose of scrutinizing and regulating a proposed plea agreement (Brockman 2010). Indeed, the *Criminal Code* does not require that the existence of a plea agreement be made known to the court in the course of such hearings; nor does the *Code* impose a duty on trial judges to investigate the circumstances underlying a plea agreement, if it comes to their attention that an agreement has, in fact, been reached between Crown and defence counsel.

Since 1992, the *Criminal Code* has required that a trial judge take steps to ensure that an accused person who pleads guilty is doing so voluntarily. More specifically, Section 606(1.1) requires that before accepting a plea of guilty, the trial judge must first be satisfied that the accused person is pleading guilty voluntarily and that he "understands that the plea is an admission of the essential elements of the offence, the nature, and consequences of the plea, and that the court is not bound by any agreement made between the accused and the prosecutor." Clearly, Section 606(1.1) only provides protection for the rights of the accused person. Unlike American judges, a Canadian trial judge is under no duty to scrutinize the facts underlying a plea agreement and is not required to hear evidence as to whether it serves the best interests of the various stakeholders concerned (including the victim(s) and the community at large).

THE ROLE OF VICTIMS IN RELATION TO PLEA NEGOTIATIONS

Since there is no formal judicial procedure for scrutinizing plea agreements in Canada, there is no opportunity for the victims of crime to express their views to a trial judge concerning the contents of a proposed plea agreement. However, victims may have a role to play at an earlier stage of the pretrial process.

Most Canadian provinces and territories have enacted legislation that entitles victims of crime to receive information concerning the status of the investigation and the prosecution of "their" cases (Roach 1999; Verdun-Jones and Tijerino 2001, 2004, 2005). However, at present, the only Canadian jurisdictions that have enacted legislation that explicitly deals with the role of victims in the plea negotiation process are Manitoba and Ontario. The Ontario legislation merely requires that victims "should have access to information" about "any pretrial arrangements that relate to a plea that may be entered by the accused at trial" (*Victims' Bill of Rights*, S.O. 1995, c. 6, s. 2(x)). It is significant that the Martin Report (Ontario Attorney General 1993), which was published two years before the enactment of the Ontario *Victims' Bill of Rights*, had recognized that victims should be consulted about plea bargains "where appropriate and feasible." However, as Roach (1999, 99) points out, the recommendations of the Martin Task Force were not designed to enhance the level of direct victim participation in the criminal justice process in Ontario, making it clear that victims should not be given the right to veto an agreement of which they disapproved. According to Roach, the report assumed that the exercise of power in plea bargaining should remain squarely in the hands of criminal justice professionals; the primary goal of the Task Force in recommending more widespread acceptance of plea bargaining was not that of victim empowerment but rather that of enhancing the efficiency of a court system that would collapse if most defendants decided to exercise their right to a full trial (ibid., 99).

Moreover, in 2000, the Province of Manitoba implemented part of a new *Victims' Bill of Rights* (C.C.S.M. c. V55), which created a right for victims to be *consulted* (as opposed to merely *informed*) about various aspects of the prosecution of "their" cases. Section 14(1) states, "If a victim requests information about the prosecution of a person for the offence, the Director of Prosecutions must ensure that information is given to the victim on," *inter alia*, "any agreement relating to a disposition of the charge." Significantly, Section 14(2) provides that "(t)he victim's views are to be considered seriously when a decision is made on any of the matters set out in subsection (1)."

Unfortunately, even when provincial legislation grants rights to victims in relation to proposed plea agreements, these rights may not be enforceable in the courts. For example, in *Vanscoy v. Ontario* (1999), a judge of the Ontario Superior Court of Justice held that Ontario's *Victims' Bill of Rights* did not create any substantive rights.[4] In this case, the complainants asserted that their right to be informed about plea negotiations had been violated when the Crown failed to inform them that a plea agreement had been reached with defence counsel. Justice Day ruled (para. 22) that the Ontario legislation did not create enforceable *rights;* rather, it articulated certain *principles:*

> I conclude that the legislature did not intend for s. 2(1) of the *Victims Bill of Rights* to provide rights to the victims of crime. The Act is a statement of principle and social policy, beguilingly clothed in the language of legislation. It does not establish any statutory rights for the victims of crime.

It is noteworthy that Manitoba's *Victims' Bill of Rights* is a trailblazing statute insofar as it creates an administrative mechanism designed to hold criminal justice officials to account if they fail to perform their statutory duties to provide information to—and consult with—victims of crime. Disgruntled victims may take their complaints to the Director of Victims' Support Services and may also seek the assistance of the provincial Ombudsperson, who must appoint a Crime Victim Investigator to deal with such complaints (Verdun-Jones and Tijerino 2005, 196).

In April 2014, the Government of Canada announced that it would introduce the *Canadian Victims Bill of Rights*. Among the proposals is an amendment to the *Criminal Code* that would require the trial judge to ask Crown Counsel if reasonable steps were taken to inform the victim(s) of the existence of a plea agreement with respect to a charge of murder or any other serious personal injury offence (Prime Minister of Canada, 2014).

RESEARCH INTO PLEA NEGOTIATIONS IN CANADA

Although plea negotiations constitute a significant element in the criminal justice system in Canada, there is a surprising paucity of recent empirical research into the phenomenon. Some evidence suggests that police officers and prosecutors are willing to admit that plea negotiations occur with frequency. For example, a study by Jonah and colleagues (1999) examined the practices, perceptions, and attitudes of 1,545 police officers across Canada in relation to the enforcement of impaired driving laws. About two-thirds of the police officers surveyed indicated that plea bargaining had occurred in impaired driving cases in which they were concerned (28.2 percent indicated it occurred in at least some cases; 36.7 percent responded that it occurred frequently). The major reason cited for plea bargaining was to "speed up the court process" (59.2 percent). Similarly, in a study of decision making by Crown counsel in relation to dangerous offender applications in British Columbia and Ontario, Bonta and colleagues (1996, 39) found that 71 percent of Crown counsel indicated that "they would consider plea bargaining as a viable option if evidentiary problems existed."

The most comprehensive Canadian study of plea negotiations was conducted some 30 years ago. Ericson and Baranek (1982, 117) employed the term *plea discussions* rather than *plea bargaining*, because the former expression makes clear that discussions may be entered into without an agreement ever being reached. They concluded that "plea discussions were a widespread and integral part of the order out of court" (121). In this respect, they found that lawyers for as many as 57 of the 80 accused said that they had entered into plea discussions (117–18).

Ericson and Baranek suggested that the existence of multiple charges appears to constitute a major element in the circumstances that lead to plea discussions taking place. Of the 23 accused whose lawyers did *not* engage in such discussions, 17 had only one charge laid against them (compared with only 9 of the 57 accused whose lawyers were involved in plea discussions). The authors believed that multiple charging is a vital component of the plea discussion process in Canada; and that without the existence of multiple charges, the defence would not be able to negotiate for the withdrawal of some charge(s) in return for the entry of a guilty plea to others. Lawyers who engaged in discussions with the Crown reported that withdrawal of charges was the major topic of conversation in plea discussions (ibid.,119).

Given the finding that there was widespread involvement of lawyers in plea discussions, what was the most likely outcome of these encounters? Ericson and Baranek discovered that although many of the lawyers engaged in plea discussions, only about one-quarter of them stated that they had reached an agreement that could be considered a bargain (143). For this group of lawyers, the most frequently mentioned agreement was one that included a sentence concession. Of the remaining lawyers who entered plea discussions, 12 percent stated that they had not reached an agreement, while lawyers for the remaining 88 percent claimed that the agreement reached brought no real advantage for the accused. More than half the lawyers (representing 23 accused) thought that an agreement had brought no tangible benefit because the charges that were withdrawn or reduced in their cases did not represent a genuine concession, but were merely the result of overcharging by the police in the first place (145).

Solomon (1983) also analyzed the data from this study and concluded that plea negotiations "did not result in important concessions for the accused." In the Provincial Court, almost 80 percent of the criminal cases that were not withdrawn by the Crown terminated with guilty pleas, and 60 percent of these cases involved plea discussions. It appears that the discussions between defence counsel and the Crown and/or police usually focused on the charges to which the accused would plead guilty, rather than on the sentence (although there was some discussion of the approach that the Crown would adopt at the sentencing stage).

Plea agreements resulted in the dropping of charges (which were often not justified in the first place) and at least a tacit agreement as to the Crown's recommendation for a sentence. However, Solomon pointed out that there was no clear relationship between the charges to which the accused ultimately pleaded guilty and the sentence handed down by the court (37). Furthermore, the sentencing recommendations made by the Crown had no direct impact on the sentence actually handed down by the court. In these circumstances, an accused person who entered into a plea arrangement with the Crown had no guarantee that her guilty plea would make any difference whatsoever to the ultimate outcome of the case.

This pioneering study by the University of Toronto criminologists provides a valuable snapshot of plea negotiations as they took place more than 30 years ago. Circumstances have undoubtedly changed considerably since then, and, as noted above, the courts are now considerably more willing to accept joint sentencing submissions from Crown and defence counsel. So it would be unwise to assume that the findings by Ericson and Baranek and the analysis by Solomon reflect the nature and scope of contemporary plea negotiations either in Ontario or in other parts of Canada. Clearly, a similar type of study needs to be conducted in contemporary circumstances.

More recent research identified a powerful reason for accused persons to seek a plea agreement with the Crown. Indeed, a study by Kellough and Wortley (2002) concluded that the detention of an accused person in custody prior to trial is a significant factor in persuading him to enter into plea negotiations with the Crown. In a study of more than 1,800 criminal court cases that came before two Toronto bail courts in a six-month period (October 1993 to April 1994), Kellough and Wortley found that accused persons who had been held in custody were more likely to plead guilty than their out-of-custody counterparts. When an accused person had been held in custody, the Crown usually refused to drop any of the original charges until the accused pleaded guilty to other charges. However, if an accused person had been released on bail into the community, she was less willing to plead guilty to any of the charges, thereby making the Crown's task of obtaining a conviction more difficult. In this respect, Kellough and Wortley (2002, 204) concluded:

> An out-of-custody accused is more likely to have all of the charges dropped but a detained accused who resists pleading guilty is more likely to spend more time in custody. In the majority of cases, being in custody prior to trial eventually means being persuaded of the wisdom of entering into plea negotiations with the Crown.

CONCLUSIONS

Plea negotiations are a well-established feature of contemporary criminal justice in Canada. The courts have accepted the legitimacy of this practice and have encouraged it by demonstrating their willingness to accept joint sentencing submissions by Crown and defence counsel. Plea negotiations are accepted as a necessary evil in a criminal justice system in which the Crown has finite resources with which to prosecute cases. Since the Crown does not have the ability to take the majority of criminal cases to a full trial, it needs to provide an incentive to criminal defendants to plead guilty to at least some criminal charges (Roberts 2000; Bjerk 2005). The strongest incentive for a guilty plea is the offer of a less severe sentence. There is no doubt that defence counsel enter into negotiations with Crown counsel in the belief that a plea agreement will make provision for a sentence that is more lenient than the sentence that is likely to be imposed should the accused person be convicted of the original charges following a full trial.

While plea negotiations have acquired a certain degree of acceptance and grudging respectability, they are still not subject to a formal process of regulation by the judiciary, as is the case in American criminal courts. As McGillivray (1997–98) has aptly commented, "Plea bargaining is a closed-door and often hasty process, unmediated by the judiciary" (para. 20). If plea negotiations are indeed an "integral element of the Canadian criminal process" (to quote the Supreme Court of Canada), it would surely constitute sound public policy for the Parliament of Canada to amend the *Criminal Code* with a view to establishing the necessary machinery for their regulation by the courts. Furthermore, there is a need to open the process of plea negotiations to public scrutiny and to create an opportunity for victims to have their views heard concerning proposed plea agreements.[5] Finally, the other Canadian provinces and territories should follow the lead of Manitoba and require prosecutors to consult with victims before entering into plea agreements with defence counsel.

Plea negotiations have certainly come of age in the 21st century. However, the criminal justice system has been excruciatingly slow in developing mechanisms to regulate plea negotiations and has failed to ensure that plea agreements serve not only the traditional interests of prosecutors, offenders, and the court bureaucracies, but also the compelling interests of the victims of crime and of Canadian society as a whole.

Further Readings

Di Luca, J. 2005. "Expedient McJustice or Principled Alternative Dispute Resolution? A Review of Plea Bargaining in Canada." *Criminal Law Quarterly* 50: 14–66.

Piccinato, M.P. 2004. *Plea Bargaining*. Ottawa: Department of Justice. http://www.justice.gc.ca/eng/abt-apd/icg-gci/pb-rpc/pb-rpc.pdf

Verdun-Jones, S.N., and A.A. Tijerino. 2004. "Four Models of Victim Involvement during Plea Negotiations: Bridging the Gap Between Legal Reforms and Current Legal Practice." *Canadian Journal of Criminology and Criminal Justice* 46: 471–500.

References

Bibas, S. 2011. "Regulating the Plea-Bargaining Market: From *Caveat Emptor* to Consumer Protection." *California Law Review* 99: 1117–61.

Bjerk, D. 2005. *On the Role of Plea Bargaining and the Distribution of Sentences in the Absence of Judicial System Frictions.* Hamilton: McMaster University, Department of Economics. http://socserv.mcmaster.ca/bjerk/-pleabargain1.pdf

Bonta, J., A. Harris, I. Zinger, and D. Carriere. 1996. *The Crown Files Research Project: A Study of Dangerous Offenders.* Ottawa: Public Safety and Emergency Preparedness Canada. http://www.publicsafety.gc.ca/lbrr/archives/ke%209434%20c7%201996-eng.pdf

Boyce, J. 2013. *Adult Criminal Court Statistics in Canada, 2011/2012.* Ottawa: Statistics Canada. http://www.statcan.gc.ca/pub/85-002-x/2013001/article/11804-eng.pdf

Brockman, J. 2010. "Offer You Can't Refuse: Pleading Guilty When Innocent." *Criminal Law Quarterly* 56: 116–34.

Caldwell, H.M. 2011. "Coercive Plea Bargaining: The Unrecognized Scourge of the Justice System." *Catholic University Law Review* 63: 61–96.

Canadian Sentencing Commission. 1987. *Report of the Canadian Sentencing Commission.* Ottawa: Supply and Services Canada.

Cohen, S., and A. Doob. 1989. "Public Attitudes towards Plea Bargaining." *Criminal Law Quarterly* 32: 85–109.

Di Luca, J. 2005. "Expedient McJustice or Principled Alternative Dispute Resolution? A Review of Plea Bargaining in Canada." *Criminal Law Quarterly* 50: 14–66.

Ericson, R.V., and P. Baranek. 1982. *The Ordering of Justice: A Study of Accused Persons as Dependants in the Criminal Process.* Toronto: University of Toronto Press.

Galligan, P.T. 1996. *Report to the Attorney General of Ontario on Certain Matters Relating to Karla Homolka.* Toronto: ADR Chambers.

Gillis, C. 2005. "Karla Homolka: Girl Next Door." *Macleans*, March 15, 2005. http://archive.today/gzep

Griffiths, C.T., and S. Verdun-Jones. 1994. *Canadian Criminal Justice.* 2nd ed. Toronto: Harcourt Brace Jovanovich Canada.

Herman, G.N. 2004. *Plea Bargaining.* 2nd ed. Charlottesville: LexisNexis.

Jonah, B., et al. 1999. "Front-Line Police Officers' Practices, Perceptions, and Attitudes about the Enforcement of Impaired Driving Laws in Canada." *Accident Analysis and Prevention* 31: 421–43.

Jones, S. 2011. "Under Pressure: Women who Plead Guilty to Crimes They Have Not Committed. *Criminology and Criminal Justice*, 11: 77–90.

Kellough, G., and S. Wortley. 2002. "Remand for Plea: Bail Decisions and Plea Bargaining as Commensurate Decisions." *British Journal of Criminology* 42: 186–210.

Lafontaine, G., and V. Rondinelli. 2005. "Plea Bargaining and the Modern Criminal Defence Lawyer: Negotiating Guilt and the Economics of the 21st Century Criminal Justice." *Criminal Law Quarterly* 50: 108–27.

Law Reform Commission of Canada. 1989. *Plea Discussions and Agreements.* Working Paper no. 60. Ottawa.

Levenson, L.L. 2013. "Peeking behind the Plea Bargaining Process: *Missouri v. Frye & Lafler Cooper.*" *Loyola of Los Angeles Law Review* 46: 457–90.

Linds, A. 2012. "A Deal Breaker: Prosecutorial Discretion to Repudiate Plea Agreements after *R. v. Nixon.*" *Queen's Law Journal* 38, no. 1: 295–323.

Lippke, R.L. 2011. *The Ethics of Plea Bargaining.* Oxford: Oxford University Press,

——— . 2013. "Adjudication Error, Finality, and Asymmetry in the Criminal Law." *Canadian Journal of Law and Jurisprudence* 26: 377–98.

Lussier, P., N. Deslauriers-Varin, & T. Râtel. 2010. "A Descriptive Profile of High-Risk Sex Offenders under Intensive Supervision in the Province of British Columbia, Canada." *International Journal of Offender Therapy and Comparative Criminology* 54: 71–91.

Manson, A. 2001. *The Law of Sentencing.* Toronto: Irwin Law.

McCoy, C. 2005. "Plea Bargaining as Coercion: The Trial Penalty and Plea Bargaining Reform." *Criminal Law Quarterly* 50: 67–107.

McGillivray, A. 1997–98. "*R. v. Bauder*: Seductive Children, Safe Rapists, and Other Justice Tales." *Manitoba Law Journal* 25: 359–83.

——— . 1998. "'A Moral Vacuity in Her Which Is Difficult if Not Impossible to Explain': Law, Psychiatry, and the Remaking of Karla Homolka." *International Journal of the Legal Profession* 5: 255–88.

Ontario, Attorney General. 1993. *Report of the Attorney General's Advisory Committee on Charge Screening, Disclosure, and Resolutions Discussions.* Toronto: Queen's Printer.

Pan, J., and M.G. Kaiser. 2001. "Thirtieth Annual Review of Criminal Procedure: Guilty Pleas." *Georgetown Law Journal* 89: 384–437.

Piccinato, M.P. 2004. *Plea Bargaining.* Ottawa: Department of Justice. http://www.justice.gc.ca/eng/abt-apd/icg-gci/pb-rpc/pb-rpc.pdf

Prime Minister of Canada. 2014. *PM Announces Legislation to Create a Canadian Victims Bill of Rights.* http://www.pm.gc.ca/eng/news/2014/04/03/pm-announces-historic-legislation-create-canadian-victims-bill-rights

Roach, K. 1999. *Due Process and Victims' Rights: The New Law and Politics of Criminal Justice*. Toronto: University of Toronto Press.

Roberts, J. 2000. *Plea Bargaining with Budgetary Constraints and Deterrence*. Working Papers from University of Toronto, Department of Economics. Toronto: University of Toronto. http://www.economics.utoronto.ca/public/workingPapers/UT-ECIPA-JOROB-00-01.pdf

Sherrin, C. 2012. Excessive Pre-Trial Incarceration. *Saskatchewan Law Review* 75: 55–96.

Solomon, P. 1983. *Criminal Justice Policy, From Research to Reform*. Toronto: Butterworths.

Thomas, J. 2010. *Adult Criminal Court Statistics, 2008/2009*. Statistics Canada Cat. no. 85-002-X, vol. 30, no. 2. Ottawa: Statistics Canada. http://www.statcan.gc.ca/pub/85-002-x/2010002/article/11293-eng.pdf

U.S. Department of Justice. 2002. *Office for Victims of Crime, Legal Series Bulletin #7: Victim Input into Plea Agreements*. Washington: Office for Victims of Crime. https://www.ncjrs.gov/ovc_archives/bulletins/legalseries/bulletin7/welcome.html

Verdun-Jones, S.N. and A. Hatch. 1985. *Plea Bargaining and Sentencing Guidelines*. Ottawa: Department of Justice Canada.

——. 1987. "An Overview of Plea Bargaining in Canada: Cautionary Notes for Sentencing Reform." In J. Dumont, ed., *Sentencing*, 71–106. Cowansville, Quebec: Yvon Blais, Inc.

Verdun-Jones, S.N., and A.A. Tijerino. 2001. *Victim Participation in the Plea Negotiation Process in Canada: A Review of the Literature and Four Models of Law Reform*. Ottawa: Department of Justice Canada.

——. 2004. "Four Models of Victim Involvement during Plea Negotiations: Bridging the Gap Between Legal Reforms and Current Legal Practice." *Canadian Journal of Criminology and Criminal Justice* 46: 471–500.

——. 2005. "Victim Participation in the Plea Negotiation Process: An Idea Whose Time Has Come?" *Criminal Law Quarterly* 50: 190–212.

Cases

Boudreau v. Benaiah (2000), 142 C.C.C. (3rd) 97 (Ont. C.A.).

R. v. Bezdan, [2001] B.C.J. No. 808 (C.A.)(QL).

R. v. Burlingham, [1995] 2 S.C.R. 206.

R. v. G.W.C., (2000) 150 C.C.C. (3d) 513 (Alta. C.A.), Supplementary Reasons, [2001] 5 W.W.R. 240 (Alta. C.A.).

R. v. Neale, [2000] B.C.J. No. 668 (C.A.) (QL).

R. v. Nixon, [2011] 2 S.C.R. 566.

Vanscoy v. Ontario, [1999] O.J. No. 1661 (Ont. S.C.)(QL).

Wellington v. Ontario (2011), 333 D.L.R. (4th) 236 (Ont. C.A.).

Endnotes

1. The principle that courts are in no way bound by a plea agreement is illustrated by the most unfortunate case of *R. v. Neale* (2000). Neale had agreed to plead guilty to a charge of robbery in exchange for the Crown's undertaking to make a submission in support of a five-year sentence, less the time already spent in custody. Unfortunately, counsel neglected to inform the trial judge that this plea agreement had been reached. Subsequently, the trial judge sentenced Neale to seven years in prison. Even though Neale did not receive the sentence recommended by the Crown (and even though the trial judge was never informed that a plea bargain had been struck), the Court of Appeal dismissed the appeal against the sentence. Justice Lambert noted (para. 14) that, in his opinion, "no injustice is being done to the appellant in this particular case through the processes before the sentencing judge." He stated that "the sentence is a fit one with the appropriate range and the circumstances of the sentencing were not such as to create any injustice."

2. Peace bonds may be imposed under Sections 810, 810.01, 810.1, and 810.2 of the *Criminal Code*. Under a peace bond, an accused person enters into a "recognizance" (a binding promise) to be of "good conduct" for a period up to 12 months (and up to two years when there is a danger of a sexual offence or a serious personal injury offence being committed). Breach of this recognizance is a criminal offence (s. 811 of the *Criminal Code*). This procedure is followed where there is a reasonable fear that the accused person will commit a serious offence—for example, a sexual assault against a child or a crime of domestic violence (see, for example, Lussier, Deslauriers-Varin, & Râtel 2010).

3. Homolka eventually served the entire 12 years of her sentence in prison. She was not granted parole or statutory release (see Gillis 2005).

4. See also *Wellington v. Ontario* (2011), a decision of the Ontario Court of Appeal.

5. The proposed *Canadian Victims Bill of Rights* would require judges to ask Crown Counsel whether reasonable efforts have been made to inform victims of the existence of a plea agreement. However, it appears that the intention of the proposed legislation is not to require consultation with victims (the precise wording of the Bill has yet to be made public).

Crime, Criminal Justice, and Aboriginal Canadians

Aboriginal Canadians are disproportionately involved in the criminal justice system in Canada, and for decades the federal and provincial governments have attempted to improve the way that the justice system treats Aboriginal Canadians. Yet correctional statistics continue to demonstrate that Aboriginal peoples are overrepresented in criminal justice statistics, particularly in the Prairie provinces. In this chapter the authors discuss the reasons why Aboriginal Canadians have been overrepresented in criminal justice statistics, including prison admissions. The chapter also reviews some of the remedies and responses that have been implemented in recent years.

Savvas Lithopoulos
Department of Public Safety Canada

Rick Ruddell
University of Regina

INTRODUCTION

Aboriginal peoples in Canada face many problems that, according to the Royal Commission on Aboriginal Peoples (1996), can be largely attributed to the effects of colonialism, past discriminatory and paternalistic government policies, and legislation intended to assimilate them into the general population. The harmful effects of colonization on the psyche of Aboriginal peoples have affected their cultural, justice, socio-economic, and political structures. These historic factors have contributed to the poverty, unemployment, alcohol abuse, and domestic violence found in Aboriginal communities today (Truth and Reconciliation Commission [TRC] 2012). The result is that Aboriginal peoples have the highest involvement in offences, arrests, and incarceration rates of any ethnic group in Canada.

The history of the government effort to assimilate Aboriginal peoples into European lifestyles, religion, and culture can be documented through a number of federal legislative and public policy decisions that were consolidated in the *Indian Act* in 1876. This Act introduced a number of practices detrimental to Aboriginal peoples, including the pass system, which restricted movement off-reserve without permission of the Indian Agent, as well as the permit system, which required Aboriginal persons to obtain permission from the Indian Agent to sell their agricultural products or purchase goods such as clothing or groceries. These practices prevented Aboriginal peoples from becoming full participants in the economic development of Canada until the late 20th century (RCAP 1996).

Another contributing factor in the assimilation process was the placement of Aboriginal children in Indian Residential Schools starting in the 1870s. Although many students attended day schools in their own communities, residential schools, operated by religious organizations under contract with the Department of Indian Affairs, were often located far away from the children's homes and families (O'Connell 2010). As a result, these youngsters grew up with little knowledge of their language, culture, religion, and identity. Corporal punishment was common, mortality rates were high, and some students were physically and sexually abused by school employees. According to the TRC (2012) the placement of these children in these schools had detrimental long-term consequences for the victims, their families, and communities. They estimated that there are 80,000 survivors of these schools alive today, as the last residential school closed only in 1996.

In the latter part of the 20th century, due to increased Aboriginal activism and positive changes in attitudes towards minority rights, federal government policy towards Aboriginal peoples shifted from de facto control to one of support for Aboriginal self-determination, self-governance, and inherent rights. For example, in 1982, "existing Aboriginal and treaty rights" were recognized in the Canadian constitution. The Royal Commission on Aboriginal Peoples was established and their 1996 report made hundreds of recommendations aimed at improving conditions for Aboriginal peoples. At about the same time, a number of federal policies were introduced that led to the creation of Nunavut; the recognition of the Métis people as a distinct Aboriginal people with rights; Canada becoming a signatory to the United Nations Declaration of the Rights of Indigenous Peoples; and the introduction of the First Nations Policing Program and the Aboriginal Justice Strategy. Governments and religious organizations also accepted responsibility for some of the misguided practices of the past, and in 2008, Prime Minister Stephen Harper apologized to former students of residential schools on behalf of all Canadians.

Despite these positive steps, many Aboriginal persons distrust the police and justice systems. LeBeuf's (2011) study of residential school survivors found that many interviewees feared rather than trusted the RCMP. There is also a lack of faith in the way that justice systems are operated; surveys conducted by the Environics Institute (2010, 99) demonstrated that "more than half of urban Aboriginal peoples have little or no confidence in the criminal justice." Those sentiments extend beyond the justice system. Grekul and Sanderson (2011, 42) noted that the long-term mistreatment and marginalization of Aboriginal peoples has resulted in "feelings of alienation, mistrust, and animosity toward mainstream institutions and authorities."

ABORIGINAL POPULATIONS

According to Statistics Canada (2013), the term *North American Indian* refers to persons who consider themselves as belonging to the First Nations of Canada, regardless of whether they are registered (that is, whether they have legal Indian status as defined in the *Indian Act*). Métis refers to people of mixed Aboriginal and non-Aboriginal ancestries. The Inuit are Aboriginal people who originally lived north of the tree line in Canada, and who self-identify as such (Statistics Canada 2013). Statistics Canada (2013) reported that in the 2011 census, 4.3 percent of the population self-identified as Aboriginal, which represents a 20.1 percent increase from the 2006 Census. In comparison, the non-Aboriginal population grew by only 5.2 percent during the same period. This growth is mainly due to an increased number of respondents who self-identified as Aboriginal and an increased birth rate. Of the total number:

851,560 (60.8%) identified themselves as a First Nation person, out of whom 637,000 (75%) were Registered Indians; 451,795 (32.3%) identified as Métis; and 59,445 (4.2%) identified as Inuit.[*]

The Aboriginal population in Canada is also young, with a median age of 27.7 compared with 40.1 years for non-Aboriginal peoples, and is increasing at a faster pace than the non-Aboriginal population (Statistics Canada 2013). Growth in the size of this youthful population has implications for justice systems given that the proportion of young males in the population is generally a good predictor of higher involvement in crime, regardless of race or ethnicity.

---

[*] Statistics Canada. 2013. Aboriginal Peoples in Canada: First Nations Peoples, Métis and Inuit. (Catalogue No. 99-011-X2011001). Ottawa: Statistics Canada.

ABORIGINAL CANADIANS: TWO WORLDS, COMMON PROBLEMS

There are two worlds when it comes to Aboriginal persons: About 30 percent of the Aboriginal population resides on First Nations reserves while the remaining 70 percent live off-reserve, and a growing number are residing in cities (Statistics Canada 2013). There are 634 federally recognized Indian Bands, commonly referred to as "First Nations," which hold 2.95 million acres of trust land (reserves) for their use. Despite their size, the average population of a reserve was only 552 residents in 2011 (Aboriginal Affairs and Northern Development Canada [AANDC] 2013). Many of these communities are geographically isolated, which is a contributing factor in terms of low income, high unemployment, substandard housing, as well as poor health and limited educational opportunities.

AANDC developed a measure of community functioning based on census data called the Community Well-Being Index (CWB). This index includes indicators of education, employment, income, and housing (quality and quantity) and has a maximum possible score of 100. O'Sullivan (2011) reported that the average CWB score for Aboriginal communities in 2006 was 57 compared to 77 for non-Aboriginal communities. Lithopoulos (2013) calculated levels of CWB by the distance and isolation from urban areas for 236 Aboriginal communities. Table 15.1 shows that the CWB index decreases as the distance from an urban centre increases. The average CWB in the most isolated communities (Geographic Zone 4) was 55, or almost 30 percent lower than the national average.

Closer investigation shows that there is a high degree of movement back and forth between First Nations and the city, a process that some call

TABLE 15.1   *Geographical Isolation and Community Well-Being*

Zone Definition	Community	Well-Being
Geographic Zone 1	The community is located within 50 km of the nearest urban area with year-round road access (n = 33).	66
Geographic Zone 2	The community is located between 50 and 350 km from the nearest urban area with year-round road access (n = 127).	60
Geographic Zone 3	The community is located over 350 km from the nearest urban area with year-round road access (n = 15).	59
Geographic Zone 4	The community has no year-round road access to an urban area (could have "winter" roads, or access in the summer by water, or accessible only by aircraft) (n = 61).	55

Sources: AANDC. 2013. Registered Indian Population by Sex and Residence, 2013. Ottawa: Aboriginal Affairs and Northern Development Canada.
AANDC. 2013. Aboriginal Populations in Canadian Cities: Why are they Growing so Fast? Ottawa: Aboriginal Affairs and Northern Development Canada.
Lithopoulos, S. 2013. First Nations Policing Policy/Program (FNPP) update: University of Regina Presentation. October 16, 2013. Regina, SK.

"churning." Similarly, the urban Aboriginal population "is growing almost five times faster than its non-Aboriginal population (AANDC 2013, 1)." Although Winnipeg has the highest proportion of Aboriginal persons of all Canadian cities (11 percent), over one-third of a million Aboriginal peoples live in just ten cities, and while the populations tend to be highest in the West, there were over 36,000 Aboriginal persons living in Toronto in 2011.

City life also presents challenges for Aboriginal peoples. Like their counterparts residing on First Nations reserves, urban Aboriginal residents are often characterized by high rates of poverty, unemployment, substandard housing, and poor participation in formal educational systems (Urban Aboriginal Knowledge Network 2013). Often these individuals reside in impoverished inner-city areas with other marginalized groups. Also, similar to life on reserve, many of these individuals suffer from chronic health problems. Rates of substance abuse are also high in these urban Aboriginal populations (Currie, Wild, Schopflocher, Laing, and Veugelers 2013). These factors contribute to a greater likelihood of involvement in youth and criminal justice systems.

ABORIGINAL PEOPLES, CRIME, AND CRIMINAL VICTIMIZATION

According to the Canadian Centre for Justice Statistics, Aboriginal peoples have the highest rates of offences, arrest, and incarceration of any ethnic group (Statistics Canada 2006). For example, on-reserve crime rates in 2004 were about three times higher than rates in the rest of the country. The difference was even greater for violent crime, with an on-reserve rate that was eight times the violent crime rate of the rest of the country. In 2004, there were about 93,000 police-reported *Criminal Code* incidents on reserves across Canada, representing 4 percent of the national total. These offences can be grouped into three categories: violent crimes, property crimes, and "other" *Criminal Code* incidents. Consistent with non-Aboriginal offenders, for crimes occurring on reserve, men were disproportionately involved in crime and were four times more likely than women to be charged with a violent offence or a property offence and five times more likely to be charged with an "other" Criminal Code offence (Statistics Canada 2006).

Statistics Canada (2011) found that Aboriginal women were almost three times more likely than non-Aboriginal women to report that they had been a victim of spousal violence, and overall these women are at higher risk of being victimized. A report commissioned by Human Rights Watch, Rhoade (2013, 25) noted that "between 1997 and 2000, the rate of homicide overall for Aboriginal women was 5.4 per 100,000 residents, compared to 0.8 per 100,000 for non-Aboriginal women—almost seven times higher." In addition, hundreds of Aboriginal women have disappeared or are missing and these cases are not included in homicide statistics. From 2010 to 2012, the province of British Columbia launched a Commission of Inquiry on these missing women. The inquiry concluded that there was systemic bias in the police response to the women who went missing from downtown Vancouver.

This bias contributed to a failure to prioritize and effectively investigate the cases (Oppal 2012).

Research has long established that Aboriginal peoples residing in large urban centres are the most vulnerable to being involved with the criminal and youth justice systems (Fitzgerald and Carrington 2008). Over 20 years ago La Prairie (1992) found Registered Indians living in large Western cities to be particularly at-risk, as were Aboriginal offenders who commit offences off-reserve. Since then, a number of scholars have raised the question of whether the disproportionate involvement of urban Aboriginal peoples is a result of zero-tolerance law enforcement practices or the over-policing of these populations (Comack 2012). In their analysis of the policing of inner-city Winnipeg, Comack and Silver (2008, 840) contend that "there are no easy or instant miracle cures for the deep and complex racialized, and crime-inducing poverty."

ABORIGINAL OVERREPRESENTATION IN JUSTICE SYSTEMS: LEGAL AND LEGISLATIVE RESPONSE

Policymakers have used legislation to attempt to address the overrepresentation of Aboriginal persons in justice systems. The responses have involved all stages of the criminal justice system, including police, courts, and corrections. Much of this legislation was a response to a series of federal and provincial inquiries that were carried out prior to 1990 and which addressed the involvement of Aboriginal persons with criminal and youth justice systems (Alberta Government 1991). Of these reports, 22 offered recommendations and the Alberta Government (1991, 4–13) summarized these into a number of key themes, including the expansion of policing services to First Nations, the need to upgrade the Band Constable Program (i.e., band bylaw enforcement officers), increased community involvement in the policing process, higher levels of cross-cultural training, and more Aboriginal persons should be hired to work in justice systems. The growing concern about Aboriginal persons and their involvement with justice systems, and especially how their communities were being policed, could not be easily dismissed, and political demands to make meaningful changes increased.

During this time, a number of legislative reforms were initiated to address the issue of disproportionate involvement of Aboriginal persons in justice systems. In 1987, for example, the Task Force report on Aboriginal People in Federal Corrections led to major amendments for Aboriginal-specific sections in the *Corrections and Conditional Release Act*. The 1991 introduction of the First Nations Police Program and the Aboriginal Justice Strategy (highlighted later in the chapter) were also intended to provide culturally appropriate policing to Aboriginal communities and effective alternatives to the mainstream justice system to decrease crime rates, victimization, and the incarceration of Aboriginal persons. Federal and provincial correctional systems introduced correctional programming that considered the distinctive needs of Aboriginal offenders. To carry out these changes, a greater priority was also placed on hiring Aboriginal persons in justice systems. Finally, in 1995, the federal government amended the sentencing principles of Section 718.2 of the *Criminal Code* by adding Subsection (e) which stipulated that "all available sanctions other than imprisonment that are reasonable in the circumstances should be considered for all offenders, with particular attention to the circumstances of aboriginal offenders (R.S.C., 1985, c. C-46)."

While legislators introduced these policies, the courts also became involved in the review of Aboriginal involvement in the justice system. The most significant legal reforms were ushered in after the 1999 Supreme Court judgment on *Regina v. Gladue*. This decision directed sentencing judges to recognize the unique circumstances of Aboriginal peoples when imposing custody. In 2012, the Supreme Court judgement in *Regina v. Ipeelee* extended the Aboriginal sentencing provisions to include breaches to long-term supervision orders. Within this context, a number of restorative justice practices, such as Circle sentencing and community justice forums (where victims and offenders met in a process akin to victim–offender mediation) were introduced to account for the circumstances of the offender and how their offences affected their victims and communities.

Despite these changes in law and legislative practices, Aboriginal peoples are still overrepresented in the criminal justice system as both victims and offenders. Although representing about 3.8 percent of the national population, Canada's Aboriginal peoples constituted 28 percent of admissions to provincial sentenced custody and 20 percent to federal custody (Statistics Canada 2014a, Table 2). Over the last 10 years the Correctional Service of Canada's overall non-Aboriginal offender population has increased by only 1 percent (161 offenders), whereas the Aboriginal offender population has increased by 31 percent (1,003 offenders). The incarcerated Inuit population has increased by 63 percent (97 to 158 offenders). In the same period, the overall incarcerated Aboriginal male population has increased 37 percent, while incarcerated Aboriginal women have increased by 107 percent (Public Safety Canada 2012). As Figure 15.1 reveals, the overrepresentation of Aboriginal peoples to sentenced custody is especially problematic in Western Canada and the Northern territories. A review of the admissions to youth custody reveals a similar pattern of Aboriginal overrepresentation (Statistics Canada, 2014b). Newell (2013) notes that the *Gladue* decision has not had the desired impact in reducing overrepresentation of Aboriginal peoples and that the introduction of the *Safe Streets and Communities Act* will increase the disproportionate involvement of Aboriginal Canadians in the justice systems (see also Roberts and Melchers 2003).

According to Public Safety Canada (2012), the typical Aboriginal offender profile differs markedly from non-Aboriginal offenders. Aboriginal offenders are more at risk for re-offending as they are:

- Younger;
- Likely to have served previous youth and /or adult sentences;

- Incarcerated more often for a violent offence;
- Have higher risk ratings (in terms of re-offending);
- Have higher needs ratings; and
- Inclined to have gang affiliations.*

FIGURE 15.1 *Aboriginal Adult Admissions to Sentenced Custody, by Province and Territory, 2011/2012*

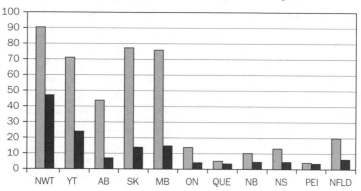

☐ Percent Aboriginal Adults Admitted to Sentenced Custody
■ Percent Aboriginal Adults in Population

Source: Statistics Canada. 2014. Adult correctional statistics in Canada, 2011/12. (Catalogue No. 85-002-X). Ottawa: Statistics Canada.

The overrepresentation of Aboriginal peoples within the Canadian criminal justice system leads to a number of negative outcomes for Canadians. First, there are increased costs to justice systems with respect to police resources, court time and costs, and the need for correctional facilities and programming. Second, crime reduces Aboriginal participation in and contributions to the economy, which results in a loss of tax revenue and increases reliance on the social safety net. Third, high crime rates have harmful psychological effects which may lead to chronic substance abuse and/or alcoholism, a lack of hope and feelings of hopelessness, low self-esteem, somatic disorders, violent tendencies, and negative attitudes towards authority figures. Taken together, these factors may lead to a greater involvement in crime (Shader 2001).

Examples of State Responses to the Problem of Aboriginal Overrepresentation

First Nations Policing Program

Canada is the only First World nation that has a national policy in place to guide the policing of Aboriginal peoples. The federal and provincial reports and reviews of Aboriginal people's involvement in criminal justice systems,

---

* Public Safety Canada. 2012. Corrections and Conditional Release: Statistical Overview. Ottawa: Public Safety Canada.

combined with a growing Aboriginal political militancy (such as the 1990 Oka crisis), led to the launch of the First Nations Policing Program (FNPP) by the federal government in 1991. The FNPP's primary goal was to provide Aboriginal communities with professional and culturally appropriate policing and replace a patchwork of different policing arrangements that were emerging throughout the nation. This was accomplished through a cost-sharing formula where the federal government incurs 52 percent of the costs of these policing agreements and provincial governments pay the remainder.

The two most common policing arrangements under the FNPP are the 38 First Nations Administered (FNA) police service agreements (839 officers) and the 122 RCMP Community Tripartite Agreements (CTA; 380.5 officers), which account for 98 percent of all funded officer positions. Much like municipal police agencies, FNA police services are operated by Aboriginal governments and are seen by many Aboriginal persons as an important step in exercising self-determination over justice systems. Initially, some of these new police services underwent serious growing pains and there were questions about their professionalism, although these agencies have improved their services over time (Public Safety Canada 2010).

As of January 31, 2014, the program consisted of 172 tripartite policing agreements funding 1,245.5 officer positions and serving almost two-thirds (62 percent) of eligible Aboriginal communities. While the total number of officers policing Aboriginal communities represented a small proportion of the 69,272 sworn officers working throughout Canada in 2013 (Statistics Canada 2014c), their roles are critical in the communities that they serve. For the 2011/12 fiscal year, the federal and provincial governments' total contribution for the FNPP was $587 per capita, which is 56 percent higher than the Canadian average of $377 (Statistics Canada 2014c).

One distinctive aspect of Aboriginal policing is the need to serve Northern and remote settlements. Health Canada (2009, 37) reported that there were 221 isolated Aboriginal communities (most residents of remote and isolated Canadian communities are Aboriginal persons). These communities are located far from urban centres and are characterized by their small populations and unforgiving environmental conditions. Few of these settlements have year-round roads and are only accessible by winter roads or by boat during the summer months, although most have year-round service. Life in these limited duration posts can be harsh for residents and officers alike. The cost of living is high and residents of many isolated places only receive their main purchases of food and household goods once a year. While the Internet has made it easier to keep in contact with the outside world, there is a lack of specialized services including health care.

Officers policing these communities have a number of challenges to overcome. Rates of crime in all Aboriginal communities are many times the national average (Statistics Canada 2006). With respect to the actual types of offences in these places, Lithopoulos and Ruddell (2011) found that officers reported high rates of violence (including domestic or family violence), feuding between different groups, and property crime. Those investigators also found that rates of social disorganization reported by these officers were also high, and included high poverty and unemployment, inadequate housing, child welfare problems, and substance abuse.

Independent reviews of the FNPP in 1996 and 2009, and a comprehensive review in 2010, found the FNPP to be relevant and on track in terms of meeting program objectives and community satisfaction with FNPP policing. According to Lithopoulos and Ruddell (2013), however, there has been comparatively little scholarly assessment of the strengths and weaknesses of the FNPP. They found that most government-funded research focused upon the administrative–bureaucratic goals of the FNPP, while relatively little government or scholarly attention has been paid to program outcomes. Over the last five years, there has also been a failure by the federal government to make a strong long-term financial commitment to the FNPP. Funding levels have not kept up with the rate of inflation and population increases in the Aboriginal communities. These problems are further compounded by short-term duration tripartite agreements, which make long-term planning by Aboriginal police services virtually impossible.

The Aboriginal Justice Strategy

In 1991 the federal government launched the Aboriginal Justice Strategy (AJS). The aim was to provide timely and effective alternatives to the mainstream justice system in appropriate circumstances—to increase the involvement of Aboriginal communities in the local administration of justice and to decrease crime rates, victimization, and incarceration of Aboriginal persons in communities with AJS-funded initiatives. Over the years, the AJS has supported hundreds of projects throughout Canada. Some examples of these include

- Increased appointments of Aboriginal judges, Justices of the Peace, corrections officers, and court workers;
- The establishment of Aboriginal Justice of the Peace courts pursuant to the *Indian Act*; and
- Cross-cultural education of non-Aboriginal judges, lawyers, police, corrections officers.

The AJS has also partnered with provincial governments to provide diversion programs for Aboriginal offenders. Some examples of these include:

- The Aboriginal Community Council Program, which is a post-charge diversion program for Aboriginal persons;
- The Community Healing Model, a holistic healing model and restorative justice program delivered to youth and adults in participating Aboriginal communities;
- Community Justice Programs, which are culturally based diversion programs delivered by local Friendships Centres to urban Aboriginal youth and adults; and

- The Gladue Services Program. The objectives of this program are to implement the Gladue principles, applicable case law, and Section 718.2 (e) of the *Criminal Code* within the court system so the court may properly take into account the circumstances of Aboriginal defendants.

In 2011, an evaluation of the AJS found that the program is still relevant and is effective in reducing short, intermediate, and long-term recidivism of Aboriginal offenders who participated in AJS-sponsored initiatives (Department of Justice 2011). In addition, the report concluded that AJS programs cost analysis on 2008–9 data "demonstrated that the average cost per community-based justice program participant was [significantly] lower than the average cost of sending an offender through the mainstream justice system (iv)." Unfortunately, the federal government's current commitment to the objectives of the AJS is questionable as the Department of Justice is no longer accepting proposals for AJS funding.

CONCLUSION

Over the last 30 years, the Canadian government has instituted a series of positive changes to reduce the Aboriginal overrepresentation in the criminal justice system. However, despite these efforts Aboriginal persons are still overrepresented in the criminal justice system as victims and offenders (Newell 2013). Some critics state that adjusting justice system policies or hiring more Aboriginal staff members in these systems merely reinforces the status quo and does not adequately address the root causes of Aboriginal crime and victimization. It is important to note that the Aboriginal population in Canada is projected to grow at a substantially higher rate than the general population. It is also important to acknowledge that Aboriginal peoples will continue to face the challenge of increased crime-related problems. Therefore, it is incumbent on governments to identify the need to reduce crime-related problems in Aboriginal communities as a high-priority policy area, and to make a strong commitment to undertake projects that address this critical issue.

As a first step, this could be accomplished by undertaking more research and evaluation into the extent and nature of crime problems as well as crime prevention in Aboriginal communities. This will assist in developing an understanding of the underlying factors concerning crime-related problems, and help identify "best practices." To this end, there is a critical need for further empirical research in this area and for more information sharing and cooperation. The existence of effective and culturally relevant criminal justice programming provides a strong foundation for healthy, prosperous, and sustainable Aboriginal communities. Indeed, an often-neglected aspect of socio-economic development, both at the community and national levels, is the crucial role of effective criminal justice in shaping economic expansion, as well as in reducing the economic and social burdens that victimization places on individuals, families, communities, and government.

Further Readings

Public Safety Canada. 2010. *2009–2010 Evaluation of the First Nations Policing Program*. Ottawa: Public Safety Canada.

Royal Commission on Aboriginal Peoples (RCAP). 1996. *Bridging the Cultural Divide: A Report on Aboriginal Peoples and Criminal Justice in Canada*. Ottawa: Supply and Services.

References

AANDC. 2013. *Aboriginal Populations in Canadian Cities: Why Are They Growing So Fast?* Ottawa: Aboriginal Affairs and Northern Development Canada.

—— . 2013. *Registered Indian Population by Sex and Residence, 2013*. Ottawa: Aboriginal Affairs and Northern Development Canada.

Alberta Government. 1991. "Justice on Trial". Retrieved from http://justice. alberta.ca/programs_services/aboriginal/Publications%20Library%20%20 Aboriginal%20Justice/CawseyReportVolumeI.aspx/DispForm.aspx?ID=15

Comack, E. 2012. *Racialized Policing: Aboriginal People's Encounters with the Police*. Winnipeg, MB: Fernwood Publishing.

Comack, E., and J. Silver. 2008. "A Canadian Exception to the Punitive Turn? Community Responses to Policing Practices in Winnipeg's Inner City." *Canadian Journal of Sociology* 33: 815–44.

Criminal Code (R.S.C., 1985, c. C-46).

Currie, C.L., T.C. Wild, D.P. Schopflocher, L. Laing, and P. Veugelers. 2013. "Illicit and Prescription Drug Problems among Urban Aboriginal Adults in Canada: The Role of Traditional Culture in Protection and Resilience." *Social Science & Medicine* 88: 1–9.

Department of Justice Canada. 2011. *Aboriginal Justice Strategy Evaluation: Final Report*. Ottawa: Department of Justice Canada.

Environics Institute. 2010. *Urban Aboriginal Peoples Study*. Toronto: Environics.

Fitzgerald, R.T., and P.J. Carrington. 2008. "The Neighbourhood Context of Urban Aboriginal Crime." *Canadian Journal of Criminology and Criminal Justice* 50: 523–57.

Grekul, J., and K. Sanderson. 2011. "'I Thought People Would Be Mean and Shout.' Introducing the Hobbema Community Cadet Corps: A Response to Youth Gang Involvement?" *Journal of Youth Studies* 14: 41–57.

Health Canada. 2009. *A Statistical Profile on the Health of First Nations in Canada: Determinants of Health*. Ottawa: Health Canada.

La Prairie, C. 1992. *Dimensions of Aboriginal Overrepresentation in Correctional Service of Canada.* Ottawa: Solicitor General of Canada.

LeBeuf, M. 2011. *The Role of the Royal Canadian Mounted Police during the Indian Residential School System.* Ottawa: Royal Canadian Mounted Police.

Lithopoulos, S. 2013. First Nations Policing Policy/Program (FNPP) update: University of Regina Presentation. October 16, 2013. Regina, SK.

Lithopoulos, S., and R. Ruddell. 2011. "Policing Isolated Aboriginal Communities: Perspectives of Canadian Officers." *Policing: An International Journal of Police Strategies & Management* 34: 434–53.

——. 2013. "Aboriginal Policing in Rural Canada: Establishing a Research Agenda." *International Journal of Rural Criminology* 2: 101–25.

National Research Council. 2004. *Fairness and Effectiveness in Policing: The Evidence.* Washington DC: National Academies Press.

Newell, R. 2013. "Making Matters Worse: *The Safe Streets and Communities Act* and the Ongoing Crisis of Indigenous Over-Incarceration." *Osgoode Hall Law Journal* 51: 199–249

O'Connell, A. 2010. "An Exploration of Redneck Whiteness in Multicultural Canada." *Social Politics* 17: 536–63.

O'Sullivan, E. 2011. *The Community Well-Being Index (CWB): Measuring Well-Being in First Nations and Non-Aboriginal Communities, 1981–2006.* Ottawa: Aboriginal Affairs and Northern Development Canada.

Oppal, Wally. 2012. *Forsaken: The Report of the Missing Women Commission of Inquiry.* Vancouver: Missing Women Commission of Inquiry.

Public Safety Canada. 2010. *2009–2010 Evaluation of the First Nations Policing Program.* Ottawa: Public Safety Canada.

Public Safety Canada. 2012. *Corrections and Conditional Release: Statistical Overview.* Ottawa: Public Safety Canada.

Rhoad, M. 2013. *Those Who Take Us Away: Abusive Policing and Failures in Protection of Indigenous Women and Girls in Northern British Columbia, Canada.* Toronto: Human Rights Watch.

Roberts, J.V., and Melchers, R. (2003) "The Incarceration of Aboriginal Offenders: An Analysis of Trends, 1978–2001." *Canadian Journal of Criminology and Criminal Justice* 45: 211–42.

Royal Commission on Aboriginal Peoples (RCAP). 1996. *Bridging the Cultural Divide: A Report on Aboriginal Peoples and Criminal Justice in Canada.* Ottawa: Supply and Services.

Shader, M. 2001. *Risk Factors for Delinquency: An Overview*. Washington DC: Office of Juvenile Justice and Delinquency Prevention, Office of Justice Programs, U.S. Department of Justice.

Statistics Canada. 2006. *Victimization and Offending among the Aboriginal Population in Canada*. Cat. no. 85-002-XIE. Ottawa: Statistics Canada.

Statistics Canada. 2011. *Violent Victimization of Aboriginal People in the Canadian Provinces, 2009*. Cat. no. 85-002-X. Ottawa: Statistics Canada.

Statistics Canada. 2013. *Aboriginal Peoples in Canada: First Nations Peoples, Métis and Inuit*. Cat. no. 99-011-X2011001. Ottawa: Statistics Canada.

Statistics Canada. 2014a. *Adult Correctional Statistics in Canada, 2011/12*. Cat. no. 85-002-X. Ottawa: Statistics Canada.

Statistics Canada. 2014b. *Admissions to Adult and Youth Correctional Services in Canada. 2011/2012*. Cat. no. 85-002-X. Ottawa: Statistics Canada.

Statistics Canada. 2014c. *Police Resources in Canada, 2013*. Cat. no. 85-002-X. Ottawa: Statistics Canada.

Truth and Reconciliation Commission of Canada (TRC). 2012. *Indian Residential Schools: An Overview*. Ottawa: Author.

Urban Aboriginal Knowledge Network. 2013. *Literature Review on Urban Aboriginal Peoples*. Ottawa, ON: National Association of Friendship Centres.

Cases

R. v. Ipeelee 2012 SCC 13, [2012] 1 S.C.R. 433.

R. v. Gladue [1999] 1 S.C.R. 688.

Criminal Justice Responses to People With Mental Illnesses

The people who are processed through the criminal justice system are different from the profile of the general population in many ways. For example, people who commit crimes and who enter the criminal justice system are more likely to come from disadvantaged social backgrounds. In addition, citizens who end up being classified as *offenders* are more like to suffer from a range of mental health problems. This suggests that mental health plays a role in their offending; breaking the law may well be a symptom of an underlying (and untreated) mental health problem. The high rates of mental disorder in the offender population create challenges for the criminal justice system. In this chapter the author discusses some of these challenges.

James D. Livingston
St. Mary's University

Rates of mental illnesses are extraordinarily high at every stage of the Canadian criminal justice system. Compared with the general population, people with severe mental illnesses, such as schizophrenia and bipolar disorders, are significantly more likely to encounter the police, incur arrests for minor crimes, acquire criminal convictions, and experience detention or incarceration in jail or prison. The coexistence of other marginalized statuses, such as being poor or an ethnic minority, only worsens this situation. Additionally, the problem grows exponentially by including other forms of mental disorder, such as substance use problems, personality disorders, intellectual disabilities, and cognitive impairment. Scholars and experts agree that the presence of people with severe mental illnesses in the criminal justice system constitutes a serious problem—on economic, medical, and humanitarian grounds—requiring urgent attention.

MYTHS AND MISCONCEPTIONS

Before discussing how the Canadian criminal justice system responds to people with mental illnesses, let us first reflect on some myths and misconceptions about the relationship between mental illness, crime, and violence. This first myth is that most people with mental illnesses engage in criminal or violent behaviour. The fact is that people with mental illnesses are more likely engage in behaviours that cause harm to themselves rather than to other people. Moreover, people with mental illnesses have an elevated risk of being victimized by crime and violence (Hiday 2006). A large body of research has found that most people with mental illnesses will never commit violent or non-violent crimes in their lifetimes.

Another misconception is that people with mental illnesses commit most of the violence in society. There are many explanations, other than mental illness, as to why people commit irrational or senseless crimes. For instance, seemingly inexplicable crimes may have been triggered by anger, frustration, desperation, or intoxication. Studies indicate that about 5 percent of violent offending in society can be attributed to individuals with severe mental illnesses; this means that 95 percent of violent crimes are committed by people without mental illness (Walsh, Buchanan, and Fahy 2002).

A third myth is that mental illness is a strong predictor of future crime and violence. Research indicates that, in comparison with other known risk factors, mental illness is a rather poor predictor of future crime (Silver 2006). Numerous other factors, such as antisocial traits and employment instability, have stronger and more robust relationships with crime and violence. Although it is true that people with mental illnesses, compared to those without mental illnesses, have an increased risk of crime and violence, the evidence indicates this is largely because they are more likely to live in disadvantaged social conditions (e.g., poverty, unemployment, disorganized neighbourhoods) that expose them to crime-producing risk factors. Very rarely is crime and violence the direct product of symptoms of mental illness (Skeem, Manchak, and Peterson 2011; Hiday 2006).

FACTORS CONTRIBUTING TO OVERREPRESENTATION

Scholars have pointed towards numerous interrelated factors, such as deinstitutionalization, criminalization, and stigma, in an attempt to explain the high rates of mental illness in the offender population (Silver 2006; Lamb, Weinberger, and Gross 1999). Some blame *deinstitutionalization*, which refers to the social movement in the mid- to late 20th century that shifted the standard approach for treating mental illnesses away from large, antiquated psychiatric institutions towards community-based care. The systematic closure of psychiatric hospitals left people with mental illnesses abandoned and left to languish in poverty and sickness without adequate care and support. Research evidence does support the notion that early efforts to transition persons with mental illnesses to the community were poorly planned and insufficiently funded. However, the findings of recent studies suggest that careful implementation of deinstitutionalization policies can mitigate adverse consequences, such as homelessness and incarceration, and may even foster favourable outcomes for people with mental illnesses, including increased life satisfaction and independent living.

Another related factor is *criminalization*, which refers to the inappropriate use of criminal justice processes, agents, and institutions to manage mental health issues. This idea is that deviant behaviour that was once handled by, and contained within, psychiatric hospitals has spilled onto the streets where it must now be handled by frontline police officers. This, in combination with deficiencies in community-based mental healthcare, contributes to the transformation and use of criminal justice processes as a means for gaining access to mental health services. For example, a mother who has a son with schizophrenia may have him arrested for a minor crime in order to get him access to mental health services. Similarly, a police officer who is tired of bringing the same individual with bipolar disorder to the emergency room every week could decide to arrest and detain the person as a means of gaining access to longer-term specialized mental healthcare.

Stigma also contributes to the overrepresentation of people with mental illnesses in the criminal justice system. Generally, stigma refers to a social process that aims to exclude, reject, shame, and devalue groups of people because of a particular characteristic—in this case, having a mental illness. This includes the rules, policies, and practices of social institutions that arbitrarily restrict the rights of, and opportunities for, people with mental illnesses—also known as structural stigma. Inequities and injustices are woven into the fabric of society, causing people with mental illnesses to have unequal access to social, economic, and political resources and power. Far too often, people with mental illnesses must live in conditions of poverty, unemployment, unstable housing, stressful life events, and unsafe neighbourhoods. Not only do these circumstances impair mental health but they also encourage criminal behaviour (Hiday 2006; Silver 2006). As such, inequities that materialize in other life domains, such as unequal access to employment or educational opportunities, can place people with mental illnesses at risk of coming into conflict with the law.

A final way to explain the high rates of mental illnesses within criminal justice populations is to consider the converging characteristics of the mental health and criminal justice systems. A major objective of both systems is to manage normative rule breaking through the identification, classification, surveillance, treatment, and containment of harmful or dangerous members of society. Canada's mental health statutes and *Criminal Code* articulate the procedures for controlling people who violate normative standards. It is no coincidence that criminal justice agents (e.g., police officers) are responsible for carrying out certain functions of the mental health system (such as responding to mental health crises or enforcing compulsory community treatment orders). Moreover, the existence of mental disorder provisions in the *Criminal Code* provides further evidence of the converging roles of the mental health and criminal justice systems. The reason why criminal justice agencies find themselves managing vast numbers of people with mental illnesses is, in part, a consequence of the conceptual overlap between crime and mental illness, as well as the intersecting functions of our mental health and criminal justice institutions.

FRONTLINE OF THE MENTAL HEALTH SYSTEM: THE POLICE

The police have a central role in handling situations involving people with mental illnesses. Estimates suggest that approximately 5 percent of all police dispatches or encounters involve persons with mental health problems, 30 percent of people with mental illnesses have had the police involved in their pathway to care (e.g., transported to hospital), and 14 percent of referrals to emergency psychiatric inpatient services involve the police (Brink et al. 2011). Attending to mental health crises, responding to people with mental illness who are witnesses and victims of crime, and diverting people to mental health services are routine duties for police officers. Additionally, officers may be called on to intervene in criminal acts involving people who appear to exhibit symptoms of mental illness—from minor nuisance- or disturbance-type offences to more serious incidents involving threatened or actual violence. Although about 40 percent of people with mental illnesses report being arrested by police at some point in their lives, studies reveal that only 14 percent of contacts between police and people with mental illnesses end in arrest (Brink et al. 2011). This suggests that most interactions are resolved by police using informal means, such as providing assistance.

To many police personnel, interacting on a routine basis with people who have mental illnesses is problematic. Several police chiefs in Canada have asserted that their officers should not be the mental health response agency of first resort. They openly complain that mental health work consumes too much time of frontline officers and diverts precious resources from core activities, including law enforcement and criminal investigations. Police officers routinely express concern about the amount of time that they must spend in hospital emergency rooms waiting for an individual with mental illness to be admitted. Additionally, police officers express frustration with deficiencies in the health and social service systems that severely constrain their ability to resolve situations effectively involving people with mental illnesses.

Research in Canada and the United States has revealed that people with mental illnesses tend to evaluate the quality of their interactions with police as being both positive and negative (Watson et al. 2008). For instance, a study of 60 people with mental illnesses in Vancouver found that, despite prevalent experiences of police use of force, the majority of participants held positive attitudes regarding their recent interactions with the police (Livingston et al. 2014). Importantly, positive perceptions were associated with interactions in which officers employed procedural justice-related skills, such as active listening, perspective taking, and fairness, rather than coercion and force. Within this study, almost all of the participants indicated the need for police officers to be better trained to handle situations involving people with mental illness.

Most police personnel and scholars concur that providing mental health training to police officers is important for reducing negative outcomes. In response to several high-profile fatal incidents and public inquiries, police services across Canada have developed specific strategies, including police training, to improve encounters with people who have mental illnesses. Changing the way in which police officers think and act in relation to mental illness is certainly a worthwhile activity; however, improving the lives of people with mental illnesses must also target the broader social and structural factors that have created the undesirable social context in which people find themselves in difficult situations (e.g., in crisis, victimized by crime, abusing substances, entrenched in poverty) requiring routine and recurrent intervention by the police. In addition to improving the quality of these interactions, perhaps more emphasis should be placed on working towards reducing the involvement of the police in the lives of people with mental illnesses.

DIVERTING PEOPLE WITH MENTAL ILLNESSES: THE ROLE OF THE COURTS

The use of criminal justice interventions is perceived to be an inappropriate, ineffective, and expensive manner for dealing with mental illnesses. The term *diversion* refers to the redirection of people with mental illnesses who have committed an offence away from the criminal justice system and towards mental health and social services. The underlying philosophy is that the offending behaviours of people with mental illnesses are more appropriately dealt with through the provision of treatment and support rather than through traditional criminal justice interventions.

Diversion strategies are designed for individuals who have been accused of crimes for whom voluntary mental health treatment and support services are a reasonable alternative to criminal justice sanctions. Accordingly, diversion programs primarily target people with an identifiable mental illness who have committed minor, non-violent, and chargeable offences. Diversion can occur at several points in the criminal justice process, including pre-arrest (e.g., police-based diversion), post-arrest (e.g., pretrial diversion), post-sentence/plea (e.g., court-based diversion), and post-incarceration (e.g., community re-entry diversion). Each of these points presents an opportunity to redirect people with mental illnesses towards appropriate services, and to prevent initial involvement or further penetration into the criminal justice system.

Court-based diversion strategies target people with mental illnesses who have not been diverted from the criminal justice system at the police or pretrial levels. These strategies can be divided into speciality mental health court and traditional court practices (Livingston 2008). Like other specialty courts, mental health courts are dedicated to handling cases involving offenders with particular problems—in this case, mental health issues. Judges and lawyers with specialized training work with mental health professionals in order to solve the problems facing offenders with mental illnesses. Although urban centres such as Toronto, Winnipeg, and Halifax have sufficient populations and resources to sustain a mental health court, many communities do not. As such, they may rely on the problem-solving approaches of judges in traditional courtrooms. There is no practical reason that problem-solving and collaborative practices used successfully in specialized courts cannot be integrated into traditional courtrooms. For instance, the court docket in a traditional courtroom can be dedicated for an afternoon to proactively and constructively deal with cases involving defendants with mental health problems. No special court is needed. The main challenge lies in changing both the traditional judicial decision-making philosophy and the adversarial, non-inclusive nature of the criminal justice system.

Diversion strategies can produce a range of desirable outcomes for people with mental illnesses, such as reducing recidivism and improving access to mental health services. However, a number of concerns have been expressed, including the overreliance on coercive interventions, as well as the potential to capture minor offenders in the criminal justice process who would have been released if diversion programs did not exist. Another issue is that many diversion strategies presume that offending behaviour is directly linked to an untreated, or ineffectively treated, mental illness that can be corrected by facilitating access to mental health services. The reality is that mental health treatment alone will not reduce reoffending for most offenders with mental illnesses, since their criminal behaviour is not caused directly by symptoms of mental illness but, rather, by factors such as poverty, employment problems, antisocial cognition, and criminal associates (Skeem, Manchak, and Peterson 2011).

CUSTODIAL AND COMMUNITY CORRECTIONS

Upwards of 80 percent of inmates have a mental disorder that includes a broad range of conditions such as adjustment disorders, substance use disorders, and personality disorders. When defined more narrowly, it would appear that 10–20 percent of inmates suffer from a severe and persistent mental illness— a rate that is two to four times greater than that of the general population (Fazel and Danesh 2002; Olley, Nicholls, and Brink 2009). Probation agencies are also responsible for managing significant numbers of people in the community who have mental illnesses, with one Canadian survey estimating the prevalence rate of mental disorders at approximately one-fifth of the community correctional population (Wormith and McKeague 1996).

When people with mental illnesses are detained, imprisoned, or being supervised in the community, opportunities arise for detecting untreated illness, reducing suffering, and improving quality of life. Not only is it good practice to provide an appropriate level of high-quality mental health services to correctional populations but also it is an ethical and legal responsibility. In Canada, this statutory obligation is enshrined in international, federal, and provincial/territorial policy and legislation. In addition to fulfilling legislative requirements, other motives for providing mental health services and supports in correctional settings include maximizing the ability for inmates to participate in the correctional programs and creating healthy environments for those who live and work in jails and prisons.

Jails and prisons are not renowned for their ability to promote mental health and well-being. Inmates with mental illnesses have great difficulty adjusting to life in correctional institutions, which can materialize as self-harming and suicidal behaviours, aggression and violence, or other institutional rule violations. In a correctional environment, the default response to individuals who engage in such behaviours is to employ segregation, fear, force, and discipline (Office of the Correctional Investigator Canada 2013). Unfortunately, these correctional approaches tend to reinforce and escalate mental health and behavioural problems. Mental health professionals who work in jails and prisons cite numerous challenges related to carrying out their duties, including the fact that their clinical decisions may be devalued, undermined, and overturned by correctional staff and leaders. Indeed, numerous philosophical and pragmatic challenges stand in the way of providing effective mental health services in correctional institutions.

The lack of appropriate, high-quality mental health services is one of the most significant problems facing Canada's provincial/territorial and federal correctional systems today (Olley, Nicholls, and Brink 2009). People who are detained in jails for brief periods should have access to mental health screening and assessment services, suicide prevention and management services, emergency and short-term mental health interventions, and services aimed at supporting inmates following their release from custody. Those who are detained in prison for longer times should also receive intermediate- and long-term mental healthcare, such as individual and group-based counselling. Beyond the walls of our correctional institutions, probationers and parolees also require access to appropriate mental health services. Traditional probation and parole agencies often lack the resources and specialized training needed to identify and appropriately deal with the needs of people with mental illnesses. To address this problem, many agencies have begun using a "specialized mental health caseload" model in which highly skilled probation officers have caseloads consisting only of people with mental illnesses (Livingston 2008). Under this innovative model, probation officers work in close partnership with mental health professionals and use non-confrontational, helpful strategies to monitor and enforce compliance.

CARE, COMPASSION, AND COERCION: FORENSIC MENTAL HEALTH SERVICES

The forensic mental health system provides specialized therapeutic and support services that aim to assess, treat, and rehabilitate people living with a mental illness who are at risk of criminal behaviour. Saying that Canada has a forensic mental health *system* is a bit of a misnomer, since the provinces and territories have their own systems that have evolved independent of one another (Livingston 2006). For instance, British Columbia organizes its forensic services using a centralized system composed of a single 190-bed secure hospital and six forensic community clinics located in urban centres throughout the province. In contrast, Ontario has a decentralized forensic system that includes more than 10 secure hospitals that have outpatient services for managing forensic clients in the community.

On the one hand, the forensic system is considered to be a compassionate way of providing necessary services and supports to persons with co-occurring mental health and legal problems. In this sense, it aims to reduce human suffering and improve quality of life. On the other hand, the forensic system has the primary objective of ensuring that society is protected from dangerous individuals. In fact, forensic mental health services are often considered a vehicle for identifying, managing, and reducing the risk of criminal and violent recidivism among people with mental illnesses. The contrasting objectives of the forensic system create many challenges for professionals who try, on a daily basis, to balance the therapeutic needs of the individual with the protective needs of the state.

The forensic mental health system can be considered a hybrid of the criminal justice and mental health systems. It operates in accordance with the requirements of federal criminal law and provincial/territorial health legislation. In Canada, the forensic mental health population consists of two legally distinct subgroups: mentally disordered offenders and mentally disordered accused. The mentally disordered offender subgroup is composed of people who are charged or convicted of crimes and who are also suffering from a mental illness, including persons living in the community (i.e., probation, parole, bail) as well as those detained in custodial settings (i.e., jail, prison). The courts have not provided offenders in this subgroup with a special mental disorder–related legal designation.

The other legal subgroup—mentally disordered accused—consists of persons who have engaged in, or have been accused of engaging in, unlawful behaviours and have been provided with a special legal designation owing to their mental illness. This subgroup includes people subsumed under the mental disorder provisions of the *Criminal Code of Canada* (ss. 16 and 672), such as persons who are court-ordered to receive forensic psychiatric assessments on issues of criminal responsibility or fitness to stand trial, as well as those who are adjudicated *Not Criminally Responsible on Account of Mental Disorder* or *Unfit to Stand Trial*. Mentally disordered accused persons are not convicted offenders; therefore, the legal system treats them differently than persons who are found guilty of an offence.

The features that distinguish the forensic mental health system from the regular mental health system are its direct interface with the legal system and its concentration on risk for violence and reoffending. Inpatient services in the forensic system are provided in secure facilities and the professionals that work with forensic patients are required to have specialized training in the assessment and management of violence risk. Community-based forensic services are provided by mental health professionals, such as nurses and social workers, who assist their clients; however, their role is also similar to that of a probation or parole officer, since they must monitor the degree to which their clients comply with legally mandated conditions, such as taking prescribed medications.

The creation of a specialized *forensic* mental health system is intended to ensure that resources are directed towards addressing the unique risk-related needs of individuals with mental disorders who are in conflict with the law. The existence of such as system also pacifies some of the public's fears related to mental illness, crime, and violence. Because of its important function in modern society, the demand for forensic services in Canada is growing rapidly. In turn, the number of hospital beds and resources allocated to the forensic system has increased steadily over the last two decades. A negative consequence of this trend is that it has the potential to perpetuate and reinforce the belief that people with mental illnesses are violent, dangerous, and require coercive interventions (Livingston, Rossiter, and Verdun-Jones 2011). Additionally, investing in forensic mental health services can divert attention and resources away from important initiatives that aim to prevent people with mental illnesses from getting involved in the criminal justice system in the first place.

CONCLUSION

Most people with mental illnesses do not commit criminal or violent acts, but they are at increased risk for coming into contact with the criminal justice system. Explanations for this are complex, involving the confluence of clinical (e.g., substance use problems), social (e.g., intolerance of social disorder), systemic (e.g., using police officers as first responders to mental health crises), and legal (e.g., punitive drug laws) factors. Throughout Canada, criminal justice agencies have developed specialized programs and strategies to respond appropriately to people with mental illnesses. Police services are developing better training for their officers and have created specialized teams that respond to mental health crises. The judicial system is building strategies and programs that aim to divert people with mental illness from the criminal justice system and to connect them with needed services.

The correctional system is finding ways to ensure that detainees, inmates, and people under community supervision have access to mental health services. The forensic mental health system is contending with increasing demands on its services. Although these developments are encouraging, it is important to keep in mind that the proliferation of specialized police teams, courts, correctional services, and forensic programs for people with mental illnesses is a telltale sign of deep-rooted social problems that have disproportionately channelled certain citizens into the criminal justice system. As a society, we must address the social injustices and inequities that contribute to the high rates of mental illnesses in Canada's criminal justice system.

Further Readings

Moran, J.E. 2013. "Mental Disorder and Criminality in Canada." *International Journal of Law and Psychiatry* 37: 109–16.

Osher, F., D.A. D'Amora, M. Plotkin, N. Jarrett, and A. Eggleston. 2012. *Adults with Behavioral Health Needs under Correctional Supervision: A Shared Framework for Reducing Recidivism and Promoting Recovery*. New York: Council of State Governments Justice Center, cited April 13, 2014. http://csgjusticecenter.org/wp-content/uploads/2013/05/9-24-12_Behavioral-Health-Framework-final.pdf

Slate, R.N., J.K. Burrington-Vollum, and W.W. Johnson. 2013. *The Criminalization of Mental Illness: Crisis and Opportunity for the Justice System*. 2nd ed. Durham, North Carolina: Carolina Academic Press.

References

Brink, J., J.D. Livingston, S.L. Desmarais, C. Greaves, V. Maxwell, R. Parent, S. Verdun-Jones, and C. Weaver. 2011. "A Study of How People with Mental Illness Perceive and Interact with the Police."

Mental Health Commission of Canada 2011, cited July 24, 2013. http://www.mentalhealthcommission.ca/English/document/437/study-how-people-mental-illness-perceive-and-interact-police

Fazel, S., and J. Danesh. 2002. "Serious Mental Disorder in 23 000 Prisoners: A Systematic Review of 62 Surveys." *Lancet* 359: 545–50.

Hiday, V.A. 2006. "Putting Community Risk in Perspective: A Look at Correlations, Causes and Controls." *International Journal of Law and Psychiatry* 29: 316–31.

Lamb, H.R., L.E. Weinberger, and B.H. Gross. 1999. "Community Treatment of Severely Mentally Ill Offenders under the Jurisdiction of the Criminal Justice System: A Review." *Psychiatric Services* 50: 907–13.

Livingston, J.D. 2006. "A Statistical Survey of Canadian Forensic Mental Health Inpatient Programs." *Healthcare Quarterly* 9: 56–61.

——. 2008. "Criminal Justice Diversion for Persons with Mental Disorders: A Review of Best Practices." http://www.cmha.bc.ca/files/DiversionBestPractices.pdf

Livingston, J.D., S.L. Desmarais, S. Verdun-Jones, R. Parent, E. Michalak, and J. Brink. 2014. "Perceptions and Experiences of People with Mental Illness Regarding their Interactions with Police." *International Journal of Law and Psychiatry*, in press.

Livingston, J.D., K.R. Rossiter, and S.N. Verdun-Jones. 2011. "'Forensic' Labelling: An Empirical Assessment of Its Effects on Self-Stigma for People with Severe Mental Illness." *Psychiatry Research* 188: 115–22.

Office of the Correctional Investigator Canada. 2014. "Risky Business: An Investigation of the Treatment and Management of Chronic Self-Injury among Federally Sentenced Women 2013," cited April 1, 2014. http://www.oci-bec.gc.ca/cnt/rpt/pdf/oth-aut/oth-aut20130930-eng.pdf

Olley, M.C., T.L. Nicholls, and J. Brink. 2009. "Mentally Ill Individuals in Limbo: Obstacles and Opportunities for Providing Psychiatric Services to Corrections Inmates with Mental Illness." *Behavioral Sciences and the Law* 27: 811–31.

Silver, E. 2006. "Understanding the Relationship between Mental Disorder and Violence: The Need for a Criminological Perspective." *Law and Human Behavior* 30: 685–706.

Skeem, J., S. Manchak, and J. Peterson. 2011. "Correctional Policy for Offenders with Mental Illness: Creating a New Paradigm for Recidivism Reduction." *Law and Human Behavior* 35: 110–26.

Walsh, E., A. Buchanan, and T. Fahy. 2002. "Violence and Schizophrenia: Examining the evidence." *British Journal of Psychiatry* 180: 490–95.

Watson, A.C., B. Angell, M.S. Morabito, and N. Robinson. 2008. "Defying Negative Expectations: Dimensions of Fair and Respectful Treatment by Police Officers as Perceived by People with Mental Illness." *Administration and Policy in Mental Health*, 35: 449–57.

Wormith, J.S., and F. McKeague. 1996. "A Mental Health Survey of Community Correctional Clients in Canada." *Criminal Behaviour and Mental Health* 6: 49–72.

Drugs and the Canadian Criminal Justice System

A significant proportion of the criminal justice budget is consumed by responses to offences involving drugs. Responding to the international drug trade, from cultivation to importation and distribution, has for many years been a major challenge, and not just for Canada. In this chapter the author takes a critical look at the criminal justice response to drugs. He argues that the prohibition-based approach, with its emphasis on punishment and deterrence, has failed.

Eugene Oscapella
University of Ottawa

Governments have many options for dealing with the vast array of mind-altering, or *psychoactive*, drugs available today. For example, they can decide to impose minimal restrictions on production, sale, and possession, as is largely the case with coffee and tea. Both beverages contain a psychoactive drug—caffeine—yet both are largely unregulated. Anyone, including a child, can purchase coffee, even though a 500-gram package of supermarket coffee contains more than enough caffeine to kill that child or even an adult.

Other drugs are regulated more strictly—for example, by limiting who can produce and buy them and where and when the drugs can be consumed. Alcohol is an example of this stricter regulation. Governments can also regulate advertising (as with alcohol) or prohibit advertising altogether (as with tobacco, which contains nicotine). Governments can tax drugs to discourage their excessive use. Again, alcohol and tobacco are examples. The criminal law comes into play only if, for example, someone drives a car or boat while impaired by alcohol. Governments also regulate drugs such as cold and allergy medications by imposing testing, quality control, and labelling standards. Still other drugs—such as sleeping pills, antidepressants, and strong painkillers—can be sold only in pharmacies and only to those holding a prescription.

Another option is to use the criminal law to prohibit the possession, production, transfer, and import or export of a drug. That is what Parliament has done with heroin, cocaine, cannabis, LSD, ecstasy, amphetamines, and hundreds of other substances. Most of these drugs are prohibited unless sold under prescription. Parliament prohibits these drugs through the *Controlled Drugs and Substances Act* (CDSA). The drugs "controlled" by this criminal law are the focus of this chapter. We commonly call them *illegal* or *illicit* drugs.

A CENTURY OF USING THE CRIMINAL LAW AND "PROHIBITION"

The *Controlled Drugs and Substances Act* came into force in 1997. It continues a century-long tradition in Canada of using the criminal law to prohibit an ever-growing range of drugs. Before 1908, when Canada first *criminalized* it, opium was legally available, as were cannabis, cocaine, and many other drugs that Parliament has since prohibited. Parliament prohibited cocaine in 1911, cannabis and heroin in 1923, and hundreds of other substances since then. Using the criminal law to deal with these drugs is largely a phenomenon of the 20th century, one that continues into the 21st. The CDSA prohibits many actions related to the substances it lists. Among the acts it prohibits are possession, sale, sharing, distribution, delivery, production, and import and export. This approach—using the criminal law—is called *prohibition*. The CDSA does not forbid drug use itself. The *Criminal Code* lists some crimes relating to drug use, such as driving while impaired by alcohol or a drug, and distributing "drug paraphernalia." But it is the CDSA that contains the bulk of Canada's provisions on illegal drugs.

Statistics Canada has reported that, in 2011, the overall rate of police-reported drug offences in Canada reached 329 incidents per 100,000 population—the highest rate in 30 years—though it declined to 314 in 2012, still the third-highest rate in 30 years. More than half of drug offences in 2012 involved cannabis, consistent with long-term trends (Statistics Canada 2013a). Despite a generally falling overall crime rate in Canada, there has been a consistent increase in the crime rate for drug offences. The overall crime rate decreased 25.9 percent between 1998 and 2011. Over that same period, the crime rate for drug offences increased 39.5 percent (Public Safety Canada 2012).

Penalties under the CDSA vary widely. Possession of a small quantity of cannabis is a criminal offence punishable by up to six months' imprisonment, a fine of up to $1,000, or both. At the other extreme, importing or exporting cannabis, heroin, cocaine, and scores of other substances is punishable by a maximum penalty of life imprisonment. Trafficking, which can include simply sharing a small quantity of a drug with a friend for no money, is punishable by up to life imprisonment for many drugs, including cocaine and heroin. The penalty for trafficking cannabis is a maximum of five years less a day if no more than three kilograms of cannabis is involved, and life imprisonment for larger amounts. Courts almost never impose these maximum penalties. However, Parliament has limited the discretion to impose shorter sentences by amending the CDSA in 2012 (*Safe Streets and Communities Act*). These amendments now force judges to impose mandatory minimum sentences of up to three years for some offences involving trafficking, production, import, or export.

Current drug laws contribute significantly to Canada's prison population. As of April 2012, just over 16 percent of federal inmates were incarcerated for "serious drug offences or conspiracy to commit serious drug offences" as their most serious offence (Public Safety Canada 2012). This figure does not include imprisonment for *acquisitive* offences committed to obtain the money to pay for illegal drugs, nor does it include imprisonment for violent crimes committed by those fighting for a share of the trade in illegal drugs. Nor does it include admissions to provincial custody for violating the CDSA, related acquisitive offences, and drug trade offences. Still, it is clear from even these limited statistics that drug laws are responsible, directly or indirectly, for a significant share of Canada's prisoners.

Criminal penalties are the most serious sanctions that the state can impose. One would expect it to base its decisions to apply these penalties on sound evidence that they will reduce the problematic use of a given drug. One would not expect decision makers to ignore evidence and instead to rely on ideology or other inappropriate considerations. Unfortunately, decisions in Canada (and in many other countries) to use the criminal law to deal with a particular drug have often flowed from prejudice, propaganda, political ideology, or historical accident, not from a rational search for ways to reduce the harms associated with the drug.

DOES THE CRIMINAL LAW REDUCE DRUG-RELATED HARMS?

In theory, the prospect of serious penalties for possessing, producing, or distributing drugs should discourage such activities. However, the evidence often points in the other direction—that the criminal law actually *increases* drug-related harms and that prohibition plants the seeds of its own failure. In other words, the criminal law causes many of the very problems it seeks to prevent. Below are discussed some of the many reasons why using the criminal law is counterproductive:

Prohibiting the supply of a drug forces users to buy it on the illegal market. The huge profits to be made in this "black" market act as an incentive to produce and sell illegal drugs and to develop new customers. The United Nations Office on Drugs and Crime (UNODC) described this illegal market as "of staggering proportions" (United Nations 2009a).

How profitable is the black market created by drug prohibition? UN figures from the mid-1990s indicated that a farmer in Pakistan received about US$90 for a kilogram of opium produced from the poppy plant. Ten kilograms of opium would be processed to yield 1 kilogram of heroin, so someone would pay about $900 for enough opium to produce a kilogram of heroin. The final retail price of that kilogram of heroin in the United States at that time was $290,000 (*Economist* 2001). This final price was more than 320 times the price paid to the farmer. That difference between the cost to produce heroin and its final retail price creates the potential for enormous profit and a powerful incentive—just the opposite of what governments want—to produce and sell heroin on the black market. In contrast, the final retail price of a pound of ground coffee beans, a legal product, might be as little as three times the price paid to the farmer who produced the beans (Miron 2003).

The funds generated by the black market help finance criminal, terrorist, and insurgent groups, adding to their power to corrupt and kill. Some RCMP reports have described the black market trade in drugs as a major, if not *the* major, source of income for most criminal groups in Canada. In 2000, RCMP Commissioner Giuliano Zaccardelli warned that for the first time, organized crime groups in Canada had accumulated so much money and power that they were threatening Canada's democratic institutions: "We are seeing signs of criminal organizations that are so sophisticated that they are focusing on destabilizing certain aspects of our society" (*National Post* 2000). Even the UNODC, long an advocate of prohibition and one of the many forces outside Canada's borders that constrain innovative drug policies in Canada, acknowledged the dramatic violence and corruption caused by current "global drug control efforts"—a polite way of saying policies and laws built around prohibition:

> Global drug control efforts have had a dramatic unintended consequence: a criminal black market of staggering proportions. Organized

crime is a threat to our security. Criminal organizations have the power to destabilize society and Governments. The illicit drug business is worth billions of dollars a year, part of which is used to corrupt government officials and to poison economies. (United Nations 2009a)

Yet the then-head of the UNODC immediately dismissed the most effective means to destroy the black market in drugs—replacing prohibition with strict regulation. "Legalization," as he simplistically described these alternatives, would be a "historical mistake" (United Nations 2009b). He did not explain why, nor did he explain what this historical mistake was. Often, support for prohibition-based approaches to drugs, even at the highest levels, seems to be based on blind faith rather than on reason and evidence.

Criminals fight to the death to control the black market and its profits. Warring groups in Colombia, often funded by huge profits from drug sales, have killed tens of thousands, as have rival drug gangs battling for control of the drug trade in Mexico (*Economist* 2010). And violence is not restricted to battles between drug lords in countries that produce and ship drugs; it reaches the consuming countries as well. A 2008 news report cited a claim in a U.S. Department of Justice report that Mexican drug traffickers posed the biggest organized crime threat to the United States. The report continued that Mexican gangs controlled distribution in most American cities and were gaining strength in areas they did not yet control (BBC 2008). These same gangs will inevitably reach into Canada, bringing further gang violence to this country. Even without the involvement of foreign criminal groups, domestic "turf" wars over control of the drug trade in Canada can be deadly. For example, a 2001 news report cited police sources for a claim that more than 150 people had been murdered in Quebec over the preceding six years in battles between criminal gangs for control of the drug trade there (*Washington Post* 2001). In 2012, 68 percent of gang-related homicides and 11 percent of non-gang-related homicides in Canada related to the illegal drug business (Statistics Canada 2013b).

In an attempt to suppress the drug trade and to confront sometimes well-armed drug gangs, the police arm themselves more heavily and develop a more aggressive style of policing. This increases bystanders' risk of death and injury during police actions. This sort of "militarization" of policing to tackle drug gangs may eventually lead to a militarization of policing generally. Law enforcement may foster violence in another way. A recent study contends that law enforcement practices that seek to disrupt drug markets may unintentionally increase market violence. Removing key players from the market may lead others to fight over the turf vacated as a result of the law enforcement action (British Columbia 2010). In addition, the black market leads to significant police and other official corruption, with police and officials sometimes actively involved in the drug trade themselves.

Law enforcement only marginally reduces the supply of drugs. In many countries, police and other government officials regularly admit that they stop only a small percentage of the illegal drugs destined for or produced in their countries. For example, a federal official told a House of Commons committee in 2001 that "law enforcement is able to stop only about 10 percent of the $7 billion to $10 billion annual trade in illegal drugs in Canada" (Connolly 2001). Even that 10 percent reduction may be futile. If there is a local glut of a drug, a 10 percent reduction may not increase prices or reduce availability or use. And even if policing does reduce the availability of one drug, users can simply switch to another of the many other illegal drugs that remain readily available.

Even what appears to be an obvious "success" in enforcing the drug laws—seizure of a large quantity of drugs—can produce harm. A large seizure may create a shortage and drive up a drug's price locally, just as a shortage of oil drives up its price. This increases the value of the drugs that remain in the market, bringing even greater profits to sellers. The higher price may lure others into selling because of the even greater profits to be made. As well, the higher price may force dependent users to commit more crimes to get the extra money they now need to buy the drug. High prices may also lead users to search for more efficient ways of using their drugs, such as by injection. Injection with equipment infected by HIV or hepatitis C—too often a reality in the world of illegal drug use—greatly increases the risk of acquiring these serious diseases. And, as noted above, users who cannot afford or get access to the drug may shift to other drugs. Users who are not familiar with these substitute drugs are more vulnerable to harm from them.

There is little evidence that the criminal law and criminal justice policies deter people from using drugs. In 2001 the Senate Special Committee on Illegal Drugs heard from Professor Peter Cohen of the University of Amsterdam that the tolerance of access to cannabis in the Netherlands has had little, if any, impact on its use:

> In terms of our national [cannabis consumption] averages, we are in the same league as Germany and France. We are considerably lower than the UK or Denmark, and much lower than the USA. The USA has levels of drug use that are double to triple the levels in the Netherlands. I do not say that this is because of drug policy, because it is my firm opinion that drug policy in itself has very little influence on the number of people who use drugs or who do not use drugs. The incredibly easy availability of cannabis-type drugs in The Netherlands has not at all changed the number of people who want to use it, because the decision to use it is based on the cultural composition of the population, who your friends are, the image of drugs and the economic situation of individuals. It does not matter what the government thinks about these drugs. (Cohen 2001)[*]

Prohibiting drugs can make their use much more dangerous than it would otherwise be. Unlike regulated drugs, prohibited drugs have no quality

---

[*] Cohen, P. 2001. Testimony before the Senate Special Committee on Illegal Drugs. May 28, 2001.

controls or labels indicating their potency. Governments discourage honest drug education for fear of "condoning" drug use. Police, rather than public health workers, often deliver the limited education that does occur. Such education provides little, if any, instruction on how to minimize the risks of using certain drugs. Much of the education preaches abstinence, abandoning to ignorance the many who do try illegal drugs.

Drug users may end up in prison for drug offences or related crimes. There, HIV and hepatitis C rates are many times higher than in open society. Users may well continue to use the drugs that are readily available there, but government authorities will not permit them access to some types of equipment, such as syringes, needed to prevent the spread of infection.

Both in and outside Canada, the stigma—indeed, outright hostility—attached to certain drugs has fostered conditions for the explosive spread of HIV and hepatitis C. Globally, millions of people have become infected as a result of government and public inattention, or outright opposition, to means for reducing the risk of disease among drug users. The failure to reduce the spread of such diseases among users leads to their spread into the general population.

The "war on drugs" mentality has led governments and the public to tolerate, and even encourage, troubling violations of rights. Violent police raids of private dwellings, increased powers of search and seizure and surveillance in homes and schools, employee drug testing, calls for long mandatory prison terms, and the encouragement of an "informer society" (once largely the mark of authoritarian regimes) are all products of this mentality. These state powers are not directed solely at drug users: all society suffers a loss of privacy and other rights. And because these measures do not work, governments may propose even greater powers of surveillance, control, and incarceration.

Conviction for a drug offence results in a criminal record (although an accused person can sometimes obtain an absolute or conditional discharge, which in theory produces no criminal record). A criminal record can result in serious collateral harms—stigma, difficulty in securing a job, complete ineligibility for some jobs, and restrictions on travel to other countries.

Money spent on enforcing drug laws and building and running prisons is not available for other, possibly more effective, programs to reduce problematic drug use. Canada's criminal justice system receives the overwhelming share of federal funds directed at the drug issue. The Auditor General reported in 2001 that "about 95 percent of the federal government's expenditures that address illicit drugs were used for supply reduction (enforcement or interdiction)." This percentage declined over the next few years, but the harsher drug penalties enacted in 2012 will require extensive new resources for the criminal justice apparatus. This will leave programs outside the criminal justice system starved of funding to deal with drug issues.

Perhaps the most fundamental flaw of prohibition is that it has failed to address the causes of problematic drug use. Prohibition assumes that the problem is drug availability and that availability can be reduced through law enforcement and punishment. This approach ignores the real issues that often underpin problematic use, such as alienation, homelessness, physical and sexual abuse, and mental illness.

WHERE IS CANADA HEADED?

There have been several attempts to move away from a prohibition-based approach to regulating drugs. In 2002 the Senate Special Committee on Illegal Drugs recommended a regulatory regime for cannabis to replace the current prohibitionist model (Senate 2002). Later that year, the House of Commons Committee on the Non-Medical Use of Drugs called for simple possession of cannabis and production of small amounts to be decriminalized. These activities would remain offences, but not *criminal* offences—those convicted would not receive a criminal record. The Commons Committee also supported supervised injection facilities where users could more safely inject the drugs on which they were dependent, and it recommended projects to provide heroin to severely dependent heroin users (House of Commons 2002).

The Liberal government in power during the first six years of the 21st century did introduce legislation to reduce penalties for simple possession of cannabis and for production of small quantities. However, Parliament never enacted the law and the Conservative government that replaced it in 2006 took a more punitive approach to illegal drugs, including cannabis, introducing mandatory minimum sentences for several drug offences, including some cannabis production and trafficking offences.

In early 2014, the federal Liberal leader proposed the possible legalization and regulation of cannabis as two American states, Colorado and Washington, have done (CBC News 2014a). The Conservative justice minister also suggested that his government was now considering allowing police officers to issue tickets to people caught with small amounts of cannabis (CBC News 2014b). To date, however, no changes to the cannabis possession provisions of the CDSA have occurred.

The former Liberal government permitted the opening of a supervised injection facility, known as Insite, in Vancouver, and it supported heroin maintenance trial projects in Vancouver and Montreal. The current Conservative government opposes a continuation of heroin maintenance projects and has attempted to block one avenue for such programs to continue—a federal initiative known as the Special Access Program. Since coming into power, the government has also opposed Insite, but to date has been unable to close it despite trying to persuade the courts to allow it to do so. In 2011, the nine judges of the Supreme Court of Canada unanimously ordered the Minister of Health to grant an exemption under the CDSA to allow Insite to continue to operate (*Canada [Attorney General] v. PHS Community Services Society* 2011). In an apparent move to impede other consumption sites from opening, the Conservative government introduced a bill in mid-2013 that imposed almost prohibitive constraints on their opening and operation (Bill C-65 2013a). That

Bill died on the Order Paper but was revived later that year (Bill C-2 2013b), although it has not yet been enacted.

In short, the Conservative government in power since 2006 has taken a highly punitive line, apart from the recent hint that it might consider lower penalties for cannabis possession. As noted above, it amended the CDSA to introduce mandatory minimum sentences for several drug offences. Government rhetoric persists with a "tough on drugs" line despite the demonstrated failure of such approaches around the world and despite a growing chorus of calls for reform by respected international figures. Unless the courts strike them down as violating the *Canadian Charter of Rights and Freedoms*, the new mandatory minimum sentencing requirements will almost certainly result in small-time drug sellers, many of them dependent users, being imprisoned, and for longer terms. Organized crime, the professed target of these minimum penalties, will remain as insulated as ever from the reach of the criminal law.

WHY PERSIST WITH SOMETHING THAT DOESN'T WORK?

Drug prohibition has not worked, is not working, and will not work to reduce drug problems. The prohibitionist system is broken. In May 2010 the head of the U.S. Office of National Drug Control Policy acknowledged this. "In the grand scheme," he said, the "war on drugs" strategy employed in the United States over the previous 40 years "has not been successful.… Forty years later, the concern about drugs and drug problems is, if anything, magnified, intensified" (Associated Press 2010).

Yet the continuing failure of prohibition has not stopped many governments—including successive federal governments in Canada—from calling for more of the same prohibitionist policies. As long as drug policy and drug laws in Canada remain driven by ideology rather than by rational discussion and evidence, it will be exceedingly difficult to mend this broken system. Another impediment to reform—perhaps the greatest impediment—is that various interests benefit from prohibition, even if it damages society as a whole. These range from "tough on crime" politicians seeking election; to organized crime and terrorist groups; to police organizations, which benefit through increased budgets to "fight drugs"; to others in what Nils Christie has called the "crime control industry."

Instead of relying on Parliament to fix the broken drug-control system, reform advocates have increasingly turned to the courts. The successful constitutional challenge to the attempt by the current Conservative government to shut down Vancouver's Insite is a case in point. Other constitutional challenges have led several courts to declare the prohibition on cannabis to be unconstitutional and forced the federal government to develop a program for access to medicinal cannabis, although higher courts later overturned some of these decisions. Reform advocates will continue to turn to the courts to undo some of the most punitive aspects of Canada's current drug laws and policies—mandatory minimum penalties, restrictions on the operation of supervised consumption sites, access to heroin maintenance programs, and problematic changes to access to cannabis for therapeutic purposes.

ALTERNATIVES TO PROHIBITION

Despite calls for reform and increasing examples from other countries, Canada's federal drug strategy remains firmly rooted in prohibition and shows continuing hostility to a dialogue on *harm reduction* measures. Even so, several harm reduction measures have established themselves in Canada, among them syringe distribution and methadone maintenance programs and education about techniques for safer drug use. More controversial programs such as heroin maintenance and supervised consumption sites still stand on shaky ground, while proposals for syringe exchange in prisons see little hope of implementation.

Several groups have described regulatory models that could replace prohibition. It is not possible in this brief chapter to explain these models in detail. Prohibition's one virtue—despite its utter failure as a policy—is its structural simplicity: simply prohibit a drug. The regulatory models that would replace prohibition are necessarily more complex, for they seek to take into account the subtleties of human behaviour; the many effects, good *and* bad, of currently illegal drugs; and the most effective ways to reduce the harms of those drugs and to enhance their benefits. Readers looking for greater insight into regulatory alternatives to prohibition can review the reports cited in the following paragraphs.

In 2002 the Senate Special Committee on Illegal Drugs called for an end to the criminalizing of cannabis users. It proposed a *criminal exemption* scheme under which the production and sale of cannabis would be licensed (Senate 2002). It also called for an amnesty for the hundreds of thousands of Canadians with a criminal record for possession of cannabis. Similarly, in 2005 the Health Officers Council of British Columbia rejected many aspects of prohibition—only this time, for all currently illegal drugs, not merely cannabis. The council called for an approach based on public health principles:

> Current conditions are right to enter into serious public discussions regarding the creation of a regulatory system for currently illegal drugs in Canada, with better control and reduced harms to be achieved by management in a tightly controlled system. The removal of criminal penalties for drug possession for personal use, and placement of these currently illegal substances in a tight regulatory framework, could both aid implementation of programs to assist those engaged in harmful drug use, and reduce secondary unintended drug-related harms to society that spring from a failed criminal-prohibition approach. This would move individual harmful illegal drug use from being primarily a criminal issue to being primarily a health issue....

Part of a public health approach includes harm reduction. Reviews of the evidence show that selected harm reduction strategies do work. Harm reduction strategies such as needle exchanges, safe injection sites and opioid substitution programs have been shown to reduce the spread of infectious diseases and the number of overdose deaths. These programs also act to draw in the otherwise marginalized drug users giving them access to health services and an opportunity to move towards risk-behavior reduction or treatment for the addiction. Harm reduction strategies have not been as effective as possible due to their implementation within the prohibition model. (Health Officers 2005, 2, 15)*

At the international level, the Global Commission on Drug Policy, whose members included former UN Secretary General Kofi Annan, four former presidents, former U.S. Secretary of State George Shultz, and former Supreme Court of Canada Justice Louise Arbour, concluded that the global war on drugs has failed, "with devastating consequences for individuals and societies around the world." Its 2011 report counselled:

- End the criminalization, marginalization and stigmatization of people who use drugs but who do no harm to others. Challenge rather than reinforce common misconceptions about drug markets, drug use and drug dependence.
- Encourage experimentation by governments with models of legal regulation of drugs to undermine the power of organized crime and safeguard the health and security of their citizens....
- Begin the transformation of the global drug prohibition regime. Replace drug policies and strategies driven by ideology and political convenience with fiscally responsible policies and strategies grounded in science, health, security and human rights—and adopt appropriate criteria for their evaluation.
- Break the taboo on debate and reform. (Global Commission 2011, 2–3)

In 2009 the British drug policy reform group Transform published its proposals for reform in what it called a *Blueprint for Regulation*. The Blueprint concluded that "both experience and research suggests that the most effective way of minimizing drug arms is regulation, based upon normative, legal frameworks rather than prohibition." The Blueprint proposed five key models, none involving prohibition, for managing drugs:

Prescription: the most controlling model, this would be an exact equivalent to current prescription models for medical drugs, and some opiate maintenance programs.

Pharmacy sales: drugs would be made available through pharmacies or pharmacy-like outlets, either on prescription or over the counter.

---

* Health Officers Council of British Columbia. 2005. Discussion Paper: A Public Health Approach to Drug Control in Canada.

Licensed sales: vendors would be granted a licence to sell specific drugs under certain, clearly defined conditions, on off-licence–like premises.

Licensed premises: vendors would be licensed to manage premises where drugs would be sold and consumed, much like public houses and bars.

Unlicensed sales: certain low risk substances could be managed through food and beverage legislation, as—for example—coffee is currently managed. (Transform 2009, 7–8)

None of the alternatives to prohibition discussed above seek to abandon drug users to a life of desperate and uncontrolled use. Instead, they seek to minimize the harms associated with using these drugs. This may include measures to help problematic users quit. At the same time, these measures avoid the grave harms to users caused by prohibition during the period when individuals are using drugs.

CONCLUSION

Canada's approach to illegal drugs demonstrates one of the sorriest misuses of the criminal law. The criminal law does not address the fundamental questions—why people use drugs, and why some of them use drugs in a way that harms them and those around them. As long as people want to alter their mental states, they will do so, whether through criminal or legal means. As this chapter has argued, the criminal law, instead of controlling problematic drug use, causes profound additional harms. Yet prohibition is so firmly entrenched as a means of dealing with certain drugs that many people and organizations do not even question its worth. As legal philosopher Douglas Husak argues in his discussion of using the criminal law to prohibit drug use, those calling for reform are always challenged to show why change is necessary. But, he says, those who support prohibition have never been called on to provide evidence that prohibition works:

> Any policy that resorts to punishment requires a justification. We should not assume that what we are doing is right unless someone can prove that it is wrong. We must always be prepared to show why what we are doing is right.... Those who favor punishments for drug users must explain why they think this policy is fair and just (Husak 2002, 13).

Further Readings

Alexander, B.K. 2008. *The Globalisation of Addiction: A Study in Poverty of the Spirit*. Oxford: Oxford University Press.

Duke, S.B., and A.C. Gross. 1993. *America's Longest War: Rethinking Our Tragic Crusade Against Drugs*. New York: Putnam.

Maté, G. 2008. *In the Realm of Hungry Ghosts: Close Encounters with Addiction*. Toronto: Random House of Canada.

References

Associated Press. 2010. "U.S. Drug War Has Met None of Its Goals." May 13, 2010.

Auditor General of Canada. 2001. "Illicit Drugs: The Federal Government's Role." Chap. 11 in *Report of the Auditor General of Canada—2001, Chapter 11, Illicit Drugs: The Federal Government's Role*. Ottawa.

Bill C-65. 2013a. *Respect for Communities Act*. 1st Session, 41st Parliament, 60-61-62 Elizabeth II, 2013.

Bill C-2. 2013b. *Respect for Communities Act*. 2nd Session, 41st Parliament, 62 Elizabeth II, 2013.

BBC News. 2008. "Mexico Drug Gangs 'Top US Threat.'" December 16, 2008.

British Columbia Centre for Excellence in HIV/AIDS, Urban Health Research Initiative. 2010. *Effect of Drug Law Enforcement on Drug-Related Violence: Evidence from a Scientific Review*. Vancouver: University of British Columbia.

CBC News. 2014a. "Justin Trudeau Watching U.S. Experience with Legalized Pot." January 23, 2014.

——. 2014b. "Pot Legislation 'Under Serious Consideration,' Peter MacKay Says." March 5, 2014.

Cohen, P. 2001. Testimony before the Senate Special Committee on Illegal Drugs. May 28, 2001.

Connolly, M. 2001. Testimony before the House of Commons Special Committee on Non-Medical Use of Drugs. October 1, 2001.

Economist, The. 2001. "Survey: Illegal Drugs." July 26, 2001.

——. 2010. "Mexico's Murder Capital: A 'Dying' City Protests." February 18, 2010.

Global Commission on Drug Policy. 2011. *War on Drugs: Report of the Global Commission on Drug Policy*.

Health Officers Council of British Columbia. 2005. *Discussion Paper: A Public Health Approach to Drug Control in Canada*.

House of Commons, Special Committee on Non-Medical Use of Drugs. 2002. *A Policy for the New Millennium: Working Together to Redefine Canada's Drug Strategy*. Ottawa.

Husak, D. 2002. *Legalize This! The Case for Decriminalizing Drugs*. London: Verso.

Miron, J.A. 2003. *The Effect of Drug Prohibition on Drug Prices: Evidence from the Markets for Cocaine and Heroin*. Cambridge, MA: National Bureau of Economic Research.

National Post. 2000. "Organized Crime Plans to Corrupt Parliament: RCMP Commissioner." September 8, 2000.

Public Safety Canada. 2012. *Corrections and Conditional Release Statistical Overview 2012*. Ottawa.

Safe Streets and Communities Act, S.C. 2012, c. 1.

Senate of Canada, Special Committee on Illegal Drugs. 2002. *Cannabis: Our Position for a Canadian Public Policy*. Ottawa.

Statistics Canada. 2013a. "Police-Reported Crime Statistics in Canada, 2012." *Juristat*, July 25, 2013.

——. 2013b. "Homicide in Canada, 2012." *Juristat*, July 25, 2013.

Transform Drug Policy Foundation. 2009. *After the War on Drugs: Blueprint for Regulation*. Bristol.

United Nations, Office on Drugs and Crime. 2009a. http://www.unodc.org/drugs/en/security-and-justice/index.html

——. 2009b. *Organized Crime and Its Threat to Security: Tackling a Disturbing Consequence of Drug Control*. Vienna.

Washington Post. 2001. "Canadian Motorcycle Gangs Gun for Control of Illegal Drug Trade." February 5, 2001.

Case

Canada (Attorney General) v. PHS Community Services Society, 2011 SCC 44.

Wrongful Convictions in Canada: Causes, Consequences, and Responses

A common perception among many members of the public is that the justice system tends to protect the rights of the accused, with the result that guilty parties too often escape conviction. However, the opposite can also occur: innocent accused persons are sometimes convicted of crimes they did not commit. This is especially disturbing when the conviction results in a long prison sentence. In this chapter, two leading Canadian researchers discuss the issue of wrongful convictions.

Kathryn M. Campbell
University of Ottawa

Myriam Denov
McGill University

Numerous procedural safeguards are presumed to protect the innocent from unintentional and/or intentional errors on the part of the police, prosecutors, and judges. Unfortunately, cases of wrongful conviction in Canada call into question the ability of our criminal justice system to distinguish between the guilty and the innocent. The devastating ordeals of wrongly convicted Canadians such as Donald Marshall Jr., David Milgaard, Guy Paul Morin, Steven Truscott, and Jamie Nelson serve as powerful reminders of the potential for error in the justice system. The media and lobby groups such as the Association in Defence of the Wrongly Convicted (AIDWYC) help in raising awareness about these cases.

This chapter begins by examining the individual and systemic factors that contribute to wrongful convictions. It then explores the effects of wrongful conviction on individuals and their families, based on in-depth interviews with two Canadians who have been wrongly convicted and falsely imprisoned. Finally, it addresses state responses to wrongful conviction, including conviction review, commissions of inquiry, and government approaches to compensation.

THE PREVALENCE OF WRONGFUL CONVICTIONS

A wrongful conviction can be defined as occurring when an individual has "been arrested on criminal charges [and has] either plead guilty to the charge or [has] been tried and found guilty; and who, notwithstanding plea or verdict, [is] in fact innocent" (Huff, Rattner, and Sagarin 1996, 10). While in the past, wrongful convictions were thought to be relatively rare, more recent estimates of the frequency of such miscarriages range from very few cases each year to 20 percent of all convictions (Holmes 2001). Innocence scholarship in the United States indicates that an accepted "estimate" is a general wrongful conviction rate between half of 1 percent and 1 percent; however, this is a subjective judgment (Zalman 2012, 230).

Furthermore, Gross and colleagues (2005, 551) found in their study of false convictions in the United States that from 1989 to 2003, any estimate of the number of wrongful convictions in that country would be in the tens of thousands. There is no reason to believe that the rate of wrongful conviction is any lower in Canada.

CAUSES OF WRONGFUL CONVICTION

Research has revealed that wrongful convictions do not occur as a result of one individual making a single grave mistake. Instead, several individual and systemic factors, alone or in concert, contribute to wrongful convictions (Castelle and Loftus 2001). These factors include eyewitness error, erroneous forensic science, false confessions, the use of jailhouse informants, professional and institutional misconduct, and racial bias.

Eyewitness Error

Psychological research shows that due to normal deficiencies in human memory, eyewitness identification is inherently unreliable (Loftus et al. 2008; Wells and Olsen 2003). Eyewitness testimony is often the sole or major source of evidence leading to a conviction; it follows that it is the single most important factor leading to wrongful convictions (Huff, Rattner, and Sagarin 1986, 1996). In the United States, through DNA forensic analysis, the Innocence Project has helped overturn 314 wrongful convictions; eyewitness misidentification was a major contributing factor in 75 percent of those cases (Innocence Project 2014).

While the inherent unreliability of human memory affects witness recall in many instances, eyewitness errors occur for other reasons, including suggestive police interviewing, unconscious transference, and the malleability of confidence (Castelle and Loftus 2001). *Suggestive police interviewing* occurs when the police communicate information to eyewitnesses that subsequently influences and ultimately contaminates their testimony. In Canada, suggestive police interviewing led to the initial convictions of Donald Marshall Jr., David Milgaard, and Thomas Sophonow. In each of these cases, witnesses were pressured by police until they abandoned their original testimony and gave false evidence (Anderson and Anderson 2009). *Unconscious transference* is witness confusion between a person seen in one situation and a person seen in another situation (Loftus 1979). The term *malleability of confidence* refers to the pliable nature of a witness's certainty of her testimony. Research has demonstrated that witnesses who identify a suspect from a police lineup or group of photos are far more confident of their choice if they receive positive feedback from authorities (cf. Wells and Bradfield 1998).

Because most jurors are unaware of the unreliability of eyewitness identification, they may place unwarranted faith in its accuracy (Sanders 1984). In Canada, defence lawyers are not permitted to call upon experts to discuss the weaknesses of eyewitness identification. It is the role of the judge to inform the jury as to the possible frailties of eyewitness testimony, as it is generally thought to be a matter of common sense. Roach points to the growing body of psychological research that raises questions about the so-called common sense intuitions about eyewitness identification (2007, 216). Moreover, when a judge plays the role of "expert" in such instances, the accused does not have a chance to refute or qualify any instructions, and a jury is likely to find any admissions from a judge about a particular issue at trial far more compelling than similar evidence from an expert witness (Bala 2001, 286). The questionable accuracy of eyewitness testimony and the undue weight it receives from criminal justice personnel make eyewitness identifications a significant contributor to wrongful convictions.

Erroneous Forensic Science

Erroneous and fraudulent forensic science has also been cited as a cause of wrongful convictions. In some cases, inadvertent human error, sloppiness, exaggeration, misinterpretation, and bias may work to contaminate evidence, whether in the forensic laboratory or at the crime scene (Castelle and Loftus 2001). More disturbing, however, are those cases in which forensic scientists deliberately tamper with evidence. For example, Stephanie Nyznyk, a laboratory technician working out of the Centre for Forensic Sciences in Ontario, suppressed information that hair and fibre samples used by the prosecution to successfully convict Guy Paul Morin of murder had been contaminated and should not have been entered as evidence (Anderson and Anderson 2009). A further example of this problem is the work of Dr. Charles Smith. While he was the chief paediatric forensic pathologist at the Hospital for Sick Children in Toronto, he made a number of significant errors in more than 40 autopsies of children whose deaths had occurred under questionable circumstances. In 2007 the Goudge Commission of Inquiry into Pediatric Forensic Pathology in Ontario examined the more egregious errors in 20 of Smith's cases, as well as the practice and oversight of paediatric forensic pathology in Ontario. The inquiry revealed that Smith made several fundamental errors: he testified outside his area of expertise; ignored the testimony of other experts that conflicted with his own; used unscientific methods in coming to his conclusions; and functioned more as a "hired gun" for the prosecution instead of presenting unbiased, objective testimony based on the facts. While a comprehensive series of recommendations emerged from this inquiry, the lives of those 20 individuals and their families were irredeemably altered and devastated by Smith's errors.

False Confessions

A confession is often viewed as the most powerful piece of evidence that the prosecution can bring against an accused. Juries are said to believe a defendant who confesses to a crime, regardless of other evidence pointing to the contrary (Leo and Ofshe 1998). While most people find it difficult to believe that anyone would confess to a crime that he did not commit, research indicates that this may not be such a rare phenomenon. Studies in the United States have found that false confessions were the leading or primary cause of wrongful conviction in anywhere from 14 to 25 percent of cases studied (Drizin and Leo 2004, 902). The Innocence Project found that for the over 300 wrongfully convicted persons they have helped to exonerate, false confessions or admissions played a role in over 25 percent of the cases (Innocence Project 2014). To understand how innocent people can come to confess to crimes they did not commit, it is important to consider the psychology behind police interrogation techniques.

Christopher Bates was wrongly convicted of murder and spent five-and-a-half years in a maximum-security prison after giving a false confession to police. Bates was arrested and charged with the murder of a shopkeeper who had been killed and robbed of $90. While in police custody, Bates was interrogated, threatened, and tormented for 17 hours. Furthermore, he was held without access to food, water, toilet facilities, and legal counsel for 72 hours. He was told that if he did not confess, child protection authorities would take his children away. After many hours of physical and psychological torture, Bates agreed to sign a declaration linking him to the robbery and murder. Bates later explained that extreme fear for his life had led him to sign the declaration. His false confession played a pivotal role in his conviction.

Bates's case illustrates a coerced false confession. However, in 1972 Romeo Phillion voluntarily confessed to a crime he did not commit. Voluntary false confessions are normally freely given to the police, with little interrogation or pressure. The literature indicates that these types of confessions are likely the result of a desire for notoriety, attention, or fame; a need to expiate guilt for real or imagined acts; an inability to distinguish between fantasy and reality; or a pathological need for acceptance or self-punishment (Gudjonsson 2002). In Phillion's case, while he was later found to have an intellectual limitation and to suffer from mental health issues, he claimed that he had confessed to killing an Ottawa area firefighter because he wanted his partner to collect the reward money. Despite having immediately retracted his confession, he served over 30 years in jail for this murder, and was exonerated only in 2010.

The Use of Jailhouse Informants

The use of jailhouse informants may also play an important role in the conviction of the innocent. Prisoner informants provide information to law enforcement officials in exchange for money, property, or the promise of leniency in sentencing. Law enforcement officials may use the testimony of such informants as a means of securing convictions. Indeed, the Innocence Project (2014) found that in over 15 percent of more than 300 cases of wrongful conviction overturned by DNA forensic analysis, an informant or jailhouse snitch testified against the defendant. Furthermore, jurors give great weight to confessions made to jailhouse informants. American studies indicate that to the average juror, there is little difference between the manner in which they receive and weigh a confession given to a police officer and a confession given to a jailhouse informant (Cory 2001).

In Canada, the case of Guy Paul Morin illustrates the dangers of relying on jailhouse informants. In 1985, Morin was charged with the murder of a young girl, Christine Jessop. While Morin was jailed without bail, two jailhouse informants who were facing charges of sexual assault and assault came forward claiming that Morin had confessed to the crime. This was the only direct evidence of Morin's guilt (Kaufman 1998, 546). Both informants—who had lengthy criminal histories, as well as histories of psychiatric problems—were desperate to get out of jail and received more lenient sentences as a result of their testimony. Morin was convicted in part because of their testimony, but his conviction was later reversed on appeal. The informants testified again at Morin's second trial, where he was convicted again. Through DNA evidence, Morin was later found to be innocent and was subsequently released from prison.

The risks of relying on jailhouse informants are obvious. In his report on the wrongful conviction of Thomas Sophonow, Justice Cory described jailhouse informants as a "uniquely evil group [who] should as far as it is possible, be excised and removed from our trial process" (Cory 2001). Informants may have much to gain and little to lose by providing false testimony to authorities. It is thus essential that this relatively common practice in the justice system be subject to limited use and that informants be prohibited from testifying. Due in large part to the difficulties revealed by these wrongful conviction cases, all 10 provinces now have safeguards in place, such as In-Custody Informant Registries, which severely circumscribe the use of such informants, as well as committees composed of attorneys that vet the testimony of jailhouse snitches.

Professional and Institutional Misconduct

Unprofessional conduct on the part of police, the prosecution, and the judiciary is an important factor in wrongful convictions (Huff et al. 1996). As a first point of entry into the criminal justice system, the police play a pivotal role in deciding whom to charge and in collecting evidence to support a charge. In building their case against a suspect, the police may suppress, lose, misinterpret, or overlook evidence that supports the defendant's claim of innocence. Such errors may occur through prejudicial identification lineups, misuse of informants, solicitation of false confessions, or reliance on poor forensic science. This unprofessional behaviour may be motivated by a sincere desire to strengthen the case against a suspect whom professionals are convinced is guilty. This set of process errors is often referred to as tunnel vision: a suspect's guilt is assumed, and evidence is then subconsciously manipulated to prove that guilt. Whether the tunnel vision occurs among police officers or the prosecution, the authorities may become so focused on one suspect that they deliberately destroy that individual's alibi and eliminate all other potential suspects from the investigation (MacFarlane 2008).

Professional misconduct can also involve withholding evidence considered favourable to the defence. The Canadian justice system prohibits police and prosecutors from pursuing a prosecution while withholding evidence that supports a claim of innocence. Both case law and policy require prosecutors to disclose to the defence all relevant evidence in their possession, and they face sanctions if they fail to do so (*R. v. Stinchcombe*). This obligation, however, does not apply to the police in exactly the same manner. Withholding evidence raises ethical questions about prosecutorial conduct and may also contribute to wrongful convictions (Rosenberg 2002).

The Canadian case of Donald Marshall Jr., who was wrongly convicted of the murder of Sandy Seale in Nova Scotia in 1971, shows how the police and the prosecution can fail to disclose information crucial to an accused's defence. Ten days after Marshall's conviction for the murder of Sandy Seale, a witness (Jimmy MacNeil) told police he had seen Roy Ebsary, not Marshall, stab Seale. The police failed to thoroughly investigate this assertion. Moreover, according to the Marshall Inquiry (Royal Commission 1989), MacNeil's claim was never disclosed by police to either Marshall's defence counsel or to the Halifax Crown counsel handling Marshall's appeal of his conviction. Had this information been presented to the Court of Appeal, a new trial would likely have been ordered (ibid.). Also, the prosecution failed to inform Marshall's defence counsel of statements from several witnesses whose stories tended to corroborate Marshall's account of the murder (Wall 1992). Marshall spent 11 years in prison for a crime he did not commit. Roy Ebsary was tried and later convicted of manslaughter for the murder of Sandy Seale, but served only one year in jail.

Judges play a role in preventing or contributing to a wrongful conviction. Judges make crucial decisions about the admissibility of evidence which can affect the outcome of a trial. At the same time, they give directions to the jury prior to deliberations where they can emphasize or downplay the importance of specific evidence or witness testimony. Judges also play a role in screening cases at the preliminary inquiry stage where they may exercise discretion regarding whether the Crown has discharged the evidential burden and can also prevent weak cases from going forward. Finally, they are able to direct verdicts of acquittal in some rare cases, where a judge finds that the Crown has not made out a prima facie case against the accused (Campbell forthcoming).

Wrongful convictions also occur in the larger institutional context. Martin (2001) identifies three institutional factors that contribute to convicting the innocent: the high-profile nature of the case, which pressures authorities to make a quick arrest; the marginalized status of the accused (an "outsider"); and the unreliable nature of the evidence. When all three factors are present in the institutional context, authorities are more likely to overlook the initial reluctance of an eyewitness, to believe an unreliable jailhouse informant, to fail to disclose favourable evidence, or to pressure a defendant into a false confession. Any one of these may precipitate a wrongful conviction.

The wrongful 22-year imprisonment of David Milgaard for the rape and murder of Gail Miller in 1970 involved police and institutional misconduct, as well as tunnel vision on the part of prosecutors. The high level of public anxiety over this brutal crime created pressure on the police to make a quick arrest. Milgaard, who had already been labelled an impulsive and marginalized "troublemaker," became the target. The case against him was based on questionable evidence obtained through police intimidation. Six years after Milgaard's release from prison, DNA forensic analysis established his innocence. Larry Fisher, a serial rapist living just blocks away from the murder scene, was subsequently convicted of the crime in 1999.

Racial Bias

Racism is a complex set of ideologies, attitudes, and beliefs claiming the supe-riority of one race over another, sometimes involving racial discrimination and disadvantage for ethnic minorities (Cashmore 1996). Racism is built into economic, political, and legal institutions, where it contributes to differential opportunities and differential treatment of racialized groups. Institutionalized racism makes racial minorities severely vulnerable to miscarriages of justice. Bedau and Radelet (1987) have shown that among 350 cases of documented wrongful convictions in the United States during the 20th century, 40 percent involved a black defendant. Racial discrimination within the criminal justice system is especially evident among blacks and Hispanics in the United States (Parker, Dewees, and Radelet 2001). Several factors, such as institutionalized racism, erroneous cross-racial identification, stereotyping, and extreme social disadvantage, help explain why racial minorities are disproportionately repre-sented among those wrongly convicted.

While little Canadian research has addressed the link between race and wrongful conviction, the prominent case of Donald Marshall Jr.—a Mi'kmaq wrongly convicted of the murder of Sandy Seale—illustrates the ways in which race is embedded in Canada's criminal justice system. The Royal Commission on the prosecution of Marshall acknowledged that Marshall had been wrongly convicted and imprisoned because, *inter alia*, he was Mi'kmaq (Royal Commission 1989, 1).

The commission's report stated that a two-tier system of justice existed in Nova Scotia and that it responded differently according to the status, wealth, and race of the person being investigated (ibid.). As a Mi'kmaq, Donald Marshall Jr. was at the bottom of the second tier (Turpel/Aki-Kwe 1992). The commis-sioners noted Marshall's second-class treatment and found that his defence counsel had failed to provide him with an adequate standard of professional representation (ibid.). Marshall's lawyers had access to whatever financial resources they required, yet they had conducted no independent investiga-tion, had interviewed no Crown witnesses, and had failed to ask for disclosure of the Crown's case against their client. The Marshall case demonstrates how stereotyping and social disadvantage can contribute to miscarriages of justice.

More recently, William Mullins-Johnson, an Ojibway Canadian, was acquitted of murdering his four-year-old niece, Valin, in 2007; but by then he had already served 12 years of a life sentence in prison. Mullins-Johnson was a victim of the errors of Dr. Charles Smith, the disgraced pathologist who found evidence of child abuse, sexual assault, and murder where there was none. Yet it was later revealed that Valin died of natural causes (see Chapter 19).

THE EFFECTS OF WRONGFUL IMPRISONMENT

The negative effects of incarceration on those serving long terms of imprison-ment have been well documented. According to Sykes (1958), the "pains of imprisonment" include the following losses: liberty, goods and services, heterosexual relationships, autonomy, and security. However, not all prisoners experience these deprivations in the same way. This section draws upon in-depth interviews with two Canadians who were wrongly convicted. Jamie Nelson was wrongly convicted of a sexual assault that never actually occurred and served more than three years in prison; Christopher Bates served more than five years for a murder he did not commit. These interviews suggest that the negative effects of incarceration are often exacerbated by a miscarriage of justice.[1]

Identity

A prison sentence constitutes a "massive assault" on the identity of the person who is imprisoned (Berger 1963). This assault is said to be especially strong for first-time inmates, who must contend with the sudden and abrupt shift in their social situation (Schmid and Jones 1991). To protect themselves and their identity, prisoners are often compelled to adopt a provisional or "suspended identity" during the period of their incarceration (ibid.). Jamie Nelson explains how it was important for him to take on a new identity in prison to ensure his survival:

> I had to build up that extra protection in prison. The other layer of Jamie wasn't there … I couldn't be Jamie. I had to be someone that I'm not, somebody that will fight, somebody that will push, somebody that doesn't give a f---. I had to wear certain hats to survive.

Many inmates attempt to suspend their pre-prison identity and formulate a provisional identity while incarcerated. However, the situation becomes highly complex for those wrongly convicted. Not only are these individuals forced to take on a prison identity that defines them as criminals when they are in fact innocent, but they may also be compelled to create a further identity, given the nature of their conviction. Jamie Nelson, who was wrongly convicted of a sexual assault, explains:

> I developed a second story right away. I certainly didn't want anybody to know I was in custody for violently raping a woman. My second story was "I beat somebody up that was trying to break into my house." I had to create a good enough lie that could explain away me going to prison for 5 to 7 years … so, it was a pretty grisly tale. I kicked him in the head a few times with steel boots, you know, I beat him up bad. That was my second story.

Nelson maintains that he could only show his true identity as an innocent man in the presence of the Parole Board members who were to determine his fate:

> I had to wear a different hat when I was with the people that made the difference [prison administration]. That's when I wore the Jamie

hat—when I was in front of the panel [Parole Board]. I never once deviated from my claim of being innocent. And that was the only time that I got to wear that hat ... I could be Jamie, behind that door, because they could not release anything to the population. I knew I was safe in that room, in that environment. It was when I was living in the community as an inmate that I ... needed to wear those different hats.

Resistance

Being wrongly imprisoned appears to produce an unfaltering resistance to all aspects of prison life. Throughout their incarceration, both Nelson and Bates resisted being labelled as criminals and maintained their innocence to the prison administration. Their constantly declaring themselves to have been wrongly convicted was often perceived by the authorities as an inability to adapt to the prison environment and as a denial of their offence. As Bates notes:

> I was obsessed about my case ... I was wrongly convicted. [My case manager] kept on making reports "the guy just denies and denies and denies, he keeps talking to you about his case...." My classification officer told me, "Jesus, you've got to stop doing this, you're never going to get out.... The parole board takes this as if you're denying the crime ... that you're not healed ... you're not fixed.... You have to admit to the crime in order to fix your problems." Sorry! I'm not guilty! I'm not denying. I'm just telling you the truth.

This unwavering resistance often created further difficulties. Nelson, who was wrongly convicted of sexual assault, maintained his credibility and status as an innocent man by refusing to apply for parole and by refusing to participate in prison programs for sexual offenders. He explains:

> I was clinging to my innocence.... I started to get myself in trouble because I wouldn't even apply for parole. You don't have to apply, it's a damn privilege last time I looked at it. I didn't want it, because I'd have to be that guilty man. So I wouldn't even apply, but then that started to go negatively against me. [They would say to me] "What are you hiding?"[1]

As a result of his refusal to self-identify as a sex offender and to participate in prison sex offender programs, he was eventually placed in segregation:

> [The administration] told me that I was going to the sexual behaviour program ... and I said, no, I wasn't. I made it clear to them that the only way that they would have me go to that program was that somebody had to drag me to it. So they ended up keeping me in the hole six months.[1]

Loss of Freedom and Consequences for the Prisoner's Family

The losses experienced by the wrongly convicted can be profound. For Jamie Nelson, these included loss of freedom and the loss of a sense of self: "I lost me, is what I lost ... my identity, who I am ... The way I viewed life." But the most significant loss appears to be the loss of family. Three of Nelson's four children were taken by child protection authorities when his wife suffered a breakdown during his incarceration. He explains the devastation of losing his family:

> What it affected was my nuclear family—wife and my children, my family. It completely devastated that. We lost our home ... I lost my kids ... I lost the care and guidance and companionship of my dad. We were extremely close ... the hardest part about being an inmate was the loss of the family.

Furthermore, the hardships that accompany losing one's family through incarceration also affect the family itself. Its members are deprived of the emotional support of their loved one and are forced to deal with the reality of having a family member in prison. They may also be deprived of an essential source of income (Ferraro et al. 1983). As Nelson explains:

> [My wife] was left living with the reality of being single, with four children, a mortgage, hydro, the groceries and other accoutrements that go with having four young children: one in school, needing to work, needing to deal with baby-sitters and, oh yeah, my husband's in prison.[1]

It is clear that the effects of a wrongful conviction and imprisonment are devastating for the individual and his family. In response, the state has proposed several methods of redress, which are outlined in the next section.

STATE RESPONSES TO WRONGFUL CONVICTION: ISSUES OF REDRESS AND COMPENSATION

When a miscarriage of justice has occurred, a number of policy responses can be instigated—by the individual or by the state—to rectify the miscarriage of justice. These include conviction review through the *Criminal Code*, commissions of inquiry, and financial compensation. However, none of these are automatically applied in cases of wrongful conviction. In addition, all occur many years after the fact and require considerable financial and emotional resources to pursue.

Conviction Review

Currently, Sections 696.1 to 696.6 of Canada's *Criminal Code* allow individuals who maintain that they have been wrongly convicted to ask the federal

Minister of Justice to review the circumstances of their case in order to ascertain whether a miscarriage of justice "likely" occurred. This remedy is also available for reviews of the dangerous offender designation. Canada relies on the Criminal Conviction Review Group (CCRG) in the Department of Justice to undertake such reviews. The criteria of eligibility regarding application for a conviction review are quite narrow. First, while this right is available to all who have been convicted of an offence, it is considered to be an extraordinary measure (Campbell 2005). Second, these individuals must have exercised all of their rights of appeal through the various courts—a process that can take many years. Finally, there must be new matters of significance that were not previously considered by the courts or that arose after the conventional avenues of appeal had been exhausted. The review process can take many years. Once all of the relevant information has been compiled and investigated, the Minister of Justice receives legal advice before making a decision. The minister does not make decisions regarding guilt or innocence, but if satisfied that a miscarriage of justice has occurred, the minister can make one of the following recommendations: (1) decline to make a remedy, (2) order a new trial or hearing, (3) order a new appeal proceeding, or (4) refer any question to the court of appeal for its opinion.

Few applications are made each year to the Minister of Justice. For example, in 2012–13, the minister's office received a total of 12 applications: three were completed, five were partially completed, and four were screened out as ineligible. During this same period, nine preliminary assessments were completed and four preliminary assessments were underway. In terms of investigations, one was completed and one was underway. Finally during this period, the minister dismissed one application and granted another, although the decision was not publicized (Department of Justice 2013). One reason for these small numbers may be the arduous application process involved. Moreover, some wrongfully convicted individuals have questioned whether it is appropriate to apply to the government for "mercy." As David Milgaard asked: "Why ask the Canadian government to give you mercy for something that you haven't done? I refuse" (Milgaard 2002).

The *Criminal Code* was amended in 2002 to clarify the ministerial review process as well as to expand the minister's investigative powers. At the same time, an independent senior individual from outside the Department of Justice, Bernard Grenier, a retired Quebec Provincial Court judge, was appointed to work with the CCRG. His role is to review all CCRG decisions, to screen applications at the assessment stage, and to provide separate advice to the minister on the merits of applications that make it as far as the investigation stage. Criticisms of the conviction review process remain: it is long and costly, it is conducted mainly in secrecy, the principle of finality in law may encourage reluctance on the part of the minister and the appeal courts to interfere with a conviction from a lower court, established rules of procedure are lacking, and conflicts of interest are possible (Braiden and Brockman 1999).

As a means of redress, conviction review has limited application and may still be inaccessible to many. In recent years there have been a number of calls to establish an independent commission of inquiry, detached from the Department of Justice, similar to Britain's Criminal Cases Review Commission. One reason put forward for establishing an independent commission is that leaving the power to revisit convictions in the hands of the Minister of Justice amounts to a clear conflict of interest (Zellick 2006, 556). However, successive Canadian governments have resisted the pressure from lobby groups for such a commission. Prior to the last amendments to the power of ministerial review to the *Criminal Code* in 2002, one of the reasons given for not establishing such a commission was that "the Canadian experience with cases of wrongful conviction bears little resemblance to that of the United Kingdom" (*Canada Gazette* 2002). Presumably, counsel was referring to the prosecution system in the United Kingdom, which differs from the Canadian system. In Britain, a head prosecutor serves the entire country; whereas in Canada, each province has an Attorney General and its own Court of Appeal. Regardless, there is merit to revisiting the idea of an independent commission for Canada.

Commissions of Inquiry

Historically, as a result of the work of various Royal Commissions or commissions of inquiry, the Canadian judiciary and public have become aware of flaws to the criminal justice process. To date, six commissions of inquiry have addressed the circumstances surrounding wrongful convictions. The Marshall Inquiry of 1989 resulted from the wrongful conviction of Donald Marshall Jr. and had a broad mandate to review and assess the administration of criminal justice in Nova Scotia and to "make recommendations" to help prevent such tragedies in the future (Royal Commission 1989). The report contained findings of fact as well as specific recommendations that addressed the role of the police and Crown attorneys, ways to ensure more equitable treatment of blacks and Indigenous peoples in the criminal justice system, and new mechanisms to deal with future wrongful convictions.

The Kaufman Inquiry of 1998 in Ontario (into the wrongful conviction of Guy Paul Morin) and the Sophonow Inquiry in Manitoba (into the wrongful conviction of Thomas Sophonow) examined police and forensic investigations and criminal proceedings that can lead to wrongful convictions. Together, these two inquiries recommended changes to police procedures regarding evidence gathering and jailhouse informants; they also called for enhanced disclosure of evidence to the defence. The Lamer Inquiry of 2006 addressed the wrongful conviction and imprisonment of three individuals in Newfoundland in the 1990s. According to its terms of reference, the inquiry was meant to investigate the administration of criminal justice regarding the arrests and prosecutions of Gregory Parsons and Randy Druken, as well as the lengthy delay experienced by Ronald Dalton with respect to the appeal of his conviction. The Commission of Inquiry into Certain Aspects of the

Trial and Conviction of James Driskell took place in 2007 in Manitoba; the Saskatchewan Commission of Inquiry into the Wrongful Conviction of David Milgaard took place in 2008.

These inquiries indicate that various provincial governments have been compelled to ascertain and address the factors that make it possible for wrongful convictions to occur in the first place. However, one must question the extent to which recommendations stemming from such commissions can realistically affect policy, since implementation of the recommendations is sporadic at best.

Compensation

When a wrongful conviction occurs, individuals often seek financial compensation for the harm they have suffered. The awarding of compensation is an attempt by the government to rectify a miscarriage of justice. Unfortunately, such awards are small consolation for the devastation to family, credibility, livelihood, and mental health that a wrongful conviction entails. With some wrongful convictions, compensation was awarded by the courts in the absence of a commission of inquiry. David Milgaard's case is one example: he served 22 years in prison for a murder he did not commit and in 1999 received $10 million in compensation from the Saskatchewan and federal governments for pain and suffering, lost income, out-of-pocket expenses, and legal fees. In recognition of the impact that wrongful convictions have on family members, Joyce Milgaard, David's mother, received $750,000 in compensation.

To date, various provincial governments have awarded from $105,000 to $10 million. The amount seems to be based largely on the number of years an individual has spent in prison and the amount of time she has waited for compensation. Many individuals have had to wait an inordinate amount of time for compensation, with extremes at both ends of the continuum. The average period has been 11.7 years from date of the original conviction (Campbell, forthcoming). In these cases, provinces have recognized errors in the administration of justice and have awarded compensation. However, these awards are difficult to obtain and come only after many years of legal and political wrangling. Even so, Canada has an obligation to provide compensation to the wrongly convicted. Besides its obligations under national laws, Canada has a binding obligation under international law, having ratified the International Covenant on Civil and Political Rights in 1976. Article 9(5) of the Covenant provides that "anyone who has been a victim of unlawful arrest or detention shall have an enforceable right to compensation." Moreover, Canada in 1988 adopted a set of federal–provincial guidelines for compensation, conditions of eligibility, and criteria for quantum of compensation (Campbell 2005). Problems regarding the kinds of cases deemed deserving of compensation as well as the amount of compensation deemed appropriate plague this process. Ultimately, financial compensation, regardless of the amount, does little to rectify the emotional, social, and financial damages wrought by a wrongful conviction.

CONCLUSION

Both individual and systemic factors contribute to errors that result in wrongful convictions in Canada. Moreover, the state's existing responses to rectify these wrongs seem unable to adequately confront and tackle these complex issues. For example, the last amendments to the *Criminal Code*'s conviction review process fall short of achieving their stated goals of enhanced transparency and accountability. Commissions of inquiry, which seek to address the issue of prevention, are often disappointing, since their recommendations are rarely implemented in full. From time to time, the media draw attention to the issue of wrongful conviction through highly controversial and publicized cases; however, this attention is often fleeting and fails to result in long-term change. Piecemeal reforms introduced to address individual errors are insufficient. There must be greater accountability among agents of the criminal justice system as a whole. Programs of education in law schools and in police academies will allow these individuals to become more aware of how their actions can contribute to wrongful convictions. Two reports by the Department of Justice regarding the prevention of miscarriages of justice offer some hope in this regard (Department of Justice 2005, 2011). As well, the voices of the wrongly convicted themselves need to be heard. Only by listening to their accounts and experiences will Canadians understand the true extent and impact of the problem.

Further Readings

Anderson, B., and D. Anderson. 2009. *Manufacturing Guilt: Wrongful Convictions in Canada*. 2nd ed. Halifax: Fernwood.

Huff, C.R., A. Rattner, and E. Sagarin. 1996. *Convicted but Innocent: Wrongful Conviction and Public Policy*. Thousand Oaks: Sage Publications.

Westervelt, S., and J. Humphrey, eds. 2001. *Wrongly Convicted: Perspectives on Failed Justice*. New Jersey: Rutgers University Press.

References

Anderson, B., and D. Anderson. 2009. *Manufacturing Guilt: Wrongful Convictions in Canada*. 2nd ed. Halifax: Fernwood.

Bala, N. 2001. "*R. v. D.(D.)*: The Supreme Court and Filtering of Social Science Knowledge About Children." *Criminal Reports* (5th), 36: 283–90.

Bedau, H.A., and M. Radelet. 1987. "Miscarriages of Justice in Potentially Capital Cases." *Stanford Law Review* 40: 21–179.

Berger, P. 1963. *Invitation to Sociology: A Humanistic Perspective*. Garden City: Doubleday Anchor.

Braiden, P., and J. Brockman. 1999. "Remedying Wrongful Convictions through Applications to the Minister of Justice under Section 690 of the *Criminal Code.*" *Windsor Yearbook of Access to Justice* 17: 3–34.

Campbell, K. 2005. "Policy Responses to Wrongful Conviction in Canada: The Role of Conviction Review, Public Inquiries, and Compensation." *Criminal Law Bulletin* 41: 145–68.

——— . (Forthcoming). *Miscarriages of Justice in Canada: Causes, Responses, Remedies.* University of Toronto Press.

Canada Gazette. 2002. *Regulations Respecting Applications for Ministerial Review—Miscarriages of Justice.* Part 1, vol. 136, no. 39. Ottawa: Queen's Printer.

Cashmore, E. 1996. *Dictionary of Race and Ethnic Relations.* London: Routledge.

Castelle, G., and E. Loftus. 2001. "Misinformation." In S. Westervelt and J. Humphrey, eds., *Wrongly Convicted: Perspectives on Failed Justice.* New Brunswick: Rutgers University Press.

Cory, P. 2001. *Commission of Inquiry Regarding Thomas Sophonow.* Winnipeg: Manitoba Justice.

Department of Justice Canada. 2005. *Report on the Prevention of Miscarriages of Justice.* Federal/Provincial/Territorial Heads of Prosecution Committee Working Group, Ottawa.

——— . 2011. *The Path to Justice: Preventing Wrongful Convictions.* Report of the Federal/Provincial/Territorial Heads of Prosecution, Sub-Committee on the Prevention of Wrongful Convictions.

——— . 2013. *Applications for Ministerial Review: Miscarriages of Justice.* Annual Report 2013, Minister of Justice. http://www.justice.gc.ca/eng/rp-pr/cj-jp/ccr-rc/rep13-rap13/rep13.pdf

Drizin, S., and R. Leo. 2004. "The Problem of False Confessions in the Post-DNA World." *North Carolina Law Review* 82, no. 3: 892–1007.

Ferraro, K.J., J.M. Johnson, S.R. Jorgensen, and F.G. Bolton. 1983. "Problems of Prisoners' Families: The Hidden Costs of Imprisonment." *Journal of Family Issues* 4: 575–91.

Gross, S., K. Jacoby, D. Matheson, N. Montgomery, and S. Patil. 2005. "Exonerations in the United States: 1989 Through 2003." *Journal of Criminal Law and Criminology* 95: 523–60.

Gudjonsson, G. 2002. *The Psychology of Interrogations and Confessions: A Handbook.* Chichester: Wiley.

Holmes, W. 2001. "Who Are the Wrongly Convicted on Death Row?" In S. Westervelt and J. Humphrey, eds., *Wrongly Convicted: Perspectives on Failed Justice*. New Brunswick: Rutgers University Press.

Huff, C.R., A. Rattner, and E. Sagarin. 1986. "Guilty Until Proven Innocent: Wrongful Conviction and Public Policy." *Crime and Delinquency* 32: 518–44.

——. 1996. *Convicted but Innocent: Wrongful Conviction and Public Policy*. Thousand Oaks: Sage.

Innocence Project. http://www.innocenceproject.org

Kaufman, F. 1998. *Commission on Proceedings Involving Guy Paul Morin: Executive Summary and Recommendations*. Toronto.

Leo, R., and R. Ofshe. 1998. "The Consequences of False Confessions: Deprivation of Liberty and Miscarriages of Justice in the Age of Psychological Interrogation." *Journal of Criminology and Criminal Law* 88: 429–96.

Loftus, E.F. (1979). *Eyewitness Testimony*. Cambridge, MA: Harvard University Press. (National Media Award, Distinguished Contribution, 1980; reissued with new Preface in 1996).

Loftus, E., J. Doyle, and J. Dysert. 2008. *Eyewitness Testimony: Civil and Criminal*. 4th ed. Charlottesville, VA: Lexis Law Publishing.

MacFarlane, B. 2008. "Wrongful Convictions: The Effect of Tunnel Vision and Predisposing Circumstances in the Criminal Justice System." Paper prepared for the Goudge Inquiry.

Martin, D. 2001. "The Police Role in Wrongful Convictions: An International Comparative Study." In S. Westervelt and J. Humphrey, eds., *Wrongly Convicted: Perspectives on Failed Justice*. New Brunswick: Rutgers University Press.

Milgaard, D. 2002. "The Voices of the Wrongly Convicted: Innocents behind Bars." November 16, 2002. Conference presentation available from Association in Defence of the Wrongly Convicted.

Parker, K., M. Dewees, and M. Radelet. 2001. "Racial Bias and the Conviction of the Innocent." In S. Westervelt and J. Humphrey, eds., *Wrongly Convicted: Perspectives on Failed Justice*. New Brunswick: Rutgers University Press.

Roach, K. 2007. "Unreliable Evidence and Wrongful Convictions: The Case for Excluding Tainted Identification Evidence and Jailhouse and Coerced Confessions." *Criminal Law Quarterly* 52: 210–36.

Rosenberg, M. 2002. "Public Inquiries: The Process and the Value." Paper presented at the Innocents behind Bars Conference, Ottawa, November 17, 2002, available from Association in Defence of the Wrongly Convicted.

Royal Commission on the Donald Marshall Jr. Prosecution. 1989. *Commissioners' Report*. Halifax.

Sanders, R. 1984. "Helping the Jury Evaluate Eyewitness Testimony: The Need for Additional Safeguards." *American Journal of Criminal Law* 12: 189–220.

Schmid, T., and R. Jones. 1991. "Suspended Identity: Identity Transformation in a Maximum Security Prison." *Symbolic Interaction* 14: 415–32.

Sykes, G. 1958. *The Society of Captives*. Princeton: Princeton University Press.

Turpel/Aki-Kwe, M. 1992. "Further Travails of Canada's Human Rights Record: The Marshall Case." In J. Mannette, ed., *Elusive Justice: Beyond the Marshall Inquiry*. Halifax: Fernwood.

Wall, B. 1992. "Analyzing the Marshall Commission: Why It Was Established and How It Functioned." In J. Mannette, ed., *Elusive Justice: Beyond the Marshall Inquiry*. Halifax: Fernwood.

Wells, G., and A. Bradfield. 1998. "Good, You Identified the Suspect: Feedback to Eyewitnesses Distorts Their Reports of the Witnesses' Experience." *Journal of Applied Psychology* 83: 360–76.

Wells, G., and E. Olsen. 2003. "Eyewitness Testimony." *Annual Review of Psychology* 54: 277–95.

Zalman, M. 2012. "Quantitatively Estimating the Incidence of Wrongful Convictions." *Criminal Law Bulletin* 48, no. 2, 221–79.

Zellick, G. 2006. "Facing Up to Miscarriages of Justice." *Manitoba Law Journal* 31: 555–64.

Case

R. v. Stinchcombe, [1991] 3 S.C.R. 326.

Endnote

1. Both Jamie Nelson and Christopher Bates gave us permission to reveal their identities and their stories.

Innocent but Presumed Guilty: The Wrongful Conviction of William Mullins-Johnson[1]

Chapter 18 discusses the phenomenon of wrongful conviction, drawing upon the research that has accumulated on this subject over the past few years. This chapter provides insight into the causes and consequences of wrongful conviction from the perspective of one individual. In 1992, Bill Mullins-Johnson was convicted of the murder of his four-year-old niece, Valin. Following an evening during which Bill babysat her, Valin was found dead in her bed the next morning. Bill quickly became the sole suspect in her murder. After being convicted almost entirely on flawed forensic evidence, he served 12 years in prison before being released and exonerated by the Ontario Court of Appeal in 2007. Bill was a victim of forensic errors made by Dr. Charles Smith, who testified to finding evidence of sexual assault and strangulation where none actually existed. Ultimately it was established that Valin had died of natural causes. In this chapter, Bill describes his experience of wrongful conviction, imprisonment, release, and subsequent exoneration.

Kathryn M. Campbell
University of Ottawa

FACTORS THAT INFLUENCED HIS WRONGFUL CONVICTION

In my own case, I believe one factor was my cultural heritage. You see, I'm Aboriginal—I'm Ojibway. I was raised most of my life on the reserve. That's my home, that's where I'm from. I don't like the word racism, myself. But that's what happens sometimes. I'm sure that this was a factor in my case—not the only factor but one of them.

People in the community were angry and emotional. What I was charged with raised a lot of emotions here. People had blind faith in what they were being told in the press and by the police. The fact that I had a previous conviction for robbery in 1989 had an impact too—it had been in the news at the time. Being arrested for a crime involving a child victim made things much worse and the community reaction at the time was significant.

I was arrested in the midst of the Bernardo[2] trial. Bernardo and Homolka were the big story at the time—everybody was up in arms about that. But at the time here in the Sault there were three cases going on,[3] including mine. We were all Aboriginal and all the cases were high profile—front page news, every one of us. So I can see how the public anger boiled over. Whether people want to admit it or not, what happens in the courtroom is sometimes influenced by public opinion. There was a rush to judge me and immediately upon my arrest, I began receiving death threats.

ARREST

They arrested me less than 12 hours after we found Valin. We found her body that morning and the cops and paramedics came and the coroner was there, too. They took her away and then everybody left except the family. Just before noon the cops came back and told everybody to leave except for Pauly [Valin's father, Bill's brother], Kim [Valin's mother, Bill's sister-in-law], and myself. They stationed two uniformed cops with us and we weren't allowed to leave the house. The police took statements from us that morning and then took me to the police station that night. That's where I spent the night, in a holding cell, and the interrogation room. The day that I was arrested and the day that they did that post-mortem, all their conclusions were made. They were made over the phone with Charles Smith. The police notes show that they had me targeted at about 8:30 that morning.

When they told me I was arrested for Valin's murder, I didn't have the words to express what that news did to me. I think I went into an immediate mental breakdown. To tell you the truth, I still suffer from it. I suffer from sleeplessness, restlessness, and anxiety attacks where I think I am about to die. My throat closes up, I can't breathe, and I think I'm dying—I can't even describe the level of distress. It would even wake me up at night and it was like that for years after my arrest.

Over the years, people have asked me, "How did you handle all that stress and pressure?" Well, when I was arrested I'd like to think it's the human spirit,

Dr. Charles Smith is a pathologist whose errors became the subject of the Inquiry into Pediatric Forensic Pathology in Ontario. In 2007 the inquiry, chaired by the Honourable Stephen T. Goudge, examined the practice and oversight of pediatric forensic pathology in Ontario, and after systemic review and assessment made a series of recommendations. The inquiry came about as a result of the Chief Coroner's Review into 45 homicide cases in which Dr. Smith had been involved. In 20 of those cases reviewers took issue with either his findings or his testimony or both.

that everybody would do this. But the arrest was so wrong to me, there was no way I was backing down from it, even if that meant I ended up serving life in prison. It was just so wrong that it changed the person that I was forever, and I knew it at the time.

BAIL

I wasn't released on bail after my arrest, it wasn't even a consideration. I didn't even ask for bail. I figured that I was safer in prison because of the death threats that I had received. I was safer in the "the hole" (administrative segregation), for my own safety.

My Family

In the beginning my family alternated between believing I was guilty or believing I was innocent—they went back and forth. But most of the time, the family closed ranks on my mom and myself. Only my mom came to visit me in prison. Whether I was awaiting trial, or doing my sentence, my mom was pretty much the only one who visited me. The family started closing ranks the day I was arrested. Maybe it was because of our conservative upbringing, the church influence, and believing in what the authorities tell you.

After I was convicted, anything I heard about the family was through mom. She would write to me every week and I called her every week, and she would come down four or five times a year. For mom's sake I maintained that contact with her just to let her know that I was still alive and kicking, but really I didn't want any contact from the street after a while.

CHARGED WITH FIRST-DEGREE MURDER

Because of the alleged assault the charge became first-degree murder. They said I had an extra charge of alleged aggravated sexual assault. But I was never convicted of that—it was pretty much withdrawn, yet they still used it, so they could get the conviction.

THE TRIAL

The trial lasted about three weeks in Sault Ste. Marie, Ontario. There was a judge and jury but there were no Indian people on my jury. There was an agreement between the defence and the Crown that no one on the jury should know anyone on the witness list. This meant that pretty much every Aboriginal person in the area was excluded, as they all knew either me or my family. It's my feeling that I was convicted by a segment of society that views me as inferior, and so you're going to have very little chance of getting a fair trial. As a matter of fact, I asked my lawyers to get a change of venue[4] because of that, just to have some Aboriginal people on the jury, but the request was refused. At the trial, there was so little evidence against me, everyone was surprised I was convicted, and as the trial went on, people started seeing that I wasn't guilty of this crime.

Dr. Smith's Testimony

Smith testified and his testimony basically was that when I killed her, I was molesting her. But he didn't perform an autopsy—he never looked at anything, just some photographs. There were two pathologists on each side and the majority of them (because of the sexual nature of the crime) deferred to Smith. But none of them could agree on the time of her death—or even if she had been molested. Since Smith was the big guy in the field, he was the star expert witness. They all deferred to him and that's pretty much why I was wrongfully convicted. Smith never had the qualifications for that job, yet his bosses didn't even look into what his training was—they built him up to be this star guy.

CONVICTION

The jury went out about 2:30 in the afternoon. They came back at about 9:00 p.m. to ask a question to confirm something. They then went back in and came back about an hour later. They told the judge that they didn't think they would be able to come to a verdict, but he sent them back to continue their deliberations. An hour later, they returned with a verdict: "guilty of first-degree murder." Maybe they felt pressured to come up with a verdict.

When I heard the verdict, I thought "I'm a dead man." I thought somebody would kill me. Because of the hierarchy of crimes in the prison population, where some crimes are targeted because of their nature, I knew that this crime of murdering a child would mark me once I was in prison. That's how I felt inside, really. When they came down with that verdict, my lawyer didn't want me to stand up for the verdict. I told him "F--- you, I'm going to stand up for this." It's a good thing I was holding on to the edge of the prisoner's box because when they came back with that verdict, I thought I was going to collapse, like my insides had been ripped out.

Dr. Charles Smith testified at Bill's trial, as well as at the trials of 19 other individuals, and serious errors were found with respect to his testimony on autopsies regarding the cause and time of death of children. The Goudge Commission of Inquiry found that among other things, Smith testified outside his area of expertise, ignored conflicting expert testimony, was chronically late with his findings, lost evidence, misinterpreted findings, and used unscientific methods. The inquiry produced 169 recommendations regarding how deaths that occurred in "questionable circumstances" should be investigated. It also called for an overhaul of the entire autopsy system.

Tammy Marquardt also served a prison sentence of almost 14 years for the alleged murder of her two-year-old son, largely based on Smith's "unscientific" evidence at trial. Her conviction was overturned by the Ontario Court of Appeal in 2011. That same year Dinesh Kumar had his conviction for criminal negligence causing death overturned in the case of the death of his infant son; Smith testified that the child died from shaken baby syndrome, which was found to be unreasonable in light of new medical evidence. In a number of the other cases, charges were laid and subsequently dropped, but not until after months and sometimes years of pretrial detention, as well as the removal of other children in the family by child protection services.

In August 2010, the Ontario government offered what it termed recognition payments to individuals who had been affected by flawed pediatric forensic pathology, aimed specifically at the individuals connected to cases examined by the Goudge Inquiry. Persons directly affected were eligible for $250,000; children removed from their homes due to these errors were eligible for payments of up to $25,000, and family members for up to $12,500. Full legal costs were also reimbursable. The time limitation on this compensation ended in August 2012 and as a result total payments were made in seven cases of those directly eligible and in 55 cases of indirect applicants or family members, totalling over $4 million (Campbell and Walker 2012). Bill received $4.25 million in compensation for his wrongful conviction.

I heard my mom break out in hysterics on my left. Someone else cried out "No," and someone cried out "Yeah," so the response was mixed. But I did make eye contact with Pauly [Bill's brother, the father of Valin] at the back of the courtroom that day. He looked right back at me and told me later that he almost attacked me right there in the courtroom. You know how certain things happen in your life that you will never forget? That was one of mine—and probably one of Pauly's. Well, I knew it wasn't me that killed her, so I had to keep looking at Pauly.

IMPRISONMENT

They sent me to Millhaven, a maximum-security prison. It was a very rough joint, but I didn't get punched out or anything like that. I guess my own character pulled me through all the years I was in there. But nobody came at me or anything like that. It was a good experience. It's weird to say that, and it's not that I felt comfortable in there, by any stretch, but the guys around me helped me through. It's odd what I experienced, but I made new friends when I was there.

I was transferred to Joyceville (a minimum-security prison) just before Christmas 1994. And by that spring I was sitting back in the "hole" waiting to get transferred again. I got bounced out of the Joyceville population because they were going to kill me. Two guys approached me and told me that the order had been sent down. But they were willing to give me a chance to walk out of Joyceville. They told me if I was still there in the general population of the prison the next day, there was nothing anybody could do. I was going to get killed the next day. So they sent me to Warkworth—a Protective Custody joint.

The majority of the prisoners there were sex offenders. I spent 10 straight years there. There were guys in there that would love to have stabbed me. But my size, I think, helped me out. I'm 250 pounds now, but at my peak I was 260 pounds of solid muscle, 6 feet 4 inches, with 20-inch arms. I was a big man, a muscular man. And fit, and with a rage in me that could bring down a mountain.

There were times, over the years, when I was nose-to-nose with guards who threatened me with violence, and I'd be inviting them to do it right on the spot. And doing this in front of other convicts too, you know, and other guards. I don't know what it is with me—I just wouldn't back down from them. That's how wrong it was, I just felt that it was so wrong that I was there and that I wasn't about to let them turn me into something I wasn't.

COPING

I did many things to cope. I tried to occupy my mind as much as I could. I would find something that could get my attention, and I would ride that momentum as far as I could until I thought of something else.

In the environment I was now in I had to understand that with all the violence, my life was now in danger. Once I understood the environment I was in, I was able to respond to it better. I didn't go through this process analytically at the time I was arrested because my emotions were shot. When I was first arrested I was in hysterics. So it wasn't a matter of sitting down and rationally thinking this through, not at all. It was a very sporadic, very unpredictable environment that I was in. And so the only thing I could do was understand that if somebody came at me, I would have to defend myself to whatever end.

My mainstay was the guitar. I taught myself to play guitar while I was in. I got involved with different groups. I was chairman of the Native Brotherhood a number of times. I was also involved with the Warkworth Literacy Council. I was vice-chairman there and helped organize symposiums. I tutored two Aboriginal high school courses. I stayed busy. I gardened and helped start a garden project for the brotherhood. We grew corn and other grains. We had a tree farm in there too. Five hundred trees were donated to street projects, neighbourhood beautification, landscaping for old folks' homes. I had my own computer and some guys helped teach me. I taught myself too—how to do basic programs—spreadsheets, databases and PowerPoint and Word. But my escape was really games, computer games. I got into gaming in a big way.

Getting exonerated did occupy my mind and my time. But I was now deep in the justice system, so I had to come back out through the same processes that got me in there in the first place. It was just a matter of filing documents properly, and going to the right people to help me. But I didn't spend days and days worrying about this or that at all. I just got an appeal lawyer, filed my appeals, lost them, and then got a hold of AIDWYC.

AIDWYC is the Association in Defence of the Wrongly Convicted. Based in Toronto, it is a pro bono, grassroots organization that fights for the release and exoneration of the wrongly convicted and that lobbies for criminal justice reform. It has a dual mandate: to prevent and rectify wrongful convictions. It was established in 1993, having grown out of the Justice for Guy Paul Morin Committee. At the present time, AIDWYC investigates convictions for serious crimes (mainly homicide) where the accused is "factually innocent" and where proof exists (through DNA or other means) that the person was not involved in any way with the crime. AIDWYC has over 30 lawyers, who work pro bono, and believes that it fills the place of an "independent" review body for claims of innocence. Where warranted, AIDWYC's lawyers will prepare an application for ministerial review for the Criminal Conviction Review Group, who reviews cases and make recommendations to the Minister of Justice. (see Chapter 20)

I guess I understood the situation I was in: I was a lifer, I accepted it. In a way I was fighting to get out. But I understood that I was a lifer now, regardless of what I say for the rest of my life. So in these small, confined boundaries I had to find happiness for myself somehow. So that's why I did so many activities. They didn't force me to take any programs. I did do some Aboriginal programs throughout the years, but there were many times when I told them I would not take their sexual behaviours program. They would say, "Well you're going to have to, because you have been convicted of a sexual crime." I said: "You show me on my file where I'm convicted of sexual assault." My corrections officer told me once, "Well, it's not there," then "F--- you" I would say. As far as I knew, that charge had been dropped because it's not on my file, being convicted of sexual assault.

I knew by refusing the program I was going to be in for the rest of my life, and I understood that. The consequence for me was that I was going to die in prison, and I understood that. But I wasn't going to give up any of the person that I was in this matter. I was an innocent man—as I told them so many times over the years that I was in prison. I would sometimes get into an argument with the guards and my parole officer and I would tell them: "I'm an innocent man in prison." But they never believed me.

The biggest myth about prison is that every convict claims to be innocent. They might for a while, but your own conscience gets you and the behaviour shows that they've accepted their own guilt. But I just refused to give in. I would not let them turn me into what they wanted me to be—a child molester, and a child killer. I was furious, I still am. I was suicidal for some time. But I learned how to deal with it better through disciplining the mind, disciplining the body, disciplining the spirit. Once I was released I cut loose a little bit, and did some partying. When I was inside I smoked pot and all that kinda stuff, but I didn't drink. I exercised a lot. I jogged, I ran, and doing weights helped me discipline my mind. You have to concentrate on doing weights rather than what's going on around you—it helps you discipline your mind. Running does the same thing.

EXONERATION

I got a hold of AIDWYC for the first time in 1994 and they told me I had to go through the appeals process first before they would get involved. So I did. I lost my Supreme Court appeal in 1998 and then I got a hold of AIDWYC again and they started slowly looking into my case and according to them, they were immediately convinced there was merit to my case. But they had to go through everything again and they reviewed it and they kinda hit a wall so to speak—they didn't know where to go after that. You know they went down [the path] … "Well if it wasn't Bill then it must have been Paul" … but that was a dead end. Maybe there was no murder at all. The last resort was to check the science in the case. That's when they started running into roadblocks from Smith's office and trying to find those slides, those tissue boxes—they had to fight with Smith for two years. When they finally got the tissue samples in early 2005, they nailed him.

An AIDWYC lawyer came and saw me. I think he was sent there to test my resolve. He had my trial transcripts open and was asking and angering me, he was pushing me about stuff. Finally I told him, "You show me in them f---ing files right there … You show me where it says I'm guilty of this … like one piece of evidence that substantially says I did this." And he said, "Well, there's none." And I said, "Then what am I doing in prison?" I said, "If you're going to help me, then help me—if not get the hell out of my life and don't ever talk to me again." And that's what convinced him that I was innocent.

I got out in September 2005 but had to wait a couple of years to get my date in the Court of Appeal. Then in October of 2007 I finally got cleared. I was in shock, I was happy—I was elated, but I was still shocked to think "I'm cleared!"

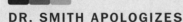

DR. SMITH APOLOGIZES

During the Goudge Inquiry, James Lockyer (Bill's lawyer) asked Dr. Charles Smith to apologize to Bill Mullins-Johnson. The following is their exchange:

Dr. Charles Smith:

"Sir, I don't expect that you would forgive me, but I do want to make it—I'm sorry. I do want to make it very clear to you that I am profoundly sorry for the role that I played in the ultimate decision that affected you. I am sorry."

Mr. William Mullins-Johnson:

"For my healing, I'll forgive you but I'll never forget what you did to me. You put me in an environment where I could have been killed any day for something that never happened. You destroyed my family, my brother's relationship with me and my niece that's still left and my nephew that's still living. They hate me because of what you did to me. I'll never forget that but for my own healing I must forgive you." (Goudge Commission of Inquiry, Executive Summary, 5)

LIFE AFTER RELEASE

Since I've been out, it's been kind of a roller coaster, but all in all, not too bad. I struggled a bit with drug abuse. I finally got my own place and it's comfortable. I was uptown last week and walking around and people are starting to acknowledge me more and more. That day about 15 people stopped me to wish me well and welcome me home. No one can believe what I've been through. Everybody I talk to is in such shock about it still. It's been almost five years since I've been out now, but everybody's still in shock, saying things like "how in the hell did that happen to you?" A few people still don't talk to me, but overall it's healing—it's just going to take some time.

I'm not working at present. Because no matter what way I expand it on my CV, there is a 12-year gap in my life that I'm going to have to explain over and over again. I don't have to spell it out to everybody all the time, but if I start getting close to somebody, I'm going to have to explain things. It's not possible to leave it behind me now, largely because I don't want to leave it in the past right now. I want to get my story out there. I want to tell people not to be so ready to believe the first thing they hear about somebody, especially an accusation as serious as the one against me. This has affected my life in ways that I don't even know yet. And I'm still in counselling because of it. I'd like to see somebody from the Attorney General's office charge the people responsible. They should have done a better investigation, to say "You know what? This little girl died of natural causes." In the end, there isn't going to be any justice for me or the other people caught up by Smith.[5] We were criminally wronged and there is nobody stepping up to protect us under the law. There's nobody representing our interests or the public's interest of equal protection and benefit of the law.

Reference

Campbell, K., and C. Walker. 2012. "Pathological Error: Reacting to the Limits of Expertise in Legal Process." *Law and Justice Review* 111: 1–38.

Endnotes

1. Thanks to David J. D'Intino for research assistance.
2. Paul Bernardo was a notorious serial killer and rapist and was convicted for two murders and two aggravated sexual assaults in 1995. He is currently serving a life sentence and has been designated a dangerous offender. All of his victims were young teenaged girls. Karla Homolka, his wife, was also implicated in the two murders and struck a controversial plea bargain with the prosecution.
3. At that time there were three other Aboriginal persons accused of killing someone in Sault Ste. Marie; one was charged with attempted murder, the other two with first-degree murder (one of these was charged with killing a police officer).
4. A motion for a change of venue involves asking a trial court to determine whether a case should be heard where it is filed or in a court in another city, county, or province. In cases where a change of venue is granted by a judge, it is normally for the sake of convenience, or—when a case is highly publicized—to ensure a fair trial.
5. He is referring to the 20 people whose cases were examined in detail at the Inquiry into Pediatric Forensic Pathology in Ontario in 2007.

Why Say Sorry When I Didn't Do It? Remorse and the Dilemma of the Wrongfully Convicted

CHAPTER

20

Most people expect wrongdoers to express remorse for their transgressions; it seems a natural way to make amends to the victim. When offenders do express remorse, it is appreciated by the victim as well as by the community in general. For this reason, the corrections system tends to be more punitive toward offenders who fail to express remorse. The criminal law reflects this attitude toward offenders by imposing more lenient sentences on remorseful offenders, such as those who plead guilty in court. But what happens when the person charged with an offence is innocent? These people can hardly be expected to express remorse for crimes they did not commit. A dilemma arises for persons who are wrongfully convicted and who then enter the correctional system: they are expected to express remorse, yet they remain adamant in their claims of innocence. As a result, they are treated more harshly by correctional authorities, who perceive them in negative terms simply because they refuse to accept responsibility and express remorse. Drawing on examples from Canada and the United States, Richard Weisman explores the question of remorse and the wrongfully convicted individual.

Richard Weisman
York University

On June 19, 1998, a young man (Mr. W.) left a party with twice the legal limit of alcohol in his blood. He got behind the wheel of his car, having refused a friend's offer to drive him home. After driving westbound on eastbound lanes for several kilometres, he collided with another vehicle, despite frantic attempts to get his attention. Three of the four passengers in the other car died and the other was critically injured (*Toronto Star* May 29, 2001). A jury convicted Mr. W. of three counts of criminal negligence causing death, criminal negligence causing bodily harm, impaired driving causing bodily harm, and exceeding the legal blood alcohol limit. When Mr. W. appeared in court to be sentenced, the assistant Crown attorney described him as unremorseful—"He expressed no remorse at any time throughout these proceedings"—and asked the court to sentence Mr. W. to 8 to 12 years in prison. Counsel for the defence asked for 3 to 5 years.

Before imposing sentence, the judge asked Mr. W. if he had anything to say. The reply was "No." The judge noted that the sentence was determined partly by the fact that Mr. W. had not shown "any remorse during the course of the trial." He added that when given the opportunity to make a statement, Mr. W. had refused to say anything: "Mr. W. is not inarticulate. He's a well-spoken gentleman who could say he was sorry. But he didn't." After that preamble, the judge imposed a sentence of 9 years, to be served in a federal penitentiary.

But, unexpectedly, just after the judge had finished speaking, Mr. W. stood up and faced those who were in attendance, declaring, "I want to address the families and friends of the deceased." The Crown attorney told him to face the other way so that the court reporter could take down his words. Mr. W. refused, saying, "I'm not interested in what you guys put on the record. What I have to say is for the families." He then made the following statement:

> I've chosen to give my statement after the judgment because it was the only way I had to show you I meant what I was saying. Despite what has been said in prior hearings, it has never been my intention to deny the accident took place nor my part in the horrific and tragic loss of lives. I have no right to request your understanding, nor do I have the right to ask for your forgiveness. But I do ask that someday you search your hearts and find that I did not intend for this to happen. I would surely surrender my life if this could return your brother, your father, your husband, your friend, your son. I'm so very sorry for the grief and sorrow I have caused your family and friends. I am truly ashamed of my actions, and all I have to offer are these words: I'm sorry.

The reporter who witnessed these events described the reaction of those who were present: "Silence ... And as everyone else in the courtroom sat stunned, unsure of what to do, a young man broke the silence. 'Thank you,' he said" (Clairmont 2001).[*]

---

[*] From Clairmont, S. 2001. "'Unrepentant' Drunk Driver Utters a Stunning Last Word." Toronto Star, May 29, A5. Permission granted courtesy of Susan Clairmont, City columnist for The Hamilton Spectator.

IMPORTANCE OF REMORSE IN CRIMINAL JUSTICE

I recount this remarkable vignette for two reasons. First, it reveals the importance that both the courts and the media place on expressions of remorse or their absence. People who show remorse are viewed as deserving of compassion and as entitled to mitigation in the form of a more lenient punishment. Those who, like Mr. W., do not show remorse (prior to being sentenced) are viewed more harshly and denied the benefits of mitigation. Second, because expressions of remorse are linked to mitigation, it is difficult to decide whether offenders say they are sorry because they mean it or because they want to obtain a more lenient sentence. Mr. W. went to great lengths to solve this problem by deliberately withholding his expression of remorse until he could not possibly obtain any benefit from it.[1]

Long before their vindication (if vindication ever occurs), the wrongly convicted are designated as persons who lack remorse, and they are separated from those who are characterized as having remorse. Just as in the case of Mr. W., they are perceived as not acknowledging responsibility for their crime and as not having any feelings of sorrow or empathy for their victim(s). This chapter examines the impact of this designation on the identity and treatment of those who have been wrongly convicted. People who have been wrongly convicted often assert their innocence and, not surprisingly, refuse to express remorse for crimes they did not commit. This chapter explores the consequences of failing to express remorse. For the purposes of this analysis, I will draw on both Canadian and American data.

The most widely publicized instances in which remorse makes a difference have involved the life-or-death decisions of jurors in capital trials in the United States. In 2003, in a trial that attracted international attention, a jury was charged with deciding whether John Muhammad, convicted of six murders—the so-called "sniper" killings—should be executed. One juror was quoted in explaining why he had voted for the death penalty: "I tried to pay attention to his demeanor the whole time. I looked for something in him that might have shown remorse. But I never saw it." The jury foreman agreed that "the lack of emotion, his [Muhammad's] failure to even acknowledge what he had done, had played into" his decision to support the death penalty as well (Dao and Bacon 2003.) A continuing research project set up in 1993—the National Capital Jury Project—used a sample of 1,155 real jurors from 340 capital trials in 14 states to establish that the offender's remorse is one of the most important determinants of whether a jury will decide in favour of death rather than a life sentence in capital trials (Sundby 1998).

The social preoccupation with remorse is also illustrated in the public response to offenders who commit offences that shock the sensibilities of their communities. No aspect of the execution of Timothy McVeigh—the man convicted of the notorious Oklahoma City bombing that resulted in 168 deaths—was more thoroughly scrutinized than whether he had shown remorse prior to his death. A search through Canadian newspapers using Factiva shows a similar interest when it comes to high-profile offenders— for example, Karla Homolka, regarding whether she felt remorse for partici- pating in the murder of her sister and of two other teenage girls, who were also raped by her husband. Thousands of news items appearing each week in the North American mass media focus on whether convicted offenders showed remorse for their wrongdoing. How people feel about their wrongful acts is as important to the courts and to the public as *why* they did it or *that* they did it.

WHY BE MORE LENIENT TOWARD PEOPLE WHO EXPRESS REMORSE?

One reason for this interest in remorse-related cases is that expressions of remorse tell us whether those who have violated the community's norms feel the same way about their misdeeds as would those who are law-abiding. Social psychologists have demonstrated that groups respond with empathy and compassion if they believe that wrongdoers are sorry for their miscon- duct. People are likely to be far more punitive if they perceive that wrong- doers feel indifferent to the harm they have caused. In this sense, when judges denounce offenders who fail to show remorse while showing mercy to those who do, they are reflecting and affirming values that are shared by the com- munity as a whole.

Another reason why courts pay so much attention to remorse is the widespread belief that offenders who feel remorse are less likely to offend again. Judges as well as members of the public tend to view remorse as revealing one's true character. If at the deepest level of feeling, offenders condemn their own actions, then it is possible that the emotional pain they experience may help deter them from further misconduct. Also, many cor- rectional authorities regard the expression of remorse as the first step toward rehabilitation.

These justifications for leniency lose their force if the expression of remorse is strategic or insincere rather than genuine. Hence, judges and juries are interested not just in the expression of remorse but also in whether, in their view, what is shown corresponds to what is felt. Since very few offenders are prepared to act as unstrategically as Mr. W., with all the risks this entails, most expressions of remorse leave room for doubt as to whether appearance corresponds to reality.

As we shall see below in the case of the wrongly convicted, this potential gap between appearance and reality can also work in the other direction. Just as a claim to feel remorse can be discredited if it seems rehearsed or unfelt, so also can a claim not to feel remorse be invalidated by what are perceived as underlying feelings of guilt or shame.

THE PROBLEM OF REMORSE FOR THE WRONGLY CONVICTED

There is much at stake in a wrongful conviction even apart from the rupture of the innocent person's life. As Huff, Rattner, and Sagarin (1996) have observed, wrongful convictions often involve a multiplicity of errors and occasional wrongdoings that may implicate different levels of the criminal justice system in "the ratification of error." Well-known Canadian cases over the past 30 years have shown that the eventual unravelling of a wrongful conviction that restores the reputation of the innocent may also challenge the credibility of those police, defence and Crown attorneys, judges, witnesses, jurors, correctional staff—even high-ranking political officials—who contributed to or condoned the injustice that led to the wrongful conviction. At the root of every wrongful conviction is a contest of credibility between an individual who asserts a claim of innocence and whose reputation and potential liberty depend upon this claim, and the justice system which claims that a conviction and the punishment that followed were justified.

Remorse is one of the issues that will determine whose definition of the situation will prevail. For the authorities, an assertion of innocence after conviction calls into question the credibility of the entire system of criminal justice; whereas a show of remorse is an affirmation that the institutions that imposed punishment did so with just cause. But for the person who has been convicted, any show of remorse subverts the claim to innocence. Even the momentary abandonment of this claim is enough to cast a lingering doubt as to its validity and thus compromise later attempts at exoneration—should the opportunity arise. The net effect of this clash of purposes is to trigger a process in which correctional staff and other officials intensify their efforts to elicit a show of remorse from the individual, while those who wish to advance a claim of wrongful conviction must embark on a project of long-term resistance.

However, this contest is decidedly unequal. Wrongly convicted persons who maintain their innocence are likely to be placed in the category of the unremorseful and to be subjected to the same deprivations as others who have been designated as lacking in remorse.[2] These deprivations are evident both in the sentencing process and in the way that the sentence is administered. Those who plead guilty to an offence are already credited with the most elemental demonstration of remorse—namely, they have acknowledged their responsibility for the commission of the offence. Those who claim innocence but are nonetheless found guilty are not allowed this credit.

These presumptions pervade all forms of sentencing, from the least to the most severe of penalties. The person who pleads guilty is officially entitled to mitigation even though the absence of remorse (as reflected in a plea of not guilty) should not result in a harsher sentence (*R. v. Ambrose*). When it comes to sentencing, pleading guilty translates into measurable and tangible reductions in the severity of sentences. More recently, it has also come to fulfill what appears to be an emerging requirement for a conditional sentence of imprisonment (served in the community) and for sentencing by sentencing circles. Because remorse in the form of acknowledgment of responsibility is taken as a first step toward rehabilitation and toward renunciation of the offending criminal conduct, those who maintain their innocence after conviction are perceived as not having accepted responsibility for their actions and, therefore, as more likely to reoffend, more dangerous, and more of a risk to the community.[3]

Moreover, the reluctance to express remorse, whatever its source, has deep cultural connotations in our society from which the law is not insulated. Individuals define themselves as members of a shared moral community to the extent that their feelings of remorse affirm the seriousness that others attach to moral transgressions. The findings of the Capital Jury Project show that jurors are more likely to impose a death sentence on persons who deny guilt on grounds of factual innocence or reasonable doubt (Sundby 1998); moreover, jurors' responses indicate a strong negative characterization of the persons who raise these defences. Especially in cases involving the death of the victim, there is a cultural expectation that those perceived as perpetrators will experience regret commensurate with the gravity of the offence. Those who do not—even on the impeccable moral ground that they were wrongly convicted—risk adverse characterization as "cold-hearted" or "utterly without feeling."[4] The moral career of the wrongly convicted thus begins not just with a harsher sentence but with the ascription of qualities that define them as more of a risk than others similarly situated and as lacking the moral sentiments—the inner emotional life—that other members of the community share.

In the context of this asymmetrical struggle for credibility, it becomes possible to better understand the pressures placed on the wrongly convicted to show remorse and the tenacity with which these pressures are often resisted. The most obvious pressures consist in deprivations, which are likely to be far greater for wrongly convicted persons who have been incarcerated than for other inmates. The annals of the wrongly convicted in Canada point to denials of parole and temporary absence because of continued assertions of innocence.[5] Even evidence that would normally favour a positive outcome, such as acquiring a skill, being active on committees, or having a record of no institutional violence, fails to outweigh the negative impact of a denial of guilt.

The pressures to show remorse are also likely to be indirect. Programs of therapy that enhance a person's eligibility for parole and other benefits typically require as a first sign of rehabilitation that the prisoner admit responsibility for the crime, even though fulfilling such a condition negates a claim of innocence. The result is that the wrongly convicted tend to accumulate a record that attests not only to their denial of guilt but also to their nonparticipation in programs designed to make them safe to return to the community.

LACK OF REMORSE VIEWED AS PSYCHOPATHOLOGY

However, no occasion touches more directly on issues of credibility than the psychological assessment and treatment of those who maintain their innocence. Here the assertion of innocence is approached less as a factual claim to be contested or rejected than as a symptom that requires therapeutic intervention. From the standpoint of the specialists—be they psychiatrists, psychologists, parole officers, or others who favour this perspective—the unwillingness to take responsibility for the crime is less a matter of defiance than of denial. An excerpt from the *Royal Commission on the Donald Marshall Jr. Prosecution* offers a revealing glimpse into how this framework was applied during Marshall's wrongful incarceration for the murder of Sandy Seale. In the following exchange, the commission was exploring a memo in which a parole officer had denied Marshall's request for a temporary absence "as it [was] felt that in light of his unstableness at the present time, he presents too high a security risk" (Hickman 1989, 110):

Q. What was his unstableness?

A. This was a period of time when his behaviour in the institution was extremely aggressive towards the staff, towards myself, and towards the other members of the case management team where in one case he threw a chair at one of the staff members.

Q. Are you able to offer any insight as to what provoked that aggressiveness?

A. I suspect that it had a lot to do with the issue of whether he was guilty or innocent of the crime. Although I was not (putting) a lot of pressure on him to admit that he was guilty, some people were.

Q. Who would these people have been?

A. Some of the other people were members of his case management team who had contact with him far more frequently than I did on a daily basis.

Q. Was it your sense that his frustration in maintaining his innocence in the face of the response that he was guilty was causing this aggression to a degree?

A. In retrospect, yes. At the time, my belief was that he was coming close to admitting that he was involved in the crime and that it was starting to come out.[*]

Because the officials presume guilt, they seek underlying disturbances that show a gap between appearance and reality in the expression of remorse and that undermine the claim of innocence. Just as overt claims of remorse can

---

[*] Hickman, A. 1989. Royal Commission on the Donald Marshall, Jr. Prosecution, vol. 1, Findings and Recommendations. Halifax: Province of Nova Scotia.

be challenged by inconsistencies between words and feelings or feelings and deeds, so also can a claim of innocence be invalidated by involuntary displays of conscience whether in the form of "aggression" or emotional turbulence.[6]

Similarly, the therapeutic approach used on Stephen Truscott during his wrongful conviction for the murder of Lynne Harper also involved a search for "abnormal" reactions. When Truscott failed to break down and admit guilt even after being administered sodium pentothal and several doses of LSD over an extended period, the psychiatric notes read as follows: "He is so controlled, so pleasant, and so objective that certainly there must be in his subconscious a tremendous control for commanding details" (Sher 2001, 376). In another log entry, the psychiatrist observed: "If he's guilty and is not admitting guilt, then this implies that there is a complete repression of the problems involved" (ibid., 395).

Yet paradoxically, the absence of these same "abnormal" reactions does not lead experts in forensic psychiatry to conclude that the person's claim of innocence may be credible. In one well-known American case of wrongful conviction, the prisoner's absence of affect resulted in the psychiatrist diag-nosing the defendant as "a sociopathic personality disorder" because of "the absolute absence of any type of guilt or remorse" (Adams 1991, 129). In another Canadian case in which the person incarcerated had long asserted his innocence, the psychologist performing the assessment observed that the defendant's "calm, confident, and remorseless exterior was consistent with the reaction of an innocent man" (Harris 1996, 397–8); but then added: "A similar presentation associated with heinous and egregious behaviour would represent a powerful indicator of psychopathy." It would seem that there is no psycho-logical model of what would be a normal reaction to a wrongful conviction.

Biographies and interviews reveal how the wrongly convicted resist these pressures to weaken their resolve. Despite maintaining their claims of innocence, most did attempt at some point to fashion a measure of relief from the restrictions, deprivations, and adverse characterizations to which they were being subjected. These actions illustrate the challenge of meeting official expectations without forfeiting one's credibility. In one instance, a man who had been wrongly convicted of sexual assault agreed to attend therapy sessions directed at sex offenders while refusing to sign a document admitting guilt (Liptak 2002, 4). Donald Marshall, after unrelenting attempts by the authorities to elicit a show of remorse, achieved a compromise of sorts when he agreed to admit to his parole officer, after being asked, that, even if he may not have committed the murder for which he was convicted, "he was the sort of individual who could have committed a murder ... a condition with which Marshall complied in hopes of improving his situation" (Harris 1990, 285).

Similarly, Stephen Truscott eventually produced a generalized state-ment in his application before a parole board in which he neither asserted his innocence nor explicitly claimed responsibility for the crime. This was in an effort to win freedom without negating the original claim of innocence

(Sher 2001, 372). Years later, even this isolated incident would have to be explained and accounted for in the application to the Minister of Justice for his case to be reconsidered (s. 690 application for retrial between Her Majesty the Queen and Steven Truscott, November 28, 2001, 115). Not until August 28, 2007, was Trustcott's appeal heard and an acquittal substituted for the conviction entered almost 50 years before, in 1959 (*R. v. Truscott* 2007).

The demand that all persons who are convicted of crimes demonstrate remorse by accepting responsibility for their offences has unintended consequences for those who have been wrongly convicted. The self-same efforts to maintain one's integrity in opposition to external pressures—actions that in other circumstances might well be viewed as virtuous—result in what Goffman (1961) referred to as the *mortification of the self*—the process by which the self is stripped of its social and psychological supports so that a new identity can replace the identity that has been lost. The treatment of the wrongly convicted illustrates this process, in which the force of criminal justice and corrections is directed toward recasting the truths claimed by those who are innocent as pathology at best and defiance at worst.

Further Readings

Medwed, D. 2008. "The Innocent Prisoner's Dilemma: Consequences of Failing to Admit Guilt at Parole Hearings." *Iowa Law Review* 93: 491.

Weisman, R. 2009. "Being and Doing: The Judicial Use of Remorse to Construct Character and Community." *Social and Legal Studies* 18, no. 1: 47–69.

——. 2014. *Showing Remorse: Law and the Social Control of Emotion*. London: Ashgate.

References

Adams, R. (with W. Hoffer and M. Hoffer). 1991. *Adams v. Texas*. New York: St. Martin's.

Clairmont, S. 2001. "'Unrepentant' Drunk Driver Utters a Stunning Last Word." *Toronto Star*, May 29, A5.

Dao, J., and L. Bacon. 2003. "Death Sentence for Muhammad: Sniper Jury Cites Lack of Sorrow." *New York Times*, November 25, A1.

Davis, S. 1997. "The Rape That Wasn't." *Alberta Report*, June 2, 30.

Goffman, E. 1961. *Asylums: Essays on the Social Situation of Mental Patients and Other Inmates*. New York: Doubleday Anchor.

Harris, M. 1990. *Justice Denied: The Law Versus Donald Marshall*. Toronto: HarperCollins.

——. 1996. *The Judas Kiss*. Toronto: McClelland and Stewart.

Her Majesty the Queen and Steven Truscott, s. 690 Application for Retrial, November 28, 2001.

Hickman, A. 1989. *Royal Commission on the Donald Marshall Jr. Prosecution*, vol. 1, Findings and Recommendations. Halifax: Province of Nova Scotia.

Huff, C., A. Rattner, and E. Sagarin. 1996. *Convicted but Innocent: Wrongful Conviction and Public Policy*. Thousand Oaks: Sage Publications.

Karp, C., and C. Rosner. 1991. *When Justice Fails: The David Milgaard Story*. Toronto: McClelland and Stewart.

Liptak, A. 2002. "Not at All Remorseful but Not Guilty Either." *New York Times*, November 3, 4.

Makin, K. 2001. "Man Jailed 29 Years Had Alibi but Police Buried It." *Globe and Mail*, November 8, 1.

——. 2008. "Baltovich Goes Free." *Globe and Mail*, April 22, 1.

Sher, J. 2001. *"Until You Are Dead": Stephen Truscott's Long Ride Into History*. Toronto: Knopf Canada.

Sundby, S. 1998. "The Capital Jury and Absolution: The Intersection of Trial Strategy, Remorse, and the Death Penalty." *Cornell Law Review* 83: 1557.

Weisman, R. 1999. "Detecting Remorse and Its Absence in the Criminal Justice System." In A. Sarat and P. Ewick, eds., *Studies in Law, Politics, and Society* 19.

Williamson, L. 2001. "A Canadian Tragedy: Money Can Never Right the Wrongs of the Thomas Sophonow Case." *Calgary Sun*, November 10, 15.

Cases

R. v. Allard (1999) 43 W.C.B. (2nd) 296.

R. v. Ambrose (2000) 271 A.R., 164.

R. v. Baltovich (1992) 18 W.C.B. (2nd) 215.

R. v. Truscott (2007) 225 C.C.C. (3rd) 321

R. v. Wood (2005) 196 C.C.C. (3rd) 155

Endnotes

1. Paradoxically, Wood did appeal his sentence partially on the grounds that the judge erred in principle in using his lack of remorse as one of the factors contributing to his relatively severe sentence. The court declined the

appeal, ruling that the sentence was fit. (See para. 24 in *R. v. Wood* (2005) 196 C.C.C.(3rd) 155).

2. Many wrongful convictions begin with a false confession rather than with a plea of not guilty. For purposes of this analysis, I am assuming that whether or not wrongfully convicted persons maintain their innocence from the outset, at some point they will have to assert their innocence in order to pursue the claim. Once they do so, they will experience the disadvantages arising from an assertion of innocence.

3. The equation of an absence of remorse with dangerousness is commonplace in Canadian and American judgments. See, for example, *R. v. Allard*, [1999] (B.C.C.A.) at para. 5: "The trial judge was quite properly concerned with protection of the public, and hence the extent to which the applicant constituted a continuing danger to those he had harmed and threatened to harm, as well as to others. For that purpose, the appellant's apparent lack of remorse was relevant ..."

4. One example is the reaction of the court to Robert Baltovich's assertion of innocence after he was convicted of murder in 1992. See *R. v. Baltovich*, [1992]18 W.C.B. (2nd) 215 at para. 25: "The record shows a cold, calculating person, and that person killed a person who had loved and trusted you"; or at para. 26: "You have high intelligence, but you are totally devoid of heart and conscience." Sixteen years later, Baltovich's conviction was overturned on appeal, a new trial was ordered, and the prosecution withdrew its case against him, resulting in a directed verdict of acquittal in 2008 (Makin 2008, 1).

5. Examples include the following: Thomas Sophonow, wrongly convicted of second-degree murder, who was refused parole and temporary absences (Williamson 2001, 15); Wilfred Beaulieu, who was wrongly convicted of sexual assault and denied temporary absence to attend the funerals of his brother and sister (Davis 1997, 30); David Milgaard, wrongly convicted of sexual assault and murder, who was turned down for parole and temporary absences many times during his 23 years in prison (Karp and Rosner 1991, 129); Donald Marshall, wrongly convicted of murder, who was refused parole for the same reasons (Harris 1990, 266). Romeo Phillion, who served nearly 35 years for a conviction that was successfully challenged and whose requests for parole were also consistently denied, was not altogether mistaken when he was quoted as saying that "parole is for the guilty, not for the innocent" (Makin 2001, 1). Subsequently, the Ontario Court of Appeal decided 2–1 to overturn Phillion's conviction on March 5, 2009, and to order that a new trial be held. However, in July 2009, the Attorney General of Ontario chose to withdraw charges, leaving Phillion in a legal limbo: neither convicted nor acquitted. Currently, Phillion is appealing to the Supreme Court of Canada to ask that a new trial be ordered so that his name might be cleared.

6. Interestingly, from this vantage point, those family members and others who believe the claim of innocence are viewed as supporting the underlying pathology; hence, continued contact is seen as problematic. Thus, one of Marshall's parole officers included in his appraisal: "There still remains the problem of Marshall himself denying his guilt and being supported in this by an overprotective mother" (Harris 1990, 283). In the case of David Milgaard, one caseworker at Stony Mountain wrote: "This writer questions how constructive familial support is. First, if the subject is guilty, familial belief in his innocence provides a firm block to subject even admitting to or working through intrapsychic aspects of offence" (Karp and Rosner 1991, 130).

The Changing Nature of Youth Justice: Assessing the Impact of the *Youth Criminal Justice Act*

Youth crime is the subject of public concern and political controversy in many countries (Roberts 2004). While almost all nations treat child and adolescent offenders differently from adults, responses to youth crime vary greatly (Tonry and Doob 2004). *The Youth Criminal Justice Act* (YCJA), which came into force in 2003, resulted in marked reductions in Canada's use of courts and custody for adolescent offenders, and without provoking an increase in youth crime. The Act has remained contentious, however, and in 2012 the Conservative government enacted amendments. This chapter reviews key provisions of the YCJA and 2012 amendments, and analyzes statistical data about the treatment of youth in Canada's justice system. The authors argue that while the federal government's rhetoric regarding youth offending is consistent with its "law and order" approach to crime in general, the 2012 amendments were relatively minor adjustments to the law and are not intended to return Canada to its previous high rates of use of youth court and youth custody. (See Bala and Anand 2012 for a fuller discussion of the YCJA and the 2012 amendments.)

Nicholas Bala
Queen's University

Peter J. Carrington
University of Waterloo

REDUCING USE OF COURTS AND CUSTODY

Prior to the introduction of the YCJA, the use of juvenile custody in Canada was higher in Canada than in most other Western nations (e.g., Bala 2003; Doob and Cesaroni 2004). The high use of courts and custody is generally acknowledged to be a more pressing issue at the juvenile level than for adults, as involvement in the formal justice system and the imprisonment of adolescents can have more profound and negative effects than for adults (Cesaroni and Peterson-Badali 2013). Community-based responses are often the most cost-effective way to deal with juvenile offenders, especially those who have committed less serious offences and who do not have an extensive history of offending. Imprisonment can often be a more punitive sentence for juveniles than for adults because young people are less able to cope with prison and may be more susceptible to the adverse effects of the inmate subculture (Cesaroni and Peterson-Badali 2005).

Furthermore, even though there is generally a greater emphasis on rehabilitation in youth custody facilities, imprisonment deprives adolescents of the social support on which they depend for their moral and psychological development. While there is a need to imprison the most serious adolescent offenders, the inappropriate use of custody is expensive, ineffective, and inhumane; indeed, imprisonment may contribute to a cycle of juvenile reoffending. Thus one of the goals of any youth justice system—reducing reoffending—can be undermined by the inappropriate use of more intensive forms of intervention, in particular custody. This conclusion is consistent with research on youth justice in other countries such as Scotland (e.g., McAra and McVie 2007). Accordingly, in introducing the YCJA in 2003, the then-Liberal federal government set as a primary goal of its juvenile justice reform a reduction in the number of juveniles being sentenced to imprisonment.

GENERAL PRINCIPLES OF THE YCJA

Preamble

The YCJA includes a preamble that makes clear the intent of the law that Canada should "have a youth criminal justice system that reserves its most serious interventions for the most serious crimes and reduces the over-reliance on incarceration for non-violent young persons."

Purpose and Nature of the Youth Justice System

The Declaration of Principle (s. 3) of the YCJA provides that the criminal justice system for youths "must be separate from that of adults." This Declaration establishes the overall purpose of Canada's youth justice system, with Section 3(1)(a) stating that:

(a) the youth criminal justice system is intended to protect the public by

(i) holding young persons accountable through measures that are proportionate to the seriousness of the offence and the degree of responsibility of the young person,

(ii) promoting the rehabilitation and reintegration of young persons who have committed offences, and

(iii) supporting the prevention of crime by referring young persons to programs or agencies in the community to address the circumstances underlying their offending behaviour....

While this statement was amended in 2012, and accountability is now listed first, the order of the statements is not legally significant, since no principle is stated to be "primary." Rehabilitation and preventing crime are equally important principles. This statement directs judges to impose sentences that facilitate the rehabilitation of young offenders, rather than custodial sentences that will merely incapacitate them.

Limited Accountability

The Declaration of Principle of the YCJA articulates a set of principles for responding to youthful offenders that places the greatest emphasis on the proportionality of the response, with Section 3(1)(c) emphasizing that "fair and proportionate" accountability is *the* central principle for responding to youth offending. The Act also recognizes, however, that it is to be limited accountability in comparison to adults, "consistent with the greater dependency of young persons and their reduced level of maturity." In its 2008 decision on the issue of whether an adult sentence should be imposed on a youth who committed a very serious offence, the Supreme Court of Canada held that because of their age, adolescents have a "heightened vulnerability, less maturity and a reduced capacity for moral judgement." Accordingly the Court concluded that the *Charter of Rights* (s. 7) and the "principles of fundamental justice" entitle youth to a "presumption of diminished moral blameworthiness" and a presumption that they will receive less severe sentences than adults who commit the same offences (*R v. D.B.*, 2008 SCC 25).

Diversion from Youth Court by Extrajudicial Measures

The YCJA encourages the diversion of cases from youth court, providing for both extrajudicial measures and extrajudicial sanctions. *Extrajudicial sanctions* are non-court, community-based programs that may result in responses such as restitution to a victim or family group conferencing. The concept of *extrajudicial measures* is broader, including extrajudicial sanctions as well as oral warnings or written cautions by the police.

The YCJA was clearly intended to reduce the number of youths appearing in youth court, particularly first offenders and juveniles accused of minor offences, as indicated by the presumption in Section 4(c): "Extrajudicial measures are *presumed* to be adequate to hold a young person accountable for his or her offending behaviour if the young person has committed a non-violent offence and has not previously been found guilty of an offence" (emphasis added). Furthermore, there is provision in the Act that a police officer "shall" consider whether to invoke an extrajudicial measure prior to commencing judicial proceedings against a young person (s. 6). The YCJA affirms the importance and stresses the range of application of extrajudicial measures, recognizing in Section 4(a) that "extrajudicial measures are often the most appropriate and effective way to address youth crime."

In many communities across Canada, extrajudicial sanctions programs have been established for minor youth offences (such as shoplifting and minor assaults). Such programs often provide for the possibility of victim–offender reconciliation or family group conferencing, and may result in an apology or restitution to the victim, community service, or counselling for the youth (Bala 2003).

Section 10 of the YCJA provides that extrajudicial sanctions may be used only if a youth "accepts responsibility" for the offence that is alleged to have been committed and consents to the imposition of the sanction. A youth who denies responsibility for the offence or who objects to a specific sanction should be referred to youth court for a hearing. In an attempt to prevent the application of these interventions to cases in which the young person is not at risk of a judicial proceeding, Section 10(2)(f) states that an extrajudicial sanction may be used only if there is sufficient evidence to prosecute a case in youth court. If the youth complies with the conditions of the extrajudicial sanction, the case against the young person cannot proceed to youth court. The record of having received an extrajudicial sanction is not technically a finding of guilt, but if in the two years following the imposition of the sanction the youth is found guilty of an offence in youth court, the existence of the prior extrajudicial sanction may be used by the youth court in considering whether to detain a youth or for imposing a more severe sentence.

The YCJA resulted in a very significant drop in the number of youth charged by police, as well as an increase in the use of various methods of police diversion. In Figure 21.1, the rates of youth apprehended by police as suspected offenders and cleared without charge are summarized in one statistic. The charge ratio, or percentage of chargeable youth who were charged, indicates the relative degree to which police are clearing cases by charge rather than by alternatives to charging. This indicator declined gently from 1991 to 2002. In 2003—the year that the YCJA was introduced—it dropped sharply from 56.4 to 44.6 percent charged: a reduction of one-fifth in one year. Since the coming into force of the YCJA the charge rate has remained relatively constant at a lower rate. This means that the YCJA has reduced the use of formal charges at the youth justice level.

FIGURE 21.1   *The Proportion of Chargeable Youth Who Were Charged, Canada, 1986–2012*

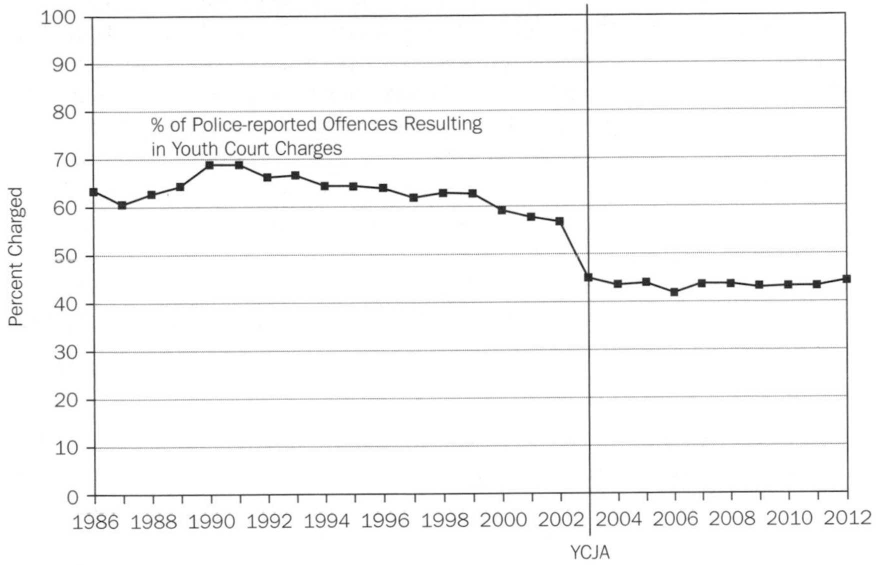

Source: Statistics Canada. Canadian Centre for Justice Statistics, Uniform Crime Reporting Survey.

PURPOSE AND PRINCIPLES OF SENTENCING

Purpose of Sentencing in Youth Court

The YCJA establishes the purpose of sentencing in youth court and then sets out specific principles of youth sentencing. Section 38(1) states that "[t]he purpose of [youth court] sentencing … is to hold a young person accountable for an offence through the imposition of just sanctions that have meaningful consequences for the young person and that promote his or her rehabilitation and reintegration." The omission of reference to general deterrence in the YCJA statement of sentencing purpose likely contributed to a reduction in the number of custodial sentences imposed in youth court (Cesaroni and Bala 2008). Its absence in the Act clearly indicates that general deterrence is not an objective when young persons are sentenced. That is, a youth should not receive a more severe sanction than otherwise appropriate in order to discourage or deter other youth from committing the same offence. However, as discussed below, in 2012, the principle of specific deterrence was added to the YCJA.

Sentencing Principles

For those youths who are charged, found guilty, and sentenced in youth court, the YCJA provides a detailed set of sentencing principles for judges to apply. Two of these principles reflect the intent of the Act to restrict the use of imprisonment for adolescent offenders. Thus Section 38(2)(d) states that "all available sanctions other than custody that are reasonable in the circumstances must be considered." Furthermore, Section 38(2)(e) requires that, subject to the requirement that sentences be proportionate to the offence, "the sentence must be the least restrictive sentence that is capable of achieving the purpose [of sentencing]." Both these general principles also apply to the sentencing of adults. However, the YCJA emphasizes the limited accountability of youth compared to adults convicted of the same offence; and it has had a much greater impact on youth incarceration than the general statements on sentencing for adults in the *Criminal Code*. Having provided youth courts with these general sentencing principles, the legislation then prescribes specific criteria that must be met before a young offender can be committed to custody.

Criteria for Imposition of a Custodial Sanction

At the adult level in Canada there are no specific offence-based criteria that must be met before an adult offender is imprisoned. In contrast, the provisions in the YCJA relating to the imposition of a custodial sentence in youth court are more restrictive, with Section 39(1) establishing four "gateways" to custody; unless one of these conditions is satisfied, a custodial sentence cannot be imposed:

A youth justice court shall not commit a person to custody ... unless

(a) the young person has committed a violent offence; [or]
(b) the young person has failed to comply with non-custodial sentences; [or]
(c) the young person has committed an ... offence for which an adult would be liable to imprisonment for a term of more than two years and has a history that indicates a pattern of findings of guilt ... or
(d) in exceptional cases where the young person has committed an indictable offence, the aggravating circumstances of the offence are such that the imposition of a non-custodial sentence would be inconsistent with the purpose and principles set out in section 38.

Thus there are only four circumstances in which a young offender may be committed to custody. As we shall discuss later in this chapter, this section has resulted in a substantial reduction in the use of custody.

Additional Restrictions Regarding the Use of Custody

If the case before a youth court satisfies one of the four "gateway" conditions in Section 39(1), a number of other custody-related principles must still be considered before a court can imprison the young offender. The first restriction is a clear reminder to judges in Section 39(2) of the principle of restraint with respect to the use of custody, even if one of the conditions of Section 39(1) is satisfied: "If [one of the criteria for custody] apply, a youth justice court *shall not impose a custodial sentence* … unless the court has considered all alternatives to custody raised at the sentencing hearing that are reasonable in the circumstances, and determined that there is not a reasonable alternative, or combination of alternatives, that is in accordance with the purpose and principles [of sentencing at the youth court level]" (emphasis added).

A second principle to be observed before a custodial sentence is imposed is designed to discourage judges from increasing the severity of the sentence in response to subsequent offending. Having imposed an alternative to custody for one offence, some judges may impose a custodial sentence if a youth appears before the court on a new charge, reasoning that the first sentence was insufficiently severe to discourage the offender. Section 39(4) attempts to constrain this judicial practice, providing that "[t]he previous imposition of a particular non-custodial sentence on a young person does not preclude a youth justice court from imposing the same or any other non-custodial sentence for another offence." While this provision does not prohibit judges from following the "step principle" logic at sentencing, the provision means that the same alternative sanction may be imposed on consecutive occasions.

A third principle that restricts the use of custody is more clearly binding on youth court judges: Section 39(5) explicitly states that a youth court "shall not" use custody as a substitute for a child protection, mental health, or other social measure. Under the previous law, a common justification for imposing a custodial sentence on troubled adolescents was that the judge could see no other way to provide the necessary social intervention for an adolescent at risk. Under the YCJA this justification for the imposition of custody is prohibited.

While the YCJA emphasizes community-based responses for the majority of youth who commit less serious offences, violent or persistent offenders may receive youth sentences of up to 3 years in custody (and up to 10 years for murder). Also, for the most serious adolescent offenders there is the possibility of an adult sentence being imposed.

Community-Based Sentences

To encourage judges to place fewer youths in custody, the YCJA added a number of community-based youth sanctions to such traditional sentences as probation, community service, or a fine. Some of these new sentences, such as requiring involvement at an "attendance centre" or "intensive supervision and support," are intended to provide youth with more support in the community, but they are relatively resource intensive and can only be imposed by a youth court if the province decides to provide the programs.

The most significant community-based sentence added by the YCJA was the "deferred custody and supervision order" (DCSO), which can be imposed by a youth court judge even without special programming being introduced by a provincial government. This sentence, analogous to the conditional sentence of imprisonment available at the adult level, allows the court to permit the youth to remain in the community for the duration of the order, subject to supervision by probation officers. In the event of an apprehended breach of the terms of release, the youth may be placed immediately in custody for the balance of the sentence without the need for another court hearing. This sentence, which can be imposed only if the youth has not committed a serious violent offence, has a maximum duration of six months. This sanction represents the last opportunity for the court to spare the offender committal to custody, and it is used quite frequently, also contributing to the decline in the use of youth custody (see Carrington, Roberts, and Davis-Barron 2011).

To summarize the sentencing provisions, the YCJA contains a number of provisions designed to discourage youth courts from imposing a term of custody on a young offender. These provisions were enacted specifically to reduce the use of imprisonment in youth courts.

Figure 21.2 shows changes over time in the use of custodial sentences in youth court, as indicated by two statistics. The rates per 100,000 show the number of custodial sentences, standardized by population, and reflect any changes in the number of cases coming to court, in the proportion of cases with a finding of guilt, and in sentencing patterns. The proportions of sentenced

FIGURE 21.2   *Rates and Proportions of Custodial Sentences in Youth Court, Canada, 1991/92–2011/12*

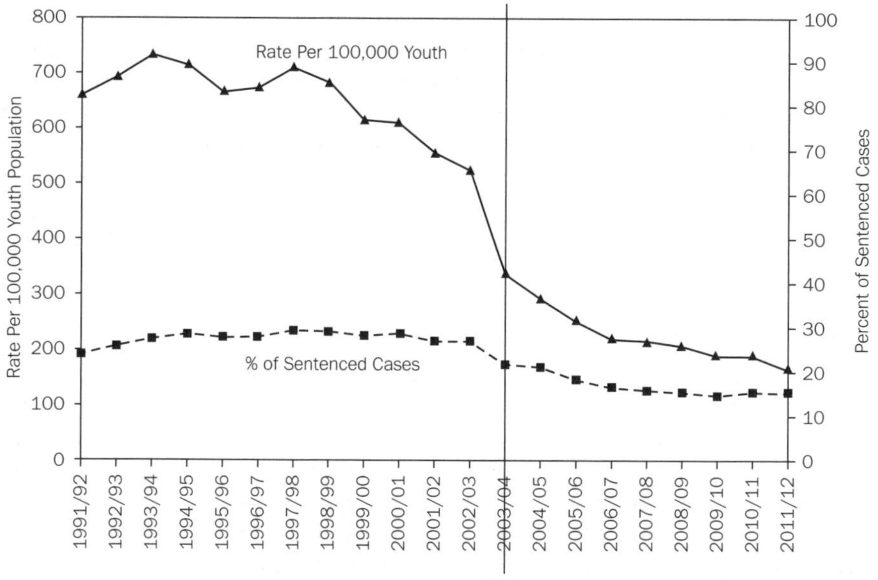

Source: Statistics Canada. Canadian Centre for Justice Statistics. Youth Court Survey and Integrated Criminal Court Survey.

cases show the use of custodial sentences, standardized by the total number of sentences handed down, and reflect only changes in custodial sentencing itself. Both indicators show a substantial drop when the YCJA came into force in 2003–4 and a slow decline thereafter. It is clear that youth courts in Canada have adopted an approach to youth sentencing that has restricted the use of custody.

The rate of custodial sentences dropped by 36 percent in 2003–4 and by a further 50 percent over the next eight years. In 2011–12, the rate of custodial sentences was 170 per 100,000 youth—less than one-third of the rate in 2002–3. The proportion of sentenced cases receiving a custodial disposition also dropped sharply—from 27 percent in 2002–3 to 22 percent in 2003–4—a drop of just under one-fifth in one year. It fell by a further 7 percent over the following eight years, with the result that in 2011–12 only 15.2 percent of sentenced youth court cases resulted in a custodial sentence. The observed reduction in the proportion of custodial sentences is strong evidence for the effectiveness of those provisions of the YCJA that restrict the use of custodial sentences.

As a result of the decrease in the volume of cases coming to youth court and in the proportion of cases with a finding of guilt that ended in a custodial sentence, the per capita rate of youth incarcerated in sentenced custody in Canada decreased dramatically after the YCJA came into force in 2003   by 53 percent from 2001–2 to 2003–4 and by a further 31 percent to 2010–11 (see Figure 21.3). In 2010–11 the rate of youth in sentenced custody was less than one-third of the rate in 2001–2. While there has been a substantial decline in use of custody for youth, there has only been a small decrease in the use of pretrial remand custody, despite the inclusion in the YCJA of provisions also intended to reduce the use of remand. This is concerning as youth placed in remand are especially vulnerable to exploitation by peers, and there is often less access to rehabilitative programming for these youth.

It is critically important to note that this reduction in the use of court and custody for young offenders has not resulted in any increase in the crime rate by young people across Canada. Critics of the previous youth justice system argued that a tougher law was needed, one that promoted rather than constrained the use of custody for young offenders. However, as can be seen in Figure 21.4, the youth crime rate across Canada has not increased since the YCJA came into force, even though the rate of youth brought to court and the use of youth custody have significantly declined (Bala and Anand 2012).

Recent Amendments to the YCJA

Despite the success of the YCJA in substantially reducing the use of courts and custody without increasing the youth crime rate, the Conservative government has maintained a critical stance towards the Act, consistent with its "law and order" rhetoric about responses to crime in general. Conservative prime minister Stephen Harper, who came into power in 2006, was an outspoken critic of the YCJA, characterizing Canada's approach to handling young offenders at the time as "an unmitigated failure" because it did not "hold

FIGURE 21.3 *Average Daily Rates of Youth in Remand and Sentenced Custody, Canada, 1996/97–2010/11*

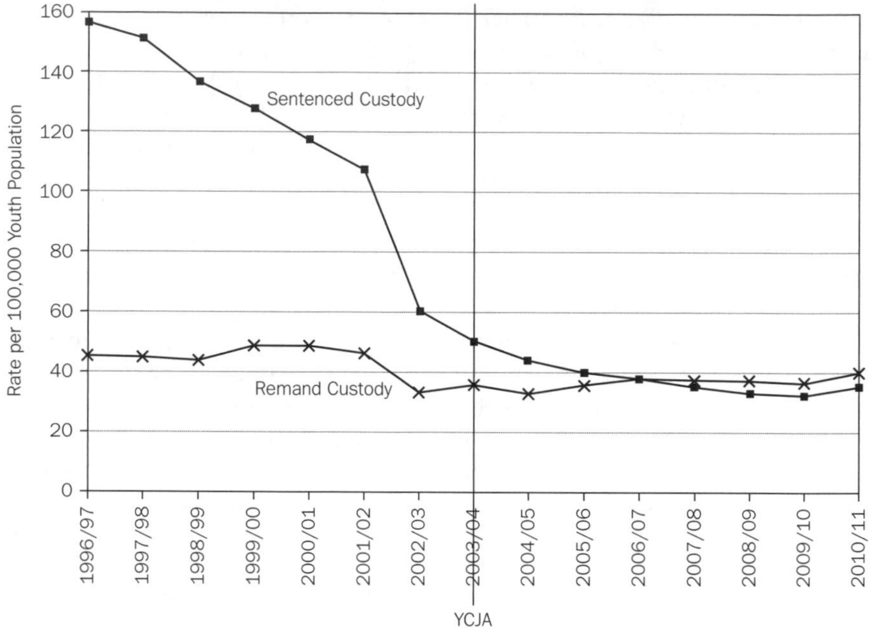

Source: Statistics Canada. Canadian Centre for Justice Statistics. Youth Key Indicators Survey.

young lawbreakers responsible for their behaviour and make them account-able to their victims and society" (Canwest 2008). In 2012 the Conservative government enacted the *Safe Streets and Communities Act* (S.C. 2012, c.1). This legislation, dubbed the Omnibus Crime Bill by commentators, primarily addressed issues related to adult offenders, but also included amendments to the YCJA.

As regards adults, this was clearly a punitive set of reforms, and included introducing a range of new offences for which there are mandatory min-imum sentences. While the full effect of this law on adults will only become clear over a period of years, and may in part depend on whether some of the provisions—for example, as regards mandatory minimum sentences—are declared unconstitutional, its intent was clearly to increase the use of cus-tody for adults. By way of comparison, the provisions of the 2012 law that amended the YCJA seem relatively nuanced and seem likely, on balance, to have little effect on youth incarceration rates. While some of the changes were clearly intended to demonstrate rhetorical support for "toughening" the YCJA and may result in small increases in sentenced custody, other changes may reduce the likelihood of placement of some youths in remand detention. Further, it is significant that in comparison to the provisions of the 2012 law that affect adults—many of which constrain judicial discretion by requiring

FIGURE 21.4   *Recorded Youth Crime Rate (Rate of Young Persons Apprehended by Police), Canada, 1986–2012*

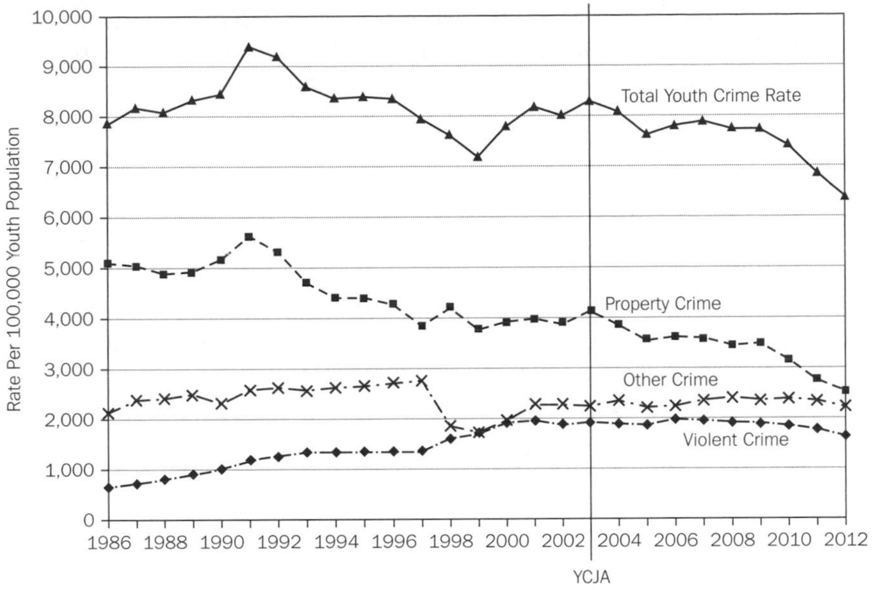

Source: Statistics Canada. Canadian Centre for Justice Statistics. Uniform Crime Reporting Survey.

minimum jail sentences and eliminating the possibility of community-based sentences for a range of offences—the 2012 YCJA amendments continue to afford judges, prosecutors, police, and probation officers discretion about how to deal with young offenders. The 2012 law did not alter the most significant restrictions on the use of custody for youth, and actually increased restrictions on use of pretrial remand.

At the time of introducing the 2012 law, the government stated its rhetorical position that the YCJA amendments were intended to be "part of its commitment to help ensure the safety and security of Canadians [with] ... proposed reforms designed to help ensure that violent and repeat young offenders are held fully accountable," noting that the public "loses confidence in the justice system when a sentence is insufficient to hold an offender accountable for his or her actions" (Department of Justice 2010). In Parliament, the Minister of Justice noted the "concern that some youth ... are out of control, are not being effectively dealt with under the current legislation" but also stated that it is only "a small number who are out of control."

An important example of the broadening of the scope in Bill C-10 for the use of custody is the expansion of the definition of the *violent offence* condition for the use of custody or detention not only to include situations where there have been physical harm or threats, but also to include cases where there may be endangerment of public safety, for example, dangerous driving. Further, the 2012 amendments allow courts sentencing youths to take account of *specific deterrence* and *denunciation* in sentencing. However, even prior to the 2012 amendments coming into force, some youth court judges were taking these factors into account. Significantly the 2012 amendments did not include *general deterrence* as a factor in youth sentencing, though general deterrence is a factor in adult sentencing. Specific deterrence is a relatively narrow concept compared to general deterrence, only requiring a court to consider whether a sentence being imposed on a youth for the offence committed is likely to be sufficient to help the youth understand that there may be significant consequences for further offending. Further, all of the sentencing principles and provisions of the original YCJA that emphasize rehabilitation and limited accountability remain in effect.

While some provisions of the 2012 amendments might make custody somewhat more likely, some of the changes to the pretrial detention provisions narrow the range of situations in which a youth may be detained. Further, the 2012 amendments provide that youth who receive an adult sentence must be kept in a youth facility at least until their 18th birthday, removing the discretion of judges to place these youth in an adult facility even before becoming adults.

The 2012 amendments may have some limited effects, especially in terms of lengthening sentences for youth who endanger public safety, or commit violent or repeat offences. However, the overall objective of enacting these amendments seems as much political or symbolic as legal. The 2012 amendments to the YCJA allow the Conservative government to claim that it has made the protection of the public a primary goal of the youth justice system. However, the actual wording of the changes suggests that their effect should be quite limited. Despite its rhetoric the Conservative government does not seem intent on significantly increasing the number of youth in custody or returning to the type of regime that existed under the YOA with its very high rates of youth custody.

CONCLUSION

The YCJA has had a significant impact on both the use of courts and custody as responses to youth crime. The law has resulted in a very significant reduction in the use of courts and custody for adolescent offenders in Canada; hence, it has allowed for a significant reduction in spending on youth courts and custody facilities, generally accompanied by a shifting of resources to community-based programs. Despite the rhetoric of Conservative politicians and the 2012 amendments, the YCJA represents a genuine success story in criminal justice in Canada.

Further Readings

Bala, N., and S. Anand. 2012. *Youth Criminal Justice Law*. 3rd ed. Toronto: Irwin Law.

Barry, M., and F. McNeill. 2009. *Youth Offending and Youth Justice*. London: Jessica Kingsley.

Doob, A.N., and J. Sprott. 2004. "Changing Models of Youth Justice in Canada." In M. Tonry and A. Doob, eds., *Youth Crime and Youth Justice*. Chicago: University of Chicago Press.

References

Bala, N. 2003. "Diversion, Conferencing, and Extrajudicial Measures for Adolescent Offenders." *Alberta Law Review* 40: 991–1027.

Canwest News Service. "Harper Vows Changes to 'Failed' Youth Justice Act," June 6, 2008.

Carrington, P., J.V. Roberts, and S. Davis-Barron. 2011. "The Last Chance Sanction in Youth Court: Exploring the Deferred Custody and Supervision Order." *Canadian Criminal Law Review* 15: 299–336.

Cesaroni, C., and N. Bala. 2008. "Deterrence as a Principle of Youth Sentencing: No Effect on Youth, but a Significant Effect on Judges." *Queen's Law Journal* 39: 447–81.

Cesaroni, C., and M. Peterson-Badali. 2005. "Young Offenders in Custody: Risk and Adjustment." *Criminal Justice and Behavior* 32: 251–77.

——. 2013. "The Importance of Institutional Culture to the Adjustment of Incarcerated Youth and Young Offenders." *Canadian Journal of Criminology and Criminal Justice* 59: 563–75.

Department of Justice Canada, Backgrounder: Sébastien's Law, March 16, 2010.

Doob, A., and C. Cesaroni. 2004. *Responding to Youth Crime in Canada*. Toronto: University of Toronto Press.

McAra, L., and S. McVie. 2007. "Youth Justice? The Impact of System Contact on Patterns of Desistance from Offending." *European Journal of Criminology* 4: 315–45.

Roberts, J.V. 2004. "Public Opinion and the Evolution of Juvenile Justice Policy in Western Nations." In M. Tonry and A. Doob, eds., *Youth Crime and Youth Justice*. Chicago: University of Chicago Press.

Tonry, M., and A.N. Doob, eds. 2004. *Crime and Justice: A Review of Research*. Chicago: University of Chicago Press.

Case

R v. D.B., 2008 SCC 25

CHAPTER 22

Young People Doing Time: Consequences of Custody for Young Offenders

Canada, like many countries, has provisions in its youth justice legislation suggesting that imprisonment should be used sparingly and only for very specific purposes. Why should Canada be reluctant to send young offenders to prison? Historically, one of the main rationales for establishing a separate youth justice system and separate custodial facilities was a belief that youth are more vulnerable than adults. Young people's special needs, their vulnerabilities, and their need to avoid stigmatization were the original impetus for the establishment of youth custody facilities in Canada. The principal reason however, is that imprisonment carries more adverse consequences for young offenders. Indeed, there is agreement around the world that custody affects young offenders more than it does adults and that it is a more severe sanction for youth. However, this belief needs to be substantiated by research. In this chapter the authors explore the effects of incarceration on young offenders, particularly girls in custody.

Carla Cesaroni
University of Ontario Institute of Technology

Holly Pelvin
University of Toronto

Although we know how many female youths are admitted to custody, for what, and for how long, little research exists on how young women actually experience and adjust to custody. The small number of girls within custodial institutions has produced the same problem that has often characterized women's prison populations: they tend to be an under-studied population. This has resulted in a lack of understanding about the experiences of female young offenders in custody, and perhaps explains the reluctance of staff to work with girls, including the perception among practitioners that girls in custody are complex and demanding (Cernkovich, Lanctot, and Giordano 2008). Despite this gap in the research literature, we do know that incarcerated girls share similar backgrounds and difficulties in adjusting to custody as boys, although there are some important differences.

For many young offenders, incarceration is the first significant period that they have spent away from their family, friends, and home community. A custodial sentence increases disengagement from family, pro-social peers, and familial/social values at a critical stage of the young offender's development. In addition, custody removes youths from local schools and therefore may affect young people who already have little commitment to their school. This may place them at risk for reoffending, delinquency, and other problem behaviours (Wasserman et al. 2003).

As a result of having been deprived of their families and social networks, younger inmates are less able to cope with the stress of imprisonment and experience much higher levels of anxiety than adult offenders. Custody ranks high among traumatic lifetime stressors for young people, right behind parental death or divorce (Frydenberg 1997). The fact that young people have generally been found to be involved in more disciplinary infractions, inmate–staff assaults, and conflicts with others than adult prisoners reflects their response to stress and difficulty coping. A youth's violence in prison is a young person's impulsive reaction to stress and may be a sign of immature coping ability (MacKenzie 1987). This may manifest in striking out at others, or in turning those difficulties inward. Unlike older prisoners—whose suicide risk is often related to psychiatric illnesses—young prisoners' suicide vulnerability can also be connected to their ability to cope with the custody environment itself (Liebling 1999). There is evidence that some coping mechanisms may be gendered. Studies have concluded that girls self-harm as a means to cope with their adjustment difficulties while incarcerated (Chesney-Lind, Morash, Stevens 2008). Incarceration exposes vulnerable individuals (in this case, youths) to additional risk because of the coping mechanisms that are required to adjust to the prison environment.

Young people differ in important ways from older adults that render them even more vulnerable while in custody. Adolescence itself challenges a young person's physical, intellectual, emotional, and social development. These challenges become more difficult with the prospect of a custodial sentence. For example, establishing a stable, integrated identity is a central task of adolescent development. It is not hard to imagine the negative impact of an onerous and highly restrictive institutional environment on the development of personal identity.

In addition, peers play a much more important role in the life of an adolescent. Given the importance of peer relationships to adolescent development, it is not surprising that the friendships a young person makes while in custody are strong predictors of later adjustment. However, relationships among adolescent peers in custody tend to be volatile. Research suggests that the friendships made by delinquents involve more arguments, more aggressive and impulsive behaviours, and greater conflict and instability than other adolescent friendships (Markus 1996). In addition, studies of delinquents' friendships suggest that delinquents are more likely to ridicule, gang up on, or reject their friends (Claes and Simard 1992).

The criminological literature on youth in custody focuses on *bullying*— the victimization of inmates by their peers (Connell and Farrington 1996). Bullying is a common activity in young offender detention centres. Between 20 and 45 percent of prisoners in young offender institutions report they have been victimized during the course of their sentence (O'Donnell and Edgar 1999). In addition, youth in custody have difficulty dealing with negative and abusive peer relationships. Of course, peer victimization can also occur in schools and local neighbourhoods, but peer abuse within custody centres differs significantly from peer abuse in other settings because it is much more difficult for youth in custody to escape their tormentors.

Most research into peer-on-peer conflict among incarcerated adolescents has involved boys. Few studies have examined how girls may handle disputes or peer-on-peer conflict in custody. When describing how boys and girls relate to their peers, particularly in the event of disagreements, it is easy to fall into gender stereotypes of male and female behaviour (Chesney-Lind et al. 2007). Typically, overt and physical forms of behaviour commonly described as violent are associated with boys, while covert behaviours that relate to a number of passive or indirect behaviours—*relational aggression* (such as spreading rumours, isolating, or ignoring someone)—are often associated with girls (Chesney-Lind, Morash, and Irwin 2007). The idea of relational aggression has been easily embraced by many because it reaffirms the stereotypical notion of the sneaky, backstabbing girl—even though there is research to suggest that boys engage in relational aggression to the same extent or even more than girls do (ibid.).

However, there is evidence to suggest that traditional notions of gender influence daily life in custody. A recent study of incarcerated boys and girls in Ontario found that boys were much more likely than girls to report that they feel it is more important to be tough while in secure detention than it is on the outside (Cesaroni and Pelvin 2013). Indeed, boys expressed ideas about masculinity that stress the importance of sticking up for themselves and not being weak, a target, or taken advantage of. Girls, on the other hand, reported that although taking care of yourself is important, acting tough is not a good strategy to use while incarcerated.

In this same study, peer-on-peer conflict was reported in ways that challenge stereotypical notions of gender. When considering overt and aggressive behaviours, girls were much more likely than boys to say that they never settle disputes through slapping, fighting, and pushing. However, almost half the girls (44 percent) said this does happens sometimes. Turning to relational aggression, girls were more likely than boys to say that they "settle beefs" by isolating someone either often or all the time (42 percent), but, interestingly, a similar percentage of boys reported the same behaviours (38 percent) following a disagreement. A similar pattern emerges when girls and boys were asked about spreading rumours (gossiping) or making fun of someone's appearance—a substantial number of girls reported engaging in this behaviour, but so do a non-trivial amount of boys.

An additional aspect of the study was an attempt to understand the social hierarchies that may exist in a youth facility. Research into the social dynamics of both incarcerated adult males and male youth has often described a hierarchy that tends to form with a "top dog," soldiers, and victims. Little research has been done on how hierarchies work in a girls' unit. The study found that in boys' units, respondents knew exactly who were "top dogs" and could describe the characteristics of the hierarchy on their unit. Boys in the study noted that status was often related to charges, reputation on the street, what neighbourhood they were from, and whether the person would stand up for themselves when threatened. When this question was posed to the girls, they were often perplexed, did not understand, or would suggest that "there is no such thing here." Instead, girls explained it was important to get along, smile, and have a sense of humour rather than be adversarial. This mirrors findings from studies on adult women in prison. For example, research by Kruttschnitt and Gartner (2003) reveals that women describe inmate relations in ways that are distinct from studies of male populations; in particular, they found that women do not relate to an inmate hierarchy. The study also supports research by Smith and Smith (2005), which suggests that secure detention or custody may sometimes provide a sense of community for female young offenders for the first time.

These findings support several conclusions: First, that girls' perceptions on how to serve time differs from that of boys—that being conciliatory and getting along has more value than conflict and toughness, and that a hierarchal structure among prisoners does not appear to be present in girls' units. Indeed, many girls suggested that if there was a "top girl" she would be the one that helped the weaker girls out. As one girl commented, "You just have to defend everyone, you have to be like a mom." The fact that girls and boys draw on notions of motherhood and toughness underscores the importance of gender-appropriate ways of "being" while incarcerated—ways that often reinforce stereotypes of masculinity and femininity. The problem with these stereotypes is that they do not always allow for reactions of anger and resistance for girls or, for the boys, emotional expressions of sadness, loss, fear, and pain.

What needs to be considered is that both girls' and boys' reactions to custody seem to be patterned by individual characteristics and pre-prison experiences, in particular in terms of culture and histories of abuse (and this is similar to findings of adult female responses to imprisonment). Though girls and boys appear to follow gendered scripts regarding perceived appropriate behaviour, further research would need to be done to understand if they ascribe the same meaning, significance, or function to these notions as those of incarcerated adult men and women.

To summarize, a custodial sentence represents a difficult challenge for any young person. The loss of freedom that custody entails and the resultant consequences that are an inevitable part of "doing time"—such as missing family and friends—may be felt more acutely by youth than by adult inmates. Experiencing custody is particularly difficult for youth who are already vulnerable. How young women and men deal with bullying and how they "do time," however, appears to differ.

THE BACKGROUND OF INCARCERATED YOUNG WOMEN

Although there has not been a focus on how girls adjust to custody, several studies have identified the fact that girls share many of the same pre-existing vulnerabilities as boys, such as poverty, dysfunctional families, problems with school, delinquent peers, and substance abuse problems.

Compared to other adolescents, youth in custody are generally vulnerable because of high levels of psychiatric problems. Among incarcerated youth, there is a high prevalence of psychiatric disorders (Ulzen and Hamilton 1998; Gretton and Clift 2011). These disorders include unipolar and bipolar depression, alcohol dependence, attention deficit hyperactivity disorder, conduct disorder, post-traumatic stress disorder, and separation anxiety disorder (Ulzen and Hamilton 1998). Several studies have estimated the prevalence of psychiatric diagnoses among young offenders in the youth justice system, but the results so far are highly variable (Kazdin 2000). However, even the most conservative results suggest that the prevalence of mental disorder is much higher among young offenders than in community samples (Ulzen and Hamilton 1998; Gretton and Clift 2011). In addition, research has demonstrated that up to 75 percent of incarcerated young offenders may have a learning disability (Henteleff 1999). Turning to differences between boys and girls, a substantial body of research suggests that regardless of race or age, female young offenders have higher rates of mental health problems—whether it be depression, anxiety, withdrawal, substance abuse (internalizing behaviours), or aggression and acting out (externalizing behaviours)—than males.

Young offenders often grow up in unstable and dysfunctional families. As a result of their family histories, young offenders are also likely to have been involved with the child welfare system prior to custody (Doob, Marinos, and Varma 1995). Yet there are many forms of family adversity that are associated with youth incarceration, including physical abuse, family breakup, and violence between parents (Goldson 2005).

However, there are clear differences between incarcerated boys and girls in terms of childhood instability and familial dysfunction. For example, a recent Ontario study of incarcerated boys and girls (Cesaroni and Pelvin 2013) found that nearly twice the proportion of girls (58 percent) were physically or sexually abused compared to boys (32 percent). The higher prevalence of both physical and sexual abuse histories for girls is in keeping with the literature on female young offenders. Girls' lives were characterized by instability, as they were more likely to have had contact with the child welfare system and demonstrate higher levels of family dysfunction than boys. Half of the sample of girls had moved four or more times in the past three years compared to only 12 percent of boys. Eighty percent of girls had child welfare involvement (compared to 48 percent of boys). Of these 80 percent of girls, 66 percent had been removed from their family homes and 54 percent had lived in a group home at some point. In contrast, only 18 percent of boys involved with child welfare had been removed from their family homes and 18 percent had lived in a group home. Dysfunction in the family home also included situations in which parents had substance abuse issues, parents had spent time in prison, and participants had suffered neglect, lived in inadequate housing, and witnessed violence in the home. On each of these measures, girls reported higher levels of vulnerability.

The results from this study are in keeping with previous research that suggests that there may be "gender specific domains" of risk/vulnerability for offending and pathways to custody or detention (Belknap and Holsinger 2006). For example, evidence suggests that family risk, physical punishment, and poor family support are more strongly associated with girls' involvement in serious delinquent activity than boys (Corrado, Odgers, and Cohen 2000). Although aspects of the family environment influence both male and female antisocial behaviour, the specific mechanisms affecting behaviour are sometimes gender-specific (Cauffman 2008). For example, among children of substance-abusing parents, parenting disruptions are linked more strongly with delinquency and drug abuse among girls than boys (Cauffman 2008).

According to Chesney-Lind et al. (2008) girls in the juvenile justice system report that their relationship with parents—not substance abuse, school problems, or boyfriends—was the primary influence in their law breaking. Girls in the juvenile justice system often lack permanent and supportive families (Corrado et al. 2000). Instability in family situations often involves moving back and forth between different relatives and child welfare and youth justice system "placements" during childhood and early teen years (Chesney-Lind et al. 2008; Corrado et al. 2000). Placements and other moves are often precipitated by young teenage girls running away from parental conflict, including chronic verbal disagreements, fighting, and violent confrontations (Chesney-Lind et al. 2008). Therefore, not surprisingly, lack of supervision, conflict over supervision, and poor emotional ties are more likely to predict antisocial behavior and delinquency in girls than boys (Cauffman 2008).

Young males in custody also experience instability and dysfunction, but in ways that highlight the influence of neighbourhood factors. For example, in the study of incarcerated boys and girls that was previously noted, boys are more likely than girls to report over-surveillance by police. In fact, well over half (57 percent) of boys reported being stopped by police "more than I can count," compared to just 18 percent of girls. Additionally, boys are likely to report that they have witnessed multiple acts of violence in their neighbourhood (54 percent; this was often tied to gang activity) compared to girls (34 percent). This finding is in keeping with previous research that suggests male young offenders are more likely to report higher exposure to community violence (Wood et. al. 2002). Therefore, both boys and girls in detention have been impacted by various forms of loss, stress, and trauma, though this seemingly occurs in different ways and settings.

OFFICIAL REPORTS AND INQUIRIES IN CANADA

Canadian research suggests that custodial sentences create unique risks for young offenders. A great deal of research on Canadian youth in custody has been done in the context of official reports or inquiries into the conditions of confinement in youth custody facilities (see Doob 1999; Law Commission of Canada 2000; Office of Child and Family Service Advocacy 2003). Many of these inquiries were responses to specific incidents in custodial facilities, including allegations of excessive use of force by staff and, in one extreme case, the death of a young person at the hands of another youth. These reports are useful because they include qualitative data that describe the youths' experiences in their own words. For example, youths who were interviewed about their first experiences in institutional facilities often spoke of "overwhelming sadness, fear of the unknown, anger, and a lack of information about what was happening to them" (Office of Child and Family Service Advocacy 1998, 8). In the words of another young person, "I cried at night, felt kind of lost" (ibid., 9). Government reports and inquiries are also useful because they describe treatment by staff, and living conditions that many youths may find stressful. They illustrate how the challenges of custody experienced by youth differ from those of adult inmates, particularly in regard to young offenders' relationships with and treatment by adult staff.

Besides concerns about basic needs and necessities (e.g., physical environment, food), concerns regarding institutional risks have also been raised. These risks relate to peer-on-peer violence, physical restraint, and placement in isolation. Peer abuse and inmate-on-inmate violence seem to be frequent features of custodial life for incarcerated youth.

Reports on conditions in Canadian institutions confirm the high frequency of peer-on-peer victimization in youth facilities. These findings are consistent with research from other Western countries. Peer-on-peer violence can occur in the context of intimidation, extortion, stealing, destruction of personal possessions, and/or verbal abuse. Youth in custody confirm the presence of several types of peer violence, including degrading activities involving bodily fluids. Descriptions of peer-on-peer violence in youth facilities are distressing, as are the descriptions of staff involvement in that violence. One researcher concluded, "From the perspective of those youth who found themselves in [these] secure facilities in Ontario, there not only is a fair amount of violence, but there is also a fair amount of staff involvement in creating or allowing this violence to occur" (Doob 1999, 30). According to youths questioned in one survey, staff involvement in violence included putting inmates at risk by "letting bad things happen" (reported by 46 percent of the sample), putting an inmate's safety in jeopardy (47 percent), and bribing inmates to "discipline" other inmates (31 percent).

As noted previously, abuse in youth detention centres is not necessarily restricted to peer abuse. Inappropriate treatment of young inmates by custodial staff is a disturbingly common aspect of institutional life. Certainly, the use of extraordinary control measures with youth in custody is necessary at times to protect staff, restrict the movement of youths, stop a youth from acting in a dangerous or aggressive manner, or confirm suspicions about contraband. Intrusive procedures may include manual restraint, mechanical restraint, isolation, and personal searches. At a minimum, youths see these incidents as "scary," "unsafe," and "unfairly applied." It is also important to note that youths frequently report injuries; incidents have been documented of youths being kicked, dragged, smashed against the floor or a table, choked, punched, or hit with batons or brooms while immobilized.

We know very little about if and how treatment by staff differs for male and female youth. However, the recent death of Ashley Smith and the subsequent coroner's inquest bring into focus serious concerns regarding the treatment of young women with mental health issues by correctional staff, including overuse of force and the use of secure isolation.

The Ashley Smith Case

Ashley Smith died on October 19, 2007, by self-strangulation with a ligature while correctional officers looked on. The officers had been told not to intervene unless she stopped breathing. Her behaviour had been labelled attention seeking and was, therefore, to be ignored. It was revealed at the inquest that in the days leading up to her death, Ashley had told staff, "It's your job to save me." The jury for the coroner's inquest into the death of 19-year-old Ashley Smith arrived at a verdict of homicide; the verdict did not imply criminal or civil responsibility, but characterized Smith's death as preventable. For almost a year, the jury had heard evidence from a number of experts that suggested that Smith's death had been the result of a number of critical failures within the Correctional Service of Canada.

Most of what the jury considered during the Smith inquest was related to the delivery of mental health services in custodial settings in complex cases. The inquest reviewed Ashley's history only while she was incarcerated in the adult system because that is where her death took place. However, Ashley was incarcerated at 15 years old, and would spent the first three years in custody in the youth justice system before being transferred to the adult system and adult prison. Ashley was initially sent to the New Brunswick Youth Centre for minor incidents including throwing crabapples at a letter carrier. She would spend almost all her time in both systems in secure isolation, which meant negligible contact with other prisoners. She would eventually accumulate so many institutional charges in the youth system (for fighting with staff and destruction of facility property—though some testified that staff contact was minor scuffles, biting, and spitting, which occurred when they would attempt to restrain her) that she would be transferred to the adult system upon her 18th birthday. Ashley objected to this transfer. She stated, "Although my record looks bad. I would never intentionally hurt anyone. I am really scared about the thought of going to an adult facility with dangerous people" (Ombudsman and Child and Youth Advocate, New Brunswick 2008, 26). A number of experts that testified at the inquest believed that Ashley's prolonged periods of isolation meant that she had little human contact, no reading material, and a security gown for clothing for most of her incarceration. It was argued that her time in segregation in both the youth and adult systems exacerbated pre-existing mental health issues.

THE IMPACT OF CUSTODY ON YOUNG OFFENDERS

Custody remains the most punitive means of holding young people accountable for their offences. Although many Canadians believe in holding youth accountable for their actions through imprisonment, it is not clear that the public would want youth to leave a correctional facility in worse condition than when they entered. In fact, many Canadians believe that assisting in the rehabilitation of a young offender is extremely important (Doob et al. 1998). Moreover, they would generally not want youth to suffer any long-term harm as a result of their time in custody. But as Steinberg, Chung, and Little (2004) argue, a rehabilitative perspective on young offenders provides challenges to both practitioners and policymakers because many custodial systems expose young offenders to harmful experiences (e.g., violence or trauma) that create more problems for youth than they had when they entered (ibid.).

Furthermore, the peer- or staff-induced harm that youth experience in custody has implications for institutional adjustment and for the likelihood of reoffending. Wasserman and colleagues (2003, 314) argue that maladjustment to confinement may make rehabilitation much more difficult: "An untreated mental disorder or emotional impairment resulting from a negative reaction to confinement might result in poorer adjustment during confinement that would negatively affect both discipline and a youth's capacity to take advantage of available programs."

What are the key predictors of adjustment to custody? Previously, authorities responsible for young inmates tended to attribute maladjustment to the "weakness" of individual youths (Goldson 2005). Contemporary approaches generally conclude that the characteristics of the individual *and* of the setting are important determinants of behaviour. Studies of youth in custody in Ontario demonstrate that those young people who entered an institution with a higher number of vulnerabilities (e.g., child welfare involvement, problems in school, delinquent peers, instability in the home) were more likely to experience subsequent difficulties with adjustment and psychological well-being (Cesaroni and Peterson-Badali 2005, 2009, 2010).

Risk factors associated with institutional life appear to have an impact on adjustment. Prison stresses (e.g., missing freedom as well as family and friends) are aspects of adjustment to custody that the institution cannot necessarily control. As most front-line staff are likely aware, many youths get used to the common difficulties associated with entry to custody (Cesaroni and Peterson-Badali 2010).

Recent comparative research reveals that there appear to be differences between incarcerated boys and girls in terms of both pre-existing and institutional vulnerabilities. While both groups have members who report a high level of pre-existing vulnerabilities and difficulties with adjustment, girls are more likely to have *higher* levels of pre-existing vulnerabilities and *higher* levels of difficulties with adjustment (Cesaroni and Pelvin 2013). Boys, however, appear to have more of a challenge when it comes to the institutional environment than girls. For example, when boys were asked about safety and fear, 43 percent worried "a little" or "a great deal" that they would be attacked while incarcerated compared to 20 percent of girls. Further, the majority of boys felt that the chance of being attacked in the institution was either "medium" (49 percent) or "high" (32 percent) compared to half of girls (50 percent) who said it was low. Additionally, 54 percent of boys either "agreed" or "strongly agreed" that they always had to watch their back. In contrast, 74 percent of girls "disagreed" or "strongly disagreed" that they always had to watch their backs. Interestingly, many of the girls remarked that they felt it was less safe for boys in the institution than girls—largely because of the perception that peer-on-peer violence or bullying among boys was inevitable.

There are two important predictors of prison adjustment over which staff have some control. First, staff can control the level of fear a youth experiences in an institution as a result of bullying or the possibility of being bullied. The consequences for the victims include not only physical injury but also psychological distress, which manifests itself in insomnia, escape attempts, and—in extreme cases—suicide (Leschied, Cunningham, and Mazaheri 1997). A study by McCorkle (1993) suggests that youths' level of fear is an extremely important predictor of their general well-being: high levels of fear in prison often undermine the correctional system's efforts to treat, educate, and train offenders. He argues that personal security is an essential requirement in any program designed to effect changes in prosocial attitudes or behaviours.

Second, staff internal support can affect a youth's adjustment. Having friends in an institution is important to a youth inmate for a number of reasons, not the least of which is knowing that there are friends in the institution who will "watch your back" (Maitland and Sluder 1996; Office of the Child and Family Advocacy of Ontario 2003). One government inquiry concluded that young prisoners who are friendless within an institution are at serious risk of victimization (ibid.). One youth from that same inquiry suggested, "Alliances and friendships make you safe. Having no friends makes you unsafe" (ibid., 35).

Although some of the violence experienced by youth in custodial institutions is staff-related, dedicated staff can play an important role in the adjustment process by providing internal support to youth in custody. Perhaps the most vital role that staff play is that of creating a climate in custody that fosters positive social interactions, a sense of stability, and a secure environment.

LONG-TERM CONSEQUENCES OF YOUTH CUSTODY

Although few studies have explored the long-term psychological consequences of the custodial experience on the life of a young person, some evidence points to long-term developmental effects. Sampson and Laub's (1997) reanalysis of the natural histories of 500 delinquents found that imprisonment had significant negative effects on job stability at ages 25 to 32. According to this study, "the structural disadvantages accorded institutionalized adolescents are so great (e.g., through dropping out of high school, record of confinement known to employers) that the influence lingers throughout adult development" (149). Incarceration appears to cut off opportunities for employment later in life, and this in turn may increase the likelihood that the young person will turn to crime. However, we do not know how these long-term impacts may differ between boys and girls.

CONCLUSION

In light of the short-term (and long-term) implications of custody on a young person's future, custody should be imposed only with great restraint. The slogan "Do the crime, do the time" is often used to argue that youth should receive the same sentences as adults convicted of the same criminal behaviour (see Roberts 2004). However, because of the impact of custodial sentences on youth, custody is in fact *more* punishing than it is for adults. This conclusion provides additional justification for treating youth differently from adults. The unique impact of custody on youth was undoubtedly the spirit behind the establishment of the first youth custody facilities in Canada and, indeed, the criteria for custody contained in the current youth justice law.

Canada has taken an important step with the YCJA in reducing the use of custody for youth in conflict with the law (see Chapter 21). However, ensuring the reduction of the use of custody may not be sufficient for the YCJA to completely fulfill its mandate. Some youths will continue to be admitted to custody. Directing how youth will do their time, not just how many youths will be incarcerated, is clearly critical to the success of the youth justice regime in Canada. Although research has clearly demonstrated the unique and gendered pathways to custody for boys and girls, our understanding of the differences in how boys and girls do their time is still developing.

Further Readings

Chesney-Lind, M., and N. Jones, eds. 2010. *Fighting for Girls*. Albany, NY: State University of New York Press.

Chesney-Lind. M., and R.G. Sheldon. 2013. *Girls, Delinquency and Juvenile Justice*. West Sussex, UK: John Wiley and Sons.

Sprott, J.B., and A.N. Doob. 2009. *Justice for Girls?* Chicago: University of Chicago Press.

References

Belknap, J., and K. Holsinger. 2006. "The Gendered Nature of Risk Factors for Delinquency." *Feminist Criminology* 1: 48–71.

Cauffman, E. 2008. "Understanding the Female Offender."*The Future of Children* 18: 119–42.

Cernkovich, S.A., N. Lanctot, and P.C. Giordano. 2008. "Predicting Adolescent and Adult Antisocial Behavior among Adjudicated Delinquent Females." *Crime and Delinquency* 54, no. 1: 3–33.

Cesaroni, C., and H. Pelvin. 2013. *Adolescent Boys and Girls in Detention: A Comparative Study*. Discussion paper prepared for the Ministry of Children and Youth Services, Research and Outcome Measurement Branch. October.

Cesaroni, C., and M. Peterson-Badali. 2005. "Young Offenders in Custody: Risk and Adjustment." *Criminal Justice and Behavior* 32: 251–77.

——. 2009. "Understanding the Experiences of Incarcerated Male Youth: The Importance of a Developmental Framework." In A. Renshaw and E. Suarez, eds., *Prisons: Populations, Health Conditions and Recidivism*. New York: Nova Science.

——. 2010. "Understanding the Adjustment of Incarcerated Young Offenders: A Canadian Example." *Youth Justice: An International Journal* 10, no. 2: 1–19.

Chesney-Lind, M., M. Morash, and K. Irwin. 2007. "Policing Girlhood: Relational Aggression and Violence Prevention." *Youth Violence and Juvenile Justice* 5, no 3: 328–45.

Chesney-Lind, M., M. Morash, and T. Stevens. 2008. "Girls Trouble, Girls Delinquency, and Gender Responsive Programming." *The Australian and New Zealand Journal of Criminology* 41, no. 1: 162–89.

Claes, M., and R. Simard. 1992. "Friendship Characteristics of Delinquent Adolescents." *International Journal of Adolescence and Youth* 3: 287–301.

Connell, A., and D. Farrington. 1996. "Bullying among Incarcerated Young Offenders: Developing an Interview Schedule and Some Preliminary Results." *Journal of Adolescence* 19: 75–93.

Corrado, R., C. Odgers, and I. Cohen. 2000. "The Incarceration of Female Young Offenders: Protection from Whom?" *Canadian Journal of Criminology* 42, no. 2: 189–207.

Doob, A.N. 1999. *The Experiences of Phase II Male Young Offenders in Secure Facilities in the Province of Ontario*. Toronto: Canadian Foundation for Children, Youth and the Law.

Doob, A.N., V. Marinos, and K.N. Varma. 1995. *Youth Crime and the Youth Justice System in Canada*. Toronto: Centre of Criminology, University of Toronto.

Doob, A.N., J.B. Sprott, V. Marinos, and K.N. Varma. 1998. *An Exploration of Ontario Residents' Views of Crime and the Criminal Justice System*. Toronto: Centre of Criminology, University of Toronto.

Frydenberg, E. 1997. *Adolescent Coping: Theoretical and Research Perspectives*. New York: Routledge.

Goldson, B. 2005. "Child Imprisonment: A Case for Abolition." *Youth Justice* 5, no. 2: 77–90.

Gretton, H.M., and R.J.W. Clift. 2011. "The Mental Health Needs of Incarcerated Youth in British Columbia, Canada." *International Journal of Law and Psychiatry* 34, no. 2: 109–15.

Henteleff, Y. 1999. *The Learning Disabled Child-at-Risk: Why Youth Service Systems Have So Badly Failed Them*. Paper presented at the Working Together for Children: Protection and Prevention Conference, Ottawa.

Juvenile Delinquents Act, R.S.C. 1970, c. J-3.

Kazdin, A. 2000. "Adolescent Development, Mental Disorders, and Decision Making of Delinquent Youths." In T. Grisso and R. Schwartz, eds., *Youth on Trial: A Developmental Perspective on Youth Justice*. Chicago: University of Chicago Press.

Kruttschnitt, C., and R. Gartner. 2003. "Women's Imprisonment." In M. Tonry, ed., *Crime and Justice: Vol. 30. A Review of Research*. Chicago: University of Chicago Press.

Law Commission of Canada. 2000. *Restoring Dignity: Responding to Child Abuse in Canadian Institutions*. Ottawa.

Leschied, A.W., A. Cunningham, and N. Mazaheri. 1997. *Safe and Secure: Eliminating Peer-to-Peer Violence in Ontario's Phase II Secure Detention Centres*. North Bay: Ministry of Solicitor General and Correctional Services.

Liebling, A. 1999. "Prison Suicide and Prison Coping." In M. Tonry and J. Petersilia, eds., *Prisons: Crime and Justice: A Review of Research*. Chicago: University of Chicago Press.

MacKenzie, D. 1987. "Age and Adjustment in Prison: Interactions with Attitudes and Anxiety." *Criminal Justice and Behavior* 14: 427–47.

Maitland, A., and R.D. Sluder. 1996. "Victimization in Prisons: A Study of Factors Related to General Well-Being of Youthful Inmates. *Federal Probation* 60: 24–31.

Markus, Robert F. 1996. "The Friendships of Delinquents." *Adolescence* 31: 145–58.

McCorkle, R.C. 1993. "Living on the Edge: Fear in a Maximum Security Prison." *Journal of Offender Rehabilitation* 20: 73–91.

O'Donnell, I., and K. Edgar. 1999. "Fear in Prison." *Prison Journal* 79: 90–9.

Office of the Child and Family Service Advocacy. 1998. *Voices from Within: Youth in Care in Ontario*. Toronto.

———. 2003. *Review of Toronto Youth Assessment Centre* (TYAC). Toronto.

Ombudsman and Child and Youth Advocate, New Brunswick. (2008). *The Ashley Smith Report*.

Roberts, J.V. 2004. "Public Opinion and the Evolution of Juvenile Justice Policy in Western Nations." In M. Tonry and A. Doob, eds., *Youth Crime and Youth Justice: Comparative and Cross-National Perspectives: Crime and Justice*. Chicago: University of Chicago Press.

Sampson, R.J., and J.H. Laub. 1997. "A Life-Course Theory of Cumulative Disadvantage and the Stability of Delinquency." In T.P. Thornberry, ed., *Developmental Theories of Crime and Delinquency*. New Brunswick: Transaction.

Smith, P., and W.H. Smith. 2005. "Experiencing Community through the Eyes of Female Young Offenders." *Journal of Contemporary Criminal Justice* 21, no 4: 364–85.

Steinberg, L., H.L. Chung, and M. Little. 2004. "Re-entry of Young Offenders from the Justice System: A Developmental Perspective." *Youth Violence and Juvenile Justice* 2: 21–38.

Ulzen, T., and H. Hamilton. 1998. "Psychiatric Disorders in Incarcerated Youth." *Youth Update* 16: 4–5.

Wasserman, G.A., et al. 2003. "Risk and Protective Factors of Child Delinquency." *Child Delinquency Bulletin Series*. April. Washington: Office of Juvenile Justice and Delinquency Prevention, U.S. Department of Justice.

Responding to Intimate Partner Violence

Violence against intimate partners is one of the most important problems facing the criminal justice system. Only in recent years, with enhancements to victimization surveys, have Canadians come to appreciate the full scale of the problem. Prior to improving methods of interviewing random samples of Canadians about their experiences of violence, the true extent of intimate partner violence, particularly violence committed against women, was unknown, since only a small proportion of incidents are ever reported to the police or other services. Devising appropriate responses to intimate partner violence has proved challenging for all sectors of the criminal justice system due to the unique nature of these crimes. In this chapter, two experts in the field of law and criminology review the principal criminal and civil law responses to this grave social problem.

Gillian Blackell
Department of Justice Canada[1]

Holly Johnson
University of Ottawa

Intimate partner violence affects a large number of women each year in Canada and commands the attention and resources of the criminal justice, health, and social service systems. For the purposes of this chapter, *intimate partner relationships* refer to marital or common law spousal as well as dating relationships, including same-sex relationships. In 2009, through a national telephone survey on crime victimization, Statistics Canada estimated that 178,000 women and 155,000 men had been victims of spousal violence in that year alone (referring to marital and common law relationships), and approximately 601,000 women and 585,000 men reported violence by a spouse in the preceding five-year period (Sinha 2013a). This survey defines *spousal violence* as encompassing threats of violence, hitting with fists or objects, or throwing objects that are likely to cause injury, choking, strangling, attempted homicide, and sexual assault. Approximately 416,100 women and 205,000 men were victims of stalking in a one-year period, and women were twice as likely as men to be stalked by intimate partners, including spouses, ex-spouses, and dating partners (20 percent for women and 11 percent for men). In addition, between 2000 and 2011, 690 women and 181 men were murdered by an intimate partner in Canada (Sinha 2013b; Boyce and Cotter 2013). Police recorded a history of family violence in 59 percent of spousal homicides against women and 78 percent of spousal homicides against men (Sinha 2013a).

Although women and men report similar prevalence rates of spousal violence committed against them, the impacts and consequences differ sharply (Sinha 2013a). Women were more than three times as likely as men to report being sexually assaulted, beaten, choked, or threatened with a gun or knife. Women were also more than twice as likely as men to be injured, six times as likely to require medical attention, five times as likely to be hospitalized, and three times as likely to fear for their lives (Johnson 2006). They were also more likely to experience 10 or more assaults and to take time off from paid or unpaid work as a result of the violence. Studies have indicated that not all occurrences of intimate partner violence are the same; they can be differentiated with respect to partner dynamics, context, and consequences, resulting in different experiences for men and women (Johnson 2008). When types of violence, psychological abuse, and consequences are combined, it becomes clear that women experience wider variation in patterns of intimate partner violence; they also experience a constellation of severe and chronic violence, coercive control, and psychological abuse with high levels of fear and injury in ways that men do not (Ansara and Hindin 2010). Even though women and men report similar levels of less severe acts of physical violence that are not embedded in coercive control, the impacts of these incidents are greater for women as well (Ansara and Hindin 2011).

The particular vulnerability of Aboriginal women to violence has now been brought to public attention through various parliamentary committees, international organizations, and advocacy by the Native Women's

Association of Canada regarding murders and disappearances of Aboriginal women (Special Committee on Violence Against Indigenous Women 2014; Amnesty International 2004). These efforts have helped shine a spotlight on the long-standing social and economic inequality that forms the backdrop to all forms of violence against Aboriginal women. The 2009 victimization survey estimates that Aboriginal women were two and one-half times more likely than non-Aboriginal women to be victims of spousal violence (Sinha 2013a). Moreover, Aboriginal women experience more severe violence and more serious consequences: spousal homicide rates are almost eight times higher for Aboriginal women than for non-Aboriginal women (4.6 and 0.6 per 100,000 population, respectively; Johnson 2006). However, this severely underestimates the prevalence of spousal homicides of Aboriginal women as in half of all homicides in Canada police do not record Aboriginal identity of victims.

Public awareness of intimate partner violence dates back to the 1970s. Domestic violence and sexual assaults in intimate relationships were historically viewed as private matters that did not necessarily warrant intervention by the criminal justice system. Over the past four decades, however, a wide range of interventions—including legislation, policies, and services—have been implemented by federal, provincial, and municipal governments as well as by community organizations in Canada to respond to the problem of intimate partner violence. These include shelters and other supports for victims, treatment for abusive partners, interagency collaboration at the community level, prevention and public awareness campaigns, specialized court processes, changes to both the criminal and the civil law, pro-charging policies for police, and pro-prosecution policies for Crown prosecutors (Johnson and Dawson 2011). Without exploring the full range of interventions to address intimate partner violence, this chapter summarizes some of the means by which the criminal and civil laws have been utilized to improve the legal response to intimate partner violence.

CRIMINAL LAW RESPONSES

While the *Criminal Code* does not contain a specific offence called *domestic* or *intimate partner violence*, a wide range of criminal offences cover violence within relationships. These include the offences of assault, sexual assault, attempted murder, homicide (murder, manslaughter), criminal negligence, forcible confinement, uttering threats, and criminal harassment. In 1983 the crimes of rape and indecent assault were replaced by the current three-tiered sexual assault provisions (ss. 271, 272, 273). The same reforms repealed spousal immunity from sexual assault charges, making marital rape a crime. In addition to substantive offences, the *Criminal Code* provides procedural protections, preventive measures, and sentencing principles applicable in spousal violence cases.

ADDRESSING CRIMINAL HARASSMENT

The offence of *criminal harassment*, commonly known as *stalking*, was enacted in 1993 following several heinous incidents of estranged male partners harassing and stalking female victims, eventually leading to their death. Although prior to 1993 police were able to charge stalkers for other offences (such as mischief, uttering threats, or making harassing phone calls), the new offence captured seemingly innocuous acts, such as watching someone's place of residence or leaving unwanted gifts on someone's doorstep. In the context of stalking, such acts can be highly threatening for the victim and often serve as precursors to physical violence. Thus, the criminal harassment offence under Section 264 of the *Criminal Code* enables police to intervene if the behaviour is repetitive or threatening and causes the victim to fear for her safety or that of someone known to her. This offence was modelled on similar offences in the United States (California was the first state to criminalize stalking, in 1990).

The offence is particularly relevant in circumstances of intimate partner abuse, where the risks of violence or the escalation of violence are often heightened during or immediately following separation. For example, according to Statistics Canada's 2004 victimization survey, half the women who were assaulted by a past partner said that the violence occurred after the couple separated; and in one-third of post-separation assaults, the violence began or became more severe after the separation. Moreover, women have a heightened risk of spousal homicide after marital separation; ex-marital partners are responsible for 28 percent of all spousal homicides perpetrated against women but for only 10 percent of homicides perpetrated against men (Johnson 2006).

Additional protections for stalking victims have been introduced since 1993. First, a 1996 amendment to the *Criminal Code* included a lifetime prohibition of firearms after a conviction for criminal harassment. Then, a 1997 amendment made a conviction for criminal harassment while under a restraining order an aggravating factor that should be reflected in sentencing (s. 264(5)); and a homicide committed in conjunction with the commission of an offence of criminal harassment became first-degree murder, regardless of whether the murder was planned and deliberate (s. 231(6)). In addition, in 2002 the maximum penalty for criminal harassment upon indictment was doubled from five to ten years. As a result, offenders convicted of criminal harassment offences can be subjected to the dangerous offender application under Section 759 of the *Criminal Code*. Finally, amendments to the *Code* in 2005 enhanced the provisions facilitating testimony by children and other vulnerable persons, including victims of criminal harassment (see below).

A strong association between stalking and intimate partner violence and homicide has been found (McFarlane et al. 1999). In the 2004 Statistics Canada victimization survey, three-quarters of women who were stalked by an ex-partner had also been physically or sexually assaulted by that partner.

Ex-partner stalkers were also found to be more dangerous and threatening than other categories of stalkers. Higher proportions of ex-partner stalkers intimidated, threatened, grabbed, or attacked their victims. Sixty percent of women stalked by an ex-partner feared their lives were in danger (Johnson 2006).

The growing phenomenon of *cyberstalking*—criminal harassment conducted through the Internet or other electronic means, such as harassing email communications, posting offensive or threatening information about the victim on the Internet, or sabotaging the victim's computer—is also an issue in intimate partner relationships. Some cyberstalkers even incite others to harass the victim by posting personal advertisements or images in the victim's name. In addition to a number of existing criminal offences, such as criminal harassment, the unauthorized use of a computer (s. 342.1), intimidation (s. 423(1)), and extortion (s. 346), a new offence prohibiting the nonconsensual distribution of intimate images is proposed in Bill C-13, *Protecting Canadians from Online Crime Act*, introduced in the House of Commons in November 2013. This will be of particular relevance in the context of intimate partner violence.

BATTERED WOMEN AND SELF-DEFENCE

The statutory law on self-defence was recently amended to replace a series of sections in the *Criminal Code* that were widely criticized as being overly complex and internally inconsistent. The *Citizen's Arrest and Self-Defence Act*, which came into force in March 2013, amended the previous Sections 34 to 37 of the *Criminal Code* with a single provision applicable to self-defence in homicide cases as well as the defensive use of force against other threats of harm to oneself or another person. The new Section 34 provides that a person is not guilty of an offence as long as the following three core elements are demonstrated: (1) a reasonable belief that either they are or another person is being threatened with force; (2) the actions taken are for the purpose of defending against that force; and (3) the actions taken are considered reasonable under the circumstances.

The new provision also includes a non-exhaustive list of factors to help determine whether the accused person's actions were reasonable in the circumstances, including how imminent the threat was and whether there were other ways in which the person might have been able to respond; the size, age, gender, and physical capabilities of the people involved; and the nature, duration, and history of any relationship between the parties to the incident, including any prior use or threat of force and the nature of that force or threat.

The new defence effectively codifies certain considerations emanating from the landmark decision of the Supreme Court of Canada (SCC) in *R. v. Lavallée*, [1990] 1 S.C.R. 854. Prior to the *Lavallée* decision, the previous law of self-defence in Canada was difficult to apply successfully in cases where battered women killed their abusive partners in self-defence. Lyn Lavallée was charged with the murder of her violent common law partner, Kevin Rust, who had regularly subjected her to physical abuse. She shot him in the back of the head as he was leaving the room after he beat her and told her that if she didn't kill him, he would kill her when their guests left. Expert evidence was introduced to demonstrate that Lavallée had been terrorized by Rust and that as a battered woman, her actions were based on a "reasonable" belief that she had no other option but to shoot him. In order to explain the perspective of the accused, the expert referred to the "battered woman syndrome," which is based on the work of Lenore Walker (1979).

Walker identified three phases of the cycle of domestic violence. The first phase, known as the *tension-building phase*, is characterized by a series of minor assaults and verbal abuse. During the second phase, known as the *acute battering phase*, the batterer is unable to control the rage and severely beats the woman. This is followed by the third phase, the *kindness and contrite loving behaviour phase*, during which the batterer behaves kindly toward the woman, asking her forgiveness and promising never to repeat the violence. This final phase provides the woman with positive reinforcement for staying in the relationship. To explain why women remain in violent relationships after the cycle has been repeated more than once, Walker argued that battered women are psychologically paralyzed because they have learned from the repeated beatings that they cannot control their circumstances. This is known as "learned helplessness." Based on the battered woman syndrome, Walker testified that Lavallée's actions constituted the final desperate act of someone who sincerely believed that she would be killed that night. The jury acquitted Lavallée. The decision was appealed to the Supreme Court of Canada, which decided unanimously to acquit her of the charge of murder.

The *Lavallée* ruling was significant for a number of reasons: (1) it made admissible expert evidence related to *battered women's syndrome*, which in turn helped dispel myths about why battered women remain in violent relationships; (2) this evidence affected the *imminency requirement* (the previous statutory requirement that the risk of attack must be imminent); and (3) the court accepted that women's experiences and perspectives in relation to self-defence may be different from those of men and that courts must now make their judgments based on the "objective" standard of the actions of a "reasonable person," rather than on the actions of the traditional legal standard, the "reasonable man" (*R. v. Malott*, [1998] 1 S.C.R 123).

While the *Lavallée* decision was initially lauded by those who work with abused women, some feminist scholars have expressed concern that it might lead to the "syndromization" of women's experiences, as has been the case in the United States (Comack 1993; Noonan 1993; Shaffer 1997; Sheehy 2001). The concerns regarding the battered women's syndrome included the risk that this would portray battered women as dysfunctional, deviant, and even pathological. Likewise, concerns were also expressed regarding the creation of a new stereotype of the "authentic" battered woman, thereby restricting the applicability of the syndrome evidence to women who fought back or did not otherwise fit the passive victim profile.

Another concern relates to the risks associated with pleading self-defence in the hopes of an acquittal, as opposed to pleading guilty to manslaughter and relying upon *Lavallée* in sentencing (Sheehy 2014). In the event that the claim fails, the woman is subject to the mandatory minimum sentence of life imprisonment for murder, whereas there is no mandatory minimum for manslaughter. Despite the concerns, the *Lavallée* ruling has contributed significantly to legislative reform and to raising awareness among the judiciary and other criminal justice personnel of the realities of battered women and is regularly cited in court decisions.

PREVENTIVE MEASURES

A number of provisions in the *Criminal Code* can be used to help prevent intimate partner violence. For instance, Section 810 allows a Justice of the Peace or a judge to issue *recognizances* (or peace bonds) to protect someone from a possible criminal offence. Peace bonds require alleged offenders to adhere to conditions, such as staying away from the victim's residence or place of work, as well as surrendering any firearms they may possess. Although the standard of proof is a civil standard—meaning that only on a balance of probabilities the applicant has reasonable grounds to fear future violence—a breach of conditions is an offence under the *Criminal Code* (s. 811). Bill C-26, the *Tougher Penalties for Child Predators Act,* which was introduced to the House of Commons in October 2013, proposes to increase the maximum penalties for a breach of a peace bond from two to four years on indictment and from six to eighteen months on summary conviction. In light of pro-charging policies in domestic violence cases, peace bonds are generally not used if there are reasonable grounds to arrest the abuser for a criminal offence.

In addition to peace bonds, the *Criminal Code* allows the justice or judge at a bail hearing to make recognizance orders or undertakings with conditions to prevent the accused from communicating with or harassing the victim or witness, in addition to other relevant conditions. In response to concerns regarding violent occurrences during the 24-hour period between arrest and the bail hearing in domestic violence cases, the *Code* was amended in 1999 to permit a Justice of the Peace who remands arrested persons into custody to order the accused not to communicate with any witness or other person between the time he is detained and his first bail hearing. A 1999 amendment also requires police officers and judges to consider a victim's safety in all bail decisions. The *Code* was further amended in 2008 to reverse the onus in bail hearings to the accused to demonstrate why bail should be granted for offences involving a firearm.

Following the mass killings at the École Polytechnique in Montreal on December 6, 1989, public pressure to update gun-control legislation significantly increased. In 1991, screening checks and safety courses for those applying for a Firearms Acquisition Certificate (FAC) were established for these certificates. Then in 1995, the federal government introduced the *Firearms Act*, which established the requirement for a licence for the possession of a firearm, a national registration system for all firearms, and a mandatory minimum sentence of four years of prison and a lifetime prohibition against the possession of restricted or prohibited firearms upon conviction of specific violent offences, including sexual assault with a weapon and aggravated sexual assault. Spouses and common-law partners, including former partners from the previous two years, are notified of FAC applications and given an opportunity to express concerns, which could lead to further investigations by the chief firearms officer. Then in September 2013, the *Ending the Long-Gun Registry Act* came into force. Although concerns have been raised about the potential impact of the repeal of the long-gun registry on domestic violence investigations, the Act did not affect the requirement for spousal notification in FAC applications.

PROTECTIVE PROCEDURAL MEASURES

It is trite to say that the criminal trial process can be gruelling for both the accused and the victim or witness. Concerns about the potential for re-victimization of victims of intimate partner violence have led to the introduction of many protective procedural measures over the past few decades. In order to protect sexual assault complainants from having irrelevant evidence of prior sexual activity admitted at trial, revised *rape shield* legislation was introduced in 1992. These amendments to the *Criminal Code* included a definition of consent for the purposes of the sexual assault provisions. The amendments clearly state that the defence of mistaken belief in consent cannot be used if the belief stemmed from the accused's drunkenness, recklessness, or willful blindness, or if the accused did not take reasonable steps to determine whether the victim was in fact consenting. The statutory requirement in Section 273.1 of the *Criminal Code* that consent to sexual activity must be expressed (i.e., not implied), ongoing, and conscious was the subject of inconsistent court rulings until the recent SCC decision in *R. v. J.A.* [2011] 2 S.C.R. 440 (Sheehy 2012). The facts in *R. v. J.A.* relate to a sexual assault in a domestic relationship context where the victim was unconscious. The majority of the court found that the legislation required ongoing conscious consent throughout the sexual activity and that advance consent to activities performed during a period of unconsciousness is not permissible in law.

The *Criminal Code* also contains a number of provisions to facilitate the testimony of vulnerable victims and witnesses. For example, although there is a presumption that criminal proceedings be held in open court, a court may exclude some or all members of the public from the proceedings, notably in cases involving sexual offences (s. 486). The court can also prohibit the publication or transmission of information that could identify a victim in cases where the victim is under 18 years of age, a victim of sexual assault, and where such a ban is deemed necessary for the proper administration of justice (ss. 486.4 and 486.5). Moreover, victims or witnesses under the age of 18 or those who suffer from mental or physical disabilities may be permitted to give evidence by way of a video recording (ss. 715.1, 715.2).

In addition, a wide range of testimonial aids are available to allow victims to testify, including closed circuit television and screens so that the accused cannot be seen by them (s. 486.2). The victim may also be accompanied by a support person at trial (s. 486.1). While many of these testimonial aids have been available since 1999 for young victims and witnesses of specified violence and sexual offences, in 2005 they were made available for adult victims of spousal abuse and sexual assault. The new Subsection 486.3(4) specifically provides for the presumptive appointment of a lawyer for cross-examination of the victim in criminal harassment cases where the accused is self-represented.

For sentencing in spousal assault cases, the *Criminal Code* provides for victim impact statements and requires that these statements be considered by courts (s. 722). Moreover, in 1995, the sentencing provisions of the *Criminal Code* were amended to provide that where an offender, in committing the offence, abuses his spouse or child or any position of trust or authority, this shall be considered an aggravating factor for sentencing purposes (s. 718.2). Since 2007, conditional sentences (including "house arrest") are no longer available for those convicted of a serious personal injury offence that carries a maximum penalty of 10 years or more, including sexual assault. The availability of conditional sentences were further restricted in 2012. Amendments have also been made to the restitution provisions of the *Code* to entitle a victim to seek restitution for actual and reasonable expenses for moving out of the offender's home to avoid bodily harm (s. 738).

DOMESTIC VIOLENCE POLICIES AND COURTS

A cornerstone of the criminal justice response to intimate partner violence has been the implementation since the 1980s in all provinces and territories of directives or guidelines for police and Crown prosecutors. These are referred to as *pro-charging* or *pro-prosecution* policies. They generally require police to lay charges in cases of domestic violence where there are legal grounds to do so. Some policies require Crown prosecutors to prosecute domestic violence cases regardless of the victim's stated desire to withdraw charges. The original aim of these directives was to send a message to abusers that spousal violence is a crime and to ensure that victims are supported and offenders treated seriously by the criminal justice system.

Then in September 2000 the Federal-Provincial-Territorial (F/P/T) Ministers Responsible for Justice requested a review of these policies, the first comprehensive review since their inception, in order to assess their effectiveness and their application and to strengthen the government response to domestic violence. The resulting 2003 report recommended the retention of pro-charging and pro-prosecution policies in spousal abuse cases, as well as the development and enhancement of supporting programs, services, and structures, including a multi-sector response to spousal violence.

In addition, in order to improve the justice system's response to partner violence, several jurisdictions have instituted domestic violence courts or court processes, which provide a range of specialized services, such as advocacy and support for victims and their children, specially trained Crown prosecutors, translation services, and treatment for abusers. The first specialized family violence court was established in Winnipeg in 1990. Since 1996 the Ontario government has introduced a domestic violence court program in all 54 court sites in the province. Dedicated domestic violence courts or court processes can also be found in the Yukon, Northwest Territories, Saskatchewan, Alberta, and New Brunswick. The Domestic Violence Treatment Option (DVTO) Courts in the Yukon and the Northwest Territories are somewhat different in that they provide a therapeutic court-based alternative to formal criminal court for responding to domestic violence crimes. Evaluations suggest that specialized court processes can result in increased reporting to police, a rise in convictions, swifter court processing, increased use of mandated treatment for abusers, enhanced training for police and prosecutors, and improved support for victims throughout the court process (Hornick, Boyes, Tutty, and White 2008; Tutty, McNichol, and Christensen 2008; Ursel and Hagyard 2008).

However, arrest, conviction, and treatment have not been shown to be effective deterrents for all violent partners. Moreover, feminist scholars have raised important questions regarding the potential for mandatory charging and prosecution policies to disempower victims by removing control of the situation from them once a report is made to police (Snider 1998; Dayton 2002–3). Some have argued that aggressive no-drop policies fail to recognize that women "use the law, purposefully and actively, as a part of a strategic process of challenge and resistance" and that a call to police does not imply an intention or need to hand over autonomy and decision-making authority to the courts (Lewis et al. 2000, 184). In addition, strict interpretation of these policies can have inequitable outcomes for women. For example, pro-charging policies that were originally designed to protect women from violent partners can work against women when a much more violent assault by a male partner is equated with self-defensive assaults by a woman and dual arrests are the result (Osthoff 2002). Many jurisdictions in Canada are attempting to prevent these situations by establishing dominant/primary aggressor policies that train police on how to determine who is the instigator of the violence and therefore which one in the couple should be charged.

The primary need of victims who call the police is to receive protection and to stop the violence from continuing (Johnson 2006). For many reasons, including financial, emotional, cultural, or child-related ones, the victim may be reluctant to have the abuser arrested and incarcerated. But regardless of the victim's wishes, calling the police puts in motion the weight of the entire criminal justice process.

One important development in the prosecution of spousal abuse cases in specialized domestic violence courts is a shift away from the notion that success in a spousal abuse case requires a conviction. Rather than defining success on this single event, prosecutors have begun to place greater emphasis on the process and on providing a service to victims. Victims are encouraged and supported when testifying against an abusive spouse; but the Crown does not proceed with the prosecution without the victim's cooperation, except in cases where there is a serious risk to the victim or the community. Reluctant victims are encouraged to consider testifying at another time (Malaviya 2008).

CIVIL LAW RESPONSES

In addition to criminal sanctions that apply across Canada, several remedies for intimate partner violence are available through the civil law. Civil remedies are provided for either through legislation or through the common law. Although historically tort was not applicable between spouses due to the doctrine of unity during marriage, torts such as assault, battery, trespass, and nuisance could now apply to a claim for damages from intimate partner violence. Tort law has not been applied often to domestic violence cases in Canada due in part to victims' fear of their aggressors (Christopher 2009). In addition to remedies for damages through the common law, many jurisdictions have criminal compensation recovery laws to which victims can turn following the conviction of the offender.

Civil Domestic Violence Legislation

Nine provinces and territories have introduced civil legislation to better protect victims in situations of domestic violence: Saskatchewan (enacted in 1995), Prince Edward Island (1996), Manitoba (1999), Alberta (1999), Yukon (2003), Nova Scotia (2003), Northwest Territories (2005), Newfoundland and Labrador (2006), and Nunavut (2008). These civil statutes are intended to complement the criminal law process, and jurisdictions are encouraged to proceed with criminal charges where applicable. The civil remedies available include emergency protection orders, orders providing temporary exclusive possession of the family home, civil restraining orders, and other provisions necessary for the protection of victims and their children. The primary value of civil domestic violence legislation is the immediacy of protection and the practical intervention it offers through remedies to victims and their children. Although the orders are civil, a violation of an order can result in a criminal charge under Section 127 of the *Criminal Code* in the absence of a specified penalty for a breach in the civil legislation. The *Family Homes on Reserves and Matrimonial Interests or Rights Act*, which will come into force in its entirety in December 2014, establishes provisional rules and procedures for emergency protection orders to be made available on reserves in respect to the temporary exclusive occupation of the family home in cases of family violence.

THE IMPACT OF INTIMATE PARTNER VIOLENCE ON CUSTODY AND ACCESS OF CHILDREN

A considerable body of clinical research has identified the negative impact on children of witnessing spousal abuse (Jaffe, Crooks, and Bala 2006). Currently in six jurisdictions (Newfoundland and Labrador, Northwest Territories, Nunavut, British Columbia, Alberta, and Ontario), family law legislation lists domestic or family violence as a factor in determining the best interests of the child for the purposes of custody and access (called *parenting orders* in Alberta and British Columbia). Yet even in the absence of specific legislative references, the courts generally consider evidence of family violence to be a relevant factor in post-separation or post-divorce custodial and parenting arrangements. Researchers have indicated that child access is often used as a window of opportunity for a partner to continue to intimidate, harass, or continue the violence against a former partner (Jaffe, Lemon, and Poisson 2003). The interplay between the family, including child protection and criminal justice systems responses to family violence, was the subject of a report by an F/P/T Working Group on Family Violence in 2014. The report examined the challenges facing families simultaneously navigating the different systems and identified some promising practices to address these challenges.

Exposing a child to spousal violence may summon child protection authorities to intervene on the grounds of emotional harm or a risk of emotional harm to the child (Wilson 2010). Moreover, child protection legislation in eight jurisdictions explicitly identifies exposure to domestic violence as a factor to be considered when determining whether a child is in need of protection (Alberta, Saskatchewan, Quebec, New Brunswick, Nova Scotia, Prince Edward Island, Newfoundland and Labrador, and the Northwest Territories). Involving the criminal justice system in responding to intimate partner violence can therefore trigger the involvement of the child protection system. Although the legislation often specifies the responsibilities of "parents" to protect children from harm, in practice mothers are often expected to protect their children from the effects of their partners' violence (Strega and Janzen 2013). Threats from child protection services to remove children may discourage women from reporting violent partners thus increasing the risk to them and their children. One innovative program that aims to alleviate these inconsistencies is Collaborative Agreement protocols between child protection services and agencies serving abused women in Ontario (Ministry of Community and Social Services 2011). By documenting the role of each agency in responding to intimate partner violence, the aim is to improve collaboration and hold abusers accountable while keeping women and children safe. A consultation with agencies that had applied the agreements concluded they were most effective in supporting cross-sectorial collaboration and communication, somewhat effective in developing procedures for keeping women safe, and least effective in holding abusers accountable.

CONCLUSION

An effective response to intimate partner violence requires multiple interventions from health, social, community, and justice service providers. Intimate partner violence continues to be a persistent and pervasive problem in Canada, and the responses of the criminal and civil law continue to evolve as they adapt to the growing body of social science research and case law on this important social problem.

Further Readings

Johnson, H., and M. Dawson. 2010. *Violence Against Women in Canada: Research and Policy Perspectives*. Toronto: Oxford University Press.

Sheehy, E. 2014. *Defending Battered Women on Trial*. Vancouver: UBC Press.

References

Ad Hoc Federal-Provincial-Territorial Working Group Reviewing Spousal Abuse Policies and Legislation. 2003. *Final Report*. Ottawa: Department of Justice Canada.

Amnesty International 2004. *Stolen Sisters: A Human Rights Response to Discrimination and Violence Against Indigenous Women in Canada*. London: Amnesty International Publications.

Ansara, D. and Hindin, M. 2010. "Exploring Gender Differences in the Patterns of Intimate Partner Violence in Canada: A Latent Class Approach." *Journal of Epidemiology and Community Health* 64: 849–54.

——— . 2011. "Psychosocial Consequences of Intimate Partner Violence for Women and Men in Canada." *Journal of Interpersonal Violence* 26, no. 8,1628–45.

Boyce, J., and A. Cotter. 2013. "Homicide in Canada, 2012." *Juristat*. Cat. no. 85-002-X. Ottawa: Statistics Canada.

Christopher, C. 2009. *Law of Domestic Conflict in Canada*. Toronto: Carswell.

Comack, E. 1993. "Feminist Engagement with the Law: The Legal Recognition of Battered Woman Syndrome." *The CRIAW Papers*. Ottawa: Canadian Research Institute for the Advancement of Women.

Dayton, J. 2002–3. "The Silencing of a Woman's Choice: Mandatory Arrest and No Drop Prosecution Policies in Domestic Violence Cases." *Cardozo Women's Law Journal* 9: 281–97.

Feder, L., and L. Dugan. 2002. "A Test of the Efficacy of Court-Mandated Counseling for Domestic Violence Offenders: The Broward Experiment." *Justice Quarterly* 19: 343–75.

Federal-Provincial-Territorial Ad Hoc Working Group on Family Violence. 2014. *Making the Links in Family Violence Cases: Collaboration among the Family, Child Protection and Criminal Justice Systems.* Ottawa: Department of Justice Canada.

Hornick, J., M. Boyes, L. Tutty, and L. White. 2008. "The Yukon's Domestic Violence Treatment Option: An Evaluation." In J. Ursel, L.M. Tutty, and J. Lemaistre, eds., *What's Law Got to Do with It? The Law, Specialized Courts, and Domestic Violence in Canada*, 172–93. Toronto: Cormorant.

Jaffe, P., C. Crooks, and N. Bala. 2006. Making Appropriate Parenting Arrangements in Family Violence Cases: Applying the Literature to Identify Promising Practices. *Research Report, 2005-FCY-3E.* Ottawa: Department of Justice.

Jaffe, P., N. Lemon, and S. Poisson. 2003. *Child Custody and Domestic Violence.* Thousand Oaks: Sage Publications.

Johnson, H. 2006. *Measuring Violence Against Women: Statistical Trends.* Cat. no. 85-570-XIE. Ottawa: Statistics Canada.

Johnson, H., and M. Dawson. 2011. *Violence against Women in Canada: Research and Policy Perspectives.* Toronto: Oxford University Press.

Johnson, M.P. 2008. *A Typology of Domestic Violence: Intimate Terrorism, Violent Resistance, and Situational Couple Violence.* Lebanon, NH: Northeastern University Press.

Lewis, R., R.P. Dobash, R.E. Dobash, and K. Cavanagh. 2000. "Protection, Prevention, Rehabilitation or Justice? Women's Use of the Law to Challenge Domestic Violence." *International Review of Victimology* 7: 179–205.

Malaviya, R. 2008. "From Shelter Worker to Crown Attorney: One Woman's Journey." In J. Ursel, L.M. Tutty, and J. Lemaistre, eds., *What's Law Got to Do with It? The Law, Specialized Courts, and Domestic Violence in Canada,* 46–68. Toronto: Cormorant.

McFarlane, J., J. Campbell, S. Wilt, C. Sachs, Y. Ulrick, and X. Xu. 1999. "Stalking and Intimate Partner Femicide." *Homicide Studies* 3: 300–16.

Ministry of Community and Social Services. 2011. *CAS/VAW Collaboration Agreements Stakeholder Consultations: Summary Report.* Retrieved March 7, 2014, from http://www.oaith.ca/assets/files/Publications/Government%20Documents/VAWCAS-consultation-report-FINAL-%20Feb-2011.pdf

Noonan, S. 1993. "Strategies of Survival: Moving beyond the Battered Woman Syndrome." In E. Adelberg and C. Currie, eds., In *Conflict with the Law: Women and the Canadian Justice System.* Vancouver: Press Gang.

Osthoff, S. 2002. "But, Gertrude, I Beg to Differ, a Hit is not a Hit is not a Hit." *Violence Against Women* 8, no.12, 1521–44.

Pottie Bunge, V. 2002. "National Trends in Partner Homicides, 1974–2000." *Juristat* 22, no. 5, Cat. no. 85-002-XIE. Ottawa: Statistics Canada.

Shaffer, M. 1997. "The Battered Woman Syndrome Revisited: Some Complicating Thoughts Five Years After *R. v. Lavallée.*" *University of Toronto Law Journal* 47: 1–33.

Sheehy, E. 2001. "Battered Women and Mandatory Minimum Sentences." *Osgoode Hall Law Journal* 39: 529–55.

——. 2012. "Judges and the Reasonable Steps Requirement: The Judicial Stance on Perpetration against Unconscious Women." In E. Sheehy, ed., *Sexual Assault in Canada: Law, Legal Practice and Women's Activism*, 483–540. Ottawa: University of Ottawa Press.

——. 2014. *Defending Battered Women on Trial: Lessons from the Transcripts.* Vancouver: U.B.C. Press.

Sinha, M. 2013a. "Measuring Violence Against Women: Statistical Trends" *Juristat.* Cat. no. 85-002-X. Ottawa: Statistics Canada.

——. 2013b. "Family Violence in Canada: A Statistical Profile, 2011." *Juristat.* Cat. no. 85-002-X. Ottawa: Statistics Canada.

Snider, L. 1998. "Struggles for Social Justice: Criminalization and Alternatives." In K. Bonnycastle and G. Rigakos, eds., *Unsettling Truths: Battered Women, Policy, Politics, and Contemporary Research in Canada*, 145–55. Vancouver: Collective Press.

Special Committee on Violence Against Indigenous Women. 2014. *Invisible Women: A Call to Action: A Report on Missing and Murdered Indigenous Women in Canada.* 41st Parliament, 2nd session.

Strega, S., and C. Janzen. 2013. "Asking the Impossible of Mothers: Child Protection Systems and Intimate Partner Violence." In S. Strega, J. Krane, S. Lapierre, C. Richardson, and R. Carlton, eds., *Failure to Protect: Moving Beyond Gendered Responses*, 49–76. Halifax: Fernwood Publishing.

Tutty, L., K. McNichol, and J. Christensen. 2008. "Calgary's HomeFront Specialized Domestic Violence Court." In J. Ursel, L.M. Tutty, and J. Lemaistre, eds., *What's Law Got to Do with It? The Law, Specialized Courts, and Domestic Violence in Canada*, 152–71. Toronto: Cormorant.

Ursel, J., and C. Hagyard. 2008. "The Winnipeg Family Violence Court." In J. Ursel, L.M. Tutty, and J. Lemaistre, eds., *What's Law Got to Do with It? The Law, Specialized Courts, and Domestic Violence in Canada*, 95–119. Toronto: Cormorant.

Walker, L. 1979. *The Battered Woman*. New York: Harper Perennial.

Wilson, J. 2010. *Wilson on Children and the Law*. Markham: Butterworths.

Cases

R. v. J. A., [2011] 2 S.C.R. 440.

R. v. Lavallée, [1990] 1 S.C.R. 854.

R. v. Malott, [1998] 1 S.C.R 123.

Endnote

1. The views expressed in this chapter represent those of the authors and do not reflect the views of Justice Canada.

Crime Victims and the Justice System[1]

For many years, crime victims were overlooked by the criminal justice system. More recently they have come to play an increasingly important role in the criminal process. This is true in Canada as well as in other common law jurisdictions, such as England, Wales, and New Zealand, and at the level of international criminal justice. Federal, provincial, and territorial governments in Canada have introduced legislation and improved services to provide victims with more "voice" in the criminal justice system.

In this chapter, Michelle Grossman and Susan McDonald, both of whom have worked in the area of victims policy and practice for many years, explore ways in which the Canadian criminal justice system has created a role for victims.

Susan McDonald
Research and Statistics Division, Department of Justice Canada

Michelle G. Grossman
University of Oxford

In recent years, federal, provincial, and territorial levels of government in Canada have made significant efforts to improve the experiences of crime victims in the criminal justice system. Despite several advances, many issues related to victims' needs and expectations in the criminal justice system require additional attention. This chapter explores several key issues relating to crime victims and the criminal justice system in Canada by examining relevant Canadian legislation as well as findings from empirical research.[2]

While this chapter does not address the impact of victimization, it is important to recognize that people react differently to crimes committed against them (for more information on impacts, see AuCoin and Beauchamp 2007; Wathen 2013; on economic impact, see Zhang et al. 2013). For example, some victims may be fearful or traumatized following the theft of a car; others will only feel annoyed and inconvenienced and will seek information from the police and others. More serious and personal violence offences have far greater impacts on victims, and longer term consequences for them. Victims are thrown into an unfamiliar justice system where they do not have a clearly articulated or understood role. For a judge or Crown attorney, a victim may be simply one more "case" or one more "witness"; but for the victim, this case will likely have affected his or her life in a myriad of ways.

When asked to identify the "players" in the criminal justice system, people often identify the police, the Crown attorney or prosecutor, the defence counsel, judge, and probation or parole officers. In legal proceedings, be they criminal, civil, or other, the people involved are generally referred to as the *parties* to the proceeding. In civil proceedings (e.g., a claim for damages for negligence), the parties are referred to as the *plaintiff* (the person "complaining" or alleging a wrong and seeking damages) and the *defendant* (the person accused of committing the alleged wrong). In criminal proceedings, the parties are the Crown and the accused. The Crown is complaining on behalf of the state or society about a wrong (i.e., a crime) allegedly committed by the accused. The roles or duties of all these parties are clear and defined. The victim (the person who actually suffered because of this wrong) is not a party in the proceedings.

THE EVOLUTION OF VICTIM "RIGHTS" IN CANADA

In Canada, the emergence of victims' voices and recognition of their concerns dates back to the early 1970s. Criminal injuries compensation programs, which provide financial awards to victims of crime, originated in some jurisdictions in the context of compensating police officers injured in the course of their duties; they then expanded to provide limited compensation from the state (i.e., the province) to other eligible victims of violent crime. To encourage the development of such programs in all provinces, the federal government began funding them and established minimum criteria for them. Federal support for these programs, which benefited some victims, coincided with government funding for legal aid programs, which benefited some accused persons.

By the early 1980s, all Canadian provinces and territories had criminal injuries compensation programs. These programs varied in terms of eligibility and the scope of financial awards. By the early 1990s, many provinces and territories were examining the effectiveness of these programs when it came to meeting the needs of victims. Most victims who qualified found the financial assistance beneficial; however, many victims were ineligible, and many other needs of crime victims were not receiving attention. Acknowledging the cost of crime to families of victims, the federal government introduced the new Federal Income Support for Parents of Murdered or Missing Children in 2013. This grant provides assistance to eligible parents who suffer a loss of income as they take time away from work to cope with the death or disappearance of a child as a result of a probable *Criminal Code* offence. Services for victims of crime, such as emergency or crisis response services, shelters, counselling, victim/witness assistance programs, and specialized services for children and for sexual assault survivors, became as important as or more so than statutory reforms.

The current victim-related provisions in the Criminal Code and in the Corrections and Conditional Release Act (CCRA) are set out below, but may be amended as a result of the *Canadian Victims Bill of Rights*. Keep in mind the distinction between the role of the federal government and that of the provincial and territorial governments. The federal government is responsible for enacting the criminal law; the provinces are responsible for enforcing the criminal law, prosecuting offences, and administering justice, which includes providing services to victims. In the territories, the federal government, through the Public Prosecution Service of Canada, is responsible for prosecuting offences as well as for court-based victim services.[3] All provinces and territories have enacted victim-related legislation addressing matters of provincial/territorial responsibility. For example, Manitoba—the first province to enact comprehensive victim legislation, in 1986—has The Victims' Bill of Rights, which defines victims' rights and specifies the obligations of the police, the Crown, and other criminal justice professionals with regard to victims.

At the federal level, the development of victims' rights in the Criminal Code has occurred largely since 1988, though the Criminal Code has, since the 1950s, contained provisions that permit restitution orders. In addition, significant reforms to Canada's sexual assault laws in the early 1980s and throughout the 1990s recognized that sexual offence complainants require special consideration. Since Canada's sponsorship of the UN Declaration of Basic Principles of Justice for Victims of Crime and its endorsement of the Canadian Statement of Basic Principles of Justice for Victims of Crime, the federal, provincial, and territorial governments have pursued victim-specific legislative reforms. The descriptions of key *Code* provisions below follow the stages of the criminal process—pretrial, preliminary inquiry, trial, sentencing, and post-sentencing.

After consultations with stakeholders across the country (see Department of Justice 2013), the federal government introduced Bill C-32, *An Act to Enact the Canadian Victims Bill of Rights (CVBR) and to Amend Certain Acts*, in spring 2014. The bill has two parts: The CVBR identifies the rights that all victims of crime would have—the right to information, the right to protection, the right to participation, and the right to restitution. The second part proposes specific criminal law amendments to the *Criminal Code*, the CCRA, and the *Canada Evidence Act* to effectively implement the CVBR. For example, under the right to protection, the availability of testimonial aids would be broadened and courts would be required to consider additional factors such as the security and protection of the witness in determining whether to order the use of a testimonial aid. As noted earlier, many of the provisions, including the definition of victim outlined below, will be affected by the new quasi-constitutional legislation.

CRIMINAL CODE PROVISIONS OF BENEFIT TO VICTIMS

Definition of Victim

In the *Criminal Code*, a crime victim is broadly defined as "the victim of an alleged offence." The definition is non-exhaustive and makes no distinctions among primary victims (i.e., the actual victim), secondary victims (e.g., spouse, parent, co-worker), and indirect victims of crime. It only clarifies that the term may properly be used even when the crime is still alleged—in other words, the term *victim* does not presume the guilt of the accused.

Consideration of Victim's Safety in Bail Decisions

When a suspect is arrested, a determination must be made as to whether the suspect should be detained in custody or released with a promise to appear for trial, sometimes with conditions (commonly referred to as *bail*). In some cases, police make these decisions; in others, a justice of the peace or a judge makes them. Regardless of who makes the decision, most victims want to know the outcome and seek assurance that their safety has been taken into account in the bail decision.

Amendments to the Criminal Code enacted in 1999 require the decision maker to ensure "the safety and security of any victim of or to the offence" at various points in the criminal justice process. In Canada, as in some other countries such as the United States, Australia, and New Zealand, risk assessment tools have been developed to assist police, judges, and justices of the peace in this decision-making process (see Northcott 2012; Millar and Ha 2014). Decision makers must consider the following factors:

- The responsible judicial officer (officer in charge, justice of the peace, or judge) must consider the safety and security of the victim.

- Where an accused is released pending trial, the judge must consider whether to make as a condition of bail that the accused abstain from any direct or indirect communication with the victim, as well as any other condition necessary to ensure the safety and security of the victim.
- The judge must consider particular concerns of the victim and highlight them in decisions when imposing special bail conditions, including in firearms prohibitions and criminal harassment measures.

Facilitating Testimony

For some victims and witnesses, judicial proceedings can be intimidating or even frightening. The *Criminal Code* contains several provisions to assist victims and reduce their anxiety when they testify. Amendments to the *Code* and to the *Canada Evidence Act* that came into force on January 1, 2006, make testimonial aids available for all victims/witnesses under the age of 18, and for vulnerable adult witnesses on application, unless such aids would interfere with the proper administration of justice. For example, these provisions:

- provide discretion for the judge to exclude members of the public from the courtroom when necessary for the proper administration of justice;
- permit a support person to accompany a witness who is under 18 years of age or has a mental or physical disability;
- allow a witness who is under 18 years of age, or who may have difficulty communicating the evidence by reason of mental or physical disability, to testify outside the court-room or behind a screen or device that prevents a view of the accused;
- restrict personal cross-examination of witnesses under 18 years of age and criminal harassment victims/witnesses by a self-represented accused (e.g., the Crown can apply for an order appointing counsel to conduct the cross-examination of the victim); *and*
- allow the admission of videotaped testimony of the witness who is under the age of 18 in specified proceedings, including sexual offences.

Other vulnerable witnesses, such as victims of spousal abuse and sexual assault or those with a disability, may apply for a testimonial aid, provided that the witness can show that in the circumstances (including the nature of the offence and any relationship between the victim/witness and the accused), he or she would not be able to provide a full and candid account of the alleged incident without the aid.

Publication Bans

While the general rule is that all criminal proceedings against an accused are held in open court, the *Criminal Code* sets out several exceptions to facilitate victims' or witnesses' participation and to protect their privacy (see Cameron 2004). Sexual offence complainants, young victims, and young witnesses are the primary beneficiaries of these special provisions. A judge can order a publication ban on the identity of a victim or witness and on any information that could disclose that person's identity, if the judge is satisfied that the order is "necessary for the proper administration of justice." The victim, witness, or Crown can apply to the court for a publication ban, stating why the order is required. The hearing to determine whether the publication ban should be granted may be held in private. In addition, a judge must order a publication ban (on application) to protect the identity of all victims of sexual offences and of all witnesses of sexual offences who are under 18 years of age. In these cases, the judge advises the victim, witness, or Crown attorney/prosecutor in advance that he or she may request this protection. In cases of child pornography, a publication ban order must be made.

Provisions for Sexual Offence Victims

Legislative reforms recognize the unique nature of sexual assault offences, the trauma suffered by victims of these offences, and the re-victimization often caused by participating in the criminal justice system in such cases. The *Criminal Code* provides a clear and commonsense definition of *consent* for the purpose of sexual assault offences. Any non-consensual sexual activity is a sexual assault; hence, proof of lack of consent is an essential element of the offence. The *Code* defines *consent* as the voluntary agreement of the complainant to engage in the sexual activity in question. Conduct short of a voluntary agreement to engage in sexual activity does not constitute consent as a matter of law. For greater certainty, the *Code* sets out specific sections where there is no consent in law. Amendments made to the *Code* in 2008 raised the legal age at which youths can consent to non-exploitative sexual activity from 14 to 16. The same amendments provided a number of exceptions to the "consent as no defence" provisions, including a "close-in-age" exception that permits 14- and 15-year-old youths to engage in consensual, non-exploitative sexual activity with a partner who is less than five years older.

Sections of the *Criminal Code* protect the victim from undue interrogation about the victim's other sexual activity. The *Code* makes it clear that evidence that a victim has engaged in sexual activity with others is not admissible to suggest that the victim was more likely to have consented to the sexual activity that is the subject matter of the current charge. The provisions restrict the admissibility of evidence to specific instances of sexual activity—those relevant to an issue at trial—and to evidence that has "significant probative value which is not substantially outweighed by the danger of prejudice to the administration of justice." In making this determination, the judge is required to consider a range of factors set out in the *Code*. The *Code* also sets out the procedure to be followed and includes provisions to safeguard the victim's privacy, including provisions for an *in camera* (closed) hearing, non-compellability of the victim at the hearing, and a publication ban on the proceedings. These provisions are sometimes referred to as the *rape shield* laws.

Finally, sections of the *Code* protect sexual offence victims and witnesses from requests for personal records, such as diaries, or records held by a third party like a doctor, therapist, or child protection agency. These provisions place the onus on the accused to establish that the records sought are likely to be relevant to an issue at trial. In addition, the trial judge is required to carefully scrutinize applications and make a decision in accordance with a two-part procedure that balances the accused's right to a defence with the victim's privacy and equality rights. This procedure is set out in the *Code* and includes safeguards for the victim's privacy: an *in camera* hearing, non-compellability of the victim at the hearing, a publication ban on the proceedings and the contents of the application, editing of the records (where ordered to be produced) to delete irrelevant personal information, and the imposition of other appropriate conditions (see McDonald and Wobick 2006 for case law on these provisions).

SENTENCING

Reforms to the sentencing provisions of the *Criminal Code* enacted in 1996 defined the purposes and principles of sentencing. Judges are directed to consider a number of objectives when sentencing offenders. Two of these objectives are directly relevant to the interests of victims:

- to provide reparations for harm done to victims or to the community; *and*
- to promote a sense of responsibility in offenders and acknowledgment of the harm done to victims and to the community.

Victim Impact Statements

Although there are only two parties in a sentencing hearing—the offender, represented by defence counsel, and the state, represented by the Crown—the victim of the crime nevertheless has a role to play. Most countries permit crime victims to submit a statement to the court detailing the impact that the crime has had upon their life. Some U.S. states go even further and allow victims to make sentencing recommendations to the court. This is not permitted in Canada. In 1988, the *Criminal Code* was amended to permit the court to consider *victim impact statements* (VISs). Since 1995, the *Code* has required the court to consider a VIS at the time of sentencing. The VIS describes the harm done to or loss suffered by the victim of the offence. The 1999 amendments to the *Criminal Code* did the following to improve the usefulness of VISs:

- ensure that the victim is permitted to read a VIS at the time of sentencing if he or she wishes to do so;
- require the judge to ask, before imposing a sentence, whether the victim has been informed of the opportunity to prepare a VIS;
- authorize adjournments to permit a victim to prepare a statement or to submit other evidence to the court about the impact of the crime;
- require that VISs be considered by courts and review boards following a verdict of not criminally responsible on account of mental disorder; *and*
- clarify that oral or written information may be provided by a victim at any proceeding to determine whether an offender sentenced to life in prison should have an earlier parole eligibility date.

In 2011, a provision in the *Code* that explicitly permits a Community Impact Statement in fraud cases came into force and effect. A Community Impact Statement may describe the losses suffered by the community, such as a neighbourhood association, business association, or seniors group, as a result of the fraud.

Federal Victim Surcharge

The *federal victim surcharge* is an additional financial penalty automatically imposed on offenders at the time of sentencing (unless the accused seeks an exception owing to undue hardship). In addition to the *federal victim surcharge*, a similar provincial/territorial surcharge exists that is automatically imposed. The federal and provincial/territorial victim surcharges are collected and retained by the provincial and territorial governments and are used to help fund programs, services, and assistance to victims of crime within the jurisdiction (see Law and Sullivan 2008). The *federal victim surcharge* was included in the 1988 amendments to the *Criminal Code*. Amendments that came into effect in the fall of 2013 provide for automatic imposition upon conviction, removing the discretion of the judge to waive the surcharge in cases of undue hardship on the offender or the offender's family. The amount of the surcharge was doubled, to 30 percent of any fine imposed on the offender. If no fine is imposed, the surcharge is $100 in the case of an offence punishable by summary conviction and $200 in the case of an offence punishable by indictment.

Restitution

The court may order the offender to pay restitution in addition to any other sentence imposed. Restitution may be ordered by the court on its own motion or on application by the Crown or victim to cover easily ascertainable monetary damages, including those resulting from bodily injury (but not for pain and suffering). In 2010, a provision was added to the *Criminal Code* to allow for an order that the offender make restitution to a victim of identity theft or identity fraud for the expenses associated with rehabilitating the victim's identity. In 2011, provisions were added to:

- require judges to consider restitution from the offender in all cases of fraud involving an identified victim with ascertainable losses and to provide reasons in cases where a victim has sought restitution but it has not been ordered;
- require Crown to advise the court if reasonable steps have been taken to provide victims with an opportunity to indicate whether they are seeking restitution for their readily ascertainable losses; *and*
- provide victims with an optional form to indicate that they want the Crown to seek restitution from the offender and to set out their ascertainable losses.

In terms of enforcement, if the restitution order is tied to a probation order or a conditional sentence, the probation officer or community corrections officer will work with offenders to ensure that they comply with the order, whether through a one-time payment or a schedule of monthly payments. In the case of stand-alone orders, the enforcement of restitution is the victim's responsibility. The victim may file the restitution order as if it were a judgment in civil proceedings and pursue civil remedies. Saskatchewan has a Restitution Civil Enforcement Program whereby state enforcement officers will assist by enforcing the restitution order in civil proceedings.

VICTIMS AND THE CORRECTIONAL SYSTEM

The *Corrections and Conditional Release Act* (CCRA) governs Correctional Service Canada (CSC), which is responsible for supervising offenders sentenced to more than two years in custody, as well as the Parole Board of Canada (PBC), which determines whether to release offenders into the community. The CCRA contains specific provisions authorizing the release of some offender-related information to victims who register with CSC and request information.

Anyone can request publicly available information, such as a description of the offence for which an offender was convicted, the sentence length, and eligibility dates for temporary absences, day parole, or full parole. But victims of crime, as defined in the CCRA, may register and request additional information, which may include the penitentiary where the offender is serving the sentence; the date of a Parole Board hearing; the nature of the conditions attached to any work release, parole, statutory release, or temporary absences; and whether the offender is in custody. Victims may request ongoing information and must ensure that CSC and the PBC have their current address for this purpose.

When victims request information from CSC and the PBC, victim liaison officers within CSC generally receive those requests and provide the information. Victims may request to attend Parole Board hearings as observers and may also have access to the PBC's decision registry. Victims may prepare and submit VISs to the Parole Board describing the physical, emotional, and financial impact of the offence upon them. PBC policy permits victims to read or otherwise present the VIS at the hearing. Victims can apply to the Department of Justice Canada for funding to attend the parole hearing.[4]

RESEARCH ON VICTIMS IN THE CRIMINAL JUSTICE SYSTEM

Legislative reforms have addressed some victim needs, and while further reforms are necessary, these reforms should be supported by research that examines both the effectiveness of the existing legislation and the broader needs of victims. An exhaustive review of all the research relating to victims of crime is beyond the scope of this chapter. Provided below is a *selection* of key research issues that are intended to inform policy, programs, and legislative reforms relating to crime victims. References for further reading are provided at the end of the chapter.

Victim Needs

The needs of crime victims range from the general to the specific and often depend on the type of victimization experienced and on the characteristics of the individual victim (see, e.g., Egbo 2009; Federal Ombudsman for Victims of Crime 2009; Fraser and McDonald 2009; McDonald and Hogue 2007). Victims frequently identify financial needs, emotional needs, practical needs, and needs related to personal safety and security to varying degrees and in varying circumstances. Research indicates that the need for information is one of the most critical and universal needs expressed by victims of crime (e.g., Meredith and Paquette 2001; Wemmers and Canuto 2002; McDonald 2010). For many people, the criminal justice process is both unfamiliar and complex, and victims often do not know how to navigate through the system. The information needs of victims and their families fall into three main categories:

1. information about the criminal justice system in general;
2. information about their specific case and their rights; *and*
3. information about services to address their other needs, such as for housing, emotional support, and financial or medical services.

For the most part, accused persons will have defence lawyers to represent them and to explain the details of the case before and during the trial. Many victims mistakenly believe that the Crown attorney/prosecutor is their personal lawyer; in fact, the Crown acts on behalf of the state, not the victim. As victims do not generally have their own lawyers to protect their interests or to assist them as the case proceeds through the system, they must rely on criminal justice system officials to provide appropriate information about how their case is proceeding and progressing. This is where victim services providers can play an important role in addressing the information needs of victims/witnesses and their families.

Child and Other Vulnerable Victims/Witnesses

Children and youth have specific needs in relation to the criminal justice system, as do victims with a physical or mental disability. It has long been recognized that children are particularly vulnerable to re-traumatization if they go through the criminal justice system as witnesses. Research (Sas 2002) has documented the cognitive development of children and addressed how the criminal justice system must adapt to ensure that children can participate effectively in the process. Testimonial aids, such as screens, support persons, or giving evidence via closed circuit television, are intended to facilitate testimony. Ongoing research continues to assess how these provisions are working in practice across the country (Northcott 2009; on vulnerable adults see Hurley 2013; Ainslie 2013).

Plea Negotiations

Plea negotiations (or plea bargains) may not seem like a topic related to victims; however, such negotiations have a significant impact on crime victims. *Plea bargaining* is defined as a "negotiation between the Crown prosecutor, defence counsel, and the accused to determine which charge will be laid or what sentence will be recommended. Typically, this negotiation is undertaken in an effort to have the accused plead guilty and avoid the need for a trial"[*] (Drislane and Parkinson 2005, 106). Plea bargaining is important since about 90 percent of criminal cases are resolved through guilty pleas, many of which are the direct outcome of plea negotiations between Crown and defence (Verdun-Jones and Tijerino 2002). However, as Verdun-Jones and Tijerino note, victims in Canada have almost no role in plea bargaining, even though the results of a plea bargain may have direct consequences for them. These researchers go on to explain that although plea negotiations play an integral role in the criminal justice process in Canada, they in fact "have no formal legal status and are not subject to direct judicial regulation" (2002, 5).

Restitution

Little research has been undertaken in Canada on court-ordered restitution. National data from Statistics Canada show that restitution orders are made

---

[*] From DRISLANE/PARKINSON. Nelson Criminology Dictionary. © 2005 Nelson Education Ltd. Reproduced by permission. www.cengage.com/permissions.

primarily in relation to property crimes (80 percent). The Department of Justice Multi-Site Survey (Prairie Research Associates 2006) included questions on restitution, with criminal justice respondents noting that the main problem is enforcement. The reason given for this is the offender's inability to pay. Research in Saskatchewan, which has the country's only Restitution Coordinator, who works with both offenders and victims, found that victims wanted more information and assistance with respect to all aspects of restitution—what they could request of the court, what happened once an order was made, and how they could enforce the order in civil court (McDonald 2010). In addition, the research found that when victims did not receive the money owed to them, this affected their confidence in the entire justice system.

Federal Victim Surcharge

Research has been undertaken to better understand how the Federal Victim Surcharge (FVS) is working in different jurisdictions. For example, Law and Sullivan (2008) found in their research in New Brunswick that the FVS was being waived in 66 percent of all cases province-wide and in 96 percent of cases with a custodial disposition. These findings were similar to those in the Northwest Territories (Warrilow and McDonald 2008), where the FVS was being waived in 70 percent of all cases territory-wide and in 94 percent of cases with a custodial disposition. As noted earlier, the FVS is collected by the provinces and territories and the revenues collected pay for services for victims. As such, it was important that the research also examined collection rates for the FVS that were not waived at sentencing. In New Brunswick, 83 percent of FVSs were being collected; similarly, 84 percent of all FVSs were being collected in the Northwest Territories. An offender's inability to pay was consistently cited by respondents in these studies as the reason for waiving the FVS.

Victim Impact Statements

Sociolegal research on VISs has been undertaken in Canada since the early 1980s, so there is a significant body of work examining how they are working from both victims' perspectives and from the perspectives of other criminal justice professionals (see Roberts 2008 for a summary). To mark the 20th year since their introduction into the *Criminal Code* (Bill C-89 in 1988), Roberts (2008) reviewed and synthesized the body of research on VISs and noted the following in terms of lessons learned:

1. Only a minority of victims submit impact statements.
2. Few victims request oral delivery of their VIS, but those who do find it beneficial.
3. Obstacles remain regarding the systematic use of statements.
4. Most victims who submit a VIS report being more satisfied with sentencing.
5. It is important to avoid creating expectations that cannot be fulfilled.

6. The mode of delivery of any VIS program is important to its success.
7. Victims require appropriate information about the purpose and nature of VISs.
8. VISs sometimes include extraneous material.
9. Judges report finding VISs useful, particularly for sentencing offenders convicted of crimes of violence.
10. Little evidence exists that VISs have adverse effects on sentencing process.*

In addition to policy research, case law continues to develop interpretations of the role of VISs at sentencing (Manikis and Roberts 2012).

CONCLUSION

The criminal justice system needs to consider justice proceedings from the perspective of individual victims. While the role that crime victims play in this system is not as clear as those of other participants in the criminal justice process, crime victims need to be considered. Although the participation of victims in the justice system has received increased attention in the research literature, as well as in policy and legislation, more work remains as evidenced by the cross-country consultations on a *Canadian Victims Bill of Rights* in 2013. Further exploration of the needs and concerns of victims, through appropriate policy research, is necessary, as are continuing efforts to evaluate the benefits of the progress already made (or initiatives already taken) to improve the criminal justice system with respect to victims of crime.

Further Readings

Johnson, H., and M. Dawson. 2011. *Violence Against Women in Canada. Research and Policy Perspectives*. Don Mills, ON: Oxford University Press.

Roach, K. 2010. *Due Process and Victims' Rights: The New Law and Politics of Criminal Justice*, 2nd ed. Toronto: University of Toronto Press.

Roberts, J.V. 2010. "The Role of the Victim at Sentencing and Corrections." In K. Reitz and J. Petersilia, eds., *The Oxford Handbook of Sentencing and Corrections*. New York: Oxford University Press.

References

Ainslie, M. 2013. *Testimonial Support for Vulnerable Adults (Bill C-2): Case Law Review (2009–2012)*. Ottawa: Department of Justice Canada.

* Victims of Crime Research Digest 2008 – Issues No. 1, Victim Impact Statements Lessons Learned and Future Priorities, Page 1:3-16, http://www.justice.gc.ca/eng/rp-pr/cj-jp/victim/rr07_vic4rr07_vic4.pdf. Department of Justice Canada, 2008. Reproduced with the permission of the Department of Justice Canada, 2014.

AuCoin, K., and D. Beauchamp. 2007. "Impacts and Consequences of Victimization, GSS 2004." *Juristat.* Statistics Canada, Cat. no. 85-002-XIE, 27, no. 1.

Cameron, J. 2004. *Victim Privacy and the Open Court Principle.* Ottawa: Department of Justice Canada.

Department of Justice Canada 2013. *News Release of December 27, 2013.* http://www.justice.gc.ca/eng/news-nouv/nr-cp/2013/doc_33022.html

Drislane, R., and G. Parkinson. 2005. *Nelson Criminology Dictionary.* Toronto: Thomson Nelson.

Egbo, R. 2009. *Memorializing the Victims of Terrorism.* Ottawa: Department of Justice Canada.

Federal Ombudsman for Victims of Crime. 2009. *Every Image, Every Child: Internet-Facilitated Child Sexual Abuse in Canada.* Ottawa: Office of the Federal Ombudsman for Victims of Crime.

Fraser, C., and S. McDonald. 2009. *Identifying the Issues: Victim Services Workers' Experiences Working with Victims with Fetal Alcohol Spectrum Disorder.* Ottawa: Department of Justice Canada.

Hurley, P. 2013. *Vulnerable Adult Witnesses: The Perceptions and Experiences of Crown Prosecutors and Victim Services Providers in the Use of Testimonial Support Provisions.* Ottawa: Department of Justice Canada.

Law, M., and M.A. Sullivan. 2008. *Federal Victim Surcharge in New Brunswick: An Operational Review.* Ottawa: Department of Justice Canada.

Manikis, M., and J.V. Roberts. 2012. "Victim Impact Statements: Recent Guidance from the Courts of Appeal." *Victims of Crime Research Digest* 5: 2–6. Ottawa: Department of Justice Canada.

McDonald, S. 2010. "Explain Please!' Working with Victims and Restitution." *Victims of Crime Research Digest* 3: 9–14, Ottawa: Department of Justice Canada.

McDonald, S., and A. Hogue. 2007. *An Exploration of the Needs of Victims of Hate Crime.* Ottawa: Department of Justice.

McDonald, S., and A. Wobick. 2006. *Bill C-46: Records Application Post-Mills, A Case Law Review.* Ottawa: Department of Justice Canada.

Meredith, C., and C. Paquette. 2001. *Summary Report on Victim Impact Statement Focus Groups.* Ottawa: Department of Justice Canada.

Millar, A., and L. Ha. 2014. *Inventory of Spousal Violence Risk Assessment Tools Used in Canada.* Ottawa: Department of Justice Canada.

Northcott, M. 2009. "Facilitating Testimony for Child Victims and Witnesses." *Victims of Crime Research Digest* 2: 17–23. Ottawa: Department of Justice Canada.

____. 2012. *Intimate Partner Violence Risk Assessment Tools: A Review*. Ottawa: Department of Justice Canada.

Prairie Research Associates. 2006. *Multi-Site Survey of Victims of Crime and Criminal Justice Professionals across Canada*. Ottawa: Department of Justice Canada.

Roberts, J.V. 2008. "Victim Impact Statements: Lessons Learned and Future Priorities." *Victims of Crime Research Digest* 1: 3–16. Ottawa: Department of Justice Canada.

Sas, L. 2002. *The Interaction between Children's Developmental Capabilities and the Courtroom Environment: The Impact on Testimonial Competency*. Ottawa: Department of Justice Canada.

Verdun-Jones, S., and A. Tijerino. 2002. *Victim Participation in the Plea Negotiation Process in Canada: A Review of the Literature and Four Models for Law Reform*. Ottawa: Department of Justice Canada.

Warrilow, L., and S. McDonald. 2008. "A Summary of Research into the Federal Victim Surcharge in New Brunswick and the Northwest Territories." *Victims of Crime Research Digest* 1: 21–4. Ottawa: Department of Justice Canada.

Wathen, N. 2013. *Health Impact of Violent Victimization on Women and Their Children*. Ottawa: Department of Justice Canada.

Wemmers, J., and M. Canuto. 2002. *Victims' Experiences with, Expectations and Perceptions of Restorative Justice: A Critical Review of the Literature*. Ottawa: Department of Justice Canada.

Zhang, T., J. Hoddenbagh, S. McDonald, and K. Scrim. 2013. *An Estimation of the Economic Impact of Spousal Violence*. Ottawa: Department of Justice Canada.

Endnotes

1. The views expressed in this chapter are those of the authors and do not necessarily represent those of the organizations with which they are affiliated. A summary of the development of the *Canadian Victims Bill of Rights* can be found at http://www.justice.gc.ca/eng/news-nouv/nr-cp/2013/doc_33022.html
2. Statistics Canada publishes a number of reports each year on the nature and extent of victimization using data from the *General Social Survey on Victimization*, and on services for victims using the *Victim Services Survey*, and the *Transition Home Survey*. For more information see http://www.statcan.gc.ca. Research from the Research and Statistics Division, Department of Justice Canada, referenced in this chapter can be accessed at http://www.justice.gc.ca
3. All three territories also provide community-based victim services.
4. For more information on financial assistance for victims to attend National Parole Board hearings see http://www.justice.gc.ca/eng/pi/pcvi-cpcv/fund-fond/app-dem.html

CHAPTER 25

Criminal (In)Justice: Responding to Corporate Crime in the Workplace

When members of the public think about crime, the offences that come to mind usually involve individual offenders committing crimes against one or two victims. Yet a great deal of crime is committed by corporations, and involves thousands of victims. Criminal justice responses to corporate offending have long been criticized for being ineffective. In this chapter Steven Bittle explores the challenges confronting the state response to offending by corporations. Although seldom in the news, corporate crimes occur every day and can affect the lives of many people.

Steven Bittle
University of Ottawa

In contemporary society it is difficult to escape the constant political, media, and popular culture chatter about the dangers of crime. Politicians regularly castigate those who make it unsafe for us to carry out our daily routines—the so-called gang members, drug dealers, and violent street predators who, according to these dominant voices, cause the most harm in society and, as such, deserve harsh punishments. This modern preoccupation with crime has resulted in the introduction of new laws aimed at "getting tough" on offenders, and calls for criminal justice officials to find more efficient crime control techniques. As David Garland (2001, 10–11) argues, in recent decades the state's crime control policy-making has shifted from cool to hot, expressing a "... collective anger and a righteous demand for retribution rather than a commitment to a just, socially engineered solution."

Virtually absent from this law-and-order rhetoric is consideration of crimes committed by the most privileged and powerful people in modern history and the corporations that they manage. Although we are taught to fear violent street crime, the reality is that we stand a much better chance of being victimized by corporate crime than traditional street crime. Globally, corporations annually kill hundreds of thousands of workers and injure millions more through:

- permitting or creating unsafe and illegal working conditions (Tombs and Whyte 2007);
- offering unsafe and dangerous products for sale in the marketplace (Friedrichs 2010);
- damaging the environment by illegally dumping toxic waste and spewing harmful pollutants into the atmosphere (Stretesky et al. 2014); and
- fraudulently stealing millions of dollars through price-fixing and illegal insider trading (Ferguson 2012).

Despite the volume and scope of these harms, they are rarely treated as crimes worthy of serious punishment. As Glasbeek (2002, 118) notes, "When corporate actors commit crimes they are rarely charged; if charged, they are rarely convicted; and if convicted, they are rarely punished severely."

Reiman (2004) likens the criminal justice system to a carnival mirror in that it reflects a "distorted image of the dangers that threaten us," drawing our collective gaze towards the threat of street crime while obscuring crimes of the powerful. This chapter uses the example of corporate crime to examine the ways in which the criminal justice system helps reproduce a distorted image of crime in society. It focuses particularly on offences by corporations that seriously injure and kill workers and/or members of the public, or what corporate crime scholars Tombs and Whyte (2007) refer to as *safety crimes*. Safety crimes provide an interesting case study in that acts of violence typically dominate discussion and debate regarding criminal justice in Canada, and yet these discussions rarely include the violence associated with workplace injury and death. Instead, when a worker is injured or killed on the job it is commonly considered an "accident," the unfortunate but largely unavoidable by-product of work in capitalist society. By exploring how safety crimes are dealt with (or more aptly, not dealt with) through the criminal justice system, this chapter will raise questions about the administration of justice in Canada and the dominant belief that we are all equally subject to the rule of law.

DEFINING CORPORATE CRIME

There is considerable variation in definitions of corporate crime. Over the years, scholars have referred to offences by corporations and/or corporate actors as *white-collar crime* (Sutherland 1940 and 1949), *corporate crime* (Braithwaite 1984; Pearce and Snider 1995), *elite deviance* (Simon and Eitzen 1986), *crimes of the powerful* (Pearce 1976), *economic crimes* (Edelhertz 1970) and *occupational crime* (Green 1990). Sutherland first introduced the concept of white-collar crime in the 1940s, arguing that crime was not simply a lower-class phenomenon and that businessmen and professionals routinely committed serious offences that went unpunished (Slapper and Tombs 1999, 3). Sutherland defined white-collar crime as "crime committed by a person of respectability and high social status in the course of his occupation" (Sutherland 1983, 7). Scholars have since built upon Sutherland's work to consider the ways in which group or organizational factors also contribute to corporate offending (Slapper and Tombs 1999). Slapper and Tombs (1999, 17) argue that definitions of corporate offending need to transcend humanist understandings of crime (i.e., decisions by individuals to commit an offence) to consider more structural factors, such as how pressures to make profit lead to decisions within a corporation to cut costs relating to workplace safety—decisions that can and do have deadly consequences.

Interest in structural factors has drawn many academics to the concept of corporate crime in order to draw attention to the ways in which an "organization's structure, its culture, its unquestioned assumptions" facilitate corporate offending (Slapper and Tombs 1999, 17). From this perspective, corporate crime is defined as "illegal acts of omission or commission of an individual or group of individuals in a legitimate formal organization, in accordance with the goals of that organization, which have serious physical or economic impact on employees, consumers or the general public" (Box 1983, 20). Corporate crimes generally fall into two categories: financial corporate crime such as insider trading, fraudulent bookkeeping, and price fixing; and social corporate crime, encompassing offences against the environment (air and water pollution) and occupational health and safety crimes (unsafe and dangerous working conditions) (Snider 1993). This chapter uses the term corporate crime to examine criminal justice responses to safety crimes.

SAFETY CRIMES IN THE WORKPLACE

Serious injuries and fatalities are a common occurrence in Canadian workplaces. For instance, from 1996 to 2008 there were on average close to 400,000 cases each year in which a worker received compensation for lost wages as a result of a work-related injury or a permanent disability (Gilks and Logan 2010; Association of Workers' Compensation Boards of Canada [AWCBC]). There are more workplace fatalities than homicides each year in Canada. For example, in 2005 there were 1,097 workplace fatalities (Sharpe and Hardt 2006) and 658 homicides (Statistics Canada 2006). And while police investigate and lay criminal charges in a majority of homicides, the same cannot be said for workplace fatalities, despite research suggesting that at least two-thirds of these incidences include some criminal culpability (Slapper and Tombs 1999, 78). What accounts for the differential treatment of safety crimes in law and in criminal justice?

REGULATING WORKPLACE SAFETY

To understand why safety crimes seldom result in criminal prosecutions, we must first consider the history of regulating workplace safety. There has been a general lack of interest, even apathy, on the part of the state when it comes to developing effective strategies for holding corporations and senior corporate officials accountable for safety crimes (Tombs and Whyte 2007). The historic reluctance to equate workplace injury and death with serious crime stems from the belief that these offences are *mala prohibitum* (wrong because the act is prohibited) as opposed to *malum in se* (inherently wrong because the act is essentially evil; Snider 2000). Workers' safety has not been totally ignored by legislators—laws have been introduced to improve workplace safety and to punish negligent employers—but unlike responses to traditional street crimes, attempts to introduce legal reforms have been slow to develop, only coming about after hard-fought lobbying by labour/unions and rarely resulting in dramatic improvements to workplace safety (Snider 1993).

Tombs and Whyte (2007, 110) characterize the history of corporate crime control as a model of criminal process that contains two distinct, yet related, spheres: on one hand there are attempts to *differentiate* corporate deviance from traditional crime by responding to it through a separate regulatory framework; on the other there are efforts to *assimilate* corporate offending into traditional criminal law/criminal justice, which is more accustomed to dealing with individual (street) offenders than corporate miscreants. Each approach is considered below.

REGULATORY JUSTICE FOR CORPORATIONS

While this book addresses issues of criminal justice concerning a variety of traditional crimes, a very different brand of justice has dominated when it comes to the state's response to safety crimes. In particular, corporate offences have been, and continue to be, dealt with primarily within the realm of regulatory justice. Regulatory justice is commonly used to deal with businesses or corporations that "fail to comply" with certain standards relating to, for instance, food safety, workplace safety, or environmental practices (Drake et al. 2010, 10). In general, regulation involves "state imposed limitation on the discretion that may be exercised by individuals or organizations, which is supported by the threat of sanction" (Stone 1982, 11; as quoted in Simpson 2002, 80). This approach emphasizes the use of persuasion and education to ensure organizations comply with regulations, relying on punishment only as a last resort if organizations fail or refuse to comply with the law (Simpson 2002, 93). Regulatory approaches stem from the belief that, on the whole, individuals are "reasonable, of good faith, and motivated to heed advice" (Braithwaite 1989, 131) and that corporations and corporate actors are not "true" criminals (Tombs and Whyte 2007).

Today, the provinces and territories are responsible for developing and enforcing regulations relating to workplace safety (except the federal government is responsible for regulating federal workplaces). While the details of these schemes differ between jurisdictions and have varied over time, they generally involve a health and safety regulatory authority with inspectors who look for instances where companies are not complying with safety regulations and issue orders to fix the problem(s), respond to complaints about workplace safety violations, and/or investigate workplace "accidents" to determine their causes. In cases where injury and/or death have occurred and a regulation has been breached, inspectors can lay charges against the company and/or individuals within the company. A finding of guilt can result in fines and/or, in rare cases, imprisonment (Snider 1993). This method of justice contains several characteristics that are germane for our examination of why safety crimes are not seen as worthy of criminal justice intervention.

First, regulatory agencies are frequently under-resourced and understaffed, meaning that they rarely have the capacity to adequately inspect workplaces to ensure that companies operate safely and comply with the law. Second, many of the regulatory laws that have been developed over the years are poorly worded, often as a result of corporate lobbying against regulations (Snider 1993). Unlike street offenders who do not have the power to influence laws directed against them, when it comes to safety crimes there is a long tradition of resistance from corporate owners and managers who argue that safety measures cost too much, interfere with management's right to develop "effective" production strategies (which do not always equate to the safest production methods), and give workers and unions too much power and control over working conditions (Noble 1995, 268). Third, critics note that regulators are susceptible to being "captured" by the industries that they are responsible for regulating—the notion that, via their efforts to educate and persuade companies to comply with the law, they begin sympathizing or identifying with the regulated, making it less likely that they will resort to punishment strategies to ensure compliance (Snider 1993).

Finally, regulatory offences are considered inchoate offences in that they focus on attempts rather than results (Wells 1993). This means that, unlike traditional crimes where the offender is charged with assault or robbery, for example, corporate offenders are charged with breaching a regulatory standard. Wells (1993) notes how workplace deaths are rarely treated as homicides, but instead as incomplete acts or attempts, such as the failure to provide safe working conditions. In the process, she argues, the language of regulation obscures the severity of injury and death in the workplace and reinforces the belief that they are "accidents," not crimes of violence (1993, 12).

Some scholars (e.g., Glasbeek 2002) question the application of the regulatory justice approach to traditional crimes. They ask us to consider, for example, a scenario in which the police catch a young person breaking into a house, and instead of arresting him for a criminal offence they ask him to reconsider his rule-breaking behaviour, or send him a letter in the mail asking him to stop this activity. The police would also inform this individual that they will observe his behaviour over the next while (don't worry, they say, we'll be sure to let you know when we are coming) and may be forced to lay criminal charges if his rule-breaking behaviour persists. As strange as this scenario seems, it is, as Glasbeek (2002, 155) notes, "precisely what, time and time again, occupational health and safety inspectors tell countless corporations that engage in rule-breaking and life-threatening practices."

REGULATORY JUSTICE

The idea that safety crimes are not "real" crimes took on new meaning during the 1980s, when self-regulation became the dominant response to corporate offending. Fuelled by the view that the free market was the most efficient means of dealing with corporate wrongdoing—that a corporation's desire to protect its reputation and competitive market forces would weed out corporate wrongdoers—there was a gradual and pronounced erosion of "formal rules of law and regulation" (Tillman and Indergaard 2005, 15–16 and 28). In essence, corporations were (re)defined as an inherent social and economic good, making it increasingly difficult to treat them as potential criminals (Snider 2000). As such, governments in most Western countries, including Canada, bought into the idea that criminal laws were ineffective in dealing with crimes of the powerful, preferring instead to employ various forms of self-regulation. As with regulation generally, self-regulation emphasizes "persuasion and bargaining" and that corporations need guidance and do not respond well to chastisement and deterrence (Slapper and Tombs 1999, 165–9). However, compared to state-centred regulation, self-regulation trusts corporations to "monitor and control their own compliance with the law under a minimalist regulatory framework" (Tombs and Whyte 2007, 166, fn. 14).

Critics charge that self-regulation by the industry has simply not been effective. In addition to the fact that corporations will not self-regulate in the absence of external pressures, corporate executives may falsify records to deceive regulators and they will only use self-regulation symbolically and under limited conditions (McMullan 1992, 89–96; Slapper and Tombs 1999, 184). What is more, in assuming that corporations are inherently good, self-regulatory approaches ignore that the imperative to accumulate corporate profit sometimes takes precedence over safety concerns (Tombs and Whyte 2007, 157). Finally, given the prevalence of corporate power, critics charge that advocates of self-regulation underestimate the relevance of regulatory capture (Tombs and Whyte 2007, 160). For many critical scholars the failure to adequately regulate workplace safety has had deadly consequences.

THE WESTRAY DISASTER

A tragic example of the failure of workplace safety regulations in Canada occurred in 1992 when 26 miners were killed following an underground explosion at the Westray Mine in Nova Scotia. Although the mine owners, Curragh Resources, were eventually charged criminally, no one was convicted, largely because of prosecutorial mishaps and difficulties determining legal responsibility (McMullan 2001). The ensuing public inquiry characterized the disaster as "foreseeable and preventable," revealing that management had been warned over 50 times prior to the explosion about workplace health and safety violations, all of which were ignored (Glasbeek 2002, 62). Tragically, the final warning came just 10 days prior to the explosion, when a Department of Labour inspector (the provincial regulator) issued the management with a written order to clean up the site to prevent a coal dust explosion or face prosecution. Unfortunately, the order's 14-day waiting period did not have a chance to expire before inspectors could take further action (McMullan 2005, 26).

As we can see from the above, regulatory justice for safety crimes works very differently from criminal justice. In many respects regulatory justice has helped to differentiate workplace injury and death from "real" crimes, downplaying their seriousness and treating them largely as "accidents," not crimes of violence worthy of criminal justice response (Tombs and Whyte 2007). The next section examines attempts to assimilate safety crimes into the realm of criminal law/criminal justice, focusing particularly on the aftermath of the Westray mine disaster and the ensuing demands to criminalize corporations that negligently injure and/or kill workers.

SAFETY CRIMES AND CRIMINAL (IN)JUSTICE

Despite the dominance of regulatory approaches to safety crimes (and corporate crimes generally), there have been attempts over the years to use the criminal law in response to these offences. One of the difficulties here is that criminal law is structured around individualistic conceptions of responsibility and sanctions, an approach that has presented unique obstacles when applied to corporate or organization offending (Slapper and Tombs 1999). As the 18th-century Lord Thurlow is said to have stated, the corporation "had no soul to damn and no body to kick" (Slapper and Tombs 1999, 26). From a criminal law perspective it was (and in many ways remains) problematic that there was not one individual to hold accountable for corporate wrong-doing, and that it was impossible for the corporation to defend itself in court (Glasbeek 2002, 128).

The difficulties of applying the criminal law to corporate offending are further complicated by the fact that the individuals behind the corporation—those who own and control it—enjoy the privilege of limited liability. The corporation has its own "legal existence" that is separate from those who invest (Yalden et al. 2008, 133). That is, the corporation is a natural, independent person, regardless of whether one or more individuals own shares in the company (Yalden et al. 2008, 135). As Nicholls notes, "A corporation can own property in its own name: it can enter into contracts; and it can sue, and be sued, too. It is, for legal purposes, a single, distinct, entity" (Nicholls 2005, 3 and 5; as quoted in Yalden et al. 2008, 32). At the same time, those who invest in the corporation have few risks beyond their monetary contribution; while they may lose their investment if the company is not profitable or goes bankrupt, they do not have to worry about taking responsibility for any corporate wrongdoing (Glasbeek 2007). This situation is particularly problematic when we consider that the limited liability corporation's main motivation is profit maximization for shareholders (Glasbeek 2004), a scenario that can and does mean that the pursuit of profits takes precedence over decisions about workers' safety.

Efforts to apply the criminal law to corporate offending surfaced as judges were faced with the realities that corporations were capable of inflicting considerable social and economic damage. In the United Kingdom in the mid-1900s, for instance, the courts introduced the identification doctrine, which effectively assigned responsibility to the corporation by equating the *mens rea* of an employee, referred to as the *controlling officer*, with that of the company itself (Slapper and Tombs 1999, 29–30). Courts in Canada soon followed suit with the Supreme Court of Canada's introduction of the *Identification Doctrine*, which assigned criminal responsibility to the corporation by tracing the crime to a senior employee(s), namely the *Directing Mind* (*Canadian Dredge and Dock Co. v. The Queen* [1985] 1 S.C.R. 662).

A person was deemed to be a directing mind when she was responsible for a particular department or unit, and the crime benefited the corporation in some way (Department of Justice Canada 2002). The problem, however, was that the identification doctrine only applied to "high-level managers with decision-making authority" (Department of Justice Canada 2002; also see Cahill and Cahill 1999), and since lower-level managers were often interpreting company policies, tracing responsibility up to senior management frequently proved impossible. This was especially difficult in large corporations where responsibility was spread throughout the corporation, making it difficult to single out a responsible individual (Cahill and Cahill 1999; Slapper and Tombs 1999).

CRIMINAL (IN)JUSTICE AND THE WESTRAY DISASTER

The Westray disaster generated renewed debate about the challenges of using the criminal law to deal with safety crimes. As noted, nobody was held to account for the death of the 26 miners and this was seen by many, particularly within the labour movement, as unacceptable. Although the subsequent Westray inquiry was not tasked with considering changes to the criminal law (the inquiry was a provincial initiative and criminal law is a federal responsibility), the inquiry chair, Justice Peter K. Richard, nevertheless sympathized with the difficulties of using the criminal law in this area and recommended that the federal government consider amendments to the *Criminal Code of Canada* to make corporate officials "properly accountable for workplace safety" (Richard 1997, 600–601). This recommendation eventually led to the enactment in March 2004 of *Criminal Code* legislation aimed at holding corporations accountable for serious injury and death in the workplace. Colloquially referred to as the Westray Bill, *Bill C-45, An Act to Amend the Criminal Code (criminal liability of organizations)*, imposes a legal duty for "all persons directing work to take reasonable steps to ensure the safety of workers and the public," attributes criminal liability to an "organization" if a senior officer knew or ought to have known about the offence, and introduces sentencing provisions specifically crafted for the organizational setting.

The Westray Bill was considered a significant development in assigning criminal responsibility to corporations for decisions and actions by representatives within the organization (a theoretically less burdensome requirement than the directing mind test; Archibald, Jull, and Roach 2004). Unfortunately, however, since the law took effect there have been only a handful of charges, two convictions, and one guilty plea—an enforcement record that hardly inspires claims of "getting tough" on corporate crime. What accounts for the lack of charges? Why are criminal justice officials not laying charges against employers who injure and/or kill workers?

In many respects, even before the Westray legislation took effect there were signs that safety crimes were not a criminal justice priority. First, unlike traditional street crimes where governments frequently and eagerly enact tough new measures, it took the federal government more than six years after the Westray inquiry report, and ten years after the disaster, before introducing the Westray Bill. What is more, in contemplating the introduction of corporate criminal liability legislation, many politicians, particularly those committed to law and order politics, were concerned with maintaining, as closely as possible, the idea that you needed a guilty mind in order to have a crime. As we have already seen, however, dominant notions of individual responsibility do not fit well with crimes committed in a corporate context. Legislators also expressed concern with the introduction of overly stringent laws that would unnecessarily impede the ability of corporations to make profits, and that some corporations might relocate outside of Canada if they perceived that they were being treated unfairly (Bittle 2012). Although these concerns did not prevent the

Westray Bill from being enacted, they nevertheless reflected a general hesitancy by legislators to criminalize corporations—a very different approach to crime control than what we commonly see with traditional street crimes.

A number of issues arising from the Westray Bill's enforcement shed further light on the view that safety crimes are not a criminal justice priority. First, many observers argue that there is poor knowledge of, and lack of interest in, this legislation among police and crown prosecutors (Bittle 2012). As Glasbeek (2002, 149) has noted, an ideological bias against criminalizing corporations and corporate actors "... saturates the efforts of the police forces, prosecutorial offices, and policy-making institutions." Second, none of the cases to date hold senior executives and board members to account and none have targeted large and complex corporations. Instead, guilty pleas and convictions have involved small, independent companies where there is little difficulty assigning criminal responsibility (Bittle 2013). For instance, in 2006, Transpavé, a small company in Quebec that manufactures concrete patio blocks, pled guilty to criminal negligence causing death and was ordered to pay a $100,000 fine after a machine that stacks concrete stones onto wooden pallets crushed a worker to death (Edwards and Conlin 2006). In 2011 the owner–operator of a small landscaping company was found guilty of criminal negligence causing death when the improperly maintained backhoe that he was operating pinned a worker against a wall, crushing him to death (Workers Health and Safety Centre 2011).

In 2012, Metron Construction, yet another small company, pleaded guilty to one charge of criminal negligence causing death after five of its workers plummeted thirteen floors when the swing stage scaffold that they were working on to repair the outside of a Toronto apartment building broke in half. Four of the workers were killed while a fifth suffered debilitating injuries (Keith 2011). Third, behind the Westray Bill's poor enforcement record is a regulatory context (as outlined earlier in this chapter) that approaches injury and death in the workplace as accidents (Glasbeek 2013). That is, the Westray Bill was introduced alongside (non-criminal) provincial workplace safety regulations, which in recent decades have been dominated by the belief that corporations will self-regulate under the influence of market forces and with some direction or persuasion from the state (Tombs and Whyte 2007). In practice this means that there are few incentives for police and Crown prosecutors to get involved in complex criminal proceedings when less complicated methods for responding to workplace "accidents" already exist (Glasbeek 2002).

As this last section reveals, criminal justice in relation to safety crimes in Canada remains largely underdeveloped. While the introduction of the Westray Bill has meant that some corporations have been, and will be, held accountable for their negligent killing of workers, the reality is that most incidences of workplace injury and death are seen as non-criminal, regulatory offences. Of course it is overly simplistic to suggest that criminal justice officials are solely responsible for the lack of interest in safety crimes; they are reinforcing broader societal beliefs that workplace injury and death are "accidents," not serious matters deserving of criminal justice attention. At the same time, however, this should not deny that choices made by governments and criminal justice officials to prioritize some crimes over others contributes to a distorted image of crime in society.

CONCLUSION: CRIMES WITHOUT OFFENDERS, VICTIMS WITHOUT A VOICE

This chapter has explored how criminal justice responses to safety crimes help reproduce a "distorted image" (Reiman 2004) of crime in Canada. In particular, it has demonstrated how the system of regulatory justice dominates the state's responses to safety crimes in the workplace, effectively downplaying their seriousness by treating them primarily as "accidents," not crimes of violence. Safety crimes are downplayed further by a criminal justice system that is unaccustomed to and/or uninterested in policing corporate wrongdoing. The state's unwillingness to use the criminal law in response to corporate wrongdoing persists despite the introduction of the Westray Bill. In the process, the criminal justice gaze remains fixed on traditional street crimes, therein reinforcing the belief that these are the "real" or only harms that require its attention.

The problems of workplace safety cannot be solved solely through criminal justice intervention. The nature and scope of workplace injury and death—including the structure of capitalist production and the relative worth of employees versus employers and shareholders—is too complicated for such a simple response. At the same time, however, the very principles of criminal justice are challenged and the seriousness of workplace injury and death is trivialized when criminal laws concerning safety crimes go unenforced. As Slapper (2013, 91) notes in reference to the lack of corporate manslaughter charges in the United Kingdom, "justice is mocked if an important law is unenforced." Questions will therefore continue to be raised about the fairness of criminal justice in Canada as long as negligent employers remain unpunished for killing workers.

Further Readings

Bittle, S. 2012. *Still Dying for a Living: Corporate Criminal Liability after the Westray Mine Disaster*. Vancouver: UBC Press.

Glasbeek, Harry. 2002. *Wealth by Stealth: Corporate Crime, Corporate Law, and the Perversion of Democracy*. Toronto: Between the Lines.

Reiman, J., and P. Leighton. 2012. *The Rich Get Richer and the Poor Get Prison: Ideology, Class and Criminal Justice*. 10th ed. London, UK: Pearson Publishing.

References

Archibald, T., K. Jull, and K. Roach. 2004. "The Changed Face of Corporate Criminal Liability." *The Criminal Law Quarterly* 48: 367–96.

Association of Workers' Compensation Boards of Canada. http://www.awcbc .org/en/statistics.asp, accessed February 15, 2014.

Bittle, S. 2012. *Still Dying for a Living: Corporate Criminal Liability after the Westray Mine Disaster.* Vancouver: UBC Press.

——— . 2013. "Cracking-Down on Corporate Crime? The Disappearance of Corporate Criminal Liability Legislation In Canada." *Policy and Practice in Health and Safety* 11, no. 2: 45–62.

Box, S. 1983. *Power, Crime and Mystification.* London: Tavistock.

Braithwaite, J. 1984. *Corporate Crime in the Pharmaceutical Industry.* Cambridge: Cambridge University Press.

——— . 1989. *Crime, Shame and Reintegration.* Cambridge: Cambridge University Press.

Cahill, S., and P. Cahill. 1999. "Scarlet Letters: Punishing the Corporate Citizen." *International Journal of the Sociology of Law* 27: 153–65.

Department of Justice Canada. 2002. *Corporate Criminal Liability: Discussion Paper.* Ottawa: Department of Justice Canada.

Drake, D., J. Muncie, and L. Westmarland. 2010. *Criminal Justice: Local and Global.* Devon, UK: Willan Publishing.

Edelhertz, H. 1970. *The Nature, Impact and Prosecution of White-Collar Crime.* Washington, DC: National Institute of Law Enforcement and Criminal Justice, Department of Justice.

Edwards C., and R. J. Conlin. 2006. "First Corporate Charged with Workplace Safety Crime Post Bill C-45." *OH&S Due Diligence Update.* Toronto, ON: Stringer Brisbin Humphrey, Management Lawyers.

Ferguson, C.H. 2012. *Predator Nation: Corporate Criminals, Political Corruption, and the Hijacking of America.* New York, NY: Crown Business.

Friedrichs, D.O. 2010. *Trusted Criminals: White Collar Crime in Contemporary Society.* Belmont, CA: Wadsworth Cengage Learning.

Garland, D. 2001. *The Culture of Control: Crime and Social Order in Contemporary Society.* Chicago: University of Chicago Press.

Gilks, J., and R. Logan. 2010. *Occupational Injuries and Diseases in Canada, 1996–2008.* Ottawa: Human Resources and Skills Development Canada.

Glasbeek, H. 2002. *Wealth by Stealth: Corporate Crime, Corporate Law, and the Perversion of Democracy.* Toronto: Between the Lines.

—— . 2004. "Enron and Its Aftermath: Can Reforms Restore Confidence?" In A.I. Anand, J.A. Connidis, and W.F. Flannagan, eds., *Crime in the Corporation*. Queen's Annual Business Law Symposium 2004. Queen's University, Kingston, Ontario, Canada.

—— . 2007. "The Corporation as a Legally Created Site of Irresponsibility." In Henry N. Pontell and Gilbert Geis, eds., *International Handbook of White-Collar and Corporate Crime*. New York, NY: Springer.

—— . 2013. "Missing the Targets: Bill C-45 Reforming the Status Quo to Maintain the Status Quo." *Policy and Practice in Health and Safety* 11, no. 2: 9–23.

Green, G.S. 1990. *Occupational Crime*. Chicago: Nelson Hall.

Keith N. 2011. "Regulators Gone Wild! OHS and Criminal Charges Laid in Christmas Eve Scaffolding Deaths." *Canadian Occupational Safety 2011* 8, no. 6 (December/January).

McMullan, J. 1992. *Beyond the Limits of the Law: Corporate Crime and Law and Order*. Halifax: Fernwood Publishing.

McMullan, J. 2001. "Westray and After: Power, Truth and News Reporting of the Westray Mine Disaster." In Susan Boyd, Dorothy E. Chunn, and Robert Menzies, eds., *[Ab]Using Power: The Canadian Experience*. Halifax, Nova Scotia: Fernwood Publishing.

McMullan, J. 2005. *News, Truth and Crime: The Westray Disaster and Its Aftermath*. Halifax, Nova Scotia: Fernwood Publishing.

Nicholls, C. 2005. *Corporate Law*. Toronto: Emond Montgomery.

Noble, C. 1995. "Regulating Work in a Capitalist Society." In F. Pearce and L. Snider, eds., *Corporate Crime: Contemporary Debates*. Toronto: University of Toronto Press.

Pearce, F. 1976. *Crimes of the Powerful: Marxism, Crime and Deviance*. London: Pluto Press.

Pearce, F., and S. Snider, eds. 1995. *Corporate Crime: Contemporary Debates*. Toronto: University of Toronto Press.

Reiman, J. 2004. *The Rich Get Richer and the Poor Get Prison*. 7th ed. London, UK: Pearson Publishing.

Richard, Justice Peter K. 1997. *The Westray Story: A Predictable Path to Disaster*. Report of the Westray Mine Public Inquiry. Justice K. Peter Richard, Commissioner. Province of Nova Scotia.

Salinger, eds., *White-Collar Crime, Classic and Contemporary Views*. New York: The Free Press, 1995, 29–38.

——. 1949. *White Collar Crime. The Uncut Version.* New Haven: Yale University Press.

Sharpe, A., and J. Hardt. 2006. *Five Deaths a Day: Workplace Fatalities in Canada: 1993–2005.* Centre for the Study of Living Standards. Research Paper 2006-04. Ottawa, ON.

Simon, David R., and D. Stanley Eitzen. 1986. *Elite Deviance.* Toronto: Allyn and Bacon.

Simpson, S. 2002. *Corporate Crime, Law and Social Control.* Cambridge University Press.

Slapper, G. 2013. "Justice is Mocked if an Important Law is Unenforced." *The Journal of Criminal Law* 77: 91–4.

Slapper, G., and S. Tombs. 1999. *Corporate Crime.* Essex, UK: Pearson Education Limited.

Snider, L. 1993. *Bad Business: Corporate Crime in Canada.* Toronto: Nelson Canada.

——. 2000. "The Sociology of Corporate Crime: An Obituary (or: Whose Knowledge Claims Have Legs?)" *Theoretical Criminology* 4, no. 2: 196–206.

Statistics Canada. 2006. *The Daily: Homicides.* http://www.statcan.gc.ca/daily-quotidien/061108/dq061108b-eng.htm, accessed February 15, 2014.

Stone, A. 1982. *Regulation and Its Alternatives.* Washington, DC: Congressional Quarterly Press.

Stretesky, P.B., M.A Long, and M.J. Lynch. 2014. *The Treadmill of Crime: Political Economy and Green Criminology.* London and New York: Routledge.

Sutherland, E. 1940. "White Collar Criminality." Reprinted in G. Geis, R.F. Meier, and L.M.

Tillman, R.H., and M.L. Indergaard. 2005. *Pump and Dump: The Rancid Rules of the New Economy.* New Brunswick: Rutgers University Press.

Tombs, S., and D. Whyte. 2007. *Safety Crimes.* Cullompton: Willan Publishing.

Wells, C. 1993. *Corporations and Criminal Responsibility.* Oxford: Clarendon.

Workers Health and Safety Centre. *Worker Death Leads to the Second C-45 Conviction.* http://www.whsc.on.ca/whatnews2.cfm?autoid=663, accessed May 20, 2011.

Yalden, R., P.D. Paton, R. Davis, J. Sarra, M. Gillen, and M. Condon. 2008. *Business Organizations: Principles, Policies and Practice.* Toronto, ON: Emond Montgomery Publications Ltd.

CHAPTER 26

Domestic Violence and Mandatory Criminal Justice Interventions: Re-Evaluating the Zero Tolerance Approach

Domestic violence is one of the most pressing problems confronting all contemporary societies. How should the criminal justice system respond to this pernicious form of violence? One of the most controversial criminal justice strategies consists of a mandatory charge policy. Mandatory charging requires police officers to lay charges in all instances of domestic violence where there is evidence to suggest an assault has occurred, regardless of whether the victim wants to press charges or not. This chapter explores this much-discussed response to the problem of domestic violence.

Rashmee Singh
University of Waterloo

DOMESTIC VIOLENCE AND THE CRIMINAL JUSTICE SYSTEM

I first met Cynthia over a decade ago while working as an Assistant Coordinator for the Victim Witness Assistance Program (VWAP) in an Ontario provincial courthouse, a position I held for several years prior to pursuing my academic career. Cynthia was a victim in a domestic violence case involving her husband. As a front-line victim service provider, my primary role at VWAP involved ensuring that victims of sexual, domestic, and child abuse were provided with ongoing information about their cases, trial preparation, safety planning, referrals to shelters, emotional support, and general assistance with navigating the criminal justice system. One of my routine responsibilities to accomplish these goals was to phone victims prior to their partners' appearances in bail court. Grabbing the stack of Crown briefs from my inbox, I began each morning with a review of my cases, focusing specifically on the police synopsis of the incident, a document that ranged anywhere between a few sentences to several pages, depending upon the details victims provided about the violence they had experienced. Although I had reviewed hundreds throughout my years at the VWAP, the four-page document of Cynthia's experience was the only one I had ever read that literally sent chills down my spine.

Cynthia's case was nowhere near the most brutal or gory incident of violence that I had come across while working as a victim advocate. However, what made it stand out for me were the extreme shows of power and control that she was subjected to by her husband, the rituals of which she relayed in explicit detail to the officer in charge of her case. I phoned Cynthia immediately and proceeded to do so every morning for each of the 30 days that her partner was held in custody without bail, an unusually harsh measure for the courts for a first-time offender with no known criminal record for domestic violence. During our many phone calls, Cynthia discussed the deterioration of her marriage since her family's migration to Canada. The demise, she explained, was largely triggered by her husband's inability to continue working in his profession due to the lack of recognition of his credentials in Canada, a systemic crisis now experienced by the vast majority of migrants in the country. Cynthia's relative success in the job market and fluency in English, she surmised, heightened her husband's sense of inferiority and his need to enforce his dominance over her. After expressing my concerns to her about her husband, as well as those of the courts, I asked whether she intended to stay with him. Holding on to her memories of their life back home, where physical violence had not been an issue in their relationship, she expressed a desire to reconcile. She believed the abuse was circumstantial and that the problem could be resolved through a combination of counselling and employment assistance.

At the end of the 30-day period, Cynthia's husband was released from jail after pleading guilty to his crime. In preparation for the drafting of his probation order, I forwarded Cynthia's input to the courts. As is routine in domestic violence cases, when victims choose to reconcile, Crown prosecutors replace conditions preventing accused persons from contacting victims with a revised condition enabling complainants to have contact with their partners with their "written revocable consent." The condition allows victims to withdraw their consent for contact at any time, in the event that the abuse continues.

After receiving a copy of her husband's probation order, I phoned Cynthia to explain his conditions to her. Along with several measures the courts imposed to ensure the system could keep a watchful eye on Cynthia's husband, the court order also required that he attend a 16-week domestic violence counselling program and report to his probation officer at least once a week. These conditions were the most the court could do at this stage of the legal process to ensure Cynthia's safety. Once a domestic violence case is resolved and the victim chooses to reconcile, the criminal justice system possesses limited ability to detain abusers.

On the day he was released, Cynthia's husband did not check in with his probation officer as ordered. Instead, he went straight home and, according to the police report, stabbed Cynthia repeatedly with a butcher knife. He then phoned the police to report his crime. When the officers attended the scene, Cynthia had already passed away as a result of her injuries. The police immediately returned her husband to custody. Although we all knew we had done our best for her, all of us—the two Crown prosecutors involved in the case, the officers in charge, and I— were still plagued by overwhelming feelings of shock and grief.

Cynthia's tragic death embodies the array of complexities and conundrums that incidents of domestic violence pose for the criminal justice system. These prosecutorial dilemmas stem from a number of factors unique to these crimes that make it very difficult for the legal system to ensure the safety of victims without compromising their autonomy. The ongoing relationship between the accused and victim is by far the most significant complication for the prosecution process. The criminal justice system assumes that both parties are not only strangers but also adversaries. However, as the discussion above illustrates, in domestic violence cases, victims and abusers are partners and couples leading intertwined lives. The reality of domestic violence is that in the vast majority of cases—although all victims undoubtedly want the abuse and violence to stop—women do not want their relationships to end. For a multitude of reasons, leaving is simply not always the only, best, and preferred decision for many victims.

Despite this reality, many may ask, are there ever any instances where the criminal justice system should override what victims want in order to ensure their safety? Having just learned about Cynthia's case, one might be tempted to embrace the view that courts should override victims' wishes. However, when we observe some of the reasons why abused women stay, they are as distinct as they are legitimate. For instance, victims often do not want to prevent their children from seeing their fathers. While many question the potential of abusers to be good fathers, the reality is that the well-being and lives of children are emotionally and materially intertwined with their parents. In addition, victims and offenders are almost always financially dependent on each other. Victims may thus require their partner's assistance to pay bills, buy food, get child care, or make rent or mortgage payments. The legal system, with its inherently adversarial approach, does not always consider these factors.

THE ZERO TOLERANCE APPROACH TO DOMESTIC VIOLENCE

The complexities just discussed all come to the fore in one of the most controversial criminal justice strategies to emerge in recent years to address the problem of domestic violence: the mandatory charge policy. *Mandatory charging*, also referred to as the *zero tolerance* approach, directs police officers to lay charges in all instances of domestic violence where there is evidence to suggest an assault has occurred, regardless of whether the victim wants to press charges or not. Given that corroborating evidence, such as physical injuries, is not always present, a victim's statement alone can suffice as evidence for the occurrence of abuse. Mandatory charging works in tandem with "aggressive" or "no drop" prosecution strategies, which operate at the level of the courts. These directives essentially prevent Crown prosecutors from dropping charges, even if victims are reluctant to pursue them. Ultimately, these policies remove discretion from all those involved in domestic violence cases, including victims, police officers, and prosecutors. Regardless of whether one is critical or supportive of the policies, there is no debating the fact that from the perspectives of victims, mandatory criminal justice intervention results in the transferring of power from the abusers to the legal system. While some abused women do in fact welcome the legal system making some very difficult decisions for them, many do not.

Given how disempowering mandatory charge and "no drop" prosecution strategies can be for abused women, the fact that these policies were initially a feminist intervention designed to help victims might come as a surprise to many. However, understanding the evolution of aggressive domestic violence prosecution strategies and their differential effects on victims illuminates an array of broader issues worth exploring when assessing the pros and cons of relying on the law more generally as a strategy to assist abused women. The issue also illuminates important divides within feminist legal theory around the possibilities and pitfalls of using the criminal justice system to address violence against women. In relaying the history of mandatory charging and prosecution, this chapter will address the following questions: Why did feminist legal reformers design an intervention that ultimately prevents victims from making their own decisions with regards to pursuing charges against their abusers? Does mandatory charging protect abused women or disempower them? Are better criminal justice strategies that guarantee protection without depriving victims of choice *possible*? To find answers, we need to first examine the social and political context in which feminist reformers involved in the battered women's movement were working. Then, we will explore the effects of the policy.

JUST LIKE ANY OTHER CRIME? DOMESTIC VIOLENCE AND THE MANDATORY CHARGE POLICY

Legal responses to domestic violence carry symbolic meaning and are intertwined with varying understandings of both the causes and solutions to the problem (Gordon 1988; Weiner 2006). Ultimately, the state and legal responses to the issue largely depend on how the problem is defined and who is defining it. Although the first Canadian laws on domestic violence emerged in the early 19th century initially under Section 292 of the *Criminal Code*, overall, the laws governing the crime were inconsistently enforced up until the mid-1970s (Martin and Mosher 1995). The critical factor in instigating the change was the advent of the Battered Women's Movement (BWM) and the increased attention to violence against women that resulted from the efforts of feminist advocates. For those involved in the movement, the abuse women endured in the private sphere of the home—and its general neglect by the police and courts—emerged as a central agenda item for improving the status of women in society. In arguing that the "personal is political," advocates in the BWM worked to draw attention to the incidence and prevalence of the problem, and the various ways in which the neglect of the issue harmed all women in society.

While advocates did not always agree on how to reform criminal justice responses to domestic violence, all were united over the fact that attitudes towards the problem—both in law enforcement and in society more generally—needed to change. One large hurdle that BWM advocates encountered in their advocacy efforts were the attitudes and institutional practices of the police. Studies on police culture (e.g., Buzawa and Buzawa 2003) highlight the longstanding neglect of domestic violence in many jurisdictions due to prevailing understandings of the crime as a "private" or family matter. As a result, a favoured police response was to encourage abusers and victims to resolve matters on their own and to refrain from laying charges. Consequently, officers rarely laid charges, and in those instances where they did, cases rarely made it through the prosecution process. These systemic deficiencies called into question the abilities of police officers to offer effective support to abused women.

The institutional responses to violence against women at the time were largely interwoven with and a reflection of larger social attitudes towards the issue. Although victim blaming is a problem that persists today, between 1950 and 1970, during a period known as the *privatization era*, abused women were often believed to have done something to "deserve" the violence they experienced. Victims were regularly stereotyped as alcoholics, irrational, or overly emotional, and just ill adjusted in general (Martin and Mosher 1995;

MacLeod 1980). Assumptions that abused women provoke violence also frequently influenced police decision making. In her review of studies conducted on police perceptions of domestic violence victims, Hilton (1993) found that officers often believed that abuse and violence were justified, if women had been unfaithful.

The systemic oversights, not surprisingly, resulted in devastating consequences. Throughout the late 1970s and the 1980s, a string of domestic homicides in the United States resulted in several class action suits against the police for failing to effectively respond to 911 calls from victims (Buzawa and Buzawa 2003). In response, the American arm of the BWM began experimenting with mandated criminal justice policies that considered the removal of police discretion when officers investigated incidents of domestic violence. Battered women's advocates in Canada launched similar campaigns. In the early 1980s, Canadian feminists instigated reform efforts aimed to convince the federal government of the importance of consistent and effective criminal justice responses to domestic violence.

Anti-violence activists advocated for mandatory charging for several reasons, the key reason being the removal of police discretion. As one might expect, feminist reformers did not trust the police to make appropriate decisions about domestic violence. In addition, just as important to the movement were the symbolic effects of aggressive criminal justice interventions. For liberal feminist strategists, who considered the law an essential tool in ensuring women's equality, effective criminal justice responses were critical to sending out the message that domestic violence was "just like any other crime"; criminalizing and enforcing the laws would send a serious message that domestic violence was intolerable. Given the social context at the time, which was laced with a general permissiveness towards wife abuse, many argued that changing social norms could not occur without a consistent and punitive criminal justice response to domestic violence. According to MacLeod (1980), laws possess "considerable influence in shaping the values of society.... When these values are in question, the law must also be put under scrutiny" (MacLeod 1980, 42). Thus, along with assisting—and possibly saving the lives of—individual victims, it was also assumed that mandatory criminal justice responses could also benefit "women as a whole."

While removing police discretion in the investigation of domestic violence incidents was not so problematic from the perspectives of feminist legal reformers, removing victim discretion was far more controversial. As noted earlier, mandatory charging and prosecution policies do not allow victims to withdraw charges once they have been laid. Proponents of these interventions cite the very real dynamics of abusive relationships as the rationale for such coercive measures. Women are often pressured by their partners, as well as family members, to drop charges; for abused women who would like to proceed with the prosecution of their cases, their removal from the decision making process is a welcome relief (MacLeod 1980; Landau 2000; Hannah 1996). Some go as far as to suggest that abused women are simply not capable of making "reasoned" arrest decisions when they are in the midst of prosecuting their cases (Wanless 1996), which is a far more problematic assumption. Nonetheless, advocates in the BWM who supported mandatory charging and prosecution genuinely believed that the removal of victim discretion would ultimately benefit all abused women and, in the most severe cases, save lives.

THE INCORPORATION OF ZERO TOLERANCE APPROACHES TO DOMESTIC VIOLENCE

Along with feminist campaigns, academic and community-based research on the policing of domestic violence played a critical role in the eventual adoption of mandatory criminal justice intervention. The research conducted by the London Coordinating Committee on Family Violence (LCCFV) in particular is cited as a key factor in the eventual development and implementation of a federal directive recommending mandatory charging and prosecution in all domestic violence cases (Hilton 1988; Hilton 1993; Department of Justice 2005). The LCCFV initiated a review of police responses in domestic violence cases throughout several divisions in London, Ontario, in 1981. The study uncovered significant systemic oversight and neglect; specifically, it found that that police arrested abusers only in less than 3 percent of cases, despite the fact that in close to 20 percent of the cases reviewed, the victims required medical attention (Jaffe et al. 1993). The findings of the LCCFV project generated significant concern within the London Police Department; consequently, in 1981, the city's police force implemented the country's first mandatory charge policy (Hilton 1988). The London Police Force's model for responding to domestic violence would soon become the favoured approach for the rest of Canada.

Although the idea of mandatory charging was initially ridiculed in Parliament in May of 1982, by July of the same year, the federal Ministry of the Solicitor General endorsed the policy and issued directives to both the Canadian Association of Chiefs of Police and the Royal Canadian Mounted Police (RCMP) to develop and incorporate it into routine police practice (Jaffe et al. 1993). By 1986, the Canadian government issued several federal directives to police and Crown Prosecutors emphasizing the importance of treating domestic violence "just like any other crime." In ensuring this commitment, prosecutors were advised to proceed with all cases in which police laid charges, "in all but the most exceptional circumstances" (Department of Justice 2005, 101). Finally, the directives emphasize the importance of removing victim discretion from the prosecution process in order to "remove the responsibility and blame from pressing charges on women, who often fear retaliation" (Department of Justice 2005, 101).

Although enforcement varies municipally, currently, all Canadian provinces deploy mandatory charging and prosecution policies, or some variation of them, in their efforts to address domestic violence. In Ontario, the policy is outlined in Section 17 of the *Ontario Policing Standards* (2000) manual. The document advises that officers should "explain to both the victims and the suspect that it is their duty to lay a charge when there are reasonable grounds to believe that an offence has been committed, and that only a Crown [prosecutor] can withdraw charges" (Ontario Ministry of the Solicitor General 2000, 7). Additional portions of the policy outline the conditions under which officers are required to lay charges and emphasize the necessity of overriding victims' wishes when laying charges. British Columbia's most recent *Crown Counsel Policy Manual* provides comprehensive guidelines to prosecutors around assessing whether or not enough evidence is present in domestic violence cases to pursue prosecution.

The document advises that lower evidentiary requirements are in effect when reviewing cases for their reasonable prospects of conviction and whether or not pursuing prosecution is in the public interest. Prosecutors are also reminded that decisions about how to address cases should "not be determined solely by the victim's wishes" (British Columbia Ministry of Justice 2013). Similarly, in Quebec and New Brunswick, police and Crown policy manuals direct charges to be laid and pursued when there is reasonable evidence supporting a claim of assault, regardless of whether victims wish to pursue charges. In these provinces, decisions to lay charges rest with the Crown prosecutor (Department of Justice 2005).

The institutionalization of mandatory charge and aggressive prosecution policies is generally perceived to be a success story for feminist legal reformers advocating for a more punitive and consistent criminal justice response to domestic violence. The transformation of domestic violence into an offense that should be taken seriously by law enforcement, rather than ignored, is certainly critical to ensuring the protection of victims entangled in abusive relationships. In addition, the assumptions upon which these interventions are based do in fact resonate with the experiences of many victims who are looking for a way out of their abusive relationships but are too afraid to pursue charges against their abusers. However, what happens when victims do not want to pursue charges against their partners or proceed with the prosecution process? As noted earlier, while all abused women want the violence in their relationships to stop, not all, for many legitimate reasons, want to end their relationships. Having just reviewed how mandatory criminal justice prosecution policies work in theory, the remaining sections of the chapter will examine these interventions in their living social context with reference to how they impact women in abusive relationships.

IMPACT OF MANDATORY CHARGE AND AGGRESSIVE PROSECUTION STRATEGIES

To truly appreciate the real impacts of these policies, it is first important to consider the legal contexts in which they transpire, and the daily realities of the criminal justice system. As is the case in most large urban jurisdictions, in

Toronto's provincial courthouses, prosecutions of domestic violence can take anywhere between a month to a year to be resolved, depending on case back-logs, and whether or not an accused wants to take his matter to trial. Cases addressed via pleas of guilt are resolved far quicker than those taken to trial. On average, in busy courthouses, cases heading to trial will likely take nine months to address, while to resolve cases in which an accused decides to plead guilty could range from as little as a week to three months.

Given that most people are unaware of mandatory charging, rarely are they prepared for the consequences when they call the police. Mandatory charging results in the abrupt removal of offenders from the household as a result of a "no contact" bail condition, which is immediately put into effect as soon as the police arrest an accused. The "no contact" bail condition ren-ders all communication and contact between the accused person and victim a criminal offense; thus, even if a victim initiates contact, or the two require some form of interaction to address, for example, child-care issues, the accused can be arrested if the authorities become aware of the communication. In addition, the abrupt removal of abusers means that victims are often left in a panic, trying to find ways to pay their rent or mortgage. Meanwhile, the added expense of additional rent when an accused moves out of the household may result in further financial difficulties for victims. Given that an accused and victim could potentially be separated for almost a year, financially, the pros-ecution process can wreak havoc on the lives of abused women.

In addition, consider a case where a victim phoned the police because she feared she was in immediate danger, yet did not want to testify against the accused or proceed with the prosecution process, either because she was too afraid or simply did not want to endure it. If the accused takes the matter to trial, the reluctant victim could be forced to testify since subpoenas are court orders. In these situations—which are far more the norm than Cynthia's case described above—the victim experiences criminal justice intervention as an extremely coercive force in her life. Whether or not the court is helping her is not entirely clear; lacking all say or autonomy in how her case should proceed, the power is simply transferred from the abuser to the system. The common denominator in both scenarios—her relationship and the criminal justice system—is her powerlessness.

ABUSED WOMEN'S PERCEPTIONS OF AGGRESSIVE CRIMINAL JUSTICE INTERVENTIONS

To date, the research on abused women's experiences with mandatory arrest and "no drop" prosecution strategies illuminates the expected divisions and a general lack of consensus over whether these policies help or harm women: unsurprisingly, while some experienced these interventions as extreme coer-cion, others considered them a saving grace. For those who fall in the former category, the court system perpetuates their re-victimization and deprives them of the ability to influence the court process. Clearly, the one-size-fits-all approach inevitable in any legal response does not work for victims who deviate from the system's typical image of an abused woman. The issue of *who* these laws work for becomes even more complicated—and controversial— when we consider the structural backgrounds of the women these interventions tend to disempower the most.

Overall, the research examining abused women's perceptions of mandatory criminal justice interventions indicates general support for mandatory charging, but extreme dissatisfaction with "no drop" prosecution policies. For example, Landau (2000) found that abused women distinguish between phoning the police for immediate assistance and taking their partners to court. Consequently, many experience "additional anxiety, frustration and disempowerment as a direct result of the strategy" (Landau 2000, 141). Landau's findings, based on interviews with 94 women, reveal these important distinctions. Of the 75 percent of women who phoned the police for assistance, most advised that they did so because they feared for their lives and wanted the police to stop the violence. Others phoned police out of concern for their children. When Landau asked her interviewees what they had hoped would occur when the police attended their homes, 30 percent acknowledged that they wanted the police to remove their spouses from their homes, and 15 percent indicated that they wanted officers to charge their partners. About the same percentage wanted officers to warn their partners and stop the assault (Landau 2000, 147). When asked directly about whether they wanted the police to charge their partners, 60 percent advised that they did. The remainder of the sample, however, did not want this outcome.

First-hand accounts from abused women illustrate the coercion they experienced during the criminal justice process poignantly. When Landau asked her interviewees to remark on their experiences with "no drop" prosecution strategies, a number of women expressed how completely overlooked, forgotten, and steamrolled they felt by the police and crown prosecutors involved in their cases. Some women also stated that prosecutors appeared to be disgusted with them for not wanting to prosecute their partners. The following quote is illustrative:

> "They should have listened to me more—show a little respect and consideration for me ... they didn't ever ask me (about issuing a no-contact order), they just did it anyway." (Landau 2000, 149)

These accounts demonstrate how traumatic mandatory arrest and prosecution policies can be if victims possess different ideas from the criminal justice system about how to address their cases.

In contrast to these narratives, a number of women in Landau's study did express support for aggressive criminal justice strategies. These stories are also important to consider. Some abused women welcomed the fact that the law essentially "did the thinking for them." In these cases, victims advised feeling extremely conflicted about how to address their cases, and appreciated that the decision-making process was entirely out of their hands. Abused women who supported the policy were adamant about the importance of removing victim discretion:

> "Women aren't in the right state of mind to make that decision (to charge) … they have other things on their minds. The law does the thinking for you." (Landau: 2000, 148)

These contrasting narratives illuminate the drastically different experiences with and perspectives on mandatory arrest and prosecution strategies among abused women. Ultimately, whether or not these policies help or harm women have much to do with, not surprisingly, whether victims actually want their partners to be charged, prosecuted, and punished. However, a number of additional factors come into play when we consider the potentially detrimental effects of these policies on abused women. As Martin and Mosher (1995) note, the potential for harm that is associated with zero tolerance approaches to domestic violence is not "evenly distributed" among women; rather, studies illuminate that "it is racial minority women, poor women and immigrant women who are likely to be exposed to the greatest risk of harm" (Martin and Mosher 1995, 35).

Case studies on the effects of aggressive domestic violence strategies on migrant women illustrate these points well. Mandatory arrest and prosecution strategies render abused migrant women far more vulnerable than Canadian-born victims for a variety of reasons. One of the most significant factors is a lack of, or uncertain, legal status. For example, victims with precarious legal status often do not want the criminal justice system involved in their cases for fear of jeopardizing their prospects of obtaining permanent residence in Canada (Martin and Mosher 1995; Singh 2010). In addition, zero tolerance strategies are often more detrimental to abused migrant women, given their lack of social and family supports (Menjivar and Salcido 2002; Smith 2005). Migrant victims are far more isolated than the majority of Canadian-born victims; consequently, the unplanned removal of partners from their homes will be far more difficult to endure. Abused immigrant women likely have fewer people in their lives to rely on in the event of financial emergencies or other crises (Wachholz and Miedmea 2000). Recent studies on immigrant women's experiences with aggressive criminal justice strategies show that poverty is a very real concern for migrant victims when they lose financial support or contributions provided by their partners for their mortgages and rent (Martin and Mosher 1995). Finally, finding additional employment as a way to cope with the sudden loss of financial resources will also be a far greater struggle for abused migrant women than victims who possess the benefits of citizenship. The failure of Canadian employers and professional associations to recognize credentials and professional experience obtained outside the country is now widely known (Bauder 2003; Girard and Bauder 2007). In addition, language barriers, discriminatory hiring practices, and systemic racism create additional obstacles for abused immigrant women to obtain jobs and the financial resources required to make ends meet. These realities remind us that when assessing whether or not these policies are a good idea, we need to consider the structural backgrounds of the women involved and the systemic barriers they confront, in addition to the wishes of individual victims.

CONCLUSION

I began this chapter with Cynthia's tragic story to illuminate the tremendous difficulties, complications, and risks associated with the policing and prosecution of domestic violence. The key point this analysis of the mandatory charge and aggressive prosecution strategies illuminates is that when it comes to domestic violence, one size clearly does not fit all. For victims who feel far too traumatized by their experiences to exercise discretion over their cases, mandatory arrest and prosecution strategies are undoubtedly helpful. However, for those who struggle with poverty, lack the protection and benefits afforded to those with full citizenship, do not have extensive social and familial supports, or who simply do not want to proceed with the prosecution process, zero tolerance approaches cause more harm than good. While liberal feminist reformers who advocated for zero tolerance strategies in the first place had the best interests of domestic violence victims in mind, they overlooked the facts that not *all* abused women experience violence similarly, nor do they all view the police and prosecutors as their protectors.

However, as Cynthia's case—as well as the numerous domestic homicides and cases of domestic violence that occur throughout North America— reminds us, domestic violence remains a serious and pressing social problem. Thus, returning to the practices of the privatization era, where the police and the courts largely ignored or excused violence against women, is absolutely not the answer. One potential solution to the dilemma is to retain mandatory charging, but to abolish the "no drop" policy to allow victims to exercise choice and discretion in the prosecution of their cases. Reforming aggressive criminal justice strategies in this way could ensure that abused women continue to receive the potentially life-saving assistance they require from the police if they are in high-risk situations, while also allowing them to determine the best course of action based of their needs, as well as the needs of their families.

Although it does not lead us to conclusive answers for the reasons and complexities described above, qualitatively examining how the mandatory charging and prosecution policies impact victims is the best mechanism for determining whether or not the intervention assists abused women. However, just as important are questions of whether zero tolerance strategies accomplish the principles of specific and general deterrence. Studies examining both processes have yet to provide conclusive results. While Sherman and Berk's (1984) study argued that arrest does prevent offenders from engaging in further violence and therefore, accomplishes the objective of specific deterrence, due to difficulties in tracking recidivism and other methodological issues, this finding is now questioned. The key problem in attempting to determine whether abusers re-offend following arrest is that indicators of recidivism are largely dependent upon the reporting of incidents, a problem that Sherman and Berk (1984) and many follow-up studies encounter in their research designs. As can be conjectured from what we know about victims' experiences with the strategy, abused women will not always report further violence to the police, particularly if they were unhappy with mandatory criminal justice intervention in the first place. In addition, some studies indicate that mandatory arrest can exacerbate violence if the abuser already has a criminal record (Hirschel and Hutchison 1992). Unemployment appears to exert a similar effect (Sherman, Schmidt, Rogan, Smith, Gartin, Cohn, et al. 1992). Overall, additional research is required to determine whether or not mandatory arrest and prosecution policies actually deter domestic violence in our society.

Further Readings

Epstein, D., M.E. Bell, and L.A. Goodman. (2003). "Transforming Aggressive Prosecution Policies: Prioritizing Victims' Long-Term Safety in the Prosecution of Domestic Violence Cases." *Journal of Gender, Social Policy and the Law* 11, no. 2: 465–98.

Mills, L.G. 1999. "Killing Her Softly: Intimate Abuse and the Violence of State Intervention." *Harvard Law Review* 113, no. 2: 550–613.

References

Bauder, H. 2003. "'Brain Abuse,' or the Devaluation of Immigrant Labour in Canada." *Antipode* 35, no. 4: 699–717.

British Columbia Ministry of Justice. 2013. *Crown Counsel Policy Manual.* http://www.ag.gov.bc.ca/prosecution-service/policy-man/pdf/SPO1-SpousalViolence.pdf, accessed April 28, 2014.

Buzawa, E., and C. Buzawa. 2003. *Domestic Violence: The Criminal Justice Response.* Thousand Oaks, CA: Sage.

Department of Justice Canada. 2005. *Final Report of the Ad-Hoc Federal-Provincial-Territorial Working Group Reviewing Spousal Abuse Policies and Legislation.* http://www.publications.gc.ca/site/eng/260385/publication .html, accessed April 29, 2014.

Girard, E.R., and H. Bauder. 2007. "Assimilation and Exclusion of Foreign Trained Engineers in Canada: Inside a Professional Regulatory Organization." *Antipode* 39, no. 1: 35–53.

Gordon, L. 1988. *Heroes of Their Own Lives: The Politics and History of Family Violence.* New York: Viking.

Hanna, C. 1996. "No Right to Choose: Mandated Victim Participation in Domestic Violence Prosecutions." *Harvard Law Review* 109, no. 8: 1857–1909.

Hilton, N.Z. 1988. "One in Ten: The Struggle and Disempowerment of the Battered Women's Movement." *Canadian Journal of Family and the Law* 7: 313–36.

——. 1993. "Police Intervention and Public Opinion." In Hilton, ed., *Legal Responses to Wife Assault: Current Trends and Evaluation*. Newbury Park, CA: Sage.

Hirschel, J.D., and I.W. Hutchison. 1992. "Female Spouse Abuse and the Police Response: The Charlotte, North Carolina Experiment." *Journal of Criminal Law and Criminology* 83, no. 1: 73–119.

Jaffe, P.G., E. Hastings, D. Reitzel, and G.W. Austin. 1993. "The Impact of Police Laying Charges." In Hilton, ed., *Legal Responses to Wife Assault: Current Trends and Evaluation*. Newbury Park, CA: Sage.

Landau, T. 2000. "Women's Experiences with Mandatory Charging for Wife Assault in Ontario: A Case against the Prosecution." *International Review of Victimology* 7: 141–57.

MacLeod, L. 1980. *Wife Battering in Canada: The Vicious Circle*. Ottawa: The Canadian Advisory Council on the Status of Women.

Martin, D.L., and J. Mosher. 1995. "Unkept Promises: Experiences of Immigrant Women with the Neo-Criminalization of Wife Abuse." *Canadian Journal of Women and the Law* 8: 3–44.

Menjivar, C., and O. Salcido. 2002. "Immigrant Women and Domestic Violence: Common Experiences in Different Countries." *Gender and Society* 16, no. 6: 898–920.

Ministry of the Solicitor General. 2000. *Ontario Policing Standards Manual*. Toronto: Queen's Printer for Ontario.

Sherman, L.W., and R.A. Berk. 1984. "The Specific Deterrent Effects of Arrest for Domestic Assault." *American Sociological Review* 49, no. 2: 261–72.

Sherman, L.W., J.D. Schmidt, D.P. Rogan, and D.A. Smith. 1992. "Variable Effects of Arrest on Criminal Careers: The Milwaukee Domestic Violence Experiment." *The Journal of Criminal Law & Criminology* 83, no. 1: 137.

Singh, R. 2010. "In-Between the System and the Margins: Community Organizations, Mandatory Charging and Immigrant Victims of Abuse." *Canadian Journal of Sociology* 35, no. 1: 31–62.

Smith, E. 2004. *Nowhere to Turn? Responding to Partner Violence against Immigrant and Visible Minority Women*. Ottawa: Canadian Council of Social Development.

Strauss, M., R. Gelles, and S. Steinmetz. 1980. *Behind Closed Doors: Violence in the American Family*. New York: Anchor Books.

Wachholz, S., and M. Baukje. 2000. "Risk, Fear, Harm: Immigrant Women's Perceptions of the 'Policing Solution' to Woman Abuse." *Crime, Law and Social Change* 34, no. 3: 301–17.

Wanless, M. 1996. "Mandatory Arrest: A Step Towards Eradicating Domestic Violence, but Is It Enough?" *University of Illinois Law Review* 2: 533–87.

Wiener, M. 2006. *Men of Blood: Violence, Manliness and Criminal Justice in Victorian England*. Cambridge: Cambridge University.

Prisoners' Rights in Canada

Imprisonment is generally reserved for offenders convicted of the most serious crimes. Offenders sentenced to the longer periods of custody—two years or more—serve their time in a federal penitentiary. The federal correctional system therefore houses the most serious offenders in the criminal justice system in Canada. How should these offenders be treated? Does the fact that they have been convicted of the most serious offences in the *Criminal Code* mean they should be deprived of many of the rights that law-abiding Canadians enjoy? In this chapter, the author reviews the rights that prisoners have and identifies the reasons why these rights should exist.

Shereen H. Benzvy Miller
M.A., LL.B.

Canada's *Criminal Code* defines hundreds of actions as crimes because they have offended public values to a degree deemed sufficient to justify criminalization. Offenders convicted of the most serious offences can be sentenced to long periods of custody. What kind of treatment can an offender expect if sentenced to serve a term of imprisonment? Do (or should) prisoners lose all their rights? Should they lose any rights—for example, the right to hold citizenship or to vote in elections? Why should we care about people who have harmed others and who have offended against our values?

Winston Churchill said: "The mood and temper of the public in regard to the treatment of crime and criminals is one of the most unfailing tests of the civilization of any country. A calm, dispassionate recognition of the rights of the accused, and even of the convicted criminal ... measure[s] the stored-up strength of a nation and [is] sign and proof of the living virtue in it."* Thus, protecting the rights of individual members of our society is at the core of Canada's constitutional and legal frameworks. And sentenced or not, offenders remain members of the society to which they will return having served their time. The criminal justice system and corrections specifically must balance the rights of the individuals involved and public safety concerns.

HAVEN'T OFFENDERS FORFEITED THEIR RIGHTS?

As noted in Chapter 2 of this text, the rights of all Canadians are set out in and protected by the Constitution and the *Canadian Charter of Rights and Freedoms* (the *Charter*). Canada's commitment to various international human rights agreements[1] has set certain standards and enshrined many of these obligations in legislation and the *Charter*. We retain these rights throughout our lives, whether we are hospitalized, serving a sentence of imprisonment, or simply enjoying life (when we are most likely to take them for granted).

Until someone tries to limit your rights, you may not think much about your rights to practise the religion of your choice, freedom of expression, freedom of peaceful assembly and association, legal counsel, a fair hearing, the presumption of innocence, and freedom from arbitrary detention and imprisonment, as well as the right not to be subjected to cruel and unusual treatment and punishment and the right not to be subjected to unreasonable search or seizure. However, these rights are fundamental to the quality of life in Canada, and we should be vigilant in ensuring that our government respects them.

Offenders retain the rights and privileges of all members of society, except those that are necessarily removed or restricted as a consequence of the sentence of the court. Statutes such as the *Corrections and Conditional Release Act* (CCRA) protect the fundamental right to life and security, fair and just treatment, and protection from discrimination and mistreatment. Other domestic legislation protects the rights of all Canadians, including offenders, such as the *Canadian Human Rights Act*; the *Privacy Act*; the *Access to Information Act*; the *Official Languages Act*; and the *Transfer of Offenders Act*. By their very nature,

---

* Statement made by Winston Churchill in the House of Commons (U.K. Parliament) on July 20, 1910.

the principles of administrative law in Canada protect individuals who enter the criminal justice system. Due process, the duty to act fairly, and strictly defined powers and delegations of authority limit what actors may do in the name of the state, be they police, prosecutors, judges, or corrections officials.

You might well ask, what does this really mean in the context of a penitentiary? After all, shouldn't prison be a painful and punitive experience? Shouldn't offenders have thought about the rights they would be losing before committing the crime? If we examine the fundamental rights listed above, it is difficult to identify more than one or two that people actually agree should be removed. The argument goes something like this: If we want our communities to be safer, we need to remove offenders from among us. But all offenders except the very few who have committed the most heinous offences will be released back into the community at some point. Thus, if our goal is to maximize safety and if those who have committed crimes will at some point be back living in society, then we should act responsibly toward them during their period of incarceration. This means that although offenders lose the right to liberty, they do not forfeit the entitlement to be treated with dignity and humanity. But what of the right to liberty?

WHY NOT SIMPLY "LOCK 'EM UP AND THROW AWAY THE KEY"?

Locking up offenders and throwing away the key might have been the strategy of some penal systems in the past and may still be how some Canadians would prefer that sentences be administered. But we should consider the purposes of sentencing when considering locking people up. These are found in part XXIII of the *Criminal Code*, which defines the purposes of sentencing:

> 718. The fundamental purpose of sentencing is to contribute, along with crime prevention initiatives, to respect for the law and the maintenance of a just, peaceful and safe society by imposing just sanctions that have one or more of the following objectives:
>
> (a) to denounce unlawful conduct;
> (b) to deter the offender and other persons from committing offences;
> (c) to separate offenders from society, where necessary;
> (d) to assist in rehabilitating offenders;
> (e) to provide reparations for harm done to victims or to the community; and
> (f) to promote a sense of responsibility in offenders, and acknowledgment of the harm done to victims and to the community.

Sending offenders to prison can serve any or all of the purposes outlined above: it can be (a) a way of expressing societal disapproval of the individual and *denouncing* the criminal conduct; (b) a means of deterring the offender and other potential offenders from further offending; (c) a way of *incapacitating* the individual and preventing him from committing further crimes in the community, at least during the period of detention; (d) an opportunity to provide treatment and rehabilitative programming to ensure safe *reintegration* of the offender back into the community when the sentence of imprisonment ends; (e) a time to repair the harm caused; and, last, (f) a means of ensuring that people are held responsible for their behaviour and actions. It is worth noting that there is no mention of sentencing providing a form of *retribution* or *punishment* for the misdeed. We are not vindictive or retaliatory in our response to crime.

In the context of a sentence that includes imprisonment, rehabilitation or social reintegration is the most difficult goal to accomplish and also the most important. It is hard to help people fit back into a community from which they have forcibly been excluded. For this reason, Canada's Parliament has defined the purpose of incarceration[2] in Section 3 of the *Corrections and Conditional Release Act* (CCRA) as follows:

Purpose of correctional system

3. The purpose of the federal correctional system is to contribute to the maintenance of a just, peaceful and safe society by

   (a) carrying out sentences imposed by courts through the safe and humane custody and supervision of offenders; and

   (b) assisting the rehabilitation of offenders and their reintegration into the community as law-abiding citizens through the provision of programs in penitentiaries and in the community.

   3.1 The protection of society is the paramount consideration for the Service in the corrections process.[3]

Providing both assistance to and control of inmates is a monumental task when one considers the correctional system's responsibilities. According to the *Departmental Performance Report* for 2012–13 prepared by the Correctional Service of Canada (CSC), on a typical day during that year, CSC was responsible for 22,762 offenders, 15,056 offenders in federal custody (including temporary detainees) and 7,706 offenders in the community. The CSC manages 56 penitentiaries of different security levels (including treatment centres and annexes within penitentiaries), 16 community correctional centres, 92 parole offices, and 4 healing lodges.[4] In addition to federally operated facilities, the CSC partners with community-based non-governmental organizations that run approximately 200 community-based residential facilities across the country (i.e., halfway houses). A fundamental value of CSC's work is *respect*: for the dignity of individuals, for the rights of all members of society, and for the potential for human growth and development. CSC assumes that people have the potential to live as law-abiding citizens. These are important assumptions if the goal is safer communities.

Incarceration is expensive, both in fiscal and human terms. Moreover, it is disruptive to families and communities and should only be used when all other options are exhausted or deemed unsafe. Courts therefore do not incarcerate all offenders in perpetuity because it is unnecessary and even counterproductive to promoting the safety of the community. Moreover, it would be dangerous to staff to try to manage people devoid of hope and with nothing to lose because the keys to the cell had been thrown away! The rehabilitation and reintegration of offenders therefore remains a top priority for the correctional system. Penitentiaries are not "warehouses" for offenders; rather, they are institutions in which a prisoner can receive treatment and participate in education and employment programs. Correctional programs are designed to address factors identified as contributing to their criminal behaviour and to help in ultimately controlling and reducing the risk that these people will present in the future.

WHY LET PRISONERS OUT OF PRISON BEFORE THE ENTIRE SENTENCE IS OVER?

Some members of the public ask why we do not require prisoners to serve every day of their sentence in prison, without being allowed to serve any part of it under supervision in the community. Most prison systems around the world have programs that permit prisoners to serve part of their sentence in the community. *Parole* is the best-known example of such early release programs. Prisoners apply for conditional release from prison, meaning that they serve the last part of the sentence in the community, subject to conditions imposed by the parole authorities. The purpose of conditional release supervision is to further protect society by providing offenders with a transitional period in which they are still being assisted and receiving programs while they adapt to life on the outside. Released offenders must adhere to certain standard conditions set out in their release certificate. The releasing provisions in the CCRA allow the parole board to impose individually crafted conditions to minimize the risk of reoffending and to increase the likelihood of success in the community. Canada and CSC have invested heavily in research in order to understand the individual needs of offenders. Good correctional practice guides the specific conditions that are imposed in order to help the offender make the adjustment back into society.

All offenders on parole must report to a parole officer and abide by a set of standard conditions which include obeying the law, not owning or possessing a weapon, and reporting any change in their domestic or financial situation. For example, offenders must travel directly to their home or to a residential facility upon release and must report regularly to their parole supervisor. The parole board may impose additional conditions including curfews, restrictions on movement, and prohibitions on drinking and on associating with certain people (such as children and former victims). Special Conditions may also be imposed where the PBC (Parole Board of Canada) considers them reasonable and necessary to further manage an offender's risk in the community, such as to abstain from the use of drugs or alcohol.

CSC parole officers can take action if they believe the offender is violating release conditions or is planning to commit another crime. They can suspend the release and return the offender directly to prison until the risk is reassessed. Some of these offenders may remain in prison. Others may be released again, but under more severe restrictions and only after more supervision or community support services are in place. Research has shown that interventions and supervision are the best ways of promoting successful community reintegration and therefore public safety.

HOW DOES CANADA ENSURE THAT THE FOCUS ON HUMAN RIGHTS REMAINS SHARP?

Many decisions affecting a federal prisoner's life are relegated to someone else's authority, such as that of correctional officers, parole officers, program managers, or institutional heads. A former inmate of Beaver Creek Institution, a minimum-security facility in Ontario, condemned CSC's power to affect a prisoner's freedom and what he called "CSC's license to trample human rights" (Melnitzer 2003, 83). Hearing such a statement makes one wonder what mechanisms exist to protect inmates from the immense power of CSC and its 15,000 employees. CSC is accountable to the public for its performance.

CSC's operations are monitored by external bodies that hold it accountable for its operations. As a federal agency, CSC is responsible to the Parliament of Canada, which upholds the rights and freedoms of all Canadians. The Auditor General monitors the proper conduct of government activities and audits CSC's financial accounts. The Information Commissioner investigates complaints from people who believe they have been denied rights under the *Access to Information Act*, which is Canada's freedom-of-information legislation. Like all Canadian citizens, offenders can exercise their right to submit complaints to the Information Commissioner. Another mechanism for external oversight is the Office of the Privacy Commissioner, which advocates for the privacy rights of Canadians.

One of the most active external oversight bodies for CSC is the Office of the Correctional Investigator (OCI). Under the *Corrections and Conditional Release Act*,[5] the Correctional Investigator acts as the Ombudsman for federal offenders. The office's principal function is to investigate and resolve the complaints of individual offenders. As well, the OCI reviews CSC's policies and procedures as they relate to inmates' complaints, and makes recommendations. The OCI publishes an annual report detailing CSC's application or non-application of the recommendations made by the OCI. It records incidents of failure to comply with its governing legislation, policies, and directives, and reports annually to Parliament.

CSC has its critics and its watchdogs. In 1994, on the recommendation of the Solicitor General, the Honourable Justice Louise Arbour was appointed to lead an Inquiry into Certain Events at the Prison for Women in Kingston. In her report, Justice Arbour wrote that CSC did not understand or respect the rule of law. Her report led to a complete reassessment of how CSC provides for women offenders, as well as a great deal of soul searching to ensure that all CSC decisions would be governed thereafter by the rule of law. In 2002, Professor Michael Jackson wrote a book titled *Justice Behind the Walls*[6] about CSC's failure to respect basic human rights in Canada's prisons. In December 2003 the Canadian Human Rights Commission (CHRC) produced a systemic review of human rights in correctional services for the federally sentenced.

The CHRC administers the *Canadian Human Rights Act* and ensures that the principles of equal opportunity and non-discrimination are followed in all areas of federal jurisdiction, including and especially in the criminal justice system. Offenders have access to the CHRC's complaint process. If it cannot resolve a complaint, the commission may investigate the case further; it may ultimately request that the Canadian Human Rights Tribunal hear the case.

In 2004, in a special report titled *Protecting Their Rights: A Systemic Review of Human Rights in Correctional Services for Federally Sentenced Women*, the CHRC wrote that female prisoners[7] continued to face systemic human rights problems in the federal correctional system. It recommended that the correctional system be tailored to the unique needs of, and lower security risks posed by, female offenders. Specifically, it called for the correctional system to take a more gender-based approach to custody, programming, and reintegration for female offenders.

In June 2008, the Correctional Investigator published a report entitled *A Preventable Death* about the death of a 19-year-old CSC inmate named Ashley Smith. His report concluded that "the Correctional Service failed to provide an acceptable level of humane professional care and treatment to Ms. Smith while she was in its custody. The Correctional Service permitted its administrative needs, its capacity issues, and its perceived security needs to over-ride Ms. Smith's very real human needs." An eight-month inquest into her death led nine jurors, in December 2013, to find that her death in custody had been a homicide. It represents a damning indictment of CSC's treatment of mentally ill inmates.

In 2009, Jackson and Stewart published a sharp critique of CSC's most recent transformation: *A Flawed Compass: A Human Rights Analysis of the Roadmap to Strengthening Public Safety*. This 200-page treatise explored CSC's history and the importance of individual rights. It reaffirmed the view that democracy can be served only when imprisonment is humane and respectful.

In addition to external mechanisms, CSC has an Offender Redress system, which is a formal internal mechanism that addresses complaints by individual prisoners or groups of inmates. The system is designed to provide offenders with access to a fair and effective redress mechanism and to recommend corrective action in cases where there is mistreatment or injustice. It helps ensure that offenders' problems and expectations are brought to the attention of personnel across the service by providing grievance-based information on trends and specific issues. There are four levels of appeals in the service, the final level being the Commissioner or her designate at National Headquarters (NHQ).

In 2011–12, the *Annual Report of the Correctional Investigator* noted that 5,789 complaints were processed. CSC serves many functions that are handled by myriad agencies and infrastructures in the outside world, from food service and mail delivery to transportation of people and personal effects around the country. When decisions are being made about all aspects of running these small cities, some people will be unhappy with them. Most complaints and grievances do not arise from misconduct or deliberate poor performance. More often, they arise from either misunderstanding a policy, misinterpreting a policy, or disagreement over a decision. The five subject areas most likely to be the subject of complaints were Health Care, Conditions of Confinement, Administrative Segregation, Transfers, and (loss of) Cell Effects. The complaint and grievance system provides managers at all levels with valuable feedback on performance as well as comprehension and communication around policies and procedures. The process is also a useful strategic planning tool, in that as concerns and values shift, the complaint and grievance process may be where such shifts are first documented. For example, the emergence of a desire for vegetarian diets based on conscience rather than religion or culture was first seen in the grievance process. A grievance on genetically modified foods, for example, might be a harbinger of another value shift.

As Winston Churchill said, "Criticism may not be agreeable, but it is necessary. It fulfils the same function as pain in the human body. It calls attention to an unhealthy state of things." Critics and oversight bodies are critical to the good health of an organization and help ensure respect for rights.

HOW WOULD A DECISION MAKER CONSIDER THE "SPIRIT" OF LAW?

The values underlying the *Corrections and Conditional Release Act* are captured in a statement of principles in Section 4. These principles help decision makers exercise their discretion properly. The most relevant principles include the following:

> 4. The principles that guide the Service in achieving the purpose referred to in section 3 are as follows:
>
> ...
>
> (*d*) offenders retain the rights of all members of society except those that are, as a consequence of the sentence, lawfully and necessarily removed or restricted;

(e) the Service facilitates the involvement of members of the public in matters relating to the operations of the Service;

(f) correctional decisions are made in a forthright and fair manner, with access by the offender to an effective grievance procedure;

(g) correctional policies, programs and practices respect gender, ethnic, cultural and linguistic differences and are responsive to the special needs of women, aboriginal peoples, persons requiring mental health care and other groups;

The law requires CSC to manage penitentiaries in a way that respects the dignity of each individual and that does not impose onerous restrictions beyond those absolutely necessary. The language previously was that CSC would use "least restrictive measures" consistent with public safety. And while the wording has been changed to denying only rights that are "necessarily removed or restricted," the intent remains the same. Offenders retain their rights as human beings, their rights as Canadians, as they are constitutionally enshrined, and CSC has an obligation to keep that intent in mind as it learns to define what is necessary when balancing the needs of care and control and limiting those rights.

Rights are not absolute: my right to swing my fist stops at the end of your nose. Communities can limit our mobility rights when justified according to law. Incarceration is not, as such, a violation of rights. The Canadian correctional system has a vast of array of law and policy as well as oversight mechanisms and complaint systems aimed at preventing needless (or malicious) limitations of rights for those who are under sentence. But as in any "people business," much depends on the exercise of judgment by individual actors in a variety of situations to ensure that limitations that are part and parcel of institutional life are not abusive or beyond the allowable level of control. Good training and supervision, strong accountability mechanisms, and a culture that emphasizes sound judgment are important for ensuring that rights are respected and that the dual responsibilities of the correctional system for both care and control are properly administered.

Some people believe there are systemic problems that need attention. Symptoms of these problems might be presented as CSC violating the rights of offenders through excessive use of force, or improper administration of segregation. These concerns can be raised in a variety of ways, such as through the annual Correctional Investigator (CI's) *Report to Parliament*. CSC submits its response to this report, along with the CI's report, to the Minister of Public Safety, who tables both reports together, making it clear that CSC has to be accountable for the questions raised by its critics. Special commissions, internal audit systems, Auditor General's audits, and internal investigations help bring other problems to the attention of the Service. These reports and responses allow for public scrutiny, which is one of the best ways to prevent abuse of authority or violation of rights. Moreover, the access-to-information legislation can expose any document produced by CSC. In a typical year, around 350–500 access-to-information requests occur in the correctional system, which means that on more than 350 occasions CSC is asked to reveal internal documents and correspondence to members of the public, adding a layer of transparency to the work done by the administration.

WHY SHOULD CANADIANS CARE ABOUT PRISONERS' RIGHTS?

Canadians should value and protect the rights of all citizens all of the time, not only because it is the moral thing to do, but also because it is good public policy. Respecting rights helps ensure that offenders have the best chance of rehabilitating themselves; this in turn makes the country a safer place. In fact there is a growing body of evidence from the field of procedural justice that suggests that when people believe they are being treated fairly, they are more likely to comply with the law (e.g., Tyler 2006). In the context of prisons, if prisoners believe that the correctional system acts fairly and respects their rights, these individuals are more likely to obey the law when they are ultimately released from prison. Conversely, prisoners who perceive they have been unfairly treated or had their rights denied are less likely to regard their punishment as legitimate and are more likely to return to a life of crime after release. In this sense, respecting prisoners' rights and treating prisoners fairly is not just a matter of justice; it contributes to a reduction in the number of crimes committed.

How civilized are Canadians compared to the standards in Churchill's quotation, cited earlier? The answer depends on a culture of respect for the rule of law, to ensure that every Canadian is safe, wherever we find ourselves in whatever circumstances.

Further Readings

Jackson, M. 2002. *Justice behind the Walls. Human Rights in Canadian Prisons*. Vancouver: Douglas and McIntyre.

Jackson, M., and G. Stewart. 2009. *A Flawed Compass: A Human Rights Analysis of the Roadmap to Strengthening Public Safety*. http://www.justice behindthewalls.net/resources/news/flawed_Compass.pdf

Melnitzer, J. 1995. *Maximum, Medium, Minimum*. Toronto: Key Porter.

References

Melnitzer, J. 2003. "Prisoners' Rights." In J.V. Roberts and M. Grossman, eds., *Criminal Justice in Canada*. 2nd ed. Toronto: Thomson Nelson.

Tyler, T. 2006. *Why People Obey the Law*. Princeton: Princeton University Press.

Endnotes

1. These international instruments include the UN's Charter; Universal Declaration of Human Rights; Convention on the Rights of the Child; International Covenant on Civil and Political Rights; International Convention of the Elimination of All Forms of Racial Discrimination; Convention Against Torture and Other Cruel, Inhumane, or Degrading Treatment of Punishment; and Standard Minimum Rules for the Treatment of Prisoners.

2. The *Corrections and Conditional Release Act* applies to offenders who are sentenced to two years or more in a federal penitentiary and who are supervised on conditional release in the community by the Correctional Service of Canada.

3. This statement of purpose was derived from the mission document that CSC developed in 1989, which reads: "The Correctional Service of Canada (CSC), as part of the criminal justice system and respecting the rule of the law, contributes to the protection of society by actively encouraging and assisting offenders to become law-abiding citizens, while exercising reasonable, safe, secure and humane control."

4. CSC also manages an addiction research centre, five regional headquarters and staff colleges, and a national headquarters.

5. See Part 3 of the *Corrections and Conditional Release Act*.

6. The book can be accessed at http://www.justicebehindthewalls.net

7. Female offenders are particularly affected by the experience of imprisonment. They are often the primary caregiver for children, and they have high rates of mental and physical disability, self-destructive behaviour (such as slashing and cutting), depression, and suicide attempts. Eighty percent report prior abuse. They experience significant poverty and have higher unemployment rates than their male counterparts and Canadian women as a whole.

CHAPTER 28

Deaths in Custody[1]

The state has a duty of care towards the people processed by the criminal justice system. This duty is particularly important when the individuals are imprisoned. Accordingly, an important function of the prison system is to ensure that inmates are housed in facilities that are safe and where their rights are respected. In this chapter the authors explore the challenges confronting the prison system in this respect, and discuss the troubling cases in which death occurs in prison.

John A. Winterdyk
Mount Royal University

Daniel Antonowicz
Wilfrid Laurier University

Corrections in Canada has a rich, dynamic, and varied history, and it has played and continues to play an integral role in the criminal justice system. And while we might sometimes criticize the effectiveness and efficiency of our correctional system, it remains the envy of many countries. For example, Correctional Services Canada (CSC) staff has consulted widely on correctional reform around the world. Nevertheless, as with any system or organization, there are always elements that can and should be improved upon. As with other Western countries, Canada has an Office of the Correctional Investigator (OCI), which was established in 1973 to serve as the watchdog (i.e., ombudsman) for any infractions that might bring into question the mandate of correctional practices in Canada's federal correctional system. The authority and mandate of the Correctional Investigator is defined under Part 3 of the 1992 *Corrections and Conditional Release Act* (CCRA). However, as noted by Sapers and Hurst (2013, 201), "The work of a prison ombudsman is often complex and varied."

Although incarceration is to be used as a sentence of last resort, between March 2010 and March 2012 the federal inmate population grew "6.8%, which is the equivalent of two large male medium security institutions" (Office of the Correctional Investigator 2012). And not only has the budget increased dramatically (i.e., 43.9 percent between 2005–06 and 2010–11) but so has the cost of keeping a federal inmate incarcerated (e.g., $88,000 in 2005–06 to over $113,000 in 2009–10). Yet, despite the expanding budget and per capita expenditures, federal prisons continue to be confronted with a growing number of complaints and issues ranging from double-bunking, a growing number of elderly inmates, access to mental and physical health care, access to programs, issues affecting federally sentenced women, the ongoing overrepresentation of Aboriginal people in federal institutions, and the prevention of deaths in custody.

During the fiscal year 2012–13, the investigative staff

- received 5,450 complaints;
- conducted more than 1,400 "use of force" reviews and 165 reviews of deaths in custody (56 cases) and serious bodily injury, including self-harm cases; and
- interviewed 1,500 offenders (Office of the Correctional Investigator 2013b).[*]

One of the more pressing issues in recent years has been unnatural deaths in custody. Such deaths, while rare, attract considerable media and public scrutiny along with the attention of the OCI. As Sapers and Hurst (2013, 213) observe, "Deaths in custody may be attributed to a variety of causes and are often impacted by any number of contributing factors." Between 2003 and 2013, 863 offenders died while in custody (Office of the Correctional Investigator 2013a). The annual numbers of unnatural deaths in custody ranged from a low of 40 in 2007–08 (the year Ashley Smith died—see box below) to a high of 65 in both 2003–04 and 2008–09. Despite various initiatives by CSC since

---

[*] Annual Report of the Office of the Correctional Investigator 2012–2013. 2013. Ottawa: The Office of the Correctional Investigator.

the inquiry following the Ashley Smith case, the number of deaths in custody has steadily increased from 49 in 2009–10 to 56 in 2012–13 (PSC 2013). Two-thirds of these deaths were attributed to natural causes. However, as the OCI recently reported, "The Office has repeatedly raised concerns about the quality, thoroughness and adequacy of the mortality review process, which the CSC has yet to address" (Office of the Correctional Investigator 2014).

When people are deprived of their liberty, under law, the state assumes responsibility for protecting individuals' human rights as well as ensuring their safety. There are four basic rationales used to protect society: deterrence, incapacitation, rehabilitation, and retribution (see Winterdyk and Miller 2013). The principles governing corrections in Canada can be found in the CCRA, as well as in provincial legislation. Key principles include the following: the rights and dignity of the offender must be respected; fair treatment and handling must be ensured; and an attempt must be made to reintegrate the offender back into the community. However, as highlighted in the case of Ashley Smith, who was 19 years old at the time of her death, the safety and security of federal inmates cannot always be guaranteed.

THE CASE OF ASHLEY SMITH: A PREVENTABLE DEATH?

Born in New Brunswick in 1988, Ashley Smith spent most of her pre-teen years living with adoptive parents. Up until age 14–15 she was a "normal" child, until she began to get involved in a range of delinquent activities. By 2002, Ashley had appeared before youth court over a dozen times but when assessed was not diagnosed as having any major psychological problems. However, over the next few years she repeatedly inflicted physical self-harm, and when she turned 18 in 2006 she was transferred to an adult facility in New Brunswick. By the end of 2007 she had been transferred 17 times between 8 different federal institutions. While being detained in the Grand Valley Institution for Women in Kitchener, Ontario, Ashley was unsuccessful in her request to be transferred to a psychiatric unit. On October 7th she committed suicide by hanging herself while guards watched and failed to intervene. The two ensuing inquests in 2011 and 2012 along with a report from the Office of the Correctional Investigator all agreed that Correctional Service Canada (CSC) had neglected to ensure the safety of Ms. Smith and that there were a number of major limitations in the protocols that CSC had in place to ensure the safety of all inmates. In December 2013, after reviewing thousands of pages of manuscripts and hearing evidence from over 100 witnesses, the coroner's jury returned a verdict of homicide in the Ashley Smith case. The coroner's report determined that the (in)actions of CSC and other key stakeholders contributed to Smith's death. Furthermore, the jury provided 104 sweeping recommendations to the presiding coroner, most of which dealt with ways to manage self-harming mentally ill females in federal detention facilities.

In Canada and internationally, there has been a growing interest in examining in-custody deaths (see Amnesty International 2012; Sapers 2010). In response to a number of high-profile unnatural in-custody deaths in Canada,[2] in police detention, in mental health facilities, and in youth-custody centres, researchers and officials have devoted increased attention to investigating the causes and circumstances of such deaths. Deaths in custody have been addressed in a number of studies in different countries.[3]

Unnatural deaths in custody are most likely to result from some form of violence such as suicide or homicide (Wobeser et al. 2002). Researchers have suggested that some of these deaths were preventable (Camilleri and McArthur 2008). In custodial settings, where people are closely monitored and supervised, some deaths, especially suicides and drug overdoses, are a failure of the state's duty of care and breach of CSC's mandate. Although in-custody deaths due to violent causes are rare, they nevertheless tend to generate considerable media scrutiny and public unease. The examination of deaths due to unnatural causes can provide valuable information on risk factors (e.g., substance abuse, mental health, and dynamic and static security features within a correctional environment) that may have contributed to these deaths.

Unfortunately, Canada has lagged behind other countries such as Australia, the United Kingdom, New Zealand, and the United States (see, for example, Cunneen 2006) in collecting detailed national data on the causes and surrounding circumstances of in-custody deaths. In Australia, for example, the National Deaths in Custody Program (NDICP) is responsible for monitoring the extent and nature of deaths in police, prison, and juvenile custody since 1980, regardless of the cause of death (Lyneham et al. 2010). The Australian Institute of Criminology (AIC) has coordinated the NDICP since its establishment in 1992, with official data on all custodial deaths between 1980 and 1992. No other country has consistently collected similar or as extensive data over such an extended period of time (Curnow and Larsen 2009).

Since 1994, in the United Kingdom, the Prisons and Probation Ombudsman (formerly known as the Prison Ombudsman) has served as the official vehicle for addressing deaths in custody and then recommending changes to the prison system. As noted in the 2010 annual report of the Ombudsman's office (as cited in Sapers 2010), there has been a notable decline in both the number of inmate deaths as well as complaints from detention facilities. Furthermore, in the UK, deaths in custody at a national level have been linked to a broader-reaching human rights standard. Article 2 of the *European Convention on Human Rights* "guarantees the right to life and places duties on the state to take steps to prevent deaths of people in detention and to establish independent investigations into deaths in custody" (*Deaths in Custody: Third Report of Session 2004–05* 2005, 5).

In response to that convention, the British House of Commons report (Forum for Preventing Deaths in Custody 2007) points out that the state (i.e., the United Kingdom) has a legal obligation to provide a comprehensive and independent review of all deaths in custody. These independent reviews are performed by the Prisons and Probation Ombudsman (PPO), and its findings are published on its website "to share the knowledge as widely as possible" (Forum for Preventing Deaths in Custody 2007). Unlike in Canada, the activities of the PPO are open to the public; in fact, in recent years the PPO has undertaken regular surveys of the families of prisoners whose deaths they have investigated. The information the PPO gathers is then used to inform reviews of, and reforms to, its policies and practices. In addition, the PPO has hired a specialist to provide assistance to PPO staff who may experience undue stress as a result of their duties and workload. As suggested by Sapers, this approach might be something that CSC may want to adopt in some manner or another as it also reflects greater collaboration between political, organizational, and public sectors, which "may create the focus necessary to bring about more lasting improvements" (Sapers 2010, 6).

It is regrettable that in Canada there is no systematic national effort to collect detailed information on in-custody deaths. Although the Canadian Centre for Justice Statistics (CCJS) collects data on deaths in federal and provincial/territorial correctional custody, the data are not as comprehensive as those maintained in other countries. CCJS data are restricted to the number of deaths and the broad causes of death. In addition to lagging behind other countries in collecting data surrounding in-custody deaths, it is disconcerting that Canada is moving away from conducting public inquiries into what are classified as natural deaths in custody. For example, in 2010 Ontario changed its regulations so that deaths deemed to be natural would not be formally investigated in a public forum. Previously published work by Wobeser et al. (2002) suggests that this may result in the loss of checks and balances for such agencies as CSC, where the primary mandate is incarceration but also where the conflicted mandate of providing healthcare to inmates is a secondary responsibility. It is important to note that healthcare in federal correctional institutions does not come under the same accreditation process regulating healthcare in the community.

OFFICIAL DATA ON UNNATURAL DEATHS IN CUSTODY

A recent annual report on Canadian deaths in custody covered the four-year period from 2003 to 2006 (Canadian Centre for Justice Statistics 2009). The annual report noted that of the 147 deaths in provincial or territorial custody, 28 percent were due to suicide while 23 percent were classified as resulting from natural causes. Approximately half (48 percent) of the deaths were classified as "Other" (Canadian Centre for Justice Statistics 2009). This category comprises accidental deaths plus cases where the cause of death could not be determined. Furthermore, out of the 165 deaths in federal custody, 18 percent were classified as "suicides" and 8 percent were registered as "murders," while the remaining deaths (73 percent) were included in the "Other" category (Canadian Centre for Justice Statistics 2009). In contrast to the "Other" category for provincial and territorial offenders, this category included both accidental deaths and deaths due to overdoses or natural causes.

Unfortunately, categories that include multiple causes of death do not permit a precise breakdown of the specific causes. It is unclear, for example, how many deaths were attributed to natural causes. The suicide statistics reported above are similar to those reported by the Office of the Correctional Investigator (2013a). This report also states that between 2003 and 2013, 536 offenders died in federal custody (a number that does not include provincial custody or police custody). Between 15 and 21 percent of these deaths were suicides. CSC data for 2012–13 shows that of the 25 unnatural deaths, one was a homicide, 12 were suicides, there were no drug overdoses, 11 were due to "unknown" causes, and 1 was an "accidental" death. Even though the rate of suicides has declined since the early 1990s, deaths as a result of suicide are still six times more common in federal prisons than among the general population (*Deaths in Custody* 2013). Similar findings have been reported in a number of international studies (see Blaauw, Kerkhof, and Hayes 2005; Fazel et al. 2008).

Several studies have extended the focus to also include other violent causes of death, such as homicides and accidental deaths. For example, Gabor (2007) examined causes of violent deaths among Canadian federal prison inmates over a five-year period (2001 to 2005). He reports a total of 82 deaths, 61 percent of which were suicides. Gabor (2007) further reported that suicides and homicides in prison occur at eight times the rate in the general Canadian population. Few studies, however, have examined all causes of in-custody deaths. Exceptions include an Ontario study by Wobeser et al. (2002) and an American study by Kim et al. (2007).

Wobeser et al. (2002) conducted one of the first Canadian studies to examine the causes of deaths in custody. A detailed review was performed of the inquest files for all custody deaths in the province of Ontario. The authors examined violent (non-natural) and natural causes of death for the time period 1990 to 1999 in the province. These included deaths in federal penitentiaries, provincial prisons, and police cells (see MacAlister 2012). Given the small number of female deaths, the researchers focused their analysis only on male deaths in custody. According to Wobeser et al. (2002), over half (59 percent) of the 283 male deaths were due to non-natural causes, such as suicide, accidental poisoning (i.e., overdoses), and homicide, while the remainder were due to natural causes. In particular, Wobeser et al. (2002, 1109) found that

"compared with the Canadian male population, male inmates in both federal and provincial institutions had a much higher rate of death by poisoning and suicide; the same was true for the rate of death by homicide among male inmates in federal institutions. The rates of death from cardiovascular disease among male inmates in federal and provincial institutions ... were also higher than the national average ... male inmates have a higher overall rate of death and a much higher rate of death from violent causes."

In 2012, Antonowicz and Winterdyk (2014) replicated and updated the findings of Wobeser et al. (2002) and provided a more representative picture of deaths in custody across three provincial jurisdictions (Alberta, British Columbia, and Ontario) from 2000 to the end of 2009. The overarching objective was to generate recommendations to prevent future unnatural deaths in custody. The key findings include the following:

- Between 2000 and 2009, 388 completed cases of deaths in custody were recorded for the three provinces (i.e., at the provincial and federal levels as well as in police custody).
- British Columbia had the largest number (150 cases, or 38.7 percent), followed by Ontario (141 cases, or 36.3 percent), and Alberta (97 cases, or 25 percent).
- In terms of gender, males were disproportionately overrepresented, with the number of males who died in custody being 356 (91.8 percent) while female deaths in custody accounted for 32 cases (8.2 percent).
- Deaths most frequently took place in prison, followed by deaths in hospitals; the smallest number of deaths occurred while offenders were being detained in police custody.
- The most frequent manner of death in custody was reported as being due to "natural causes" (181 cases, or 46.6 percent). The second-most-common manner of death was "suicide" (78 cases, or 20.1 percent). Homicides accounted for less than 5 percent of the cases.
- Analysis of causes of death revealed that for 19.1 percent of the cases, drug or alcohol abuse was listed as the primary cause of death across federal, provincial, and municipal detention centres; in 21.1 percent of the cases, a history of intravenous drug use was identified. This is not surprising since it is well documented that drug and substance abuse among inmates is a significant problem in the offender population (see Weekes et al. 2009).
- Just over 62 percent of those who died while in custody had a history of a prior medical condition. Of those, 19.3 percent had "multiple medical problems," 23.2 percent had "drug related medical problems," 22.9 percent had "mental health problems," and 5.7 percent had "multiple diagnoses" of mental health disorders.*

CONCLUSION

Although correctional facilities are mandated by law to ensure the safety and well-being of their populations, certain risks to personal safety are to be anticipated given the nature of the population, their pre-existing medical conditions, and the dynamics within a correctional/detention facility. The question is, To what extent can, or should, the numbers be reduced? Of those

---

* Antonowicz, D. and Winterdyk, J. 2014. A review of deaths in custody in three Canadian provinces. Canadian Journal of Criminology and Criminal Justice, 2014, 56(1): 85–104.

deaths that are "preventable," should there be different standards or expectations between the different types of correctional/detention facilities? For example, it is recognized that even in the medical profession patients die as a result of "medical errors."[4] As reported in the 2010–11 OCI annual report: "Preventing deaths in custody is challenging work. There are no shortcuts. Even the slightest errors or omissions ... can lead to tragic, if unintended consequences.... it is ... complicated by the constant necessity to balance security concerns against a legal duty of care" (26). Nevertheless, even though the research shows that approximately two-thirds of deaths in custody are the result of natural or accidental causes, any unnatural deaths raise concerns about the protocols that CSC has in place to reduce the risk of such events. Hence, in addition to upholding the core values and mission of CSC, reducing incidents of self-inflicted deaths and/or self-harm should continue to be a key priority of prison staff.

To its credit, CSC has implemented its own Independent Review Committee (IRC) and has introduced a number of measures and policy procedures in an effort to learn from deaths in custody and develop suicide and self-harm prevention and/or intervention strategies that are sustainable. Hence, independent investigations such as those conducted by OCI and by the IRC for CSC can serve an important role for drawing such events to the attention of CSC. In addition to conducting independent inquiries OCI is also able to address any concerns that might be raised by the deceased's family member(s).

The rate of unnatural deaths among Canadian inmates is higher than that of the general population. Furthermore, despite recent efforts of CSC to address its dynamic and static procedures to reduce the rate of unnatural deaths in custody, these rates have not significantly declined—especially in the aftermath of the Ashley Smith case"Various reports have offered a range of recommendations. Even though it is recognized that CSC responds to and treats any deaths in custody seriously, like any organization, there are disparities in the operations of correctional institutions that lead to risks or opportunities for unnatural deaths to occur. Therefore, any attempts to reduce the risk of unnatural deaths should focus on a "systems" approach that better enables CSC to comply with Section 19 of the *Corrections and Conditional Release Act*, which states that the safety and security of all inmates be of paramount priority. Furthermore, a 2013 OCI report on mortality recommended that any "sudden" or "unexpected" fatalities should be subject to a National Board of Investigation (NBI) so as to enhance the quality, accountability, and transparency of CSC's investigations (Office of the Correctional Investigator 2013a). As evidenced in this chapter and documented in various OCI reports, "preventable" deaths do occur; by subjecting such incidents to a more accountable process, the incident rate of such deaths may be reduced.

Furthermore, the creation of an NBI should include all levels of government in order to enhance the quality of investigative reports and processes and to strengthen information sharing not only between institutions but also between clinical and front-line staff. In addition, consideration should be given to appointing a senior manager who would be responsible for safe custody practices (Sapers 2013) and the development of uniform standards to deal with death inquiry practices.[5] Finally, efforts could be made to share lessons learned through "best practices" internationally and learned across other services (see Gabor 2007; MacAlister 2012).   Countries such as the United Kingdom, Australia, and the United States have all developed protocols that have reduced the rates of deaths in custody. However, if CSC fails to fully embrace and commit to addressing the problem of unnatural deaths in custody, the incidence of such deaths will only increase"

Further Readings

Office of the Correctional Investigator. 2013. *Annual Report of the Office of the Correctional Investigator 2012–2013*. Ottawa: The Office of the Correctional Investigator.

Sapers, H., and C. Hurst. 2013 "Oversight and Accountability in Federal Corrections: The Office of the Correctional Investigator." Chap. 8 in J. Winterdyk and M. Weinwrath, eds., *Adult Corrections in Canada*. Whitby, ON: de Sitter Pub.

Winterdyk, J., and M. Weinwrath, eds. 2013. *Adult Corrections in Canada*. Whitby, ON: de Sitter Pub.

References

Amnesty International. 2012. *Amnesty International Report 2012: The State of the World's Human Rights*. London: Amnesty International.

Antonowicz, D., and J. Winterdyk. 2014. "A Review of Deaths in Custody in Three Canadian Provinces." *Canadian Journal of Criminology and Criminal Justice* 56, no. 1: 85–104.

Blaauw, E., A.J.F. Kerkhof, and L.M. Hayes. 2005. "Demographic, Criminal, and Psychiatric Factors Related to Inmate Suicide." *Suicide Life-Threatening Behaviors* 35: 63–75.

Bureau of Justice Statistics (BJS). http://bjs.ojp.usdoj.gov/content/dcrp/dictabs.cfm

Camilleri, P., and M. McArthur. 2008. "Suicidal Behavior in Prisons: Learning from Australian and International Experiences." *International Journal of Law and Psychiatry* 31: 297–307.

Canadian Centre for Justice Statistics. 2009. *Adult Correctional Services Survey in Canada: 2005–2006*.

Canadian Mental Health Association, Ontario. 2010. *Annual Report 2009–2010*. Reference Tables. Ottawa: Canadian Mental Health Association.

Cunneen, C. 2006. "Aboriginal Deaths in Custody: A Continuing Systematic Abuse." *Social Justice* 33: 37–51.

Curnow, J., and J.J. Larson. 2009. *Deaths in Custody in Australia: National Deaths in Custody Program 2007*. Monitoring Reports No. 3. Canberra: Australian Institute of Criminology.

Deaths in Custody: Third Report of Session 2004–05, Volume I. 2005. House of Lords and the House of Commons London: The Stationery Office Limited.

Deaths in Custody. 2013. Ottawa, ON: The Office of the Correctional Investigator. http://www.oci-bec.gc.ca/cnt/priorities-priorites/deaths-deces-eng.aspx, accessed January 07, 2014.

Fazel, S., J. Cartwright, A. Norman-Nott, and K. Hawton. 2008. "Suicide in Prisoners: A Systematic Review of Risk Factors." *Journal of Clinical Psychiatry* 69: 1721–31.

Forum for Preventing Deaths in Custody. *Annual Report 2006–2007*. 2007. www.preventingcustodydeaths.org.uk/forum_for_preventing_deaths_v_4.pdf, accessed December 18, 2013.

Gabor, T. 2007. *Deaths in Custody*. Report prepared for the Office of the Correctional Investigator. Ottawa. http://www.oci-bec.gc.ca/cnt/rpt/oth-aut/oth-aut20070228-eng.aspx, accessed December 26, 2013.

Kim, S., A. Ting, M. Puisis, S. Rodriguez, R. Benson, C. Mennella, and F. Davis. 2007. "Deaths in the Cook County Jail: 10-Year Report, 1995–2004." *Journal of Urban Health: Bulletin of the New York Academy of Medicine* 84: 70–84.

Liebling, A., and T. Ward, eds. 1994. *Deaths in Custody: International Perspectives*. London: Whiting & Birch Ltd.

Lyneham, M., and C. Andy. 2011. *Twenty Years of Monitoring by the National Deaths in Custody Program since the Royal Commission into Aboriginal Deaths in Custody*. http://aic.gov.au/publications/current%20series/mr/1-20/20.html, accessed December 27, 2013.

Lyneham, M., J.J. Larson, and L. Beacroft. 2010. *Deaths in Custody in Australia: National Deaths in Custody Program 2008*. Monitoring Reports No. 10. Canberra: Australian Institute of Criminology.

MacAlister, D. 2012. *Police Involved Deaths: The Need for Reform*. Vancouver, BC: B.C. Civil Liberties Association.

Mumola, C.J. 2005. *Suicide and Homicide in State Prisons and Local Jails*. NCJ 210036. Washington, DC: U.S. Department of Justice, Bureau of Justice Statistics,.

Office of the Correctional Investigator. 2010. *Annual Report of the Office of the Correctional Investigator 2009–2010*. Ottawa: The Office of the Correctional Investigator.

Office of the Correctional Investigator. 2011. *Annual Report of the Office of the Correctional Investigator 2010–2011*. Ottawa: The Office of the Correctional Investigator.

Office of the Correctional Investigator. 2012. *Annual Report of the Office of the Correctional Investigator 2011–2012*. Ottawa: The Office of the Correctional Investigator.

Office of the Correctional Investigator. 2013a. *An Investigation of the Corrections Service's Mortality Review Process*. December 18. Ottawa: The Office of the Correctional Investigator.

Office of the Correctional Investigator. 2013b. *Annual Report of the Office of the Correctional Investigator 2012–2013*. Ottawa: The Office of the Correctional Investigator.

Office of the Correctional Investigator. 2014. *Backgrounder: An Investigation of the Correction Service of Canada's Mortality Review Process*. January 20. Ottawa: The Office of the Correctional Investigator.

Public Safety Canada. 2013. "2012 Corrections and Conditional Release Statistical Overview." http://www.publicsafety.gc.ca/cnt/rsrcs/pblctns/2012-ccrs/index-eng.aspx, accessed December 26, 2013.

Sapers, H. 2010. *Towards a Canadian Forum in Preventing Deaths in Custody*. Justice Report, 8–9.

——. 2013. "Preventing Deaths in Custody: Recommendations, Impacts and Change." Paper presented at the 13th Biennial CCJA Congress, Vancouver, BC, October 5, 2013.

Sapers, H., and C. Hurst. 2013. "Oversight and Accountability in Federal Corrections: The Office of the Correctional Investigator." Chap. 8 in J. Winterdyk and M. Weinwrath, eds., *Adult Corrections in Canada*. Whitby, ON: de Sitter Pub.

Weekes, J., A. Moser, M. Ternes, and D. Kunic. 2009. *Substance Abuse among Male Offenders*. Research Snippet Number 09-2: Ottawa: Correctional Service Canada.

Winterdyk, J., and A. Miller. 2013. "Adult Corrections within a Canadian Context. " Chap. 1 in John Winterdyk and Michael Weinwrath, eds., *Adult Correction in Canada*. Whitby, ON: deSitter Pub.

Wobeser, W.L., J. Datema, B. Bechard, and P. Ford. 2002. "Causes of Death among People in Custody in Ontario, 1990–1999." *Canadian Medical Association Journal* 167: 1109–13.

Endnotes

1. Parts of this chapter derive from an article in the 2014 *Canadian Journal of Criminology and Criminal Justice* 56, no. 1: 85–104.

2. Between 2002–03 and 2012–13 the annual number of unnatural deaths (i.e., suicide, accident, murder, overdose, use of force, and unknown causes) ranged from a low of 10 in 2007–08 to a high of 25 in 2012–23. The mean number of unnatural deaths between 2002–03 and 2012–13 is just over 18 deaths per year (Sapers 2013a).

3. These include the following: Lyneham, Joudo Larsen, and Beacroft (2010); Lyndham and Andy (2011); and Cunneen (2006) led studies in Australia. In Canada, Gabor (2007) and Wobeser, Datema, Bechard, and Ford (2002) have studied this issue. Kim et al. (2007); Mumola (2005); and Liebling and Ward (1994) have done studies in the United States. In the United Kingdom, see the "Forum for Preventing Death in Custody" (2007).

4. A 2004 report noted that some 195,000 people die in American hospitals due to a "medical error" each year (see www.medicalnewstoday.com/articles/11856.php, accessed October 07, 2011). A similar report found that between 9,000 and 24,000 people die annually in Canadian hospitals due to some type of medical error (see http://www.medicalnewstoday.com/articles/8609.php, accessed December 17, 2013).

5. This is especially important for federal inmates who are sometimes transported between provinces, since autopsies are conducted by provincial medical examiners or coroners.